This catalogue is published on the occasion of the exhibition:

Evelyn Dunbar (1906-1960)
The Lost Works

Pallant House Gallery

9 North Pallant
Chichester
West Sussex PO19 1TJ

3 October 2015 - 14 February 2016

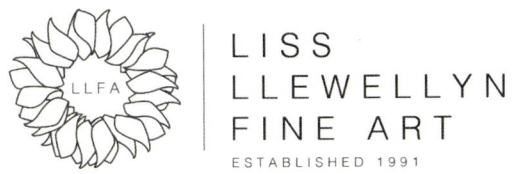

  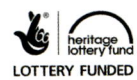 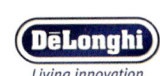

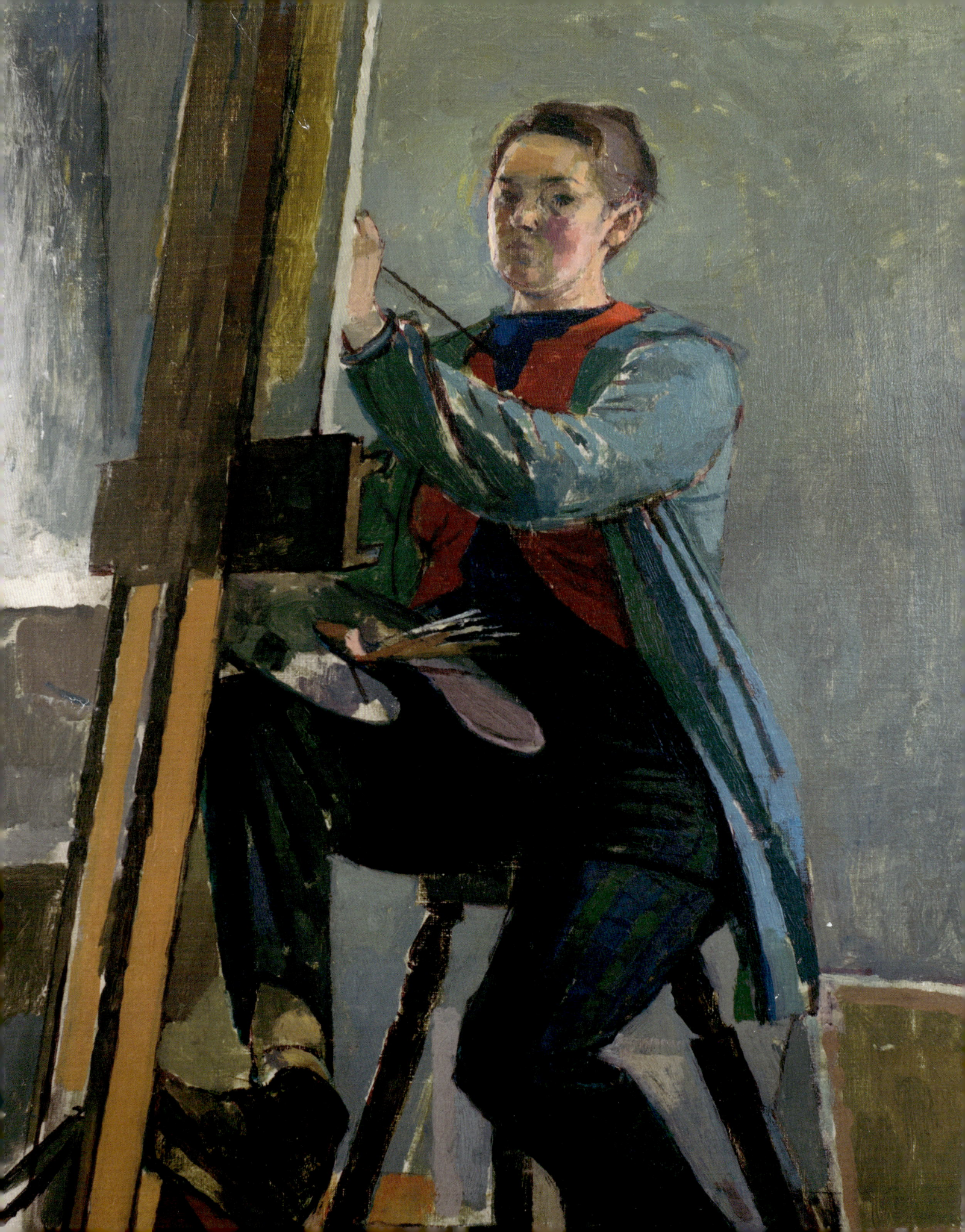

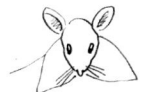

Evelyn Dunbar (1906-1960)
The Lost Works

Edited by Sacha Llewellyn & Paul Liss

For Alasdair

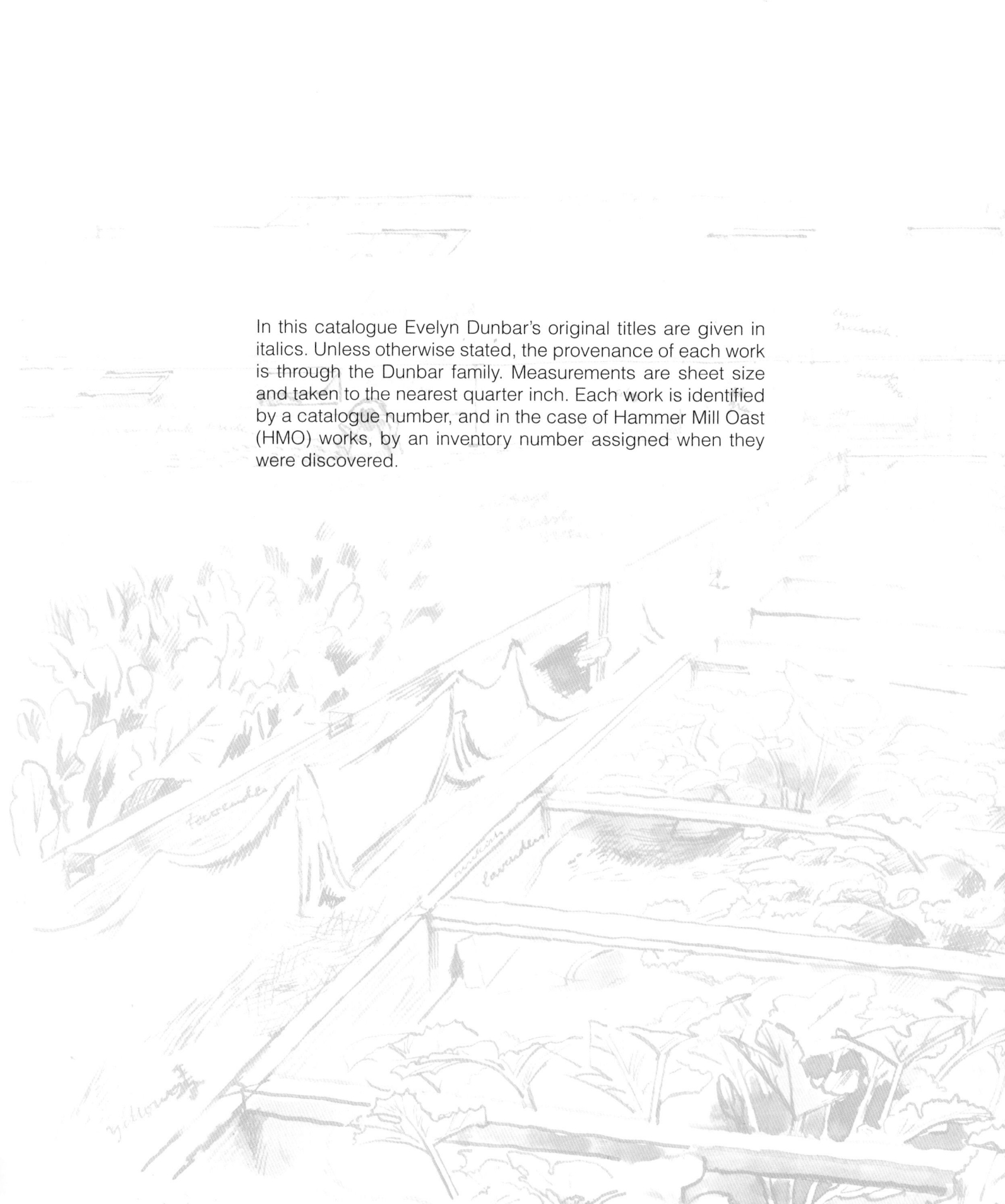

In this catalogue Evelyn Dunbar's original titles are given in italics. Unless otherwise stated, the provenance of each work is through the Dunbar family. Measurements are sheet size and taken to the nearest quarter inch. Each work is identified by a catalogue number, and in the case of Hammer Mill Oast (HMO) works, by an inventory number assigned when they were discovered.

CONTENTS

ACKNOWLEDGEMENTS 6

LOST & FOUND 8
Simon Martin

IN SEARCH OF THE ENDURINGLY POWERFUL 10
Sacha Llewellyn & Paul Liss

THE SIGNIFICANCE OF LOST WORKS: 12
A BIOGRAPHER'S PERSPECTIVE
Gill Clarke

EVELYN DUNBAR: SUCH A GIFTED ARTIST 14
Andrew Lambirth

CATALOGUE

Section essays by Alan Powers & Peyton Skipwith
Catalogue notes by Christopher Campbell-Howes & Paul Liss

Early Work & Family Portraits 35
The Brockley Murals 53
Gardens & Landscape 69
Gardeners' Choice 83
Gardener's Diary 1938 & Related Paintings 99
The Children's Shop & Commercial Design 117
Wartime 131
Post War 155
Sketchbooks & Ephemera 169

CHRONOLOGY 184

Christopher Campbell-Howes

Acknowledgements

This exhibition is the result of a happy convergence of three serendipitous events: the discovery by Ro Dunbar of over 500 previously unrecorded works by Evelyn Dunbar and the subsequent meeting of Ro and Christopher Campbell-Howes after his twenty year quest for the lost works; along with the vision of Simon Martin in bringing the exhibition to Pallant House Gallery.

The support of back-up teams has been essential – at every stage in this project Christopher Campbell-Howes has been unfailingly supported by Josephine Campbell-Howes. Christopher's diligence in discovering new works and researching every aspect of Dunbar's life has played a vital role in moving Dunbar scholarship forward.

Ro Dunbar and her two daughters Lucy and Jessica have lent their support and have had the benefit of Heather and Charles Trollope's advice.

Simon Martin, Artistic Director at Pallant House Gallery, has depended upon the initiative and resourcefulness of his team: Katy Norris who has been responsible for curating the exhibition; Anna Zeuner for handling the PR; Harriet Judd for overseeing the publication, sourcing images and copyright clearance; the further assistance of Cheryl Gaydon Chilton and Sarah Norris has been invaluable.

We would also like to acknowledge our debt to Gill Clarke; her book, *Evelyn Dunbar: War and Country* (Bristol: Sansom & Co., 2006), published to coincide with an exhibition at the St. Barbe Museum, Lymington, played a vital role in re-establishing Dunbar's reputation. We are especially grateful to Andrew Lambirth, Alan Powers and Peyton Skipwith for their essays.

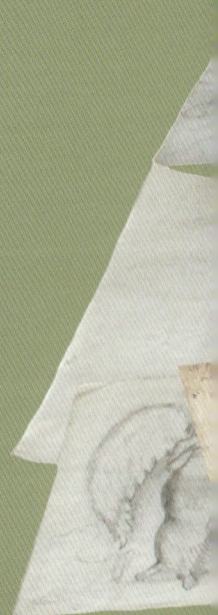

This exhibition has been greatly enhanced by the addition of a key number of loans. We are indebted to Jane England, Brian Webb and Iain and Bunny Smedley for being so generous in lending their paintings.

It has been a great pleasure to work with David Maes on this publication, who has, as always, designed the catalogue with sensitivity and precision.

James Folley has been most generous in granting full copyright agreement.

This project has been greatly enhanced by additional contributions from Anne Barrett, Nicola Beauman, Erika Brandl, Ruth Bubb, Elizabeth Bulkeley, Richard Campbell-Howes, Nick Higbee, Robert Imhoff, David Lacy, Rupert Maas, Steven Maisel, Emmanuel Pédeneau, Pernille Richards, Andrew Sim, David Thompson and Farang Wren.

Sacha Llewellyn & Paul Liss, June 2015

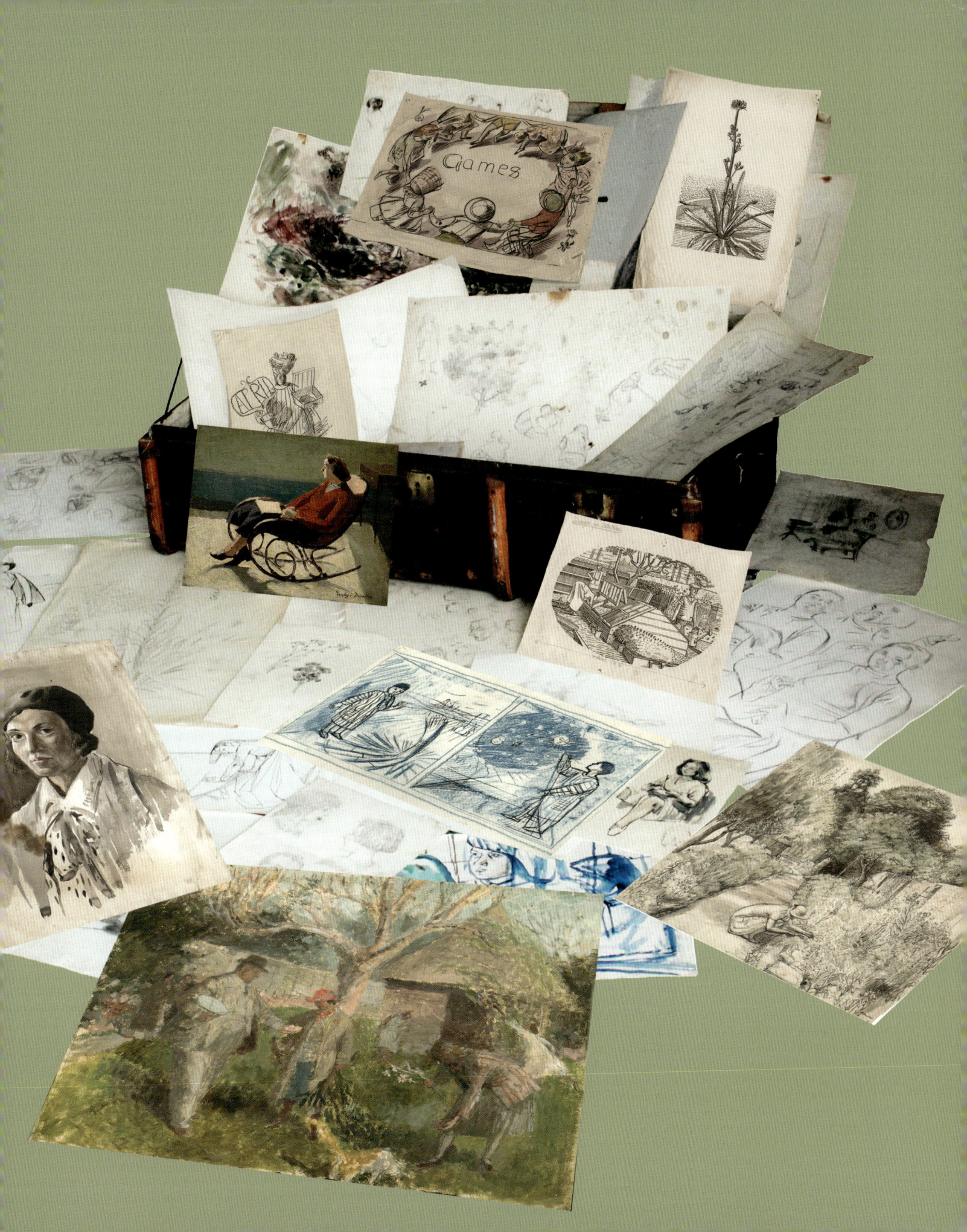

Lost & Found

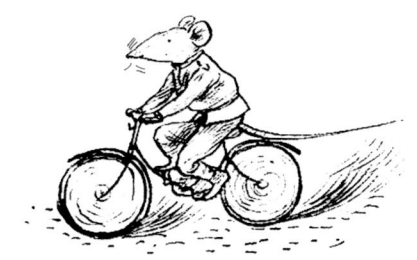

For a curator it is a rare and precious thing to be able to present a previously unknown artwork to the public. So often, monographic exhibitions in public galleries are predominantly of artworks that are well-known, recorded in catalogue raisonnés, or widely published. Perhaps there is an expectation that if an exhibition is to be significant the contents must be deemed 'iconic' and within the canons of art. But whilst there is a comfort in seeing much-loved and familiar works, encountering a previously unknown work for the first time carries a charge that could be described as the 'shock of the new', even if the work was created many years earlier. However, the discovery of 'unknown' works is an infrequent occurrence; when it happens it can animate and punctuate a show, bringing freshness and providing new insights into an artist's working methods and deepening our understanding of their life and work.

What then, when the entire show is composed of 'lost works', not seen in public for decades, if ever? It is an exciting proposition and immediately stirs up curiosity: all kinds of questions about why the work is not known and has not been seen, and the privileged feeling of being one of the first set of eyes to gaze upon the work. So it is with this remarkable collection of previously unknown works by Evelyn Dunbar. At Pallant House Gallery we have developed a reputation for reappraising the careers of artists whose work merits greater attention, and mounting exhibitions on themes in Modern British art that warrant deeper examination, often for the first time. Reflecting the Gallery's identity as a 'collection of collections' we also hold exhibitions of particular private collections, integral to which is the story of how and why the collection was formed.

The rediscovery of this important collection of works by Evelyn Dunbar is a particularly engaging story. When in September 2012 the BBC *Antiques Roadshow* was held at Cawdor Castle, amongst the dolls, items of furniture and bric-a-brac that were brought by the queues of people waiting in the inevitable rain was a painting by Dunbar. It was the kind of moment that the television producers must cherish. The Neo-Romantic painting entitled 'Autumn and the Poet' (1960) (CAT 114) had been brought to the roadshow by a relation of the artist and after it was appraised by Rupert Maas before the cameras it was sold and subsequently donated, through the initiative of Liss Llewellyn Fine Art, to Maidstone Museum and Bentlif Art Gallery. Ordinarily this outcome might have been the happy ending to a story, but in this case it was only the beginning.

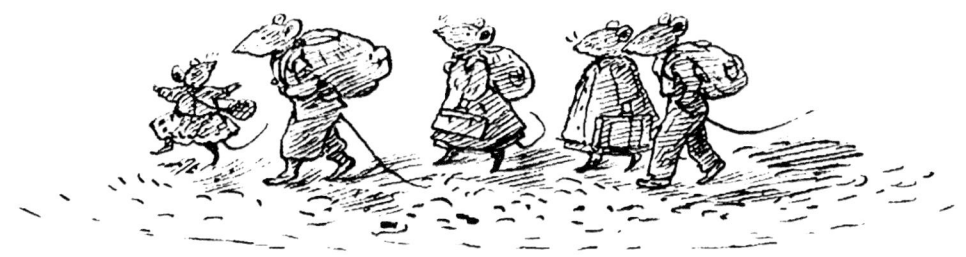

Seeing Dunbar's painting on the *Antiques Roadshow* caused Ro Dunbar to reflect on the extraordinary number of paintings, drawings and studies in her possession, and in turn led to her meeting the Dunbar enthusiast Christopher Campbell-Howes, himself the artist's nephew. None of the works in her collection had previously been recorded, and so it is a remarkable discovery underpinning her position as one of the most significant female figurative artists working in Britain during the twentieth century. Within the collection are studies for some of her most celebrated paintings as a War Artist such as *Milking Practice with Artificial Udders* (FIG 6) in the collection of the Imperial War Museum, studies for her mural scheme at Brockley School and her *English Calendar* (CAT 71).

We are delighted to be able to present these works for the first time at Pallant House Gallery. On behalf of the Trustees of Pallant House Gallery and my Co-Director Marc Steene, I would like to express my gratitude to Paul Liss and Sacha Llewellyn, to Ro Dunbar and James Folley, to the other lenders, the contributors to the catalogue: Gill Clarke, Andrew Lambirth and Christopher Campbell-Howes, to David Maes the designer of this beautiful catalogue, our Curator Katy Norris and the team at the Gallery who have worked on the show. Finally we thank the patrons and supporters, and to our headline sponsor De'Longhi for their ongoing support of the Gallery.

Simon Martin
Artistic Director Pallant House Gallery
June 2015

Illustrations:

Line drawings from *An Episode in the History of the Lake District* (1941), written by Roger Folley and illustrated by Evelyn Dunbar, from the original held in the Tate Archive. This was a journal of a wartime climbing holiday, with the protagonists presented as mice. Left: Folley's cousin Moira Rayner. Right: Folley, Dunbar, Dunbar's former student friend Margaret Goodwin, Folley's former student friend Glynn Burton, and a small girl showing the party the way to the station.

In Search of the Enduringly Powerful

Sacha Llewellyn & Paul Liss

> *'As with any artist's work, it fluctuates: there are great pictures and interesting ones, some enduringly powerful and some tired and slipshod.'*
>
> William Boyd, *The Guardian Newspaper,* 4 June, 2006

Evelyn Dunbar threw very little away and on her unexpected death in 1960, when she was 53, her husband Roger made a point of giving the remaining contents of her studio for safe keeping to her brother Alec (CAT 10). Subsequently they were put into an oast house attic in Kent where they remained unseen for a generation. This lost studio of Evelyn Dunbar only re-emerged in 2013. Consisting of several hundred previously unrecorded works this remarkable haul – christened the Hammer Mill Oast (HMO) collection – increased overnight the known body of Dunbar's work by more than 50%.

Discovering a large quantity of work by a little-known artist is not an entirely rare event – it is the fate of many artists to die with most of what they produced. But to discover a large body of work by a highly regarded and relatively well-documented artist is altogether rare.

In her essay *The Significance of the Lost Works* (pp.12-13) Gill Clarke documents, from a biographer's point of view, the importance of this newly discovered group. In *Evelyn Dunbar: Such a Gifted Artist*, (pp.14-31), Andrew Lambirth offers a compelling introduction to Dunbar concluding that, 'the more one sees of her work the more impressive and assured it looks'.

What sort of works are typically found in an artist's studio? The contents of a studio can broadly be divided into three groups:

1) Archival material: letters, photographs, newspaper cuttings, exhibition catalogues, pictures by other artists (reproductions or original works) sketch books, props and general ephemera broadly constitute the first category of work found. The significance of this material in piecing together the story of the artist is invaluable. Establishing the provenance of works – something that so often gets destroyed when a studio is thrown into auction – provides a vital link in the chain of reassessing the significance of individual works as well as the value of an artist's body of work as a whole. Items on which commercial value is traditionally so rarely placed – the original artwork for advertisements, illustrations, and creations associated with the decorative rather than fine arts – are amongst the greatest treasures to be uncovered in a studio. It is in works such as *The Children's Shop* sign (CAT 76), the Shell advertisements (CAT 82-84), or the *Opportunity* needlework (CAT 75), that we are offered the most complete but rarest glimpse of Dunbar's personality.

2) The *Salon des refusés* – pictures that failed to sell and therefore remained with the artist – constitute the second category of works typically found in a studio. Today it seems inexplicable that *An English Calendar* (CAT 71), certainly one of Dunbar's masterpieces, failed to sell during her lifetime; she eventually gifted it to Wye College some two decades after it had first been offered for sale at Wildenstein's. With the benefit of

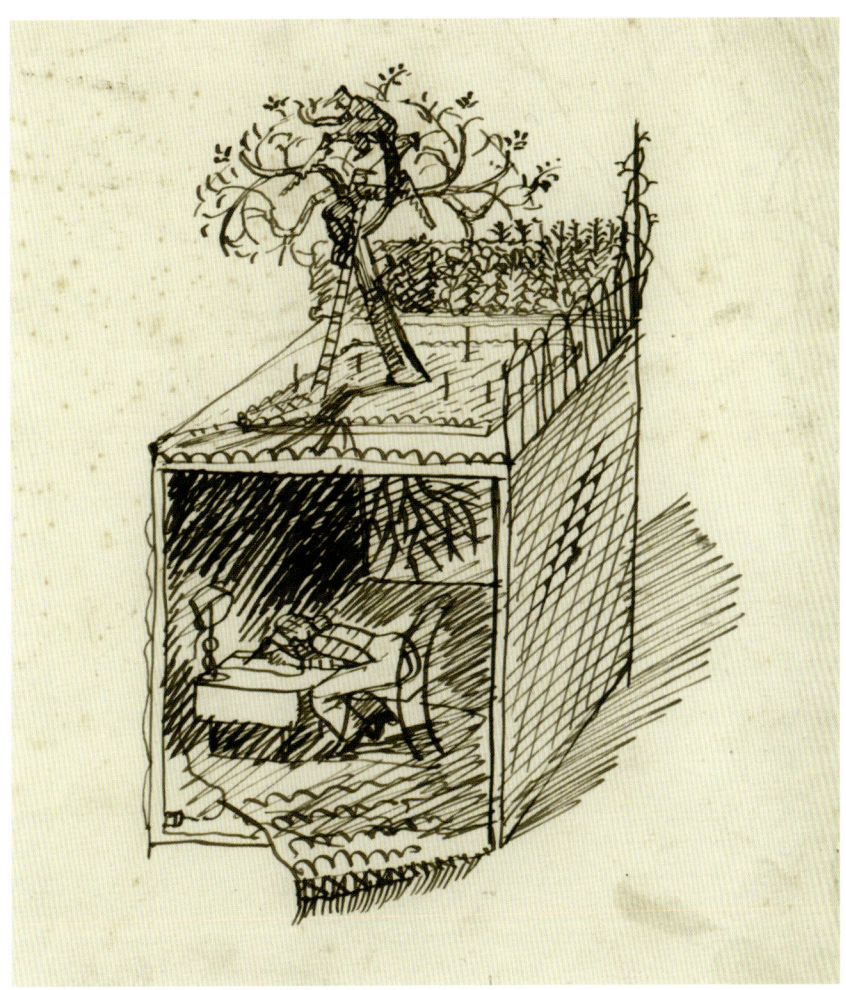

CAT 1 [HMO 223]
An Allegory of the Nature of Creation, 1940s-1950s,
Pen and ink on paper,
9 x 6 ¾ in. (22.8 x 17.5 cm)

hindsight it is sometimes hard to distinguish between these works and their near relatives: pictures that remained in the artist's studio because they were never offered for sale, including works to which the artist, or artist's family, attached a special importance. Pictures that fall into this category are Dunbar's late self-portrait (CAT 113) and *Autumn and the Poet* (CAT 114).

3) The largest category of pictures typically found in a studio consists of what might be described as work in progress: working drawings, compositions that were never quite resolved, projects that were either abandoned or temporarily put to one side to be returned to at a later date or that remained incomplete at the artist's death, such as *The Old Schoolmistress* (CAT 110). In seeing the full range of media used and the artist's methodology, (for instance the use of squaring, CAT 18), the process through which compositions evolved becomes clearer. Exhibiting these works raises an interesting issue; the artist might not have agreed with the idea of putting them on display and in a context that was never intended for them. The beauty of a work might depend simply on chance: drips of paint (CAT 22), a collision of motifs (CAT 64), or the unfinished nature of a study (CAT 68). This gives these works a curious frisson – a form of cultural voyeurism – as the moment of creative genius is laid bare. *An Allegory of the Nature of Creation* (CAT 1) opens up a view onto the enduringly powerful universe that occupied Dunbar's mind. The fact that works such as these have survived – through good chance and fortuitous custodianship – is today a cause for celebration.

The Significance of Lost Works: A Biographer's Perspective

Gill Clarke

Ten years ago I wrote the first biography of the artist Evelyn Dunbar; described by her Principal at the Royal College of Art (RCA), Sir William Rothenstein, as having real 'genius'. *Evelyn Dunbar: War and Country* was published by Sansom & Company and accompanied the exhibition I curated at St. Barbe Museum & Art Gallery, Lymington, which showcased over 30 works from national, regional and private collections to show her work as muralist, painter, illustrator and Official War Artist. That 2006 exhibition was the first devoted to Evelyn Dunbar's work, which I had initially been drawn to owing to my longstanding interest in the Women's Land Army – a subject that she recorded with keen understanding during the Second World War.

Given that Dunbar's life and work had been neglected I sought to retrace her footsteps both literally and visually so as to develop an understanding of the person who could compose such lyrical work. It was a process facilitated by Roger Folley, Evelyn's husband whom I got to know well during my visits to Wye, Kent. Additionally, Elizabeth Bulkeley, Charles Mahoney's daughter allowed me access to Dunbar's intimate and beautifully illustrated letters to her father, who had taught Dunbar and with whom she had collaborated on a number of projects. Many visits to, and interviews with, family, friends, colleagues and sitters ensued.

If a catalogue raisonné of Dunbar's work had been compiled before the discovery of the lost works there probably would have been fewer than two hundred and fifty pictures in public and private hands to record. The discovery of the Hammer Mill Oast collection represents a significant increase (in quantitive terms) in the known body of work. It was with much interest therefore that I viewed these works – what insights might they offer, what impact would they have on my view of the significance of Dunbar's work? The early paintings and photographs were a delight; especially those of family members which revealed from the outset the place given to her garden – a locale that was to remain an inspiration for much of her later work. I particularly enjoyed seeing the photograph of the family home, The Cedars (which features in her memorable painting *Winter Garden* (FIG 2) at Tate Britain) as Roger and I had climbed the tower where Dunbar had toiled over many of her wartime commissions.

The drawings associated with The Children's Shop were of interest too and may be linked to a book that Dunbar was collaborating on with her former English teacher about children's games. In connection with this in 2007 I received a letter from someone who had worked with Jessie Dunbar at The Children's Shop from 1948-55, she recalled 'the sectional' *An English Calendar* (CAT 71), hanging over the fireplace and confirmed that the models for the months were Dunbar's sisters, brothers and family gardener. *April* (CAT 69) and *February* (CAT 65) are delightful and evidence of her imagination and depth of feeling.

While Dunbar's work from the Home Front is now better known it is valuable nonetheless to see many of her preliminary sketches. Those for *A Land Girl and the Bail Bull* (FIG 19) are fascinating revealing the genesis of and process and intentions behind perhaps her most accomplished work from that wartime period. They also demonstrate her powers of observation and fine draughtsmanship and why she was ideally suited to provide the illustrations for *A Book of Farmcraft* (1942) (FIG 16), which was designed with neophyte Land Girls in mind. It was helpful too to see Dunbar's *My little WAAF* (CAT 96), one of the few of her works rejected by the War Artists' Advisory Committee in March 1945 on the grounds that it was not of very great interest nor added much to the war records and the sitter not a very good one.

Also illuminating were works that hitherto were only titles in catalogues. The allegorical *Flying Applepickers* (CAT 107) with its sense of other-worldliness is one such example. The finished work was exhibited at Black Hall, Oxford as part of the exhibition '5 Painters' in 1949.

I recently discovered two letters that relate to Dunbar's work. The first (9/12/49) from Dunbar when she was living in Enstone, some 10 miles from Oxford, to her friend from the RCA Margaret Goodwin, making reference to being full of ideas chiefly 'poetical & imaginative. (Not abstract though) and having a much clearer attitude to painting'. The second from Percy Horton, Ruskin Master of Drawing (21/5/60) to Mahoney written shortly after attending Dunbar's funeral, commenting on how she would be missed at the Ruskin where she was a stimulating and popular teacher but also questioning whether something prevented her from being as good as she might, such as isolation in the country away from stimulating influences.

Thus the lost works are particularly significant and help us to better judge whether this was indeed the case. For me, and I suspect many others, these new works will serve to convince that Dunbar did have a unique imaginative power which is strangely compelling and which enabled her to add much to the spirit and practice of English art in the mid 20th century.

Evelyn Dunbar: Such a Gifted Artist

Andrew Lambirth

Evelyn Dunbar, who was part of a generation which did not seek publicity for their work, rarely exhibited her paintings, was not able to view them as an essential source of income and was happy in later years to give them away. This apparently modest self-valuation has been all too readily accepted by subsequent generations, and her work had, until recently, all but disappeared from accounts of 20th century British art. She continued to feature in histories of War Art, but that limited categorization has not done much for her work as a whole. It is, of course, indicative of how little her art was valued or esteemed that a large cache of it should be immured for decades in an oast house, and only just been re-discovered. However, now that her work is appearing regularly in museums and the commercial sector, she is even the subject of admiring websites and blogs by enthusiastic youngsters, who have termed her 'an absolute inspiration, hero, icon'. So, who was Evelyn Dunbar?

One of the biggest problems for students (or indeed professors) of 20th century British art has been the lack of material on Dunbar. Gill Clarke's pioneering book on her came out in 2006, accompanying an exhibition devoted to Dunbar at the St Barbe Museum in Lymington. St Barbe does a brilliant job, but this small museum is not on everyone's beat, and is certainly not as widely-known as it deserves to be. Only now, as more of Dunbar's work reappears, and as its consistently high standard becomes apparent, can her achievement be properly reassessed.

Undoubtedly she died too young (she was 53), which allowed her only a relatively short career, but then she outlived her near contemporary Eric Ravilious by 18 years, and his early death has not stood in the way of an extraordinary recent revival and mounting nationwide popularity. And it could be argued that she had done her best work years before her death. But even that assertion could be questioned, for little research has yet been done on her post-war work. Her best-known and best-documented period is the war, but her art was highly thought of both before and after that particular watershed. Perhaps her artistic independence has told against her. Dunbar was never part of a movement or clique, but the English – rank individualists – are not very good

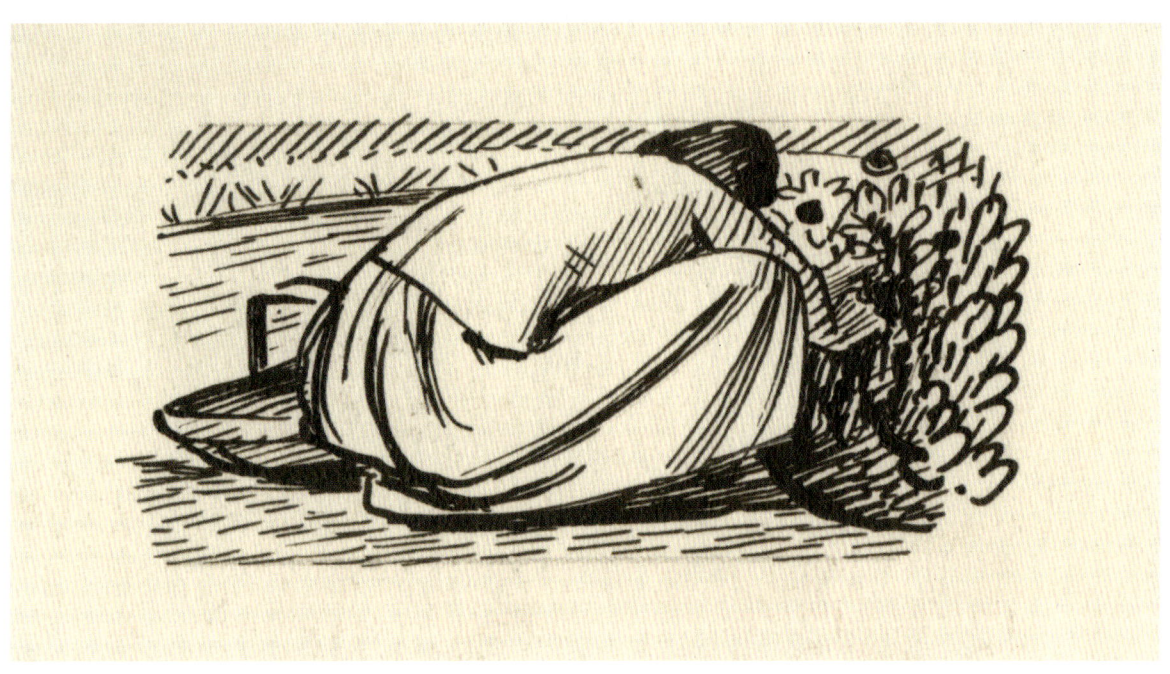

CAT 60 [HMO 200]) 'Studies for gardening vignettes', detail (See page 101)

at associations of artists or belonging to movements. Her work was probably too subtle and idiosyncratic for the mainstream, and could scarcely register against the clamorous post-war developments of Kitchen Sink Realism and Pop Art.

These are some of the reasons why we need to look again at Evelyn Dunbar, an unfairly neglected English 20th century painter. But was she just a respectable talent, or something more? Only prolonged study of her work – in all its aspects – will enable us to decide that, which is why it is so important to be able to see and contemplate such a body of paintings and drawings as the present one. Certainly she was a painter who loved the English countryside, but particularly her native Kent with its generously opulent landscape, the garden of England, wide-skied and fertile. Her favourite terrain was the Weald – the fields and beech woods of the North Downs – and she painted it not just with deep affection, but with an understanding of place (the numinous quality of landscape) that can rival such artists as Paul Nash or Graham Sutherland. Dunbar does it in a less overt and demonstrative manner – perhaps in a less masculine way – but the magic, and the authoritative perception, are undoubtedly there.

To position her fairly one must try to imagine an intersection of three such disparate artists as Edward Bawden, Eric Ravilious and Stanley Spencer. The Bawden of the *Ambrose Heath* illustrations (I'm thinking particularly of *Good Food*, 1932), the Ravilious of *Downs in Winter* (c.1934) and *Beachy Head* (1939), and the Spencer of the early religious paintings and the Sandham Memorial Chapel at Burghclere. (Also perhaps the pen drawings for the 1927 *Chatto & Windus Almanack*.) Then add overtones (and undertones) of Paul Nash, such as might be present in *Wood on the Downs*, 1929 and *Landscape of the Megaliths*, 1937, but with the tinge of mysticism translated into pure spirituality. Add to this rich mix the work of Paul's seriously underrated younger brother John. In fact John Nash at his finest (for example *The Cornfield*, 1918, *Dorset Landscape*, c.1930 and *Iken, Suffolk*, 1934) offers perhaps the nearest single parallel to Dunbar, though she tends to people her landscapes, whereas Nash prefers his empty, and there is a different kind of intensification to her clipped and tender imagery. John Nash is adept at the unvarnished poetry of the seasons, the natural cycle. Dunbar tempers this with the intended benefits of human intervention. Her landscapes are curiously more controlled than Nash's. In the end, her work might be defined as reportorial matter-of-factness, tinged with lyricism: richness with restraint.

Where did such discriminating sensitivity come from? Consider the distinction of her biography, however plainly recounted. She first rose to prominence in the early 1930s, working as a muralist. An exceptionally gifted student, she came to the attention of several tutors at the Royal College of Art: Cyril (or Charles) Mahoney, Allan Gwynne-Jones, the Professor of Painting, and finally William Rothenstein, the Principal. Mahoney, another underrated artist, was a major influence on her. He and Dunbar collaborated on an ambitious series of mural paintings for Brockley School in south London (FIG 1), and during their execution (1933-36) developed an intimate relationship, which lasted until 1937. Their love affair was as much about the land as it was about personalities, specifically in terms of the gardens they planned, planted and endlessly discussed. Out of this intense dialogue came a remarkable illustrated book, the jointly-authored *Gardeners' Choice* (CAT 35-55). And it was this highly developed appreciation of growth and nurture that continued to sustain Dunbar's work in years to come.

In this period, gardening seemed to go particularly well with art. During the 1930s, Bawden and Mahoney exchanged plants and seeds. And then there were the revered artist-plantsmen of Essex and Suffolk: John Nash, Cedric Morris and John Aldridge. Mahoney was a passionate artist-gardener and under his tutelage and coming from the background she did (the Dunbars had a large garden at Strood, near Rochester),

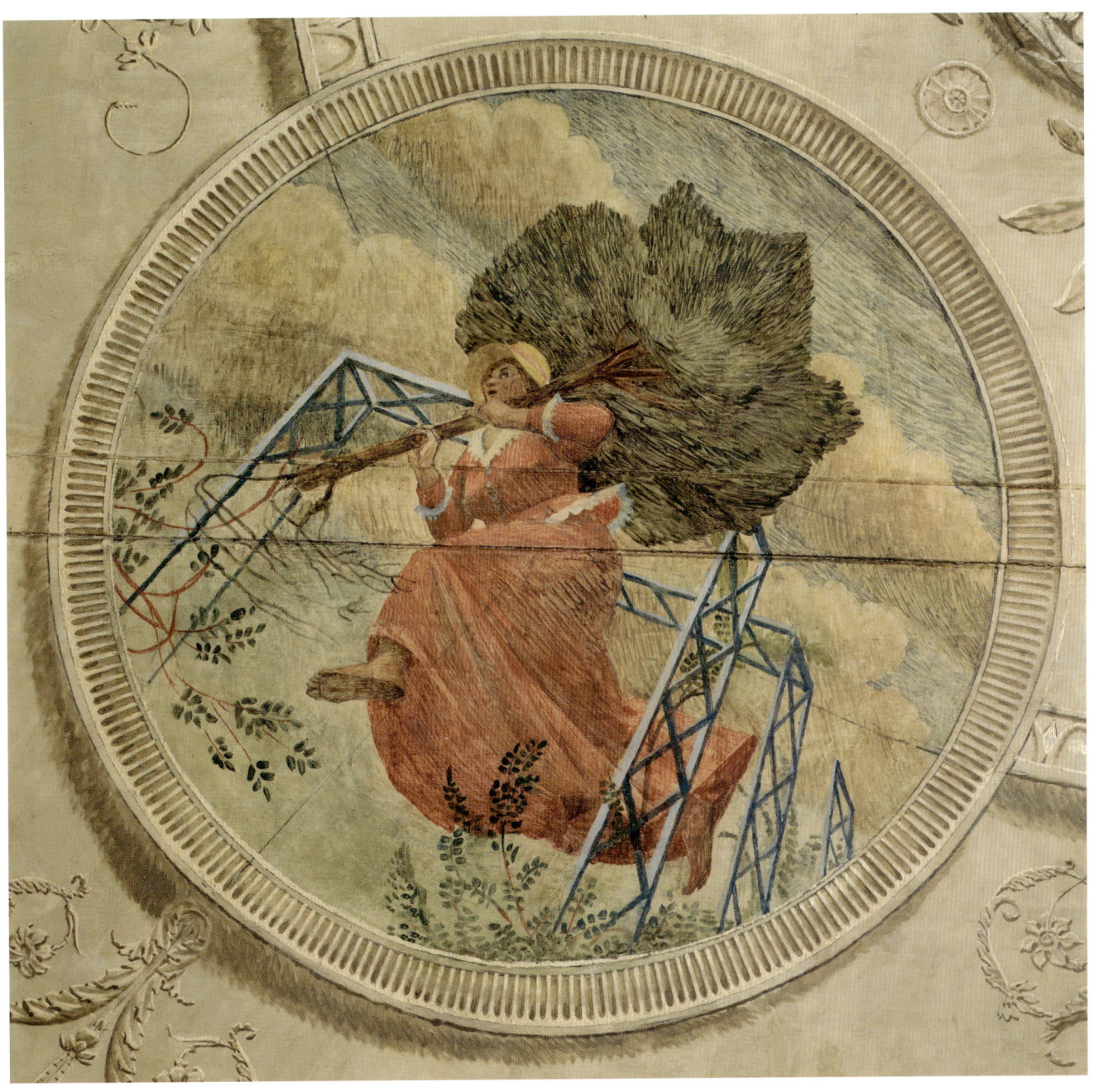

FIG 1 Detail from the Brockley School murals: *Minerva and the Olive Tree*
Photograph: Richard Valencia, © Christopher Campbell-Howes

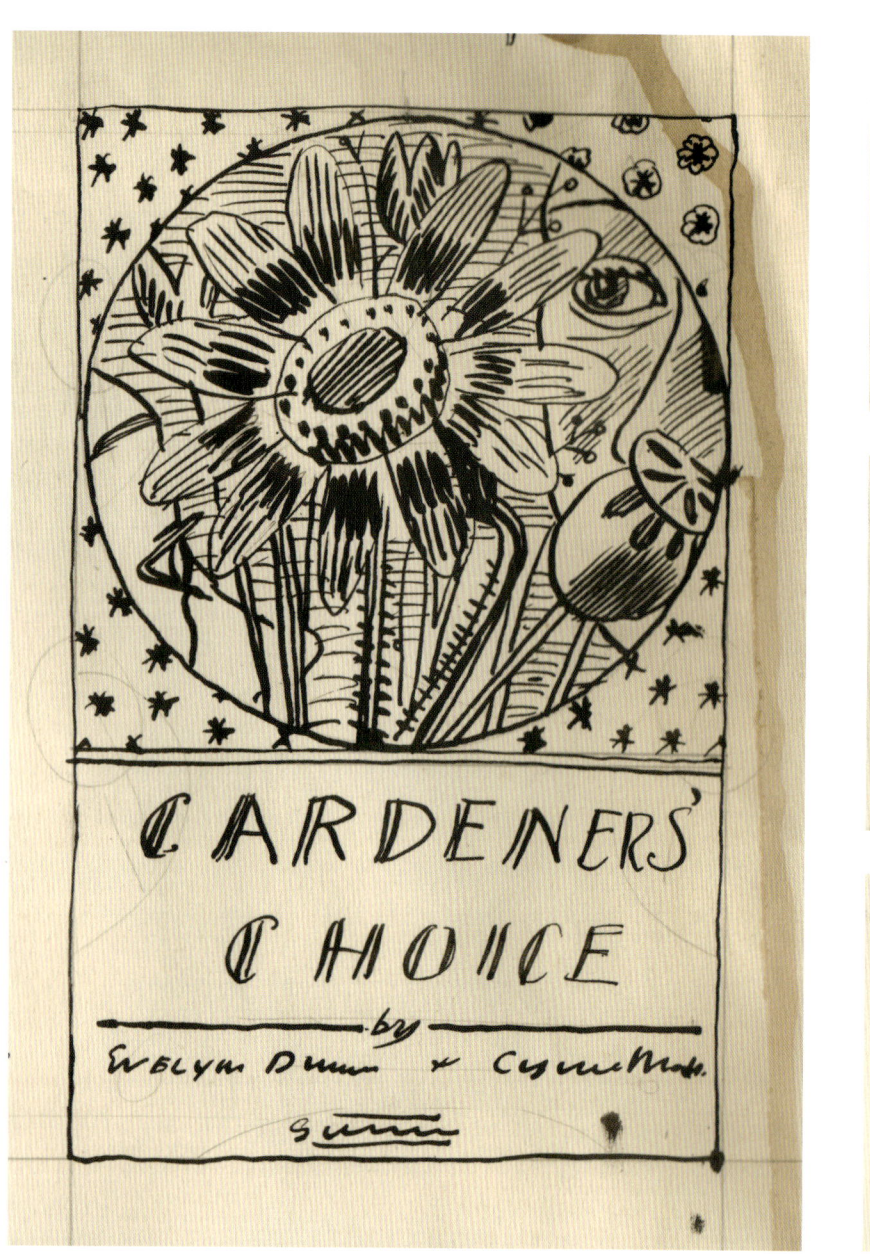
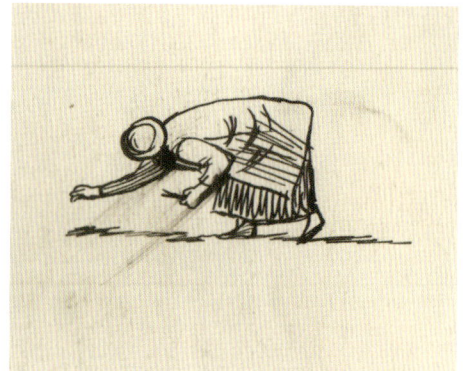
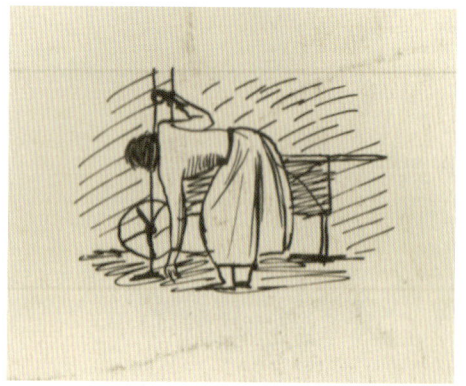
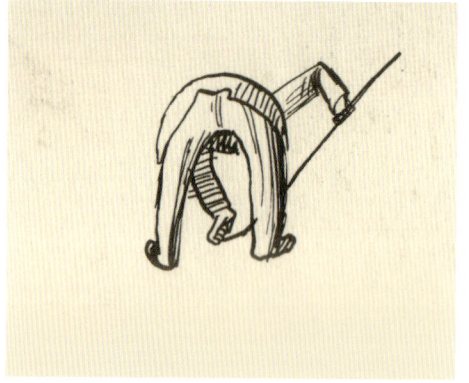

CAT 35 [HMO 363] & CAT 60 [HMO 200] Details of studies for *Gardeners' Choice* and gardening vignettes (See pages 85 and 101)

Dunbar was able to match his enthusiasm. In a very real sense, gardening became their common ground, the locus of their love. It is perhaps not surprising that Dunbar in later years seems not to have taken the same interest in making and tending gardens herself. This activity was part of her pact with Mahoney, and when that came to an end, he was the one who remained devoted to his garden.

Sir William Rothenstein in his memoir *Since Fifty* (1939) referred directly to the Brockley murals and that Mahoney offered to carry them out with 'one of his most gifted students, Miss Evelyn Dunbar'. Rothenstein noted that for three years the pair worked on the murals, 'among the best, to my mind, conceived since Madox Brown's wall paintings at Manchester.' Rothenstein goes on: 'Unfortunately, Brockley is some eight miles from the centre of London, and these fine paintings remain unknown and unvisited.' The situation remains much the same today. Although still in existence (unlike many of the murals designed for public or private buildings), the Brockley paintings remain little known, hidden away in a suburb of south London. Rothenstein concluded: 'It is lamentable that such gifted painters as Cyril Mahoney and Evelyn Dunbar should be unused. Our economics are unsound; such neglect is unpolitic economy.'

Of course Rothenstein's book was published in 1939, when Dunbar was indeed under-employed, but for the next six years she was to be almost constantly employed as a war artist, producing some of the best work of her career, and painting at the height of her powers. Later in his memoir Rothenstein listed his top students, beginning with Henry Moore and Mahoney, and continuing with such luminaries of 20th century British art as Ravilious, Bawden, Barnett Freedman and Edward Le Bas, and including Dunbar amongst the final names. Rothenstein's support was not limited to fine words. In February 1936 the City Art Gallery in Carlisle, whose Honorary Adviser he was, bought Dunbar's cartoon for the panorama at Brockley and two oil sketches. Rothenstein's advisory role to Carlisle lasted nine years, and during that time he recommended some 100 works by artists as diverse as Wyndham Lewis and Stanley and Gilbert Spencer, as well as by his expected favourites, among whom Gwynne-Jones, Ravilious, Bawden, Freedman, Percy Horton and Mahoney all featured.

Further family support ensued. In March 1936, John Rothenstein (Sir William's oldest son) wrote an article for *The Studio*, entitled 'Scope for Young Artists', which discussed the Brockley murals and the achievement of Mahoney and Dunbar. 'In the work of both of them', Rothenstein junior wrote, 'is manifest that grand austerity linked with an intense devotion to nature which has been the inspiration of so large a part of our greatest poetry, but which, curiously enough, is rarely met within our painting.' Mahoney and

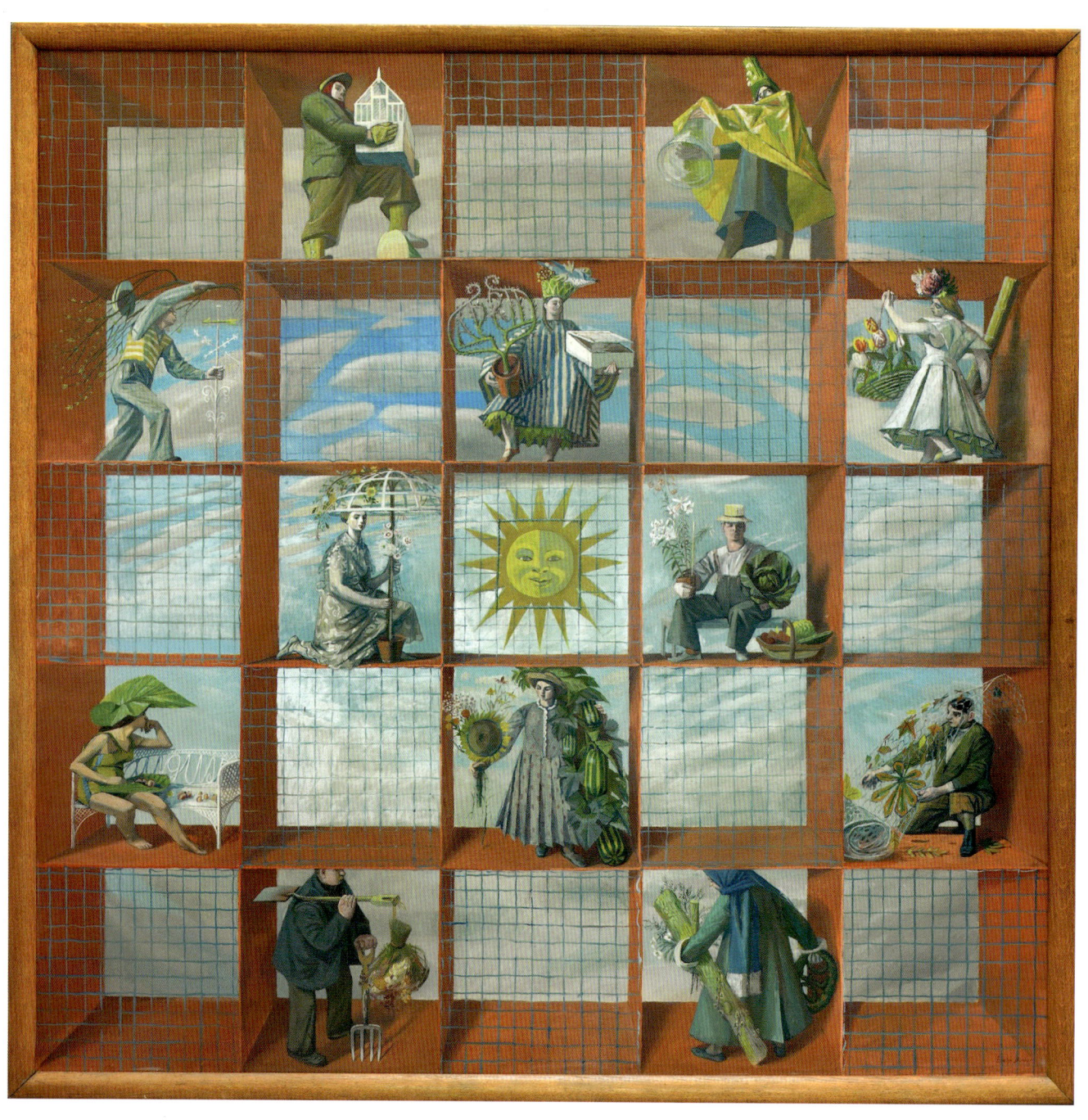

CAT 71 *An English Calendar*, 1938, oil on canvas, 72 x 72 in. (183 x 183 cm) (See pages 110-111)
Collection: Archives Imperial College London

Dunbar were seen as part of the pastoral, romantic tradition that flourished in the 1930s before Neo-Romanticism became the movement of the moment.

There were also official appearances. In March-April 1938, Dunbar was included in an exhibition at Wildenstein & Co in New Bond Street entitled *Cross-Section of English Painting*, and staged by Gwynne-Jones. It included such painters as William Coldstream, Rodrigo Moynihan, Victor Pasmore and Vivian Pitchforth. Dunbar was the only woman artist, and among her exhibits were *An English Calendar* (CAT 71) (now in the possession of Imperial College) and *Winter Garden* (FIG 2) (now in the Tate). Percy Horton, who reviewed the show in his column for *Left Review*, was of the opinion that the exhibition did not represent the current state of English painting, and accused Dunbar's work of being suburban and petit-bourgeois. But inclusion in the exhibition was a distinct accolade for Dunbar, whatever Horton thought.

Perhaps Horton's criticism was intended, in some peculiarly personal way, as a means of showing solidarity with his friend Mahoney. To an unknowable extent Dunbar's relationships with Mahoney's friends must have been damaged – or at least qualified – by the end of their affair. How did it affect her? Gwynne-Jones certainly seemed to continue supportive. Besides selecting her for the Wildenstein show, as a Tate trustee he was no doubt instrumental in persuading the gallery's governors in 1940 to buy two of Dunbar's paintings, *Winter Garden*, and an early student work entitled *Study for Decoration: Flight* (1930) (FIG 3).

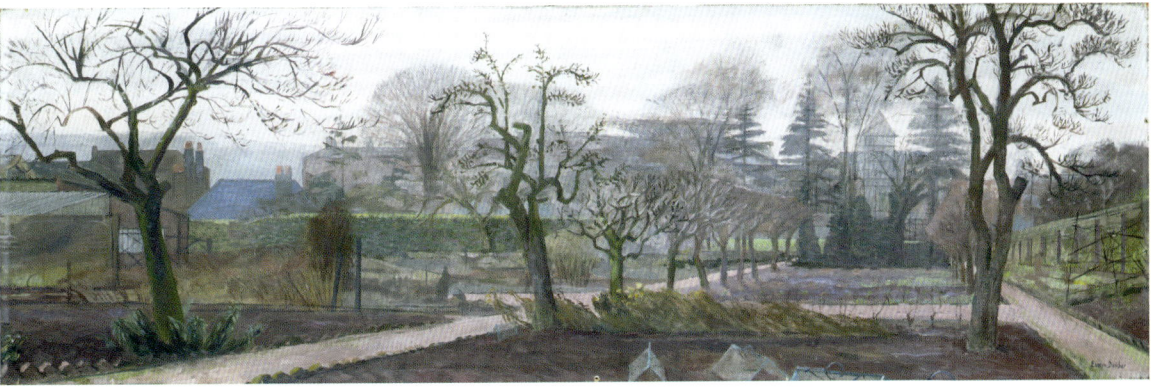

FIG 2 *Winter Garden*, c.1929-37, oil on canvas, 12 x 36 in. (30.5 x 91.4 cm)
Collection: © Tate, London 2015

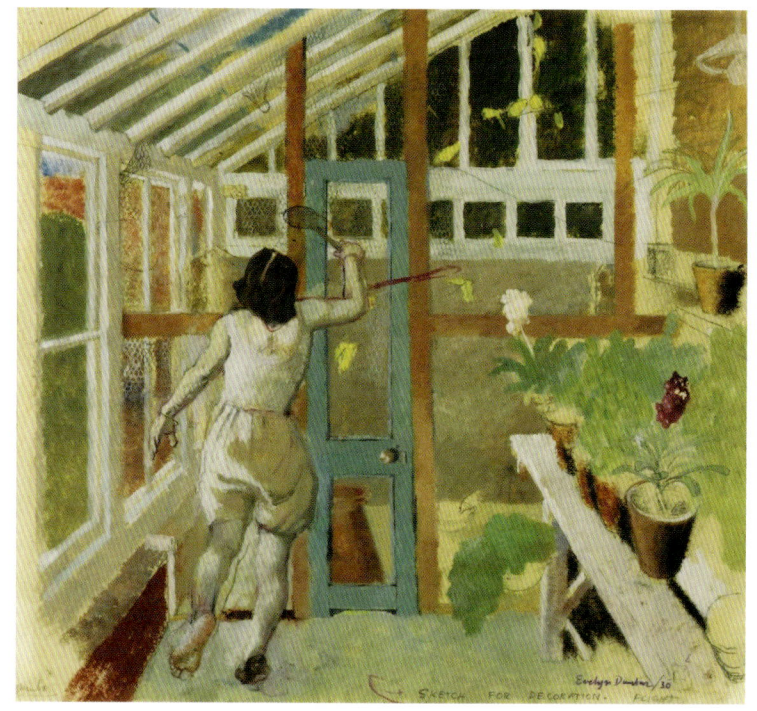

FIG 3
Study for Decoration: Flight, 1930
Oil and watercolour on paper
15 x 15 ½ in. (38.1 x 39.4 cm)
Collection: © Tate, London 2015

Then, in a bold attempt to carry modern art to the Kentish heartlands, in March 1939 Dunbar opened The Blue Gallery above the shop her sisters ran in Rochester, with an exhibition including work by Bawden, Mahoney, Gwynne-Jones, Kenneth Rowntree and Freedman. It was praised in the local paper (*The Chatham, Rochester & Gillingham News*) as 'remarkably catholic', but not 'a bombshell of modernity'. The timing could scarcely have been more unfortunate, with war looming on the horizon, and the gallery closed after a few months. Very soon, other issues would preoccupy them all.

Dunbar's wartime career is key to an understanding of her art. She was the only woman working for the War Artists' Advisory Committee (WAAC) on a full-time salaried basis, and her brief as a war artist was to record the Home Front, by documenting in paint civilian contributions to the war effort, with particular reference to the Women's Voluntary Service and the Women's Land Army. Her special achievement lies in the unsentimental depiction of ordinary women adapting to unfamiliar work, painted with sympathetic but arresting intensity. By the end of the war some 40 paintings by Dunbar had been accepted by the WAAC. Evidently she supplied work which pleased the commissioners, but did her art express war consciousness, a somewhat disputed quality that clearly exercised the minds of officials?

An examination of her major war paintings leaves little doubt as to her keen awareness of war and ability to express its moods, even when the subjects were ostensibly agricultural. There is, in much of Dunbar's work, a certain piquant strangeness, which represents the action of the imagination on a closely-observed scene. This is the artist's curiosity (and perhaps empathy) transforming the outward record into art. Eric Newton wrote: 'The most successful of our war artists are not so much eye-witnesses of spectacular happenings as poets trying to catch the mood below the surface.' Again and again, Dunbar succeeds in this. However, one of her most pastoral and idyllic paintings, the exquisitely beautiful *Men Stooking and Girls Learning to Stook* (CAT 100), was turned down by the WAAC – presumably for not saying enough about the war effort.

In July 1940 the first exhibition of wartime art at the National Gallery included Dunbar's *Putting on Anti-Gas Protective Clothing* (FIG 4). This painting, a six-frame serial image and

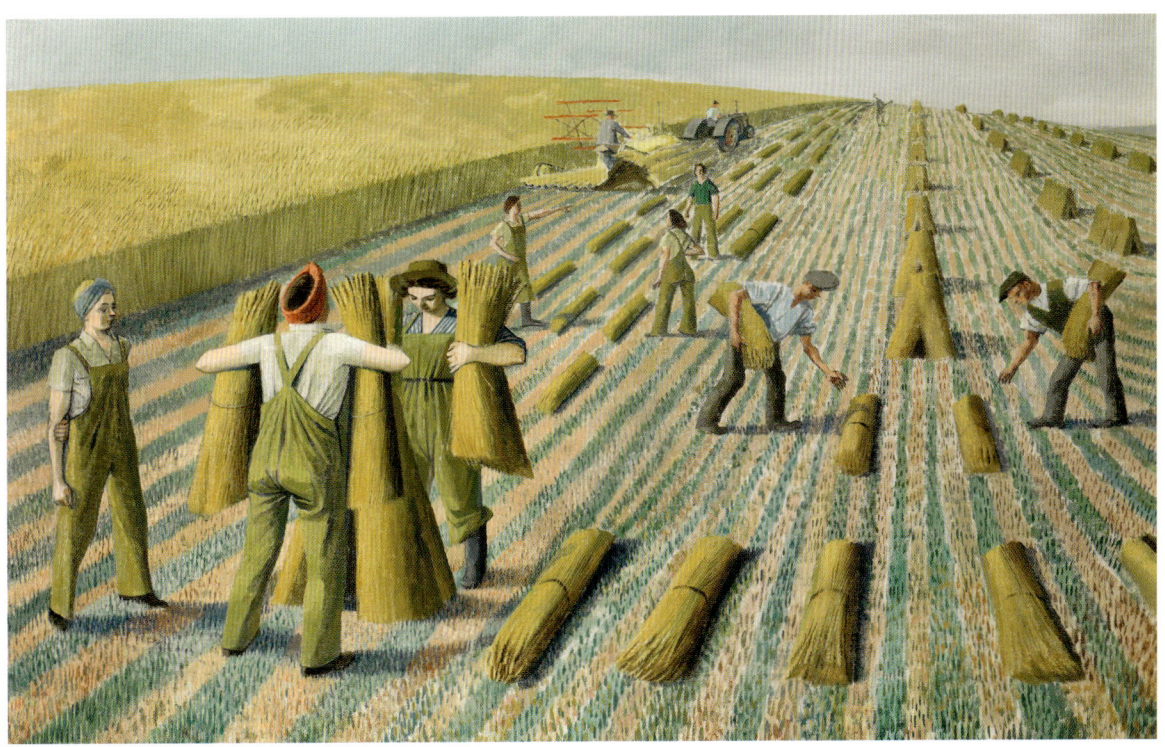

CAT 100 *Men Stooking and Girls Learning to Stook*, oil on canvas, 29 ½ x 19 in. (75 x 49 cm)
Private collection (See pages 146-147)

something of a favourite, was also shown in 1941 at MOMA New York (and illustrated in the sumptuous hardback American catalogue, *Britain at War*). Dunbar had her own very definite ideas about what made a good war painting and what didn't, and was not hesitant about expressing an opinion. When she went in 1940 to see the exhibitions *War Pictures by British Artists* and *British Painting since Whistler*, Dunbar claimed to enjoy most the work of Bawden and Anthony Gross, and admitted in a letter to Mahoney that she found 'the incessant round of John Nash's and Eric Ravilious a bit tedious'.

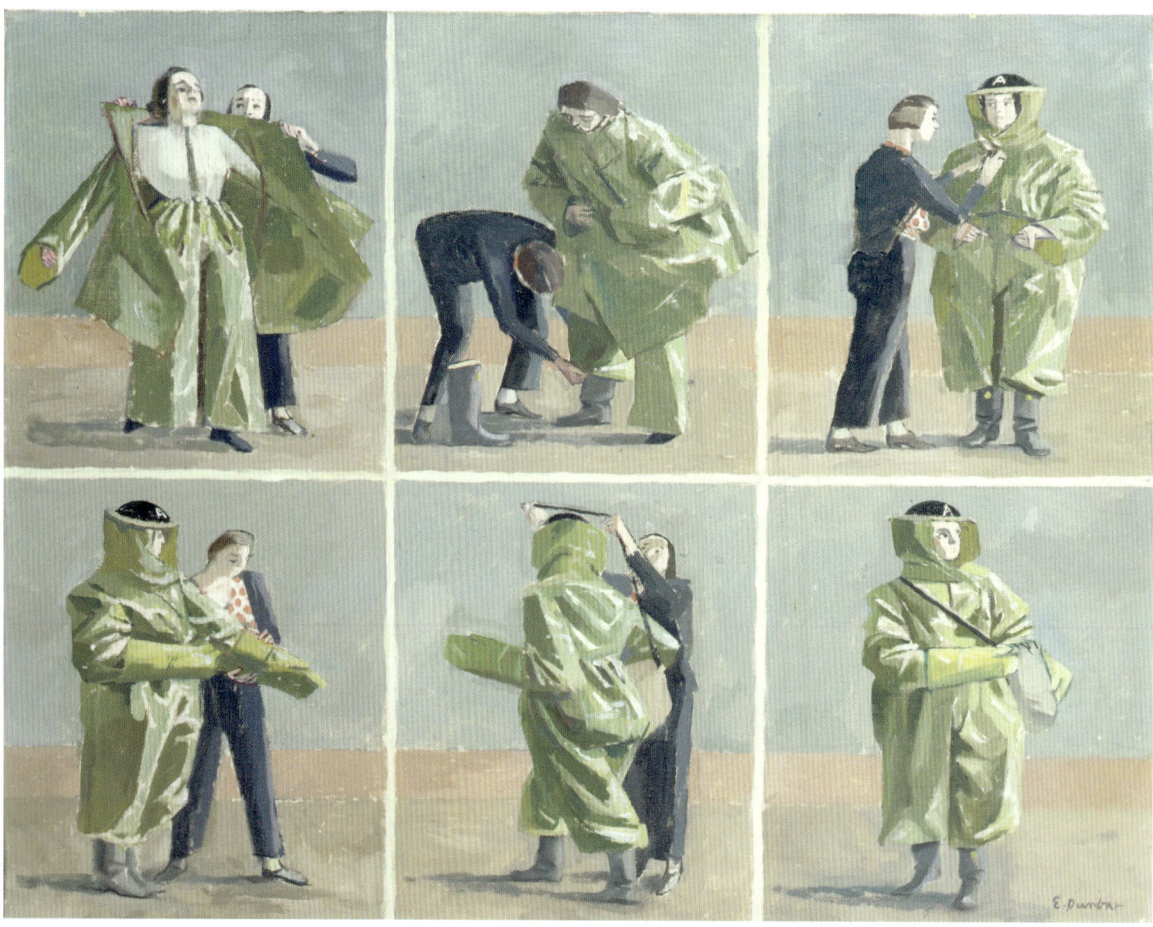

FIG 4 *Putting on Anti-Gas Protective Clothing*, 1940, oil on canvas, 24 x 30 in. (60.9 x 76.2 cm)
Collection: © Imperial War Museums (Art.IWM ART LD 247)

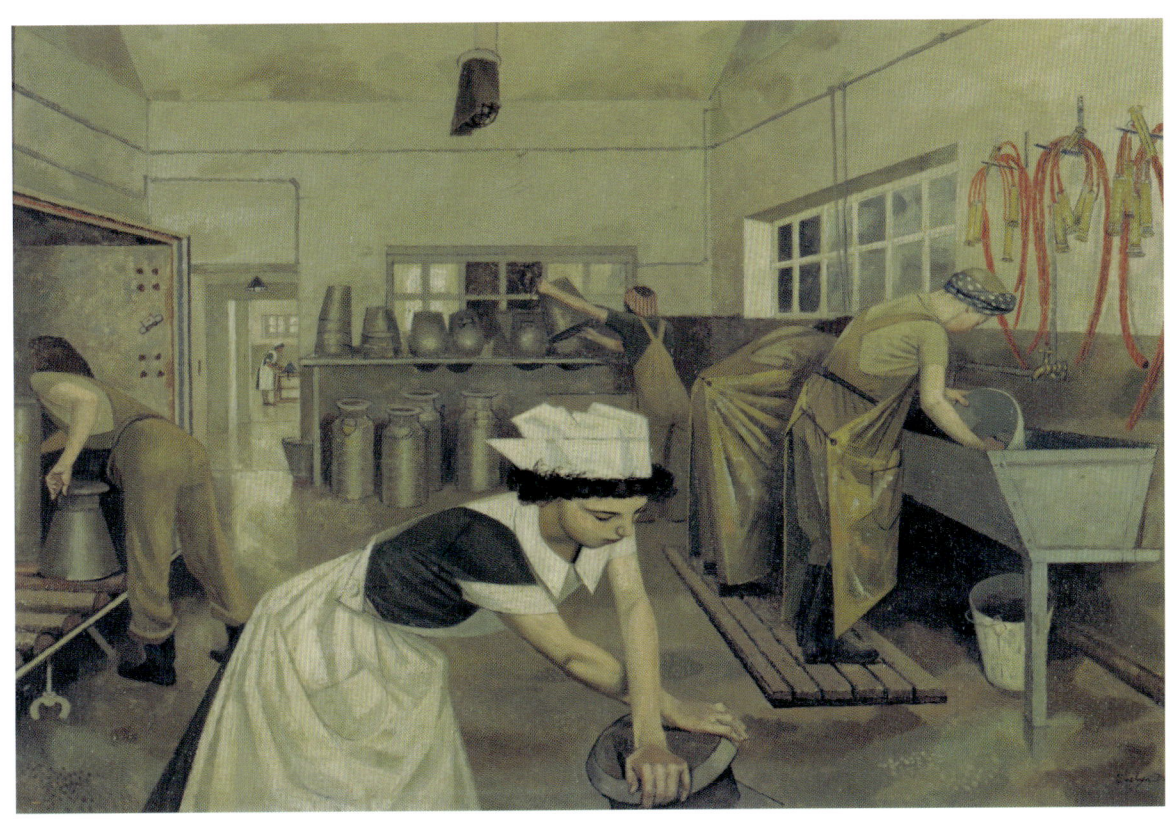

FIG 5 *Women's Land Army Dairy Training*, 1940, oil on canvas, 20 x 30 in. (50.8 x 76.2 cm)
Collection: © Imperial War Museums (Art.IWM ART LD 767)

Her own work appears in two of the eight paperback war-time volumes entitled *War Pictures by British Artists*, firstly *Blitz* (1942) and then *Women* (1943). *Blitz* features her single painting *Putting on Anti-Gas Clothes* (as it was here called), while *Women* carries four images, including the memorable *Women's Land Army Dairy Training* (FIG 5), and *Milking Practice with Artificial Udders* (FIG 6). In 1944, Dunbar was included in Jill Craigie's black and white documentary film, *Out of Chaos*, about the work of the WAAC. Several of her paintings were shown, although more time was given to better-known artists such as Paul Nash, Graham Sutherland, Stanley Spencer and Henry Moore.

Evelyn Dunbar was modest and self-effacing. However charming and likeable these traits are in friends and acquaintances, they do not help an artist to be well-known or

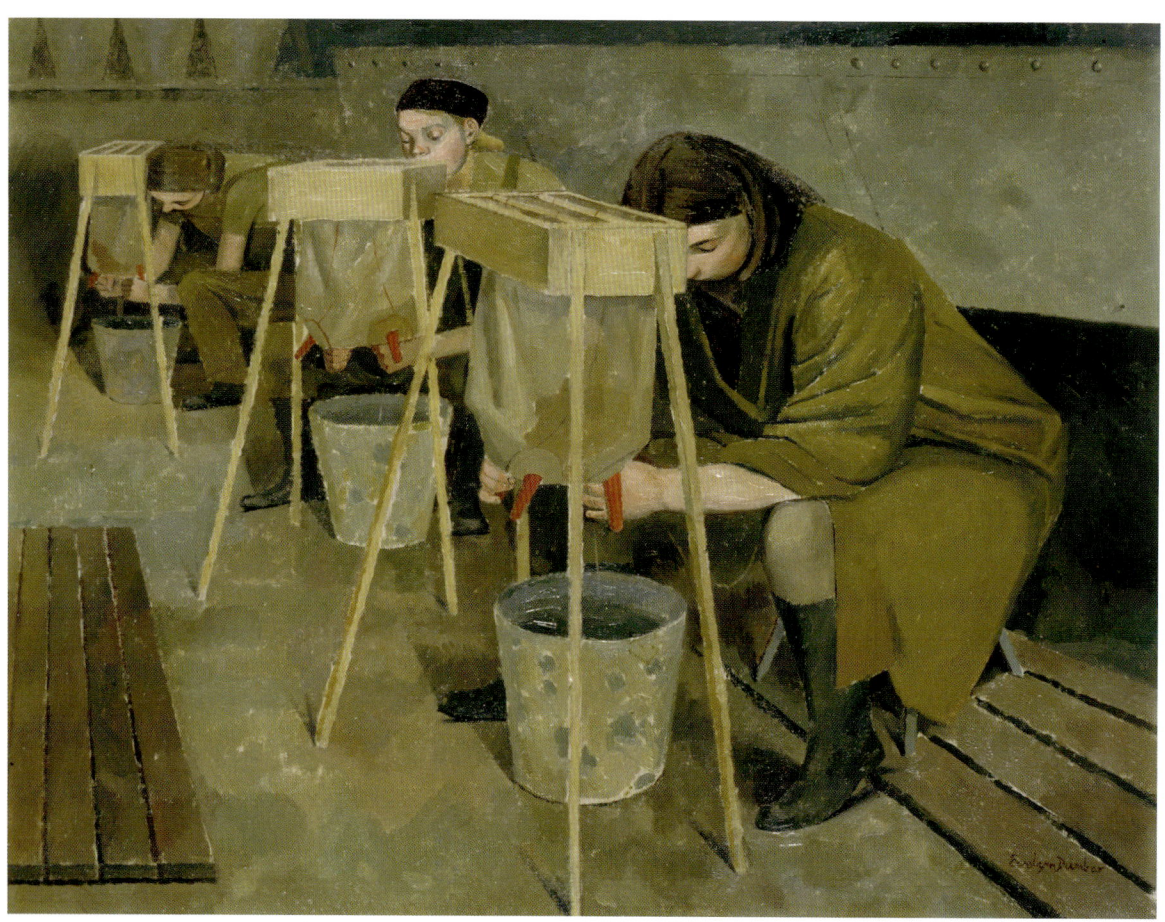

FIG 6 *Milking Practice with Artificial Udders*, 1940, oil on canvas, 24 ¼ x 30 in. (61.7 x 76.6 cm) (See page 130) Collection: © Imperial War Museums (Art.IWM ART LD 766)

appreciated. People are only too ready to take you at your own valuation, and in art, the unassertive go to the wall. This is a huge irony, as the sensitivity required to be an artist would seem to be totally at odds with the toughness required for self-promotion. The lesson Dunbar had already learnt was that you don't get rich and famous painting murals. Even Spencer's superb Burghclere murals are little-known – or were until they were recently taken out of the chapel for which they were expressly painted and toured around the country by the National Trust. After the war, for Dunbar as for so many others, it must have been very much a question of, what next?

In the summer of 1947, Dunbar met Albert Rutherston, the younger brother of Sir William Rothenstein. Rutherston, who had Anglicized his name, was then Master of Drawing at the Ruskin School in Oxford, a position he had held since 1929, though Percy Horton would in fact soon replace him. Rutherston asked Dunbar to join the part-time staff, which she duly did in October 1947. Teaching at Oxford brought her back into contact with earlier friends and associates from Mahoney's circle: Horton, Gwynne-Jones, Rowntree and Freedman. Of this group, Gwynne-Jones was perhaps the most high-powered. Certainly, Dunbar met Stanley Spencer, and his younger brother Gilbert, through Gwynne-Jones.

Looking at Dunbar's work, one or two critics presciently identified the 'Neo-primitive' influence of Stanley Spencer. (RH Wilenski was one such.) Dunbar knew Spencer's murals at Burghclere from first-hand visits, and she also kept up with his more regular easel output, visiting, for instance, his exhibition at Arthur Tooth in July 1936. As Spencer used Cookham, so did Dunbar use the Kent countryside or Strood High Street. The latter features in *The Queue at the Fish Shop* (FIG 18), one of her most celebrated paintings. Neither Spencer nor Dunbar painted literal uninflected transcriptions of people and places, but both developed imaginative reinterpretations of the loved and familiar. This was their power.

Look at Dunbar's painting *A Knitting Party* – who else was doing this sort of thing? (FIG 7) You can imagine Ardizzone drawing it in a more amusing and jokey way, but Dunbar takes it straight, and her painting is the more affecting because of it. The taut sparseness of the composition, and the quiet authority of the palette, put me in mind of Henry Walton (1746-1813) and his marvellously atmospheric painting *Sir Robert and Lady Buxton and their daughter Anne* (Norwich Castle Museum). In the same way, Dunbar's picture is a full but subtly understated account of a particular social (wartime) ritual, but also a brilliantly composed painting.

Is Dunbar a Modernist? Kathleen Palmer writing in *Women War Artists* (Tate, 2011) seems to think so. 'With her innovative and original style, Evelyn Dunbar was developing a reputation as a leading female modernist', she writes. Certainly Dunbar was admired by her peers, and by the art establishment, as demonstrated in this essay, but it is perhaps rather beside the point to discuss her in terms of Modernism. She is not a Modernist along the lines of Ben Nicholson, for instance, with his complex understanding and interpretation of international abstraction. She is much closer to the attitude of Stanley Spencer, and was he a Modernist? Again, this is not really the issue. With both Dunbar and Spencer we are talking about artists who delved so deeply into the human condition, its hopes and celebrations, as well as its tragedies, that their work is timeless in its relevance. It does not belong to a particular era or movement, but joins that idiosyncratic band of great individualists that makes up the history of British art.

It can also be said that Dunbar avoided the disputes and crippling intolerances of Modernism by the useful expedient of her early training. After all, she was a top-of-the-range artist-craftsman, mural painting and illustration equipping her perfectly for such a designation. Artist-craftsmen did not have to waste time considering the proposed utopias of Modern Art, they could simply get on with painting; particularly if, like Dunbar, they believed they were already living in Eden. Her strong belief as a Christian Scientist underlies her vision as a painter. In her view, the earth was a paradise, and nature was good, unchangeable, bountiful. In this scheme of things there was no room for a man-made eldorado.

Perhaps there was a certain innocence here, a degree of trust and acceptance that the modern world does not usually accept or foster. But Dunbar's work was built on celebration of the land, on husbandry. This is why her vision does not really fit within the Neo-Romantic remit, because for her paradise was here and now – not lost, or confined to the past. She identified more with the Pre-Raphaelites (as did Stanley Spencer, of course), and shared their desire for a painting to tell a positive story or point an uplifting moral. Not for her the sombre mood of most Neo-Romantic art, the gloom and destruction, the ruined buildings and troubled undergrowth.

And yet, there are other factors at work. Dunbar's interest in compartmented images obviously derives from the registers and divisions in Italian Renaissance fresco cycles, though a more contemporary interpretation would include the comic strip as well. Thus, in an unexpected way, Dunbar's painting foreshadows the cartoon narratives of Pop Art. This can be seen perhaps most clearly in *A 1944 Pastoral: Land Girls Pruning at East Malling* (FIG 8). In this strange painting, part eclogue, part illustrated farming guide, the central image of women pruning is framed by vignettes of hands clipping and sawing. (You can imagine a caption: 'The Seven Correct Pruning Positions for Secateurs.') The eventual outcome of this activity, a bowl and two plates of apples, are also included in the surrounding frieze, thus collapsing the time lag between pruning and fruiting, and adding a disconcerting touch of Modernist simultaneity to the image. As is the case with much of Dunbar's work, the more you look at this painting, the odder it appears.

Dunbar had an instinct for the revealing aspect of a subject, for the dramatic and eye-catching. She had a good visual memory, remembering details to supplement the drawings she made on site for her paintings. She also had a powerful visual intelligence, and was good at analysing and organizing the structure of figure compositions or the way

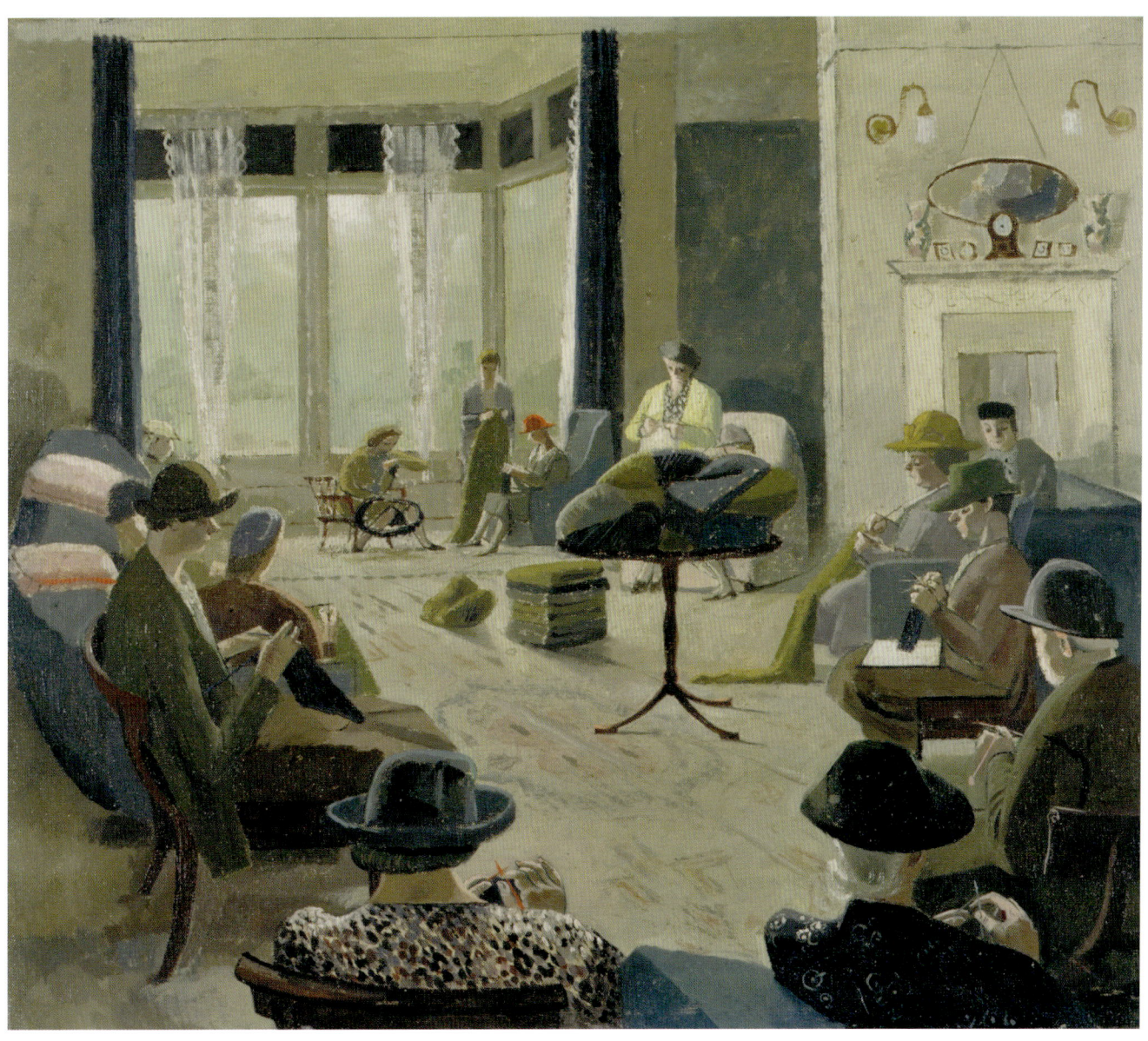

FIG 7 *A Knitting Party*, 1940, oil on canvas, 18 x 20 in. (45.7 x 50.8 cm)
Collection: © Imperial War Museums (Art.IWM ART LD 768)

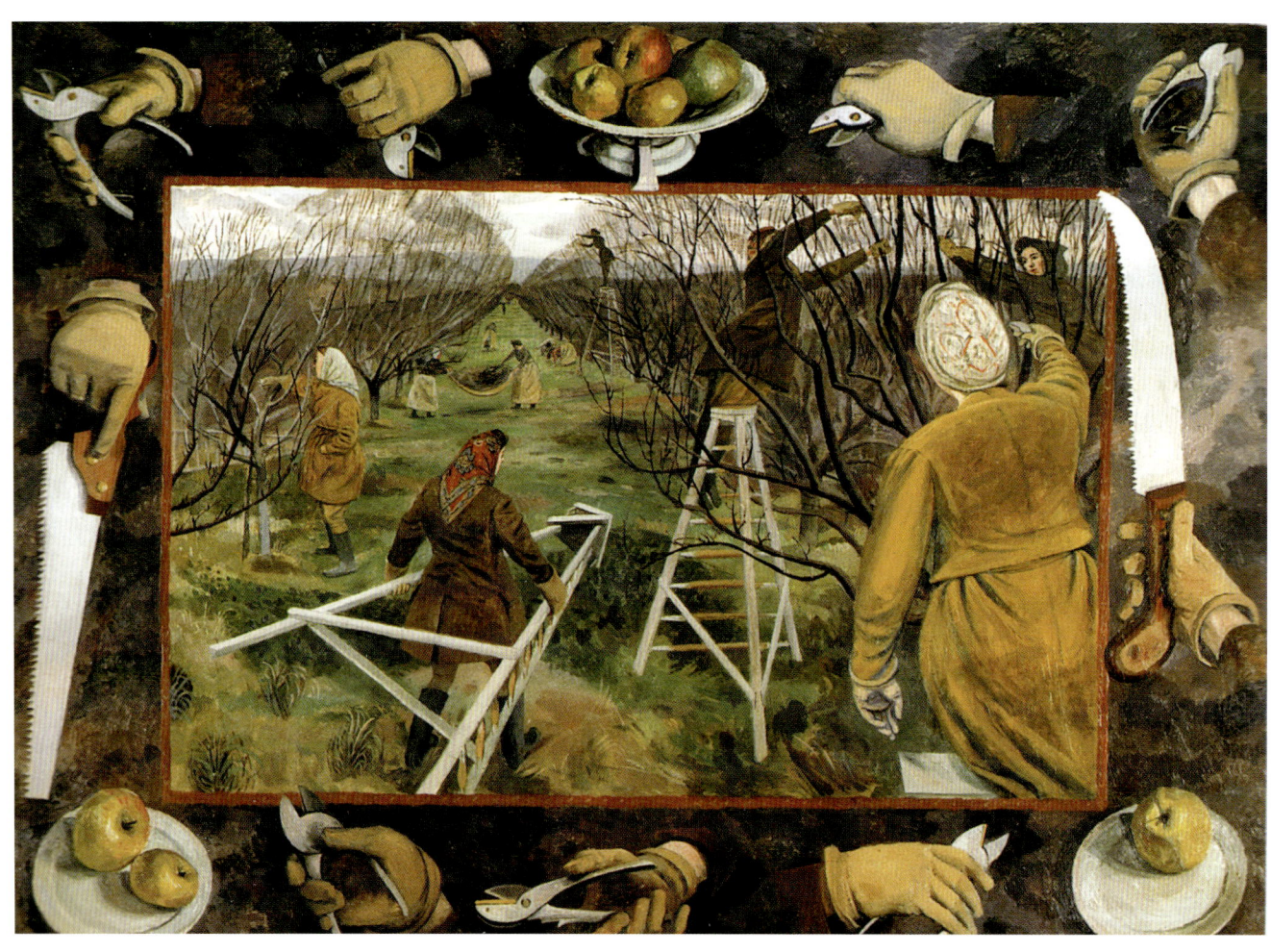

FIG 8 *A 1944 Pastoral: Land Girls Pruning at East Malling*, oil on canvas, 36 x 48 in. (91.3 x 121.8 cm)
Collection: Manchester Art Gallery

landscape should spread out and recede. This formal compositional discipline, though presumably answering a need within herself, no doubt also owed a considerable debt to the teaching at the Royal College of Alan Sorrell, who was nicknamed 'Old Angles' because of his passion for pictorial structure. For Dunbar, the depth and opacity of the paint was as important as the pictorial design, the surface texture as essential a part of the product as the patterns of light and colour.

Although elected to various associations, Dunbar was, as already noted, never part of any artistic movement. Of course, this did not militate entirely against recognition, and John Nash is always put forward as an example of an independent who made good. But actually Nash was a member of the Cumberland Market Group with Bevan, Ginner and Gilman, as well as the London Group, and he enjoyed a close association in early years with his extremely well-connected and ambitious brother, Paul, just at the point when he needed to launch his own career. These advantages were of undeniable use to him, and if in later years he was a man alone, the consequent dropping off of his public profile is in fact all too discernible. John Nash was a war artist in both wars, which certainly helped to boost his reputation and establish him in the public eye, and this is the chief career asset that Dunbar also shared. Aside from that, she was very much an artist alone.

We are still at the beginning of Dunbar studies and I don't think it's wise just yet to make too many large or definitive statements about her place in the history of 20th century British art. We need to get more used to her very particular vision, to seeing her in the company of others, to weighing her interpretations of people and places against her contemporaries. Her work must settle into place rather than be forced to adopt a position. But from what we have now, in terms of re-discovered work and thoughtful scholarship, despite her relative newness to the spotlight, it can reasonably be maintained that she is a substantial artist whose work deserves much more attention than it has so far received. In fact, the more one sees of her work, the more impressive and assured it looks, and that cannot be said for a number of artists whose reputations currently stand much higher than hers.

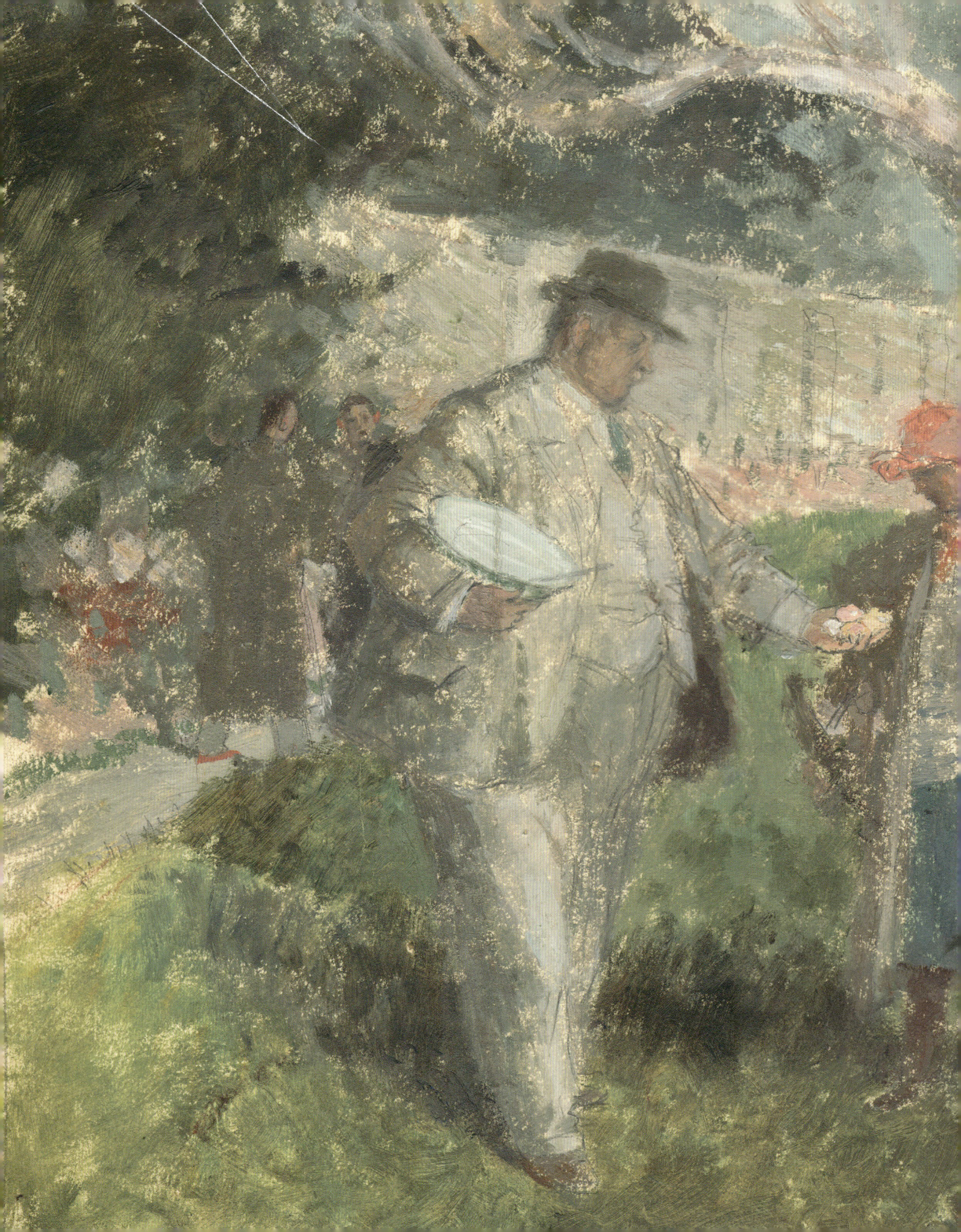

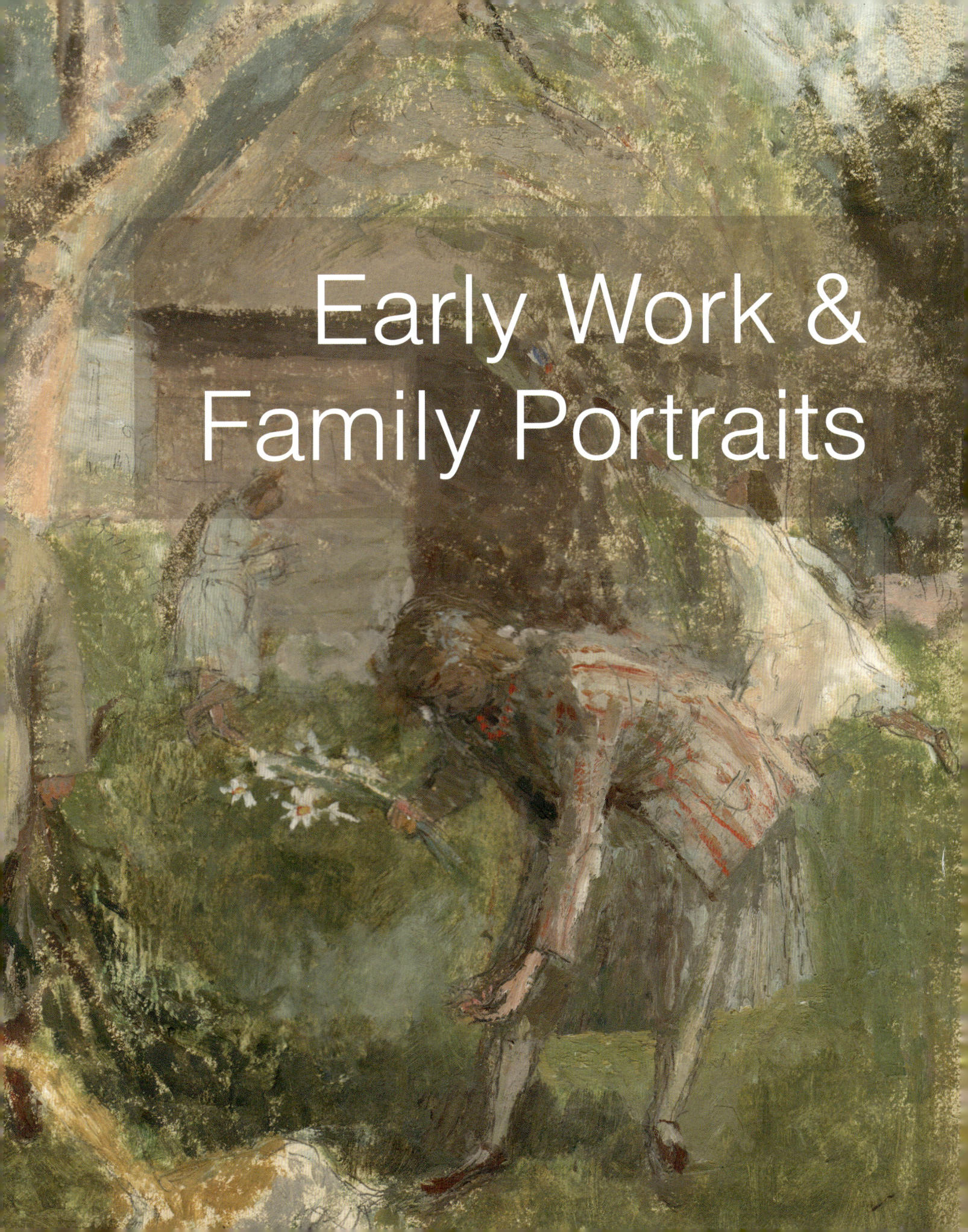

Early Work & Family Portraits

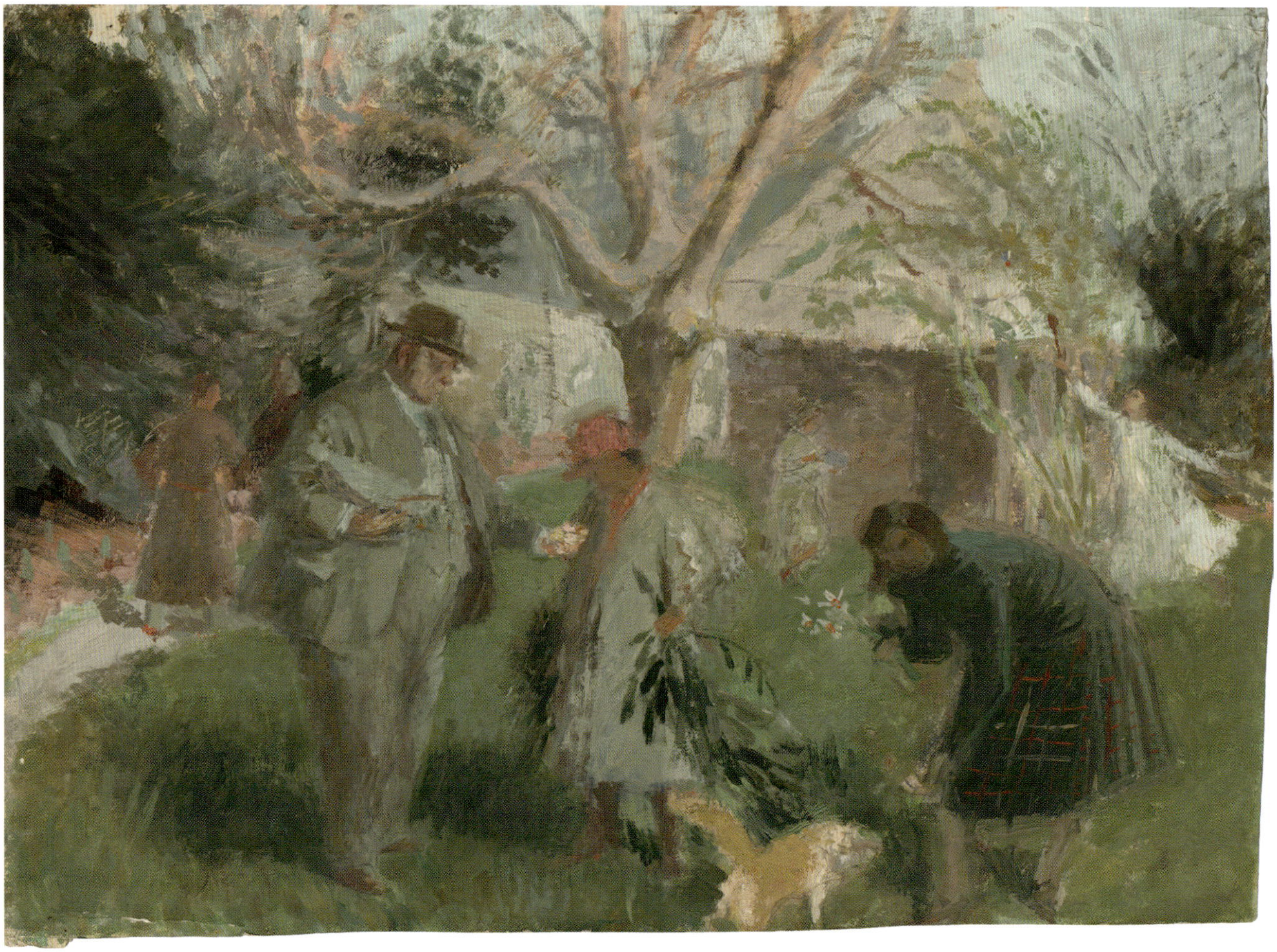

CAT 2 [HMO 74] The Dunbar family in the Garden at The Cedars, Spring (Version 2), c.1928,
Pencil and oil on paper, 14 ½ x 19 ½ in. (37 x 50 cm)

This composition depicts William Dunbar, Evelyn's father, showing eggs to Evelyn's mother Florence. Majorie, Evelyn's sister, is in the foreground (wearing a blazer) whilst her brothers Alec and Ronald are seen on the path on the left-hand side. Evelyn is playing badminton with her sister Jessie in the background.

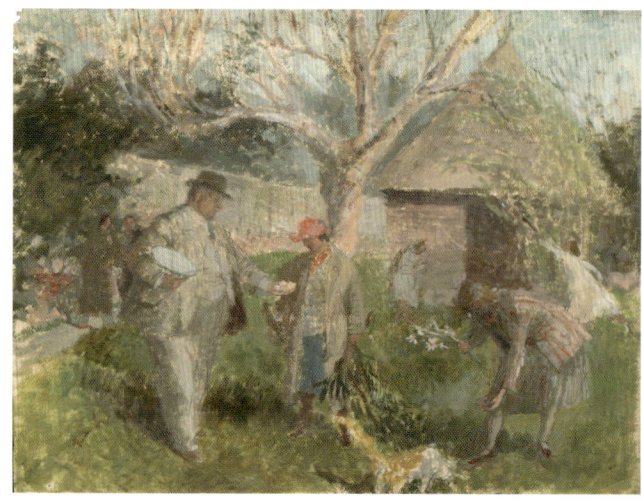

CAT 3 [HMO 75]
The Dunbar family in the garden at The Cedars, Spring
(Version 1), c.1928,
Pencil and oil on paper, 15 x 19 in. (38,2 x 48.5 cm)

Early Work & Family Portraits

It is remarkable how consistent and complete the art training available in England could be at the beginning of the twentieth century, following the replacement of the old 'South Kensington' system by more imaginative and intelligent methods. Winning prizes from the Royal Drawing Society while she was at Rochester Grammar School, Dunbar progressed to the local art school, and thence to London and the Royal College.

The early work that has survived gives an insight into the effectiveness of this training, of which the foundations were laid down at the Slade in the late nineteenth and early twentieth centuries, based on a reciprocal balance of observational drawing and learning from the paintings of the past. In Evelyn Dunbar's time, Modernism, looming over the English Channel, was still largely considered an alien disruption, foreign by nationality – then so were most of the artistic models on which British art was formed – but more significantly foreign to the moral and aesthetic standards that prevailed in most art schools across the rest of Europe as well. So insistent did the claims of Modernism become, and so pervasive do they remain in the body of knowledge and literature, that we need to rely on instinct to judge the relative qualities of the more conservative art that Dunbar represented, and to go back and understand what she and her contemporaries were trying to achieve.

The basis of this pedagogy was the imaginative composition, in a neo-Renaissance tradition, involving a number of figures in a credible but also idealized space. It barely differed from the definition of 'istoria' given in Leon Battista Alberti's essay 'On Painting' in 1435. Here Alberti argued that a composition with multiple figures was the noblest form of art, because it was the most difficult, and had the power to engage and move spectators. Dunbar's work, more even than that of many of her contemporaries raised according to the same tradition, follows Alberti's instructions.

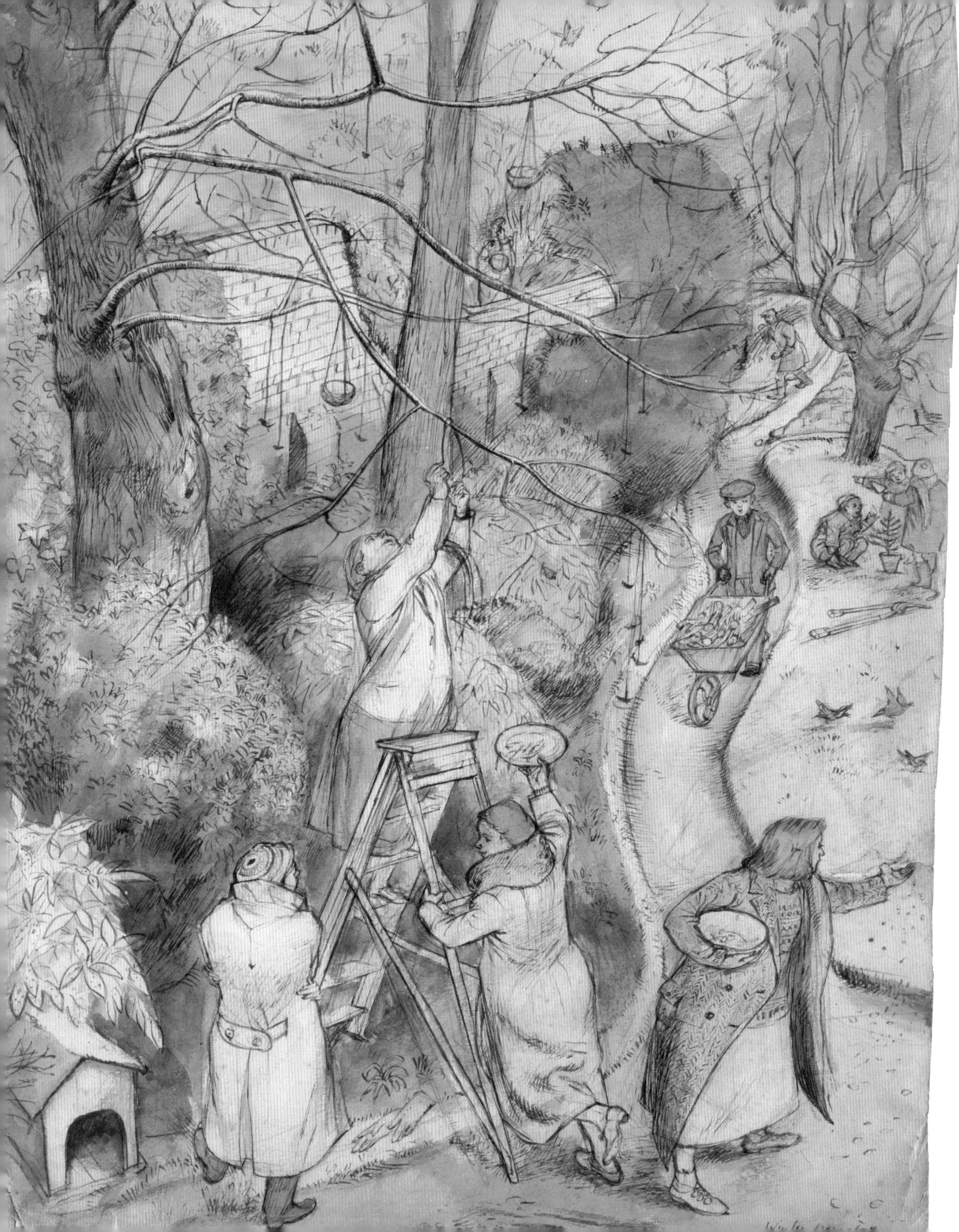

The compositions of her family in the garden belong in a special genre of back garden subjects from this period, and demonstrate how classical techniques of composition could knit together a seemingly casual family group, allowing scope for gentle humour. This group of works shows how easily she managed the transition between drawing and painting, with a mixture of detail and broad handling that later informed her work in illustration. Her self-portrait (CAT 11) is watchful, suggesting a cool critical gaze that gives all her work an individual edge, while the portrait of Ida Shepherd (CAT 6) anticipates by a couple of years the quietly intense Euston Road School approach. The 10 minute sketch of her father (CAT 12), meanwhile, shows her accomplishment in working rapidly in oil, something not encouraged at Euston Road. Bright light and sharply observed body language in the portrait of Florence Dunbar (CAT 14) reveal Dunbar's skill in catching character at a distance, a talent notable in her work as a war artist.

Alan Powers

CAT 4 [HMO 53] *Winter from Above*, c.1927, inscribed with title recto, Pencil, pen & ink and wash on paper, 22 ¼ x 14 ½ in. (56.5 x 37 cm)

The viewpoint of this composition is taken from a first floor window of The Cedars, the Dunbar family house in Strood, Kent. The artist's mother Florence, on a stepladder steadied by her oldest daughter Jessie, is tying bird food to a branch. Marjorie, her second oldest daughter, is reaching out of the picture. Alec, fourth of the five surviving Dunbar children, has his back to the viewer. Other figures are neighbours' children and gardeners.

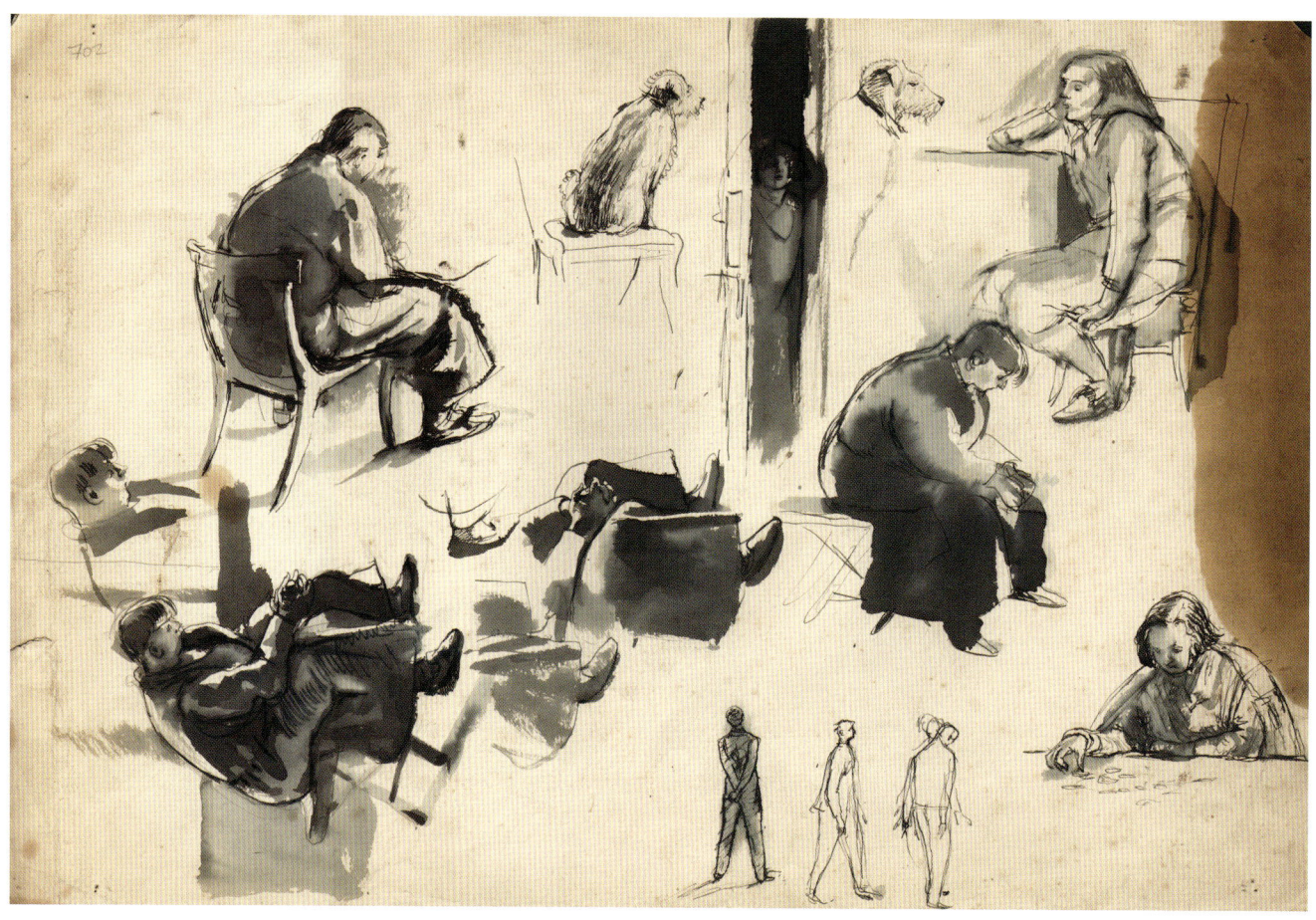

CAT 5 [HMO 702] Studies of the Dunbar family, c.1927,
Pen & ink and blue wash on paper, 15 x 22 in. (38.2 x 56 cm)

This sheet includes studies of the artist's sisters Marjorie (with head on hand), Jessie (playing patience) and Felbridge (the dog) sitting on a chair, etc.

CAT 6 [HMO 775]
Portrait of Ida Shepherd, c.1933, signed 'ED', inscribed on frame 'IDA DUNBAR THE CEDARS STROOD'.
Oil on canvas, 18 x 14 in. (45.7 x 35.6 cm)

Ida was a friend of Evelyn's during her Rochester days.

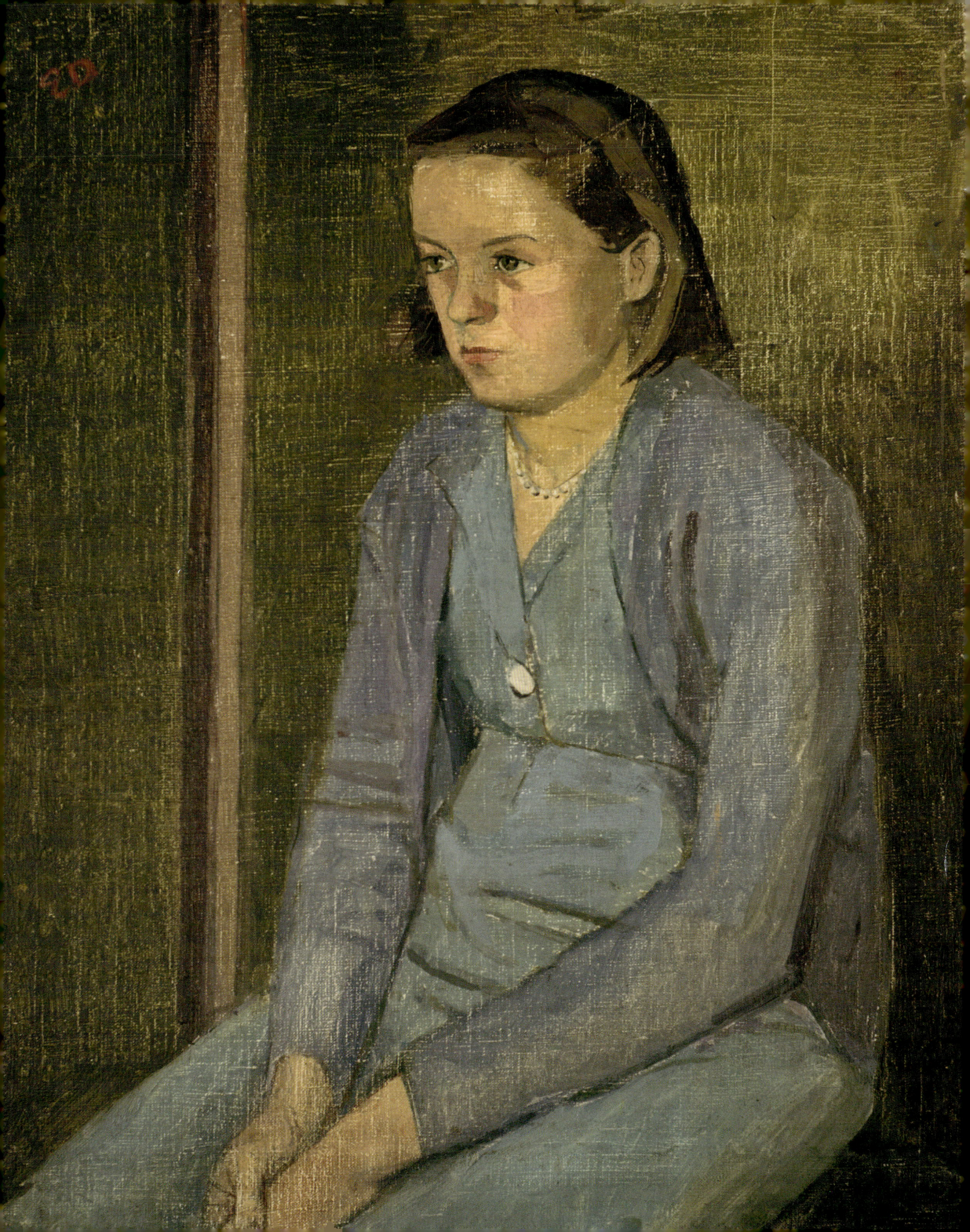

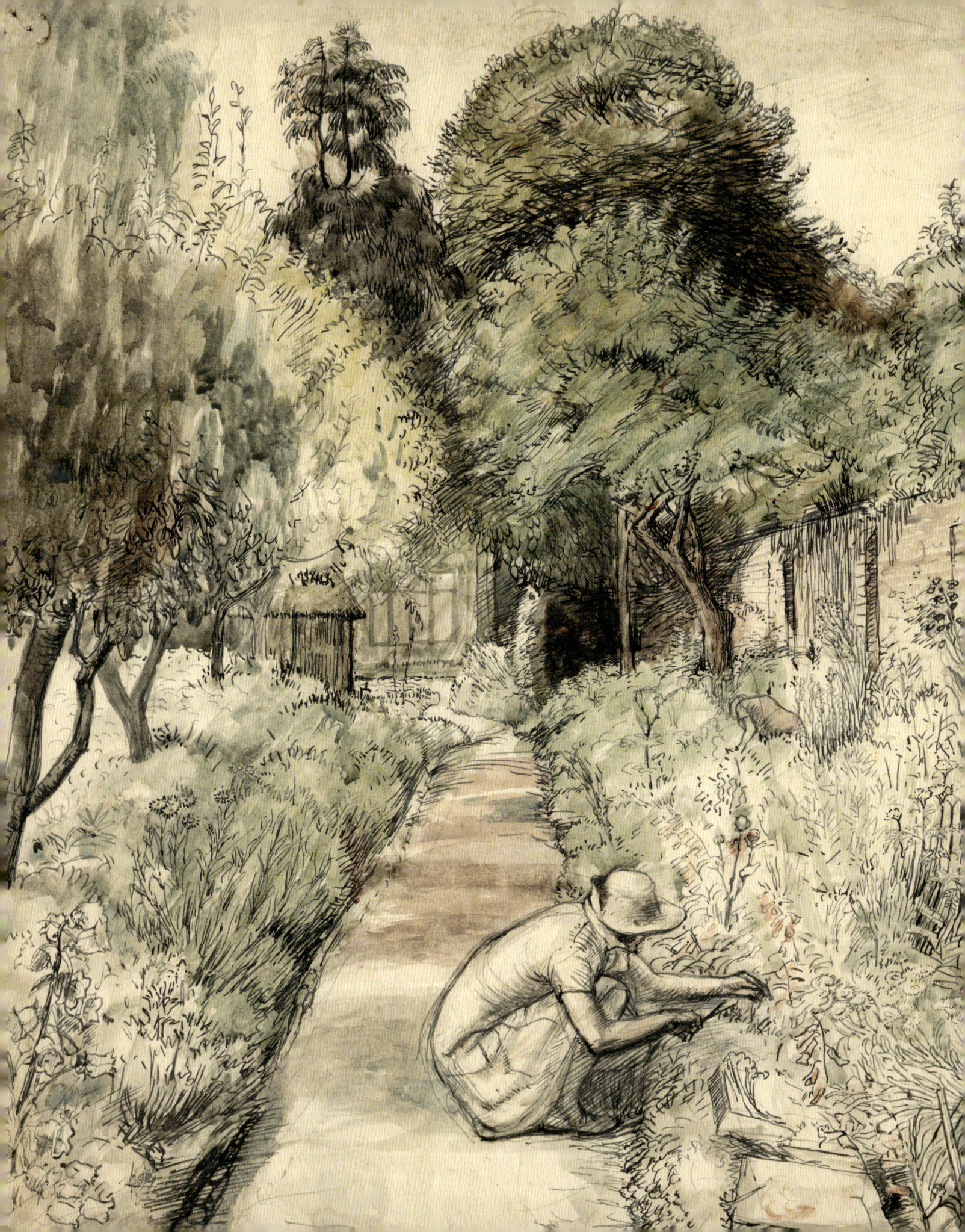

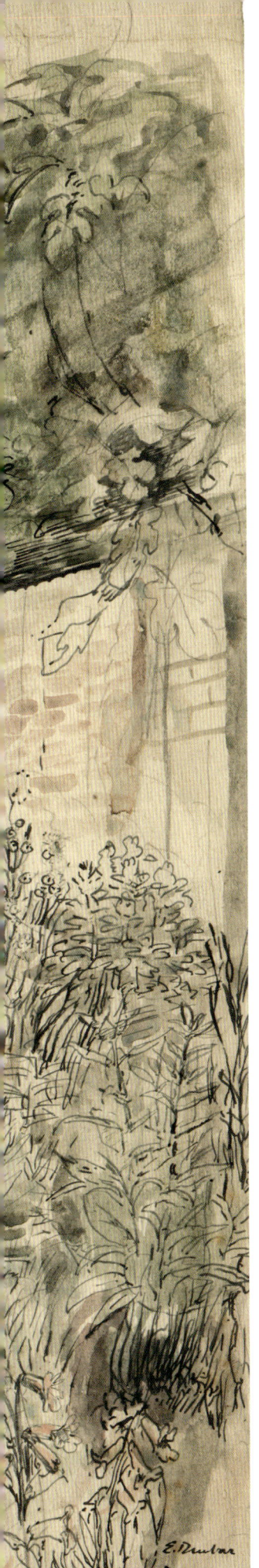
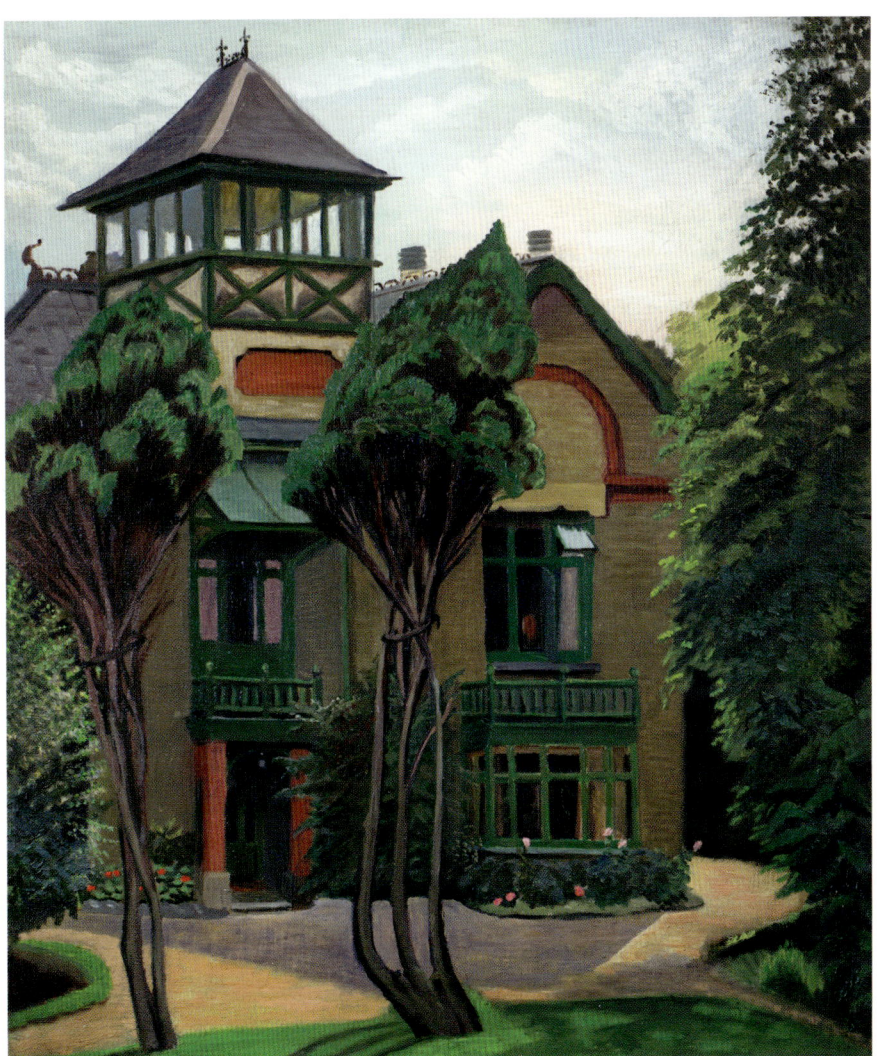

CAT 8 [HMO 767]
The Cedars, the Dunbar family home in Strood, Rochester from 1924-1946,
Oil on canvas, 22 x 18 in. (56 x 46 cm)

Dunbar probably painted this early study of The Cedars shortly after her father William Dunbar bought it in 1924. The tower was equipped as a studio to be shared by his wife Florence, an indefatigable amateur painter of floral still lifes, and by Evelyn, then 17. An early photograph of The Cedars appears in the Chronology at the end of this catalogue. The house is still standing, although bereft of its former dignity. What was the garden is now a housing estate.

CAT 7 [HMO 68] The Herbaceous Border at The Cedars, signed 'E. Dunbar', c.1934,
Pencil, pen & ink and watercolour on paper,15 ½ x 15 in. (39.5 x 38 cm)

If they are not actually portrayed, the figures tending the herbaceous border are likely to be based on the artist's sisters Marjorie (foreground) and Jessie (almost hidden in the middle ground). The buttressed brick wall often features in Dunbar's pictures of The Cedars garden, while beyond the summer house, seen from the front in CAT 2 and 3, the sitting room window is evident. This large window is seen from the inside in *A Knitting Party* (CAT 126). In the later 1920s and 30s The Cedars garden was a constant source of delight and inspiration for Dunbar.

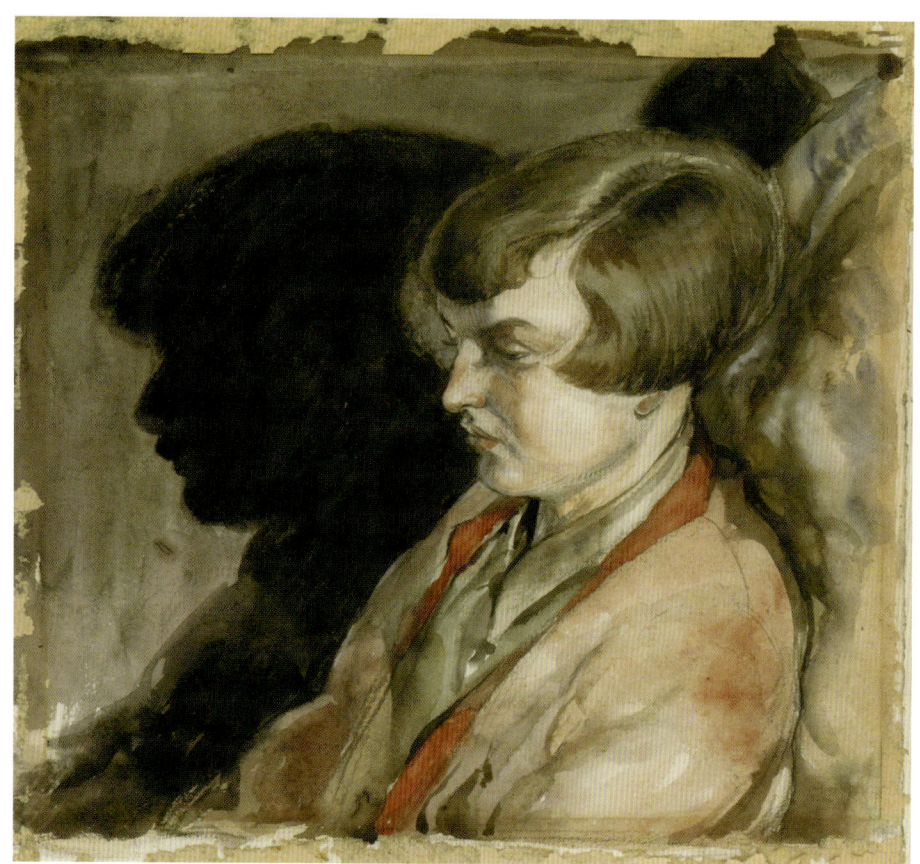

CAT 9 [HMO 790]
Portrait of Jessie Dunbar, c.1925,
Watercolour on paper,
9 x 9 in. (22.8 x 22.8 cm.)

Jessie was the older of Evelyn's two sisters and of her siblings the one who modelled for her most often. She is invariably seen in profile because she suffered from a strabismus which she felt disfigured her.

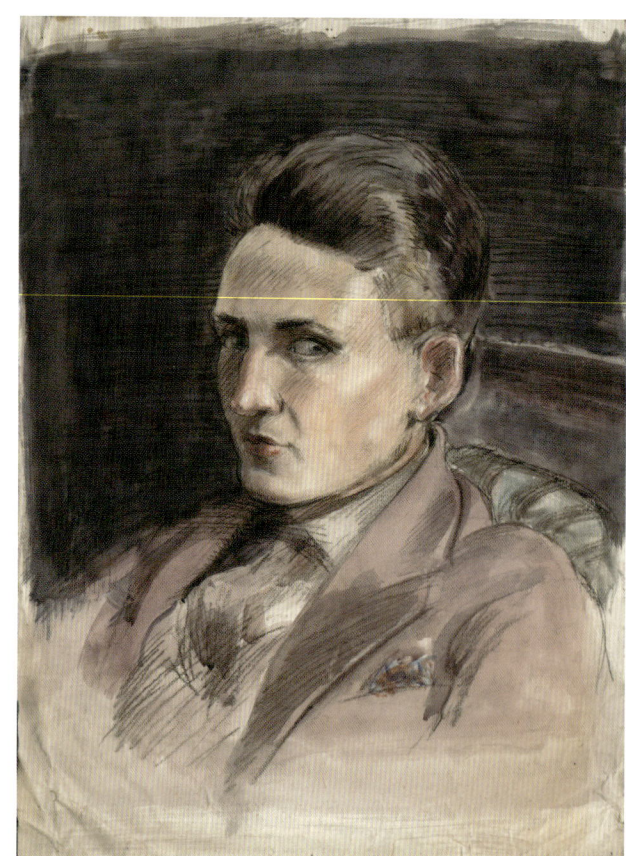

CAT 10 [HMO 80]
Portrait of Alexander James Dunbar ('Alec'), c.1928,
Pencil and watercolour on paper,
15 x 22 in. (38.4 x 55.5 cm)

Alec Dunbar, the younger and of the artist's two brothers, inherited their father William's entrepreneurial spirit, but not always to the same good effect. It was to Alec Dunbar that Roger Folley, the artist's husband, consigned the contents of her studio after her death in 1960.

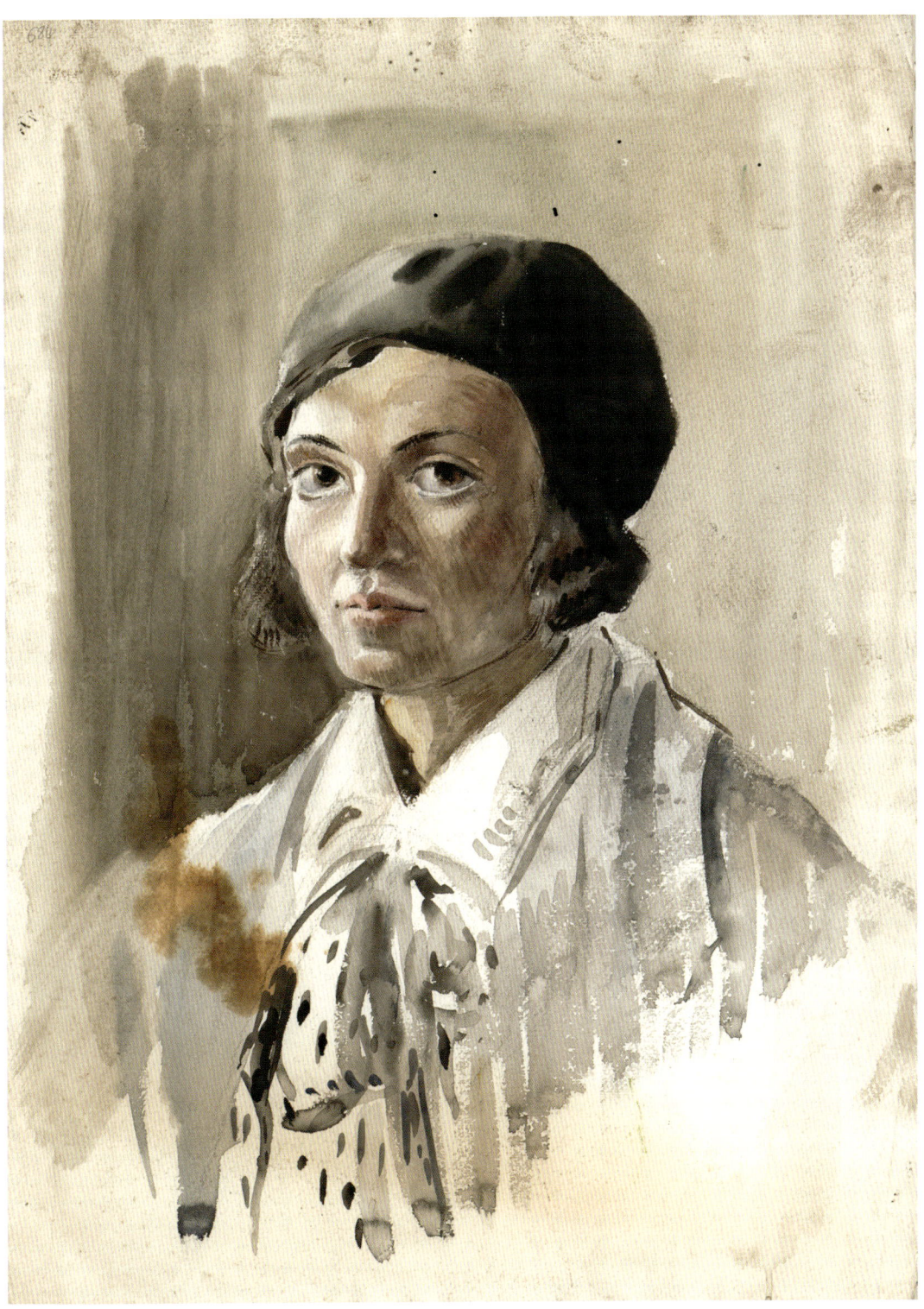

CAT 11 [HMO 684] Self-portrait, c.1930,
Pencil and watercolour on paper, 15 x 22 in. (38.4 x 55.5 cm)

This self-portrait was probably one of a student portfolio of six water-colours submitted for exhibition at the Royal College of Art, December 1930. The other contents of this portfolio, representing work with the Royal College of Art holiday sketching club the previous summer, are lost. Tantalisingly, one was entitled *The Miracle*. In the oils section Dunbar included *The Onion Bed*, also lost, presumably originating from The Cedars vegetable garden.

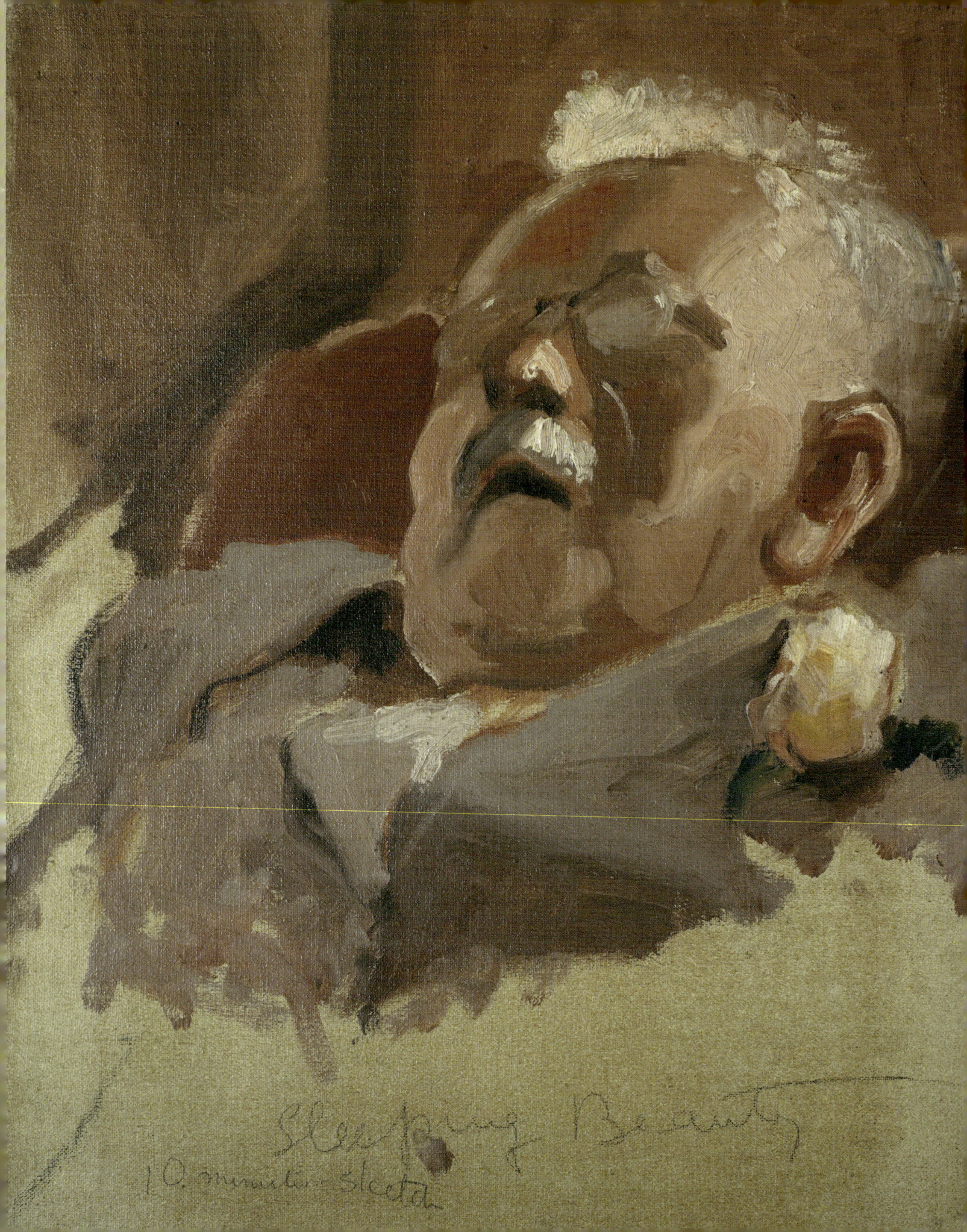

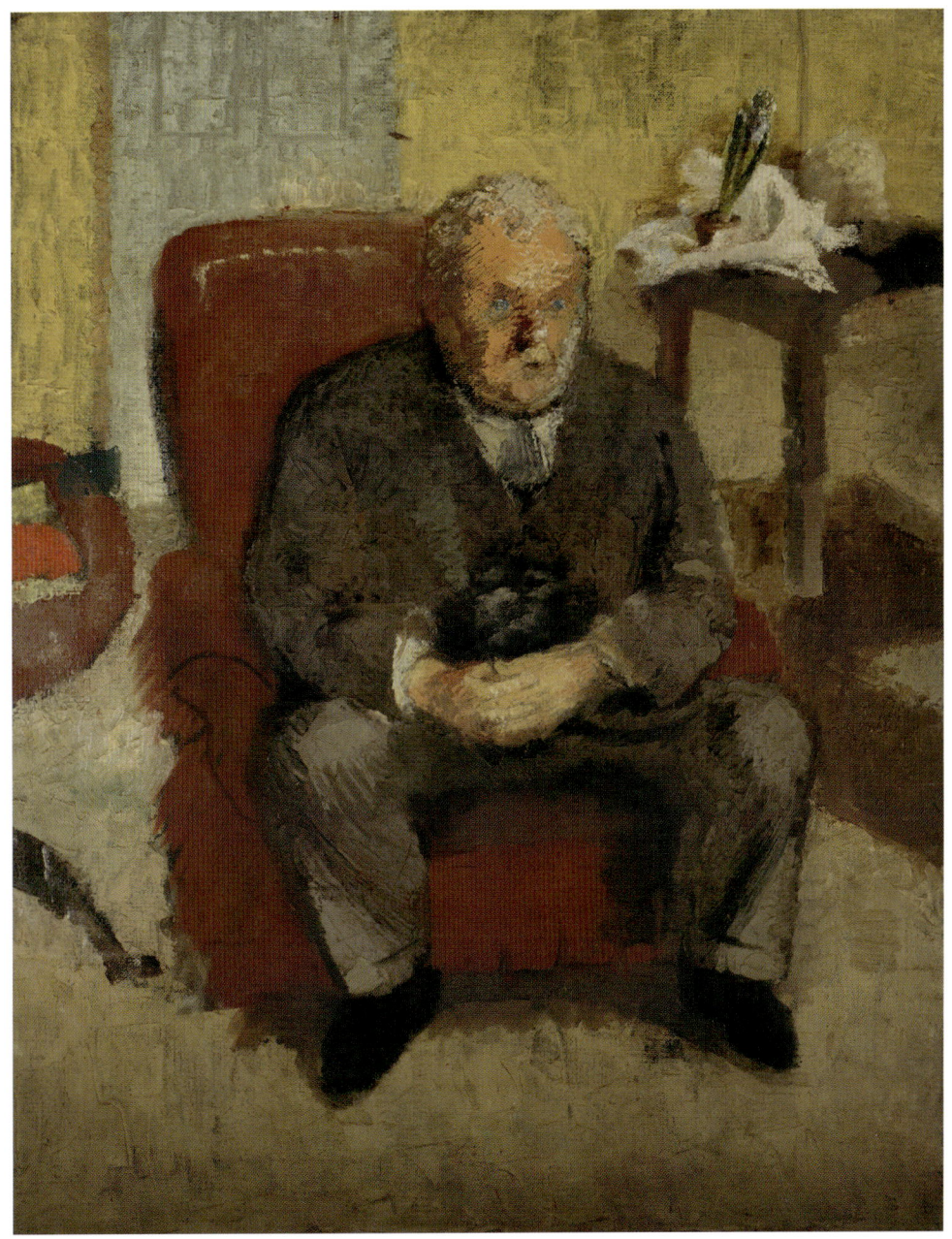

CAT 13 [HMO 848] Portrait of William Dunbar, c.1928,
Oil on canvas, 24 x 18 in. (61 x 45.7 cm)

This canvas depicts the artist's father in the winter of 1928-29 with the Dunbar's newly-acquired Scottish terrier 'Paul' on his lap.

CAT 12 [HMO 786] *Sleeping Beauty, 10 minute sketch*, c.1928,
Inscribed in pencil recto, probably by Jessie Dunbar, with title,
Oil on canvas, 19 x 13 in. (48 x 33 cm)

This is a portrait of the artist's father, asleep after lunch, William Dunbar, a crofter's son from Cromdale, Morayshire, took advantage of an 1870s apprenticeship scheme for young Scots and bound himself to a Reading tailor. He prospered, bought the business and eventually sold it prior to setting up a similar business in the Medway Valley in 1908. He died in 1932 at the age of 70.

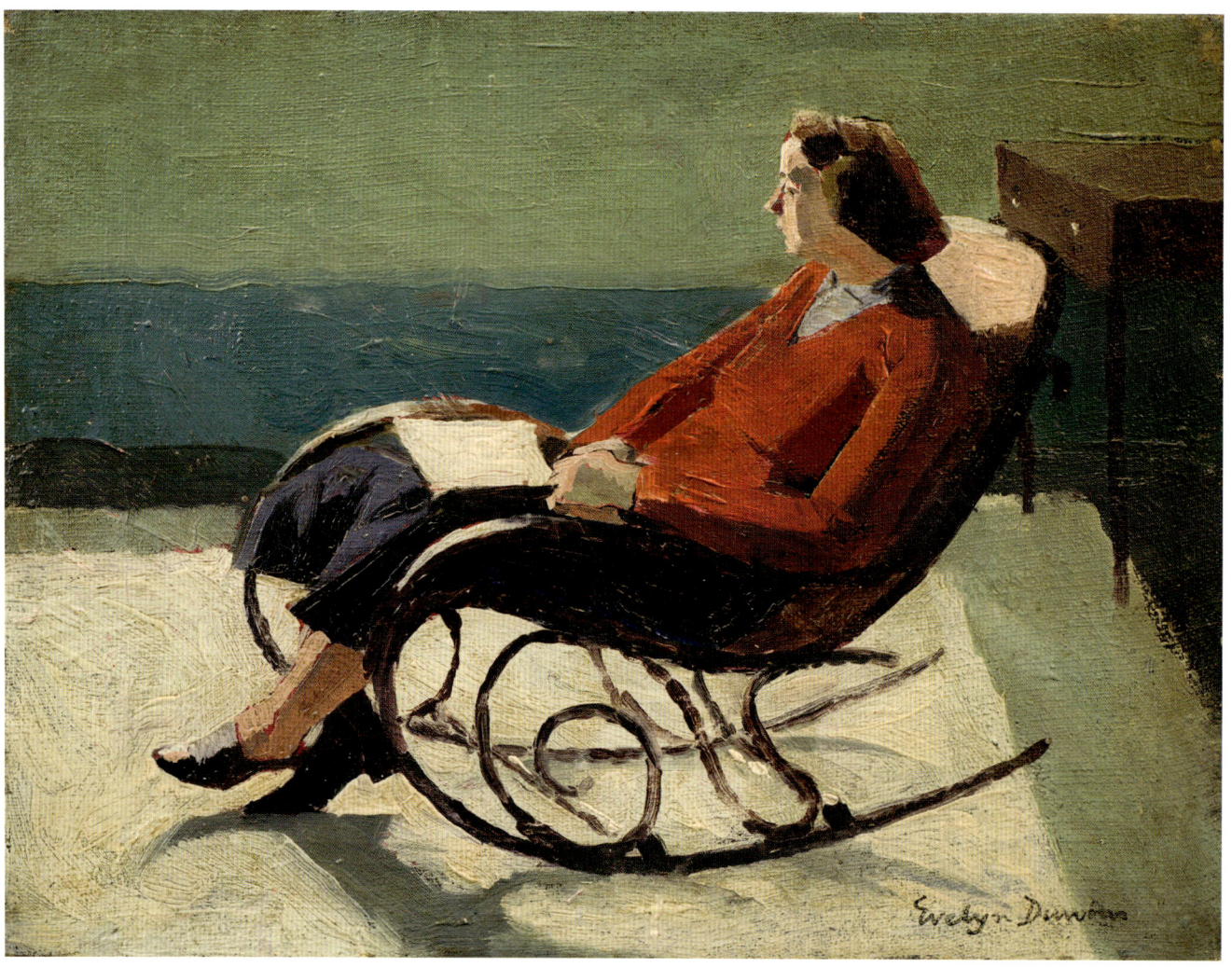

CAT 14 [HMO 797]
Portrait of the artist's mother, Florence, on a bentwood rocking chair, c.1930,
Studio stamp "Evelyn Dunbar",
Oil on canvas, 8 x 10 in. (20 x 25.4 cm)

Florence Dunbar, née Murgatroyd, was the daughter of a Bradford woolmaster. She met William Dunbar on one of his frequent visits to Bradford for textiles for his Reading bespoke tailoring and household linen business. They married in 1895. A tireless and green-fingered gardener, she also painted innumerable floral still lifes. Evelyn owed much to her unceasing encouragement. She died in 1944.

CAT 15 [HMO 761]
Portrait probably of Jessie Dunbar (recto), c.1925, with sketches of two female heads (verso)
Oil on canvas, 24 x 17 in. (61 x 45.1 cm)

An early portrait of Jessie Dunbar, in the same slightly primitive style as The Cedars (CAT 8). Jessie Dunbar had a squint, about which she was very sensitive. She modelled frequently for her sister Evelyn, her final appearance being as the principal subject in *The Land Girl and the Bail Bull* (FIG 19). Dunbar is always careful to avoid direct reference to her sister's strabismus: here she shows her with eyes lowered demurely.

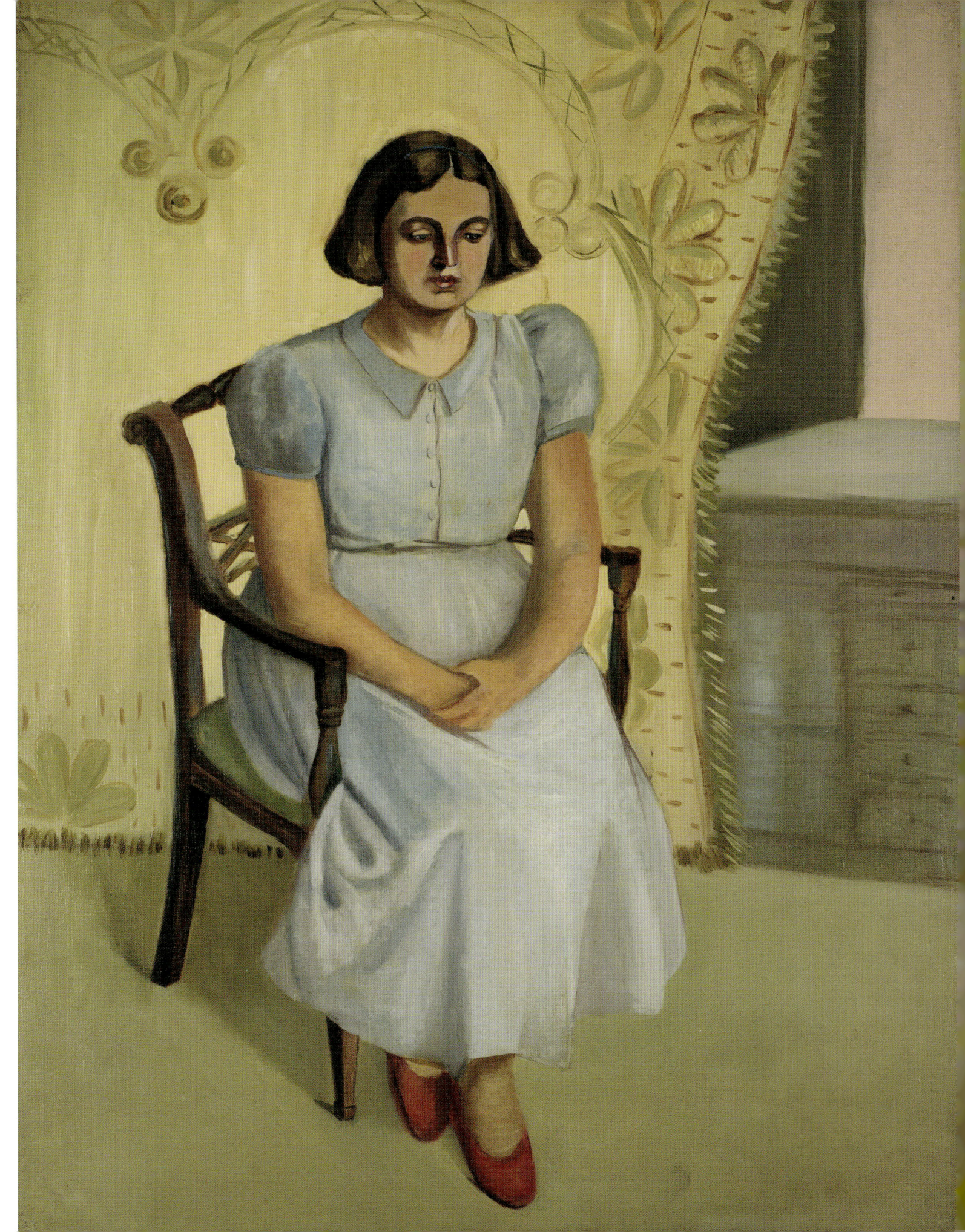

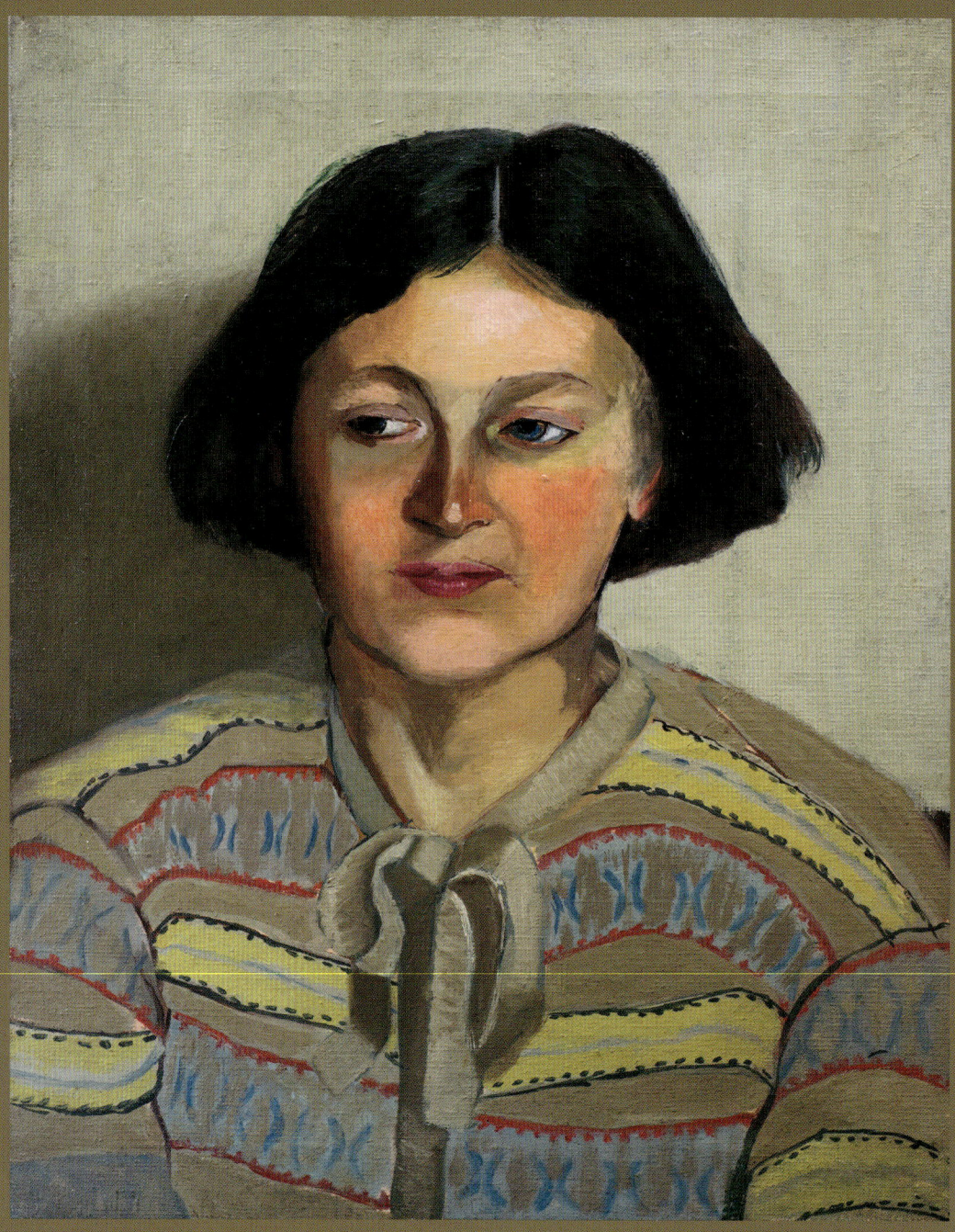

CAT 16   [HMO 771] Portrait of a woman wearing a Fair Isle cardigan, c.1932,
Oil on canvas, 18 x 14 in. (46 x 35.5 cm)

The subject is probably the artist's cousin, Vera Swain (née Murgatroyd), who spent much of her life in Sri Lanka. It is likely that she modelled for *Spring* (see CAT 63, page 104)

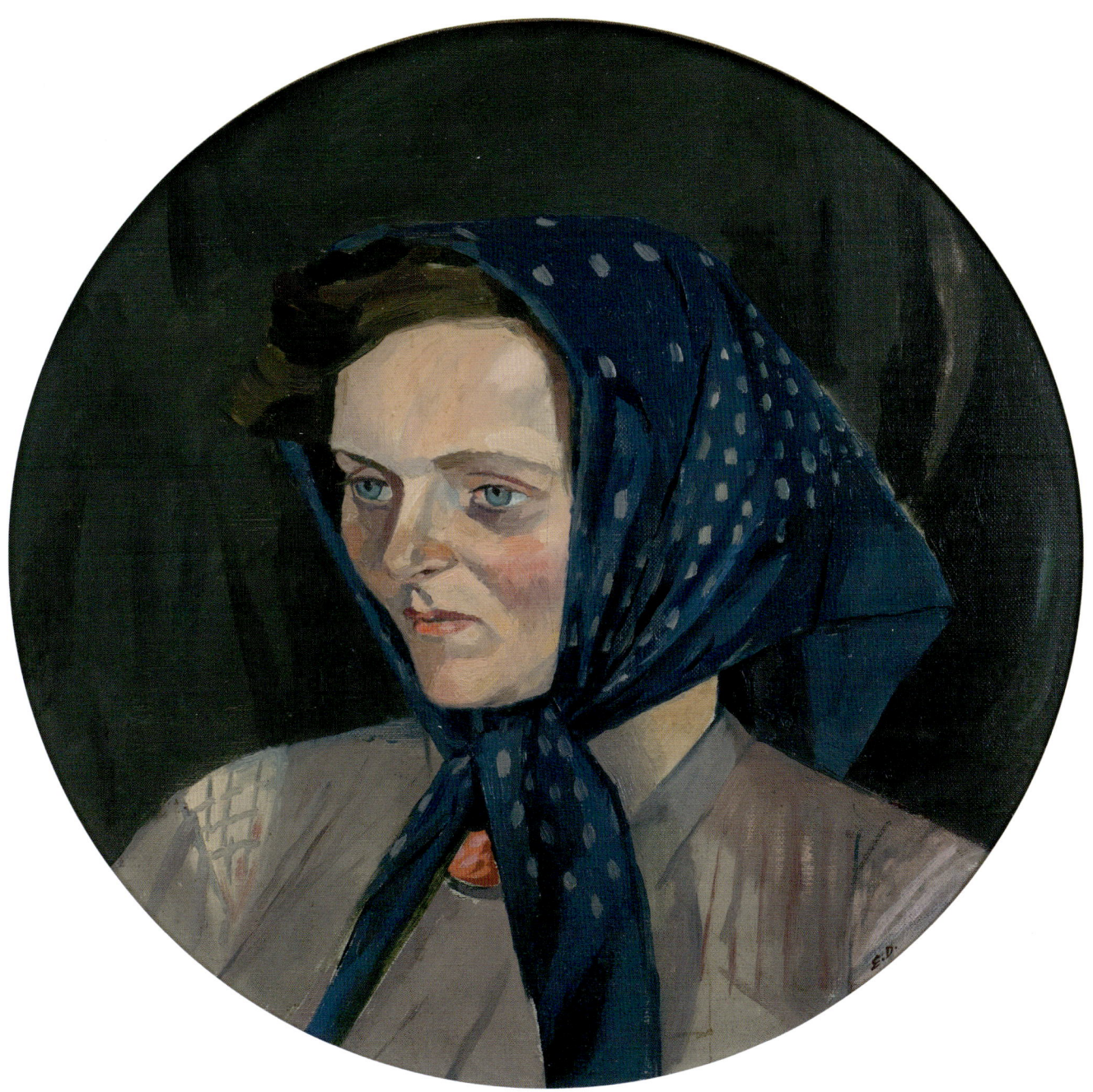

CAT 17 [HMO 770]
Portrait of Jill Dunbar, c.1939, Signed 'E.D.'.
Oil on canvas, 17 in. (43.2 cm) diameter

Emily Dunbar, née Brush and always known as Jill, became the artist's
sister-in-law after her marriage in 1936 to Dunbar's brother Alec. (see CAT 10).

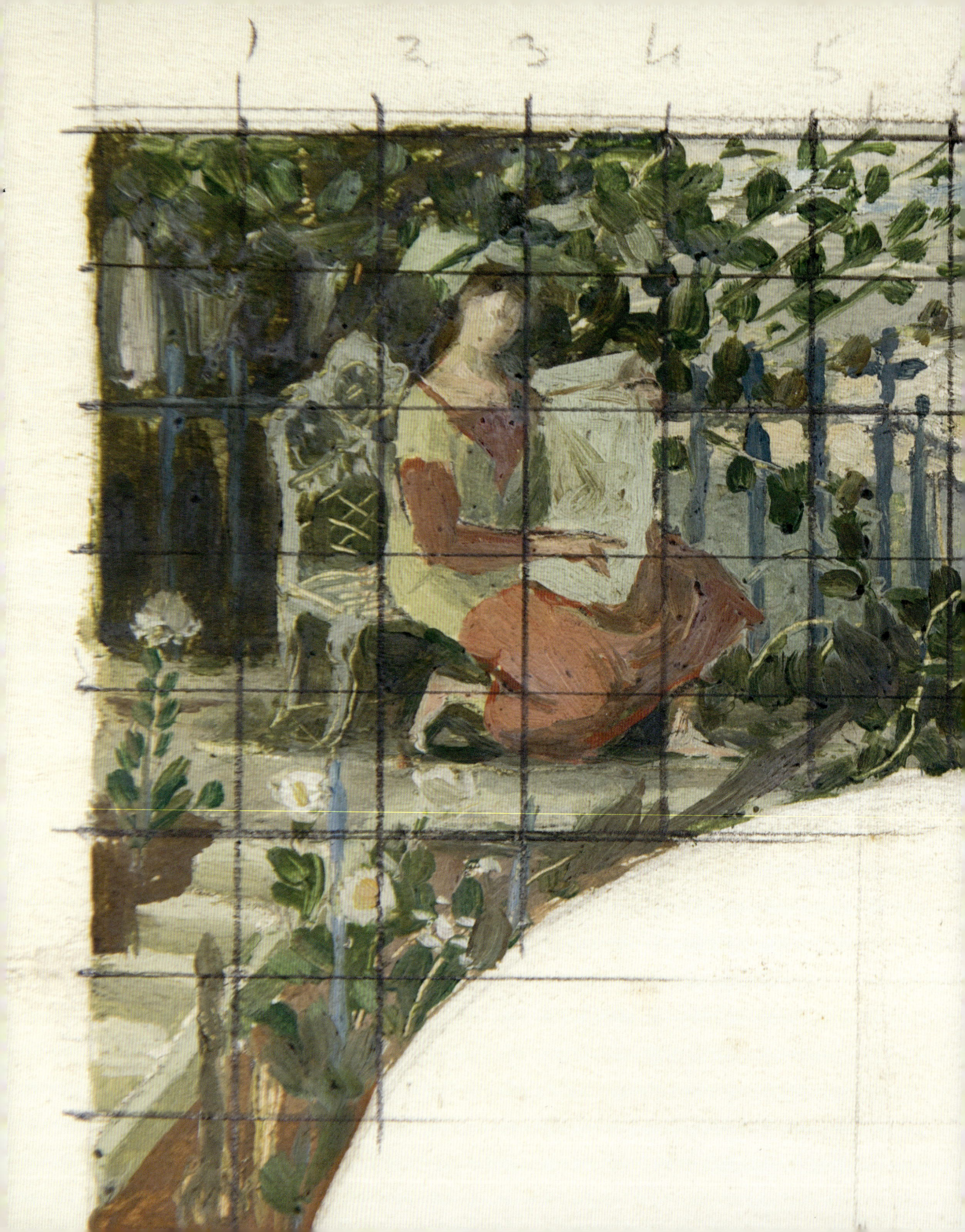

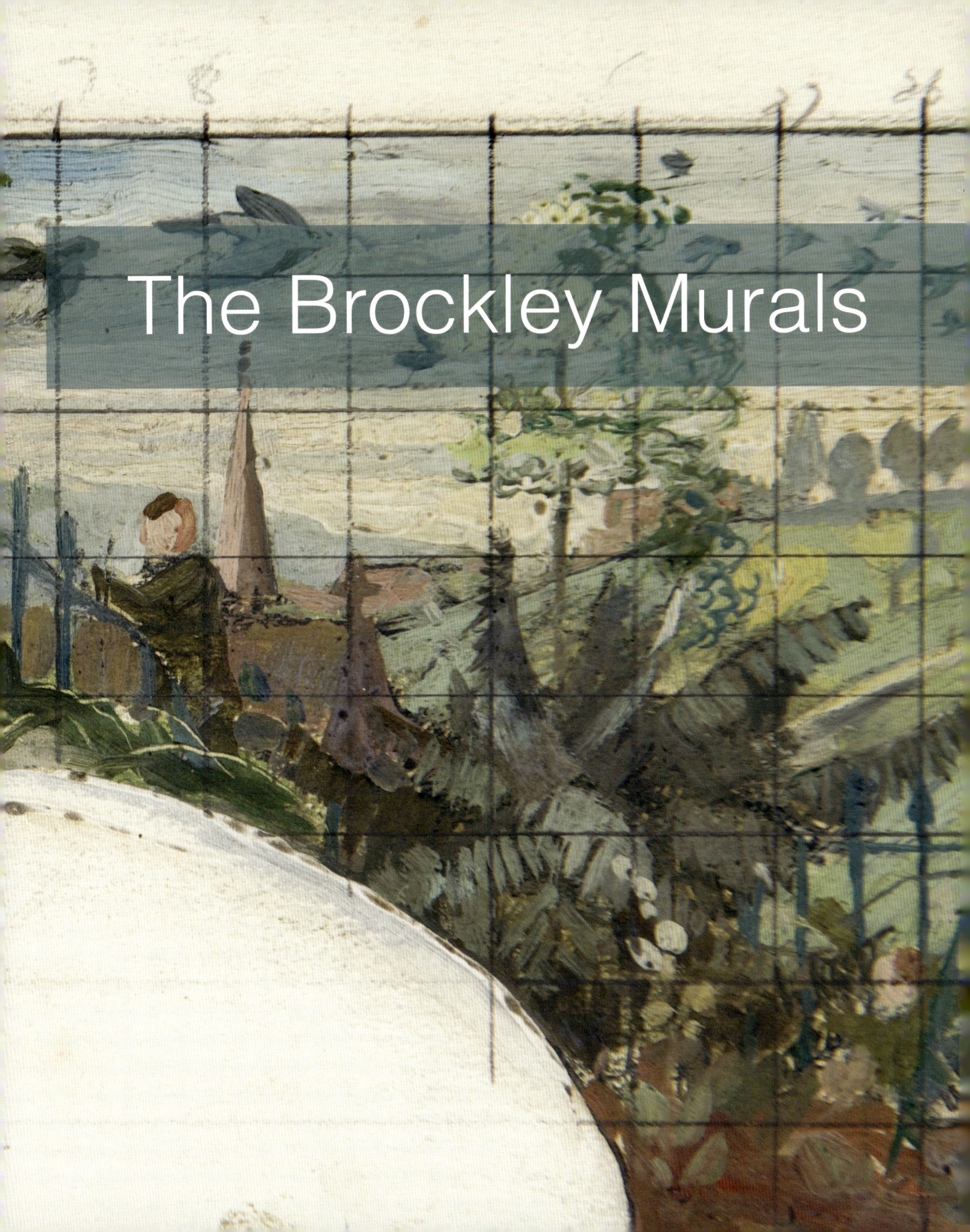
The Brockley Murals

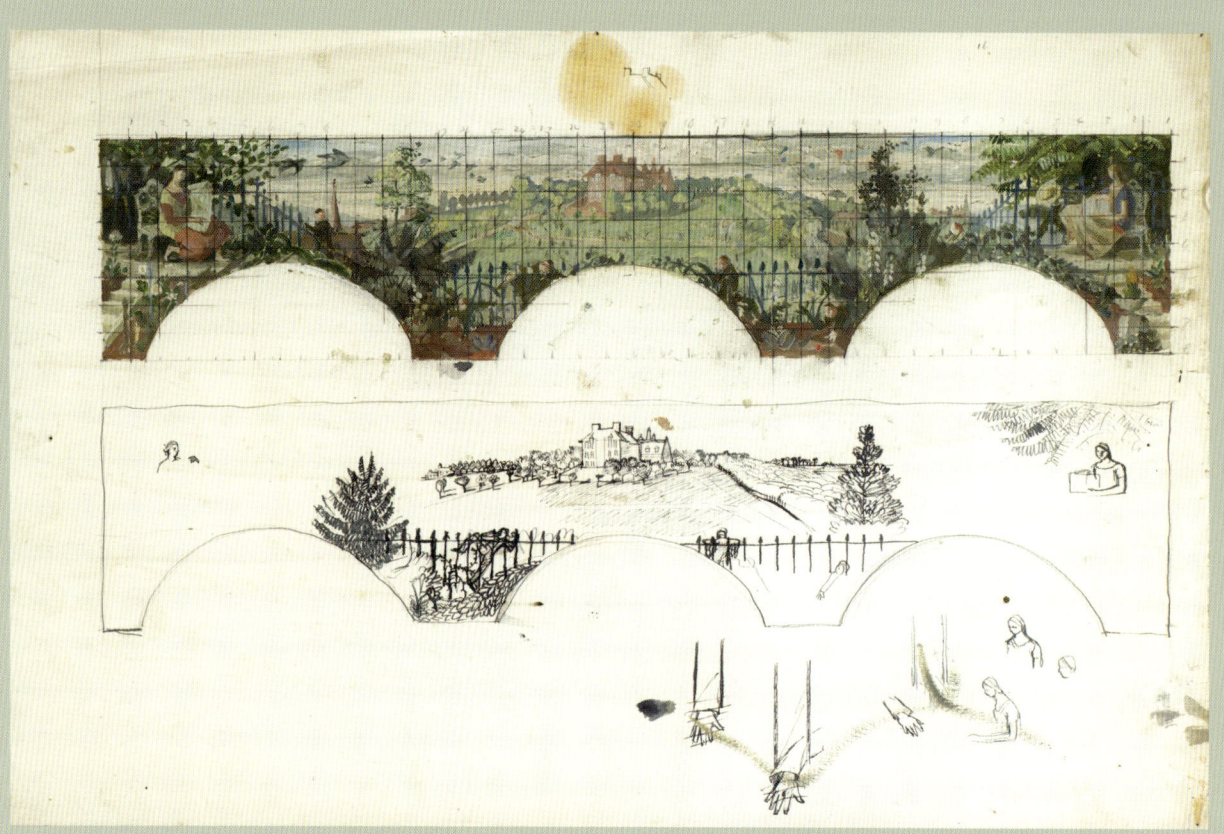

CAT 18 [HMO 428] Colour sketch for the Hilly Fields mural frieze at Brockley County School for Boys, 1933, Pencil and oil on paper, 15 x 22 ½ in. (38 x 57 cm)

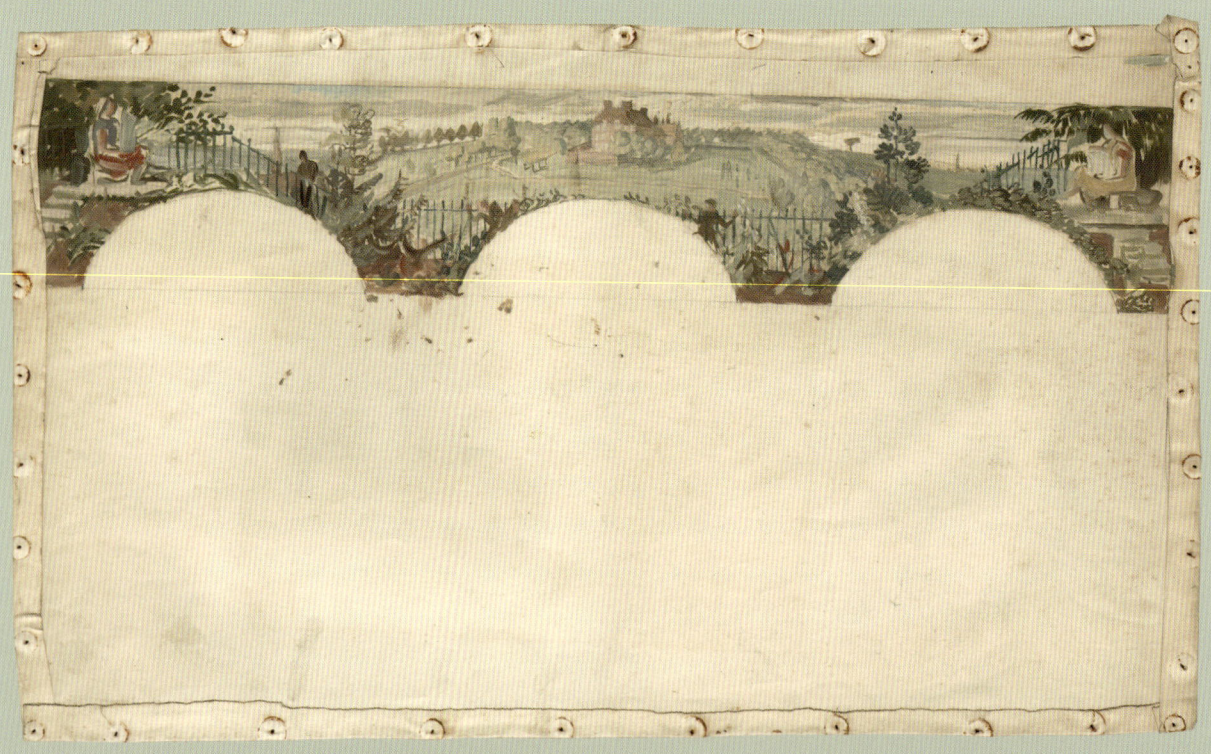

CAT 19 [HMO 525] Colour sketch for the Hilly Fields mural frieze at Brockley County School for Boys, 1933, Pencil and oil on paper, 12 x 20 in. (30.5 x 50.5 cm)

The Brockley Murals

Art educators saw murals both as a training method in the classical tradition, and as an affirmation of the value of artists to society. Sir William Rothenstein, the Principal of the Royal College of Art, made a broadcast in 1932 on 'The English Artist and the English Public', stressing the value of honestly painted everyday subjects from nature as a counterweight to Modernism on one hand, and the devotion even of topographic painters to foreign places on the other. 'Being in daily touch with students', Rothenstein told his listeners, 'I know that there is no lack of blossom; that the English genius for rich content still persists.' Dr. Sinclair, the headmaster of the Brockley County School for Boys in the London borough of Lewisham, then the suburban fringe of Kent, responded by offering his school hall, with its five arched recesses, and a balcony with a vaulted underside. The result, in Rothenstein's view, was the best mural cycle since Ford Madox Brown's work in Manchester Town Hall.

Charles Mahoney, as a tutor at the RCA, assembled a team of younger women collaborators, with Dunbar as the senior among them, and two who were still students: Violet Martin and Mildred 'Elsie' Eldridge. According to Eldridge's memory in the 1980s, they were united chiefly by their dislike of London and yearning for the country. The chosen theme was *Aesop's Fables*, which gave scope for narrative themes in landscape settings. Dunbar painted 'The Country Girl and the Pail of Milk', one of five large arched panels, in which the main story in the foreground is perhaps less dramatic than the before-and-after episodes of the fable drama in the background. It is fascinating, in the light of this work, to see two of Dunbar's newly discovered schemes for the panels on the facing wall. Both have the same spatial design, with a winding road containing the main subject at the bottom, and additional figures. Hercules, the god of the title, is contained in a tondo shape, filling the arched top, (CAT 24) while in *The Woodcutter and the Bees* (CAT 25), a carefully observed rural scene, the chicken hut peforms an equivalent role in the composition, while a visually intriguing framework of green branches fills out the bottom right corner.

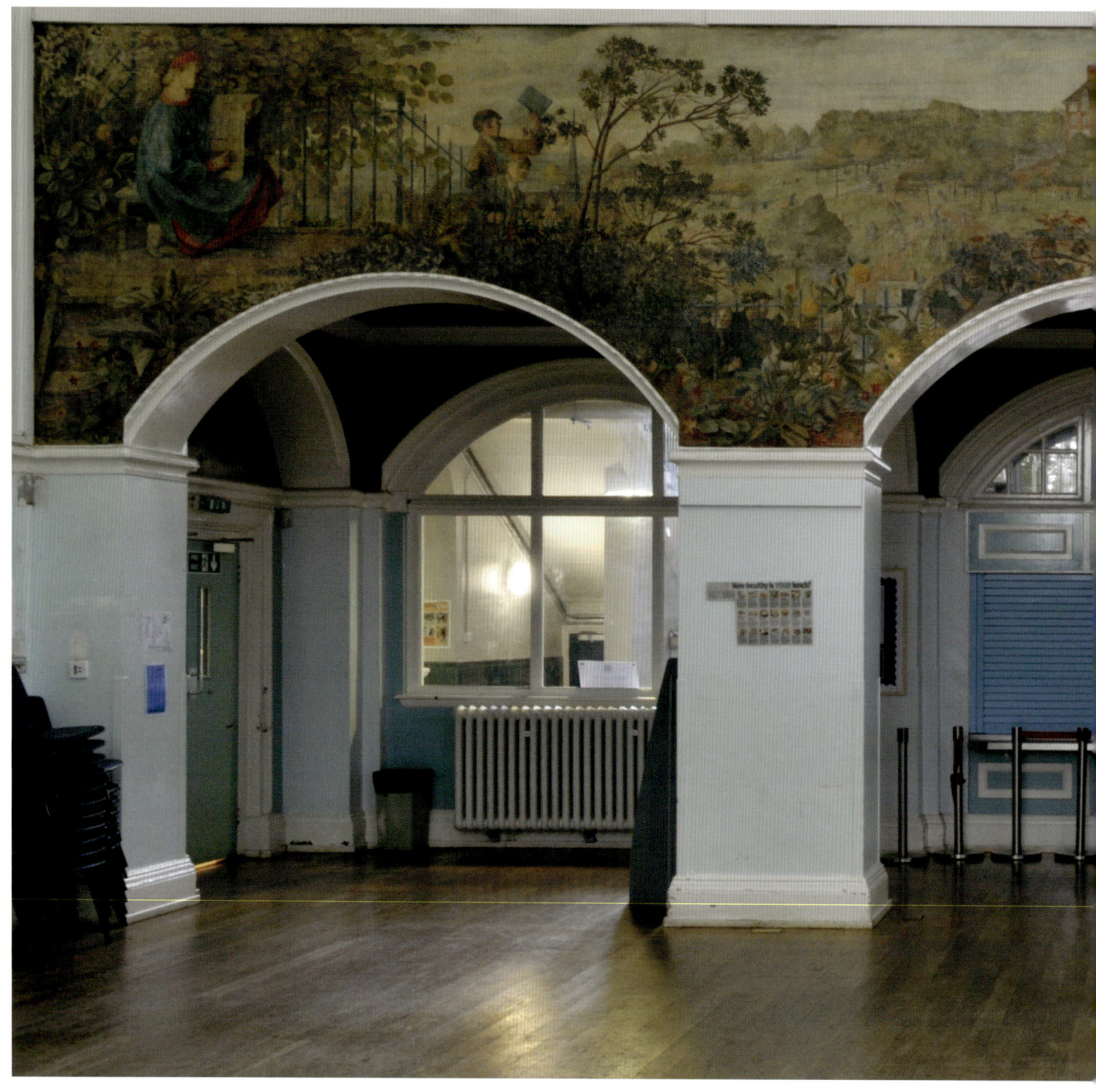

FIG 9 Evelyn Dunbar's frieze for Brockley School (now Prendergast School, Lewisham), c. 1932-3, *in situ*, photo: Nigel Green

In addition to her main panel, Dunbar did the broad fascia of the balcony with a frieze showing the school across the park. So naturally did she invent foreground detail that the odd shape she had to fill hardly bothers the eye. Schoolboys in uniform moving behind the railings convey a Carel Weight sense of mild menace, yet without histrionics. Her seated allegorical figures to either side add the level of strangeness found in similar subjects by Alan Sorrell, one of the younger RCA tutors. The drawings and composition

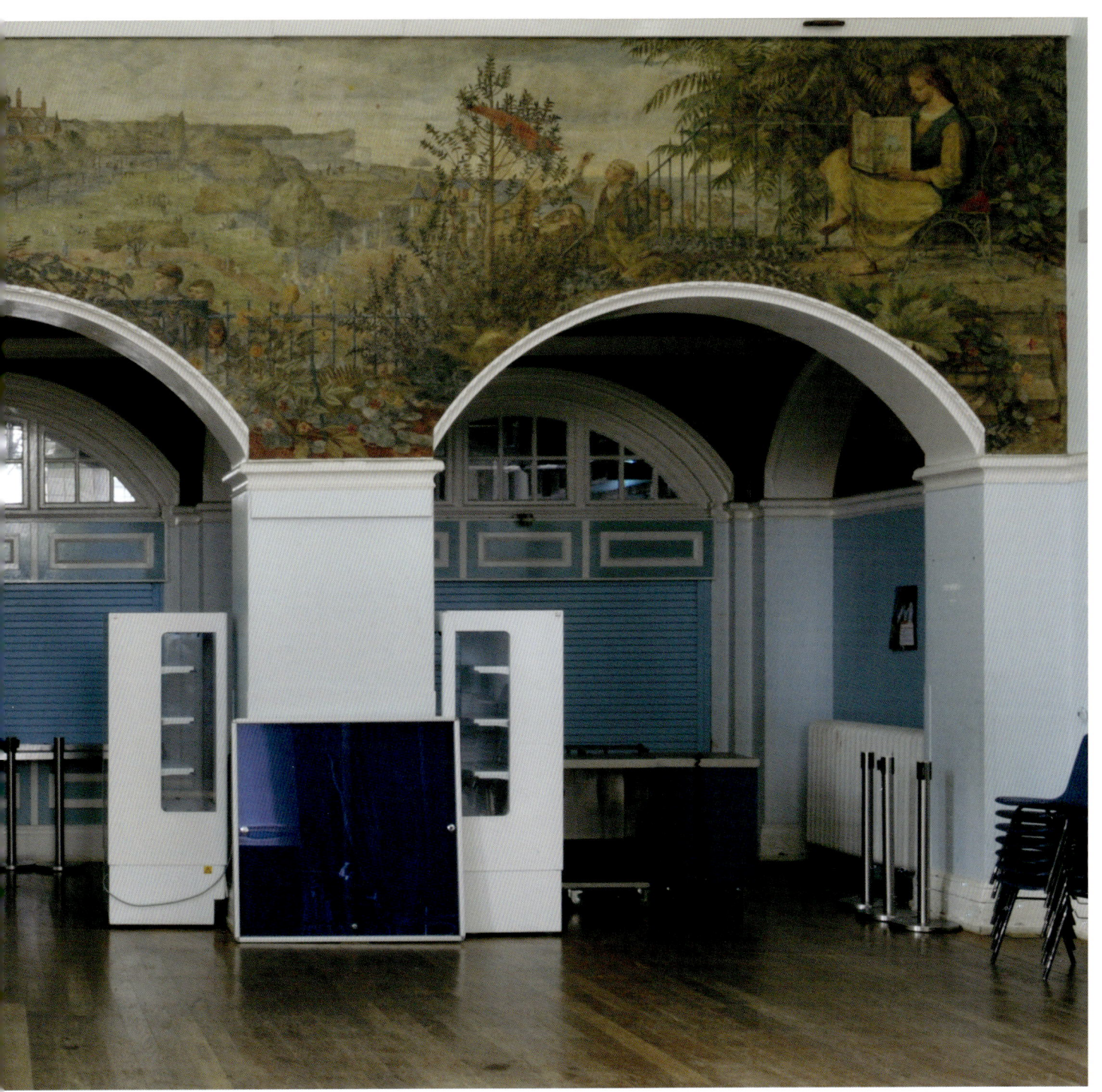

studies reveal the academic discipline of the RCA in action, and miraculously the finished work, while not easy to view in situ, retains freshness in its Pre-Raphaelite detail. In addition, Dunbar painted most of the vaulted underside of the balcony, where the most delightful and imaginative parts of the whole scheme can be found.

A.P.

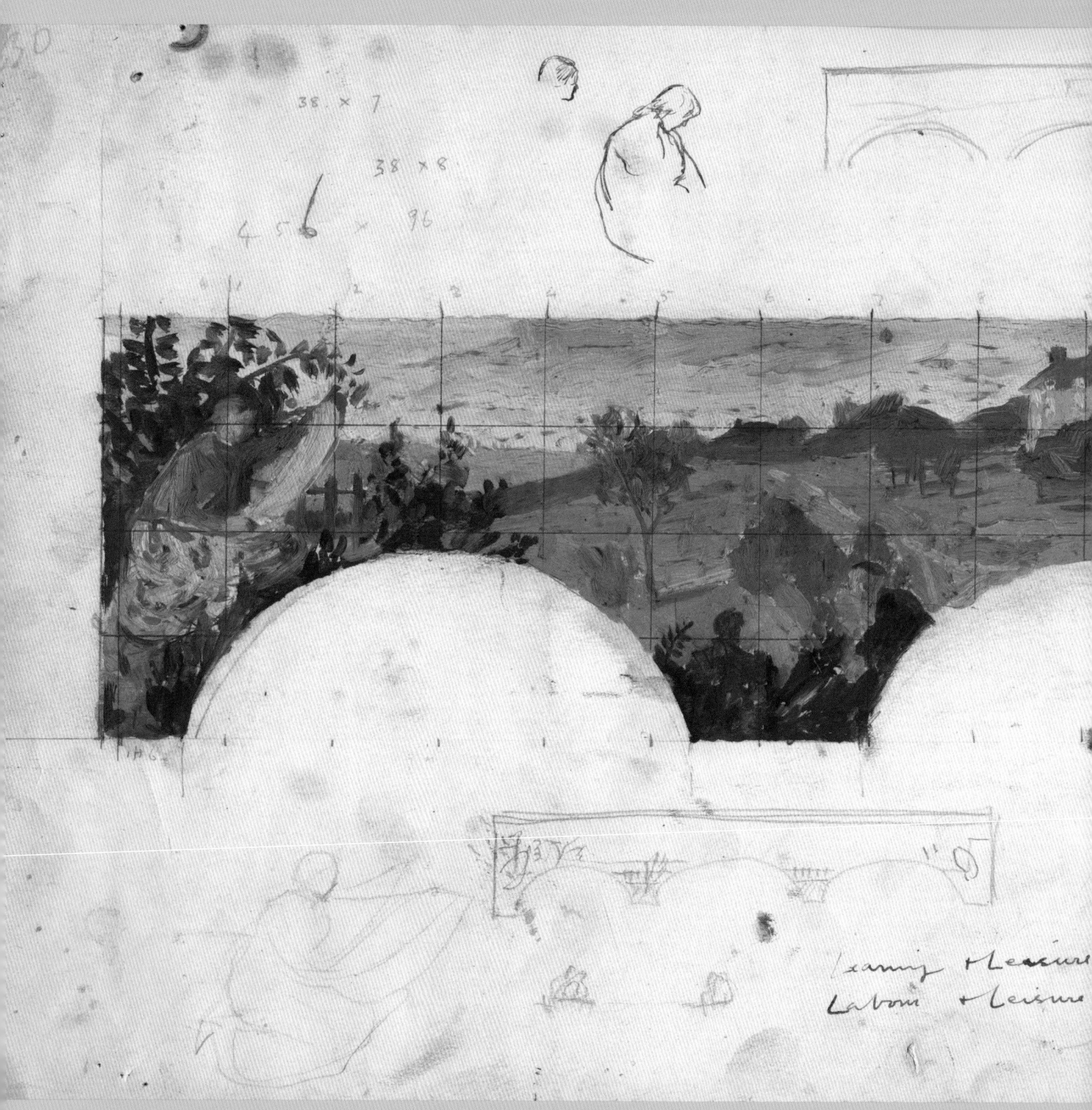

CAT 20 [HMO 430] Colour sketch for the Hilly Fields mural frieze at Brockley County School for Boys, including incidental sketches, squared, 1933,
Inscribed recto 'Learning & leisure/Labour & leisure', referring to later addition of two schoolboys above the frieze.
Pencil, pen & ink and oil on paper, 10 ¼ x 23 in. (26 x 58 cm)

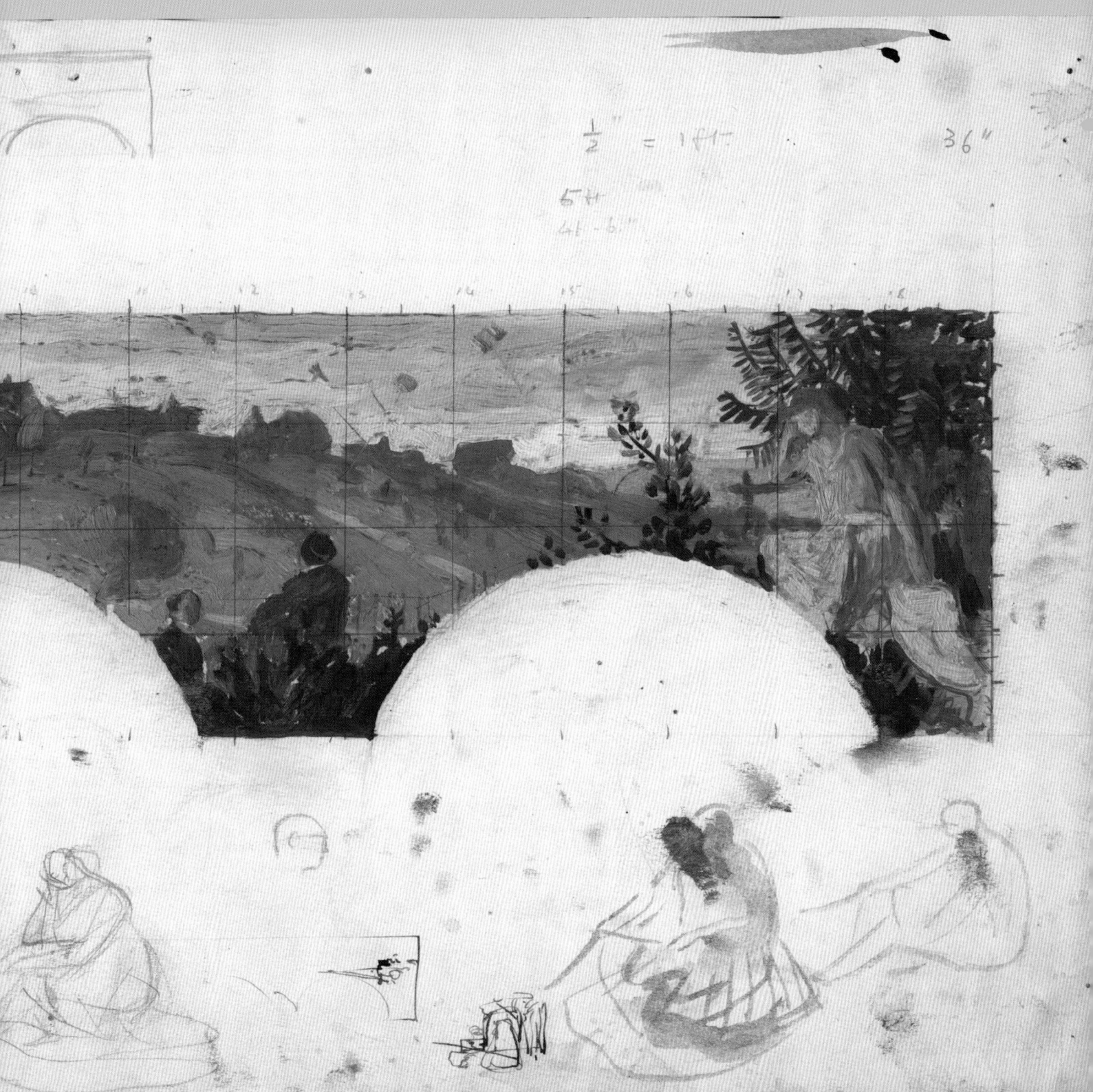

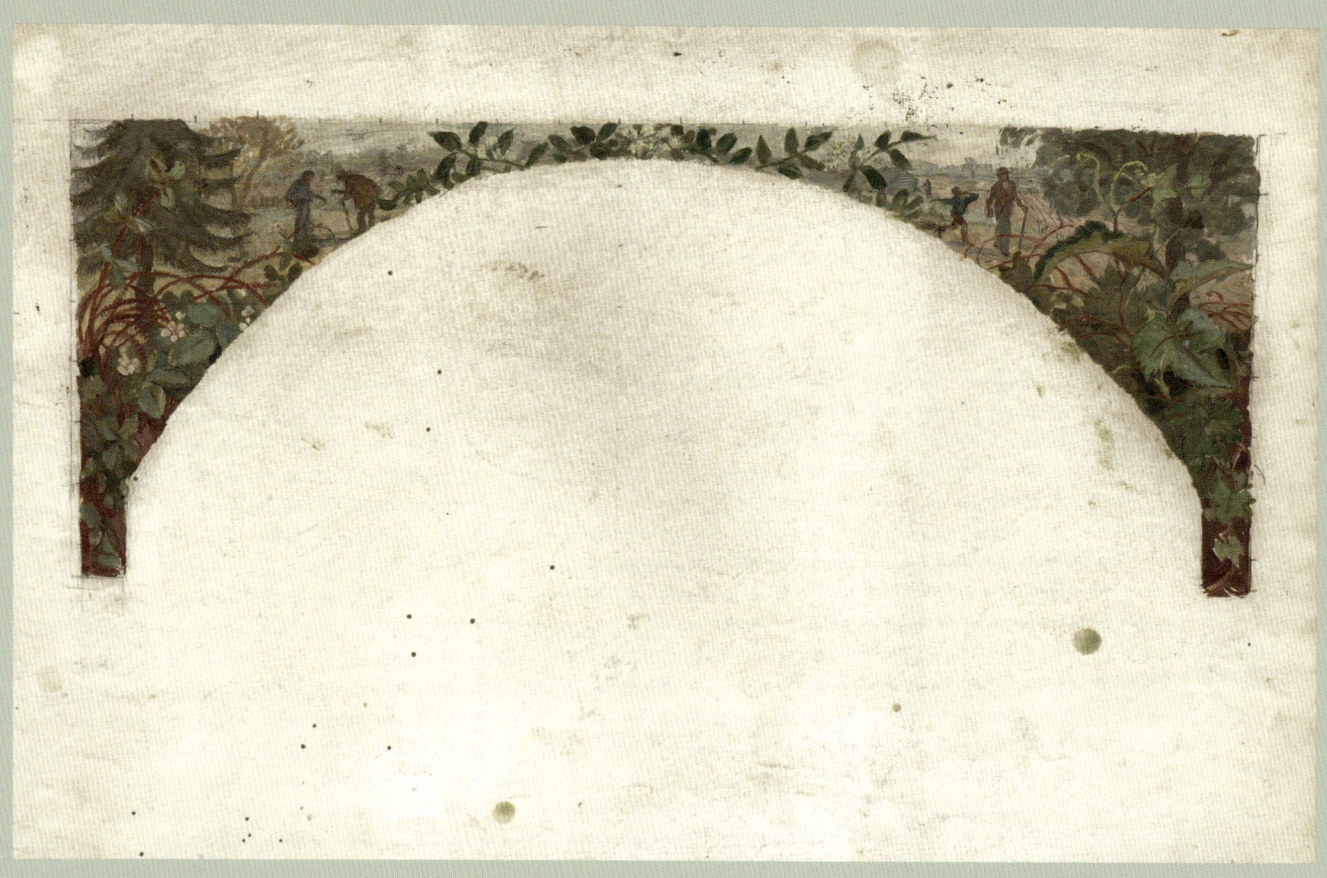

CAT 21 [HMO 551] Colour study for the adjoining sub-gallery spandrels, 1935,
Pencil and oil on paper, 15 ¼ x 22 ¼ in. (39 x 56.5 cm)

The adjoining sub-gallery spandrels illustrate the fables *The Fir Tree and the Bramble* (after Aesop, left) and *The Elm Tree and the Vine* (from Ovid, *Metamorphoses*, right). While *The Fir Tree and the Bramble* is not greatly edifying, *The Elm Tree and the Vine* is an early example of Dunbar's fondness for literary allusion, together with a certain autobiographical element: in Ovid's telling of the legend, the Vine (i.e. Dunbar) actively seeks the support of the Elm (i.e. Mahoney). (Classical Mediterranean vineyards often had elm supports.) In this light, this spandrel is a declaration of love.

CAT 22 [HMO 645]
Studies for the Brockley mural panel *The Country Girl and the Pail of Milk*, 1933,
Pencil, pen & ink and oil on paper, 22 x 15 in. (55.8 x 38.2 cm)

The artist's sister, Jessie, modelled for the 'Country Girl'
in the various episodes of the fable.

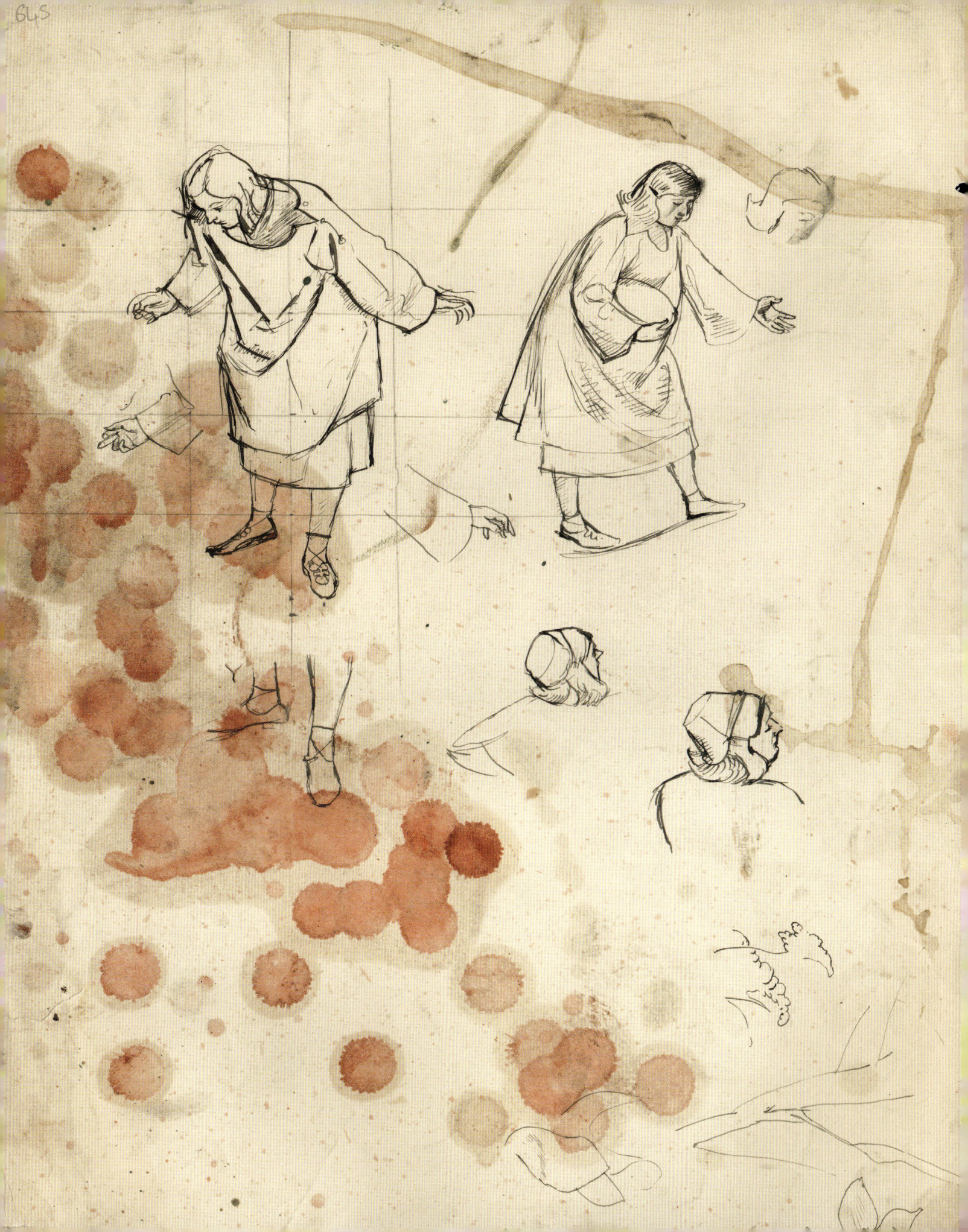

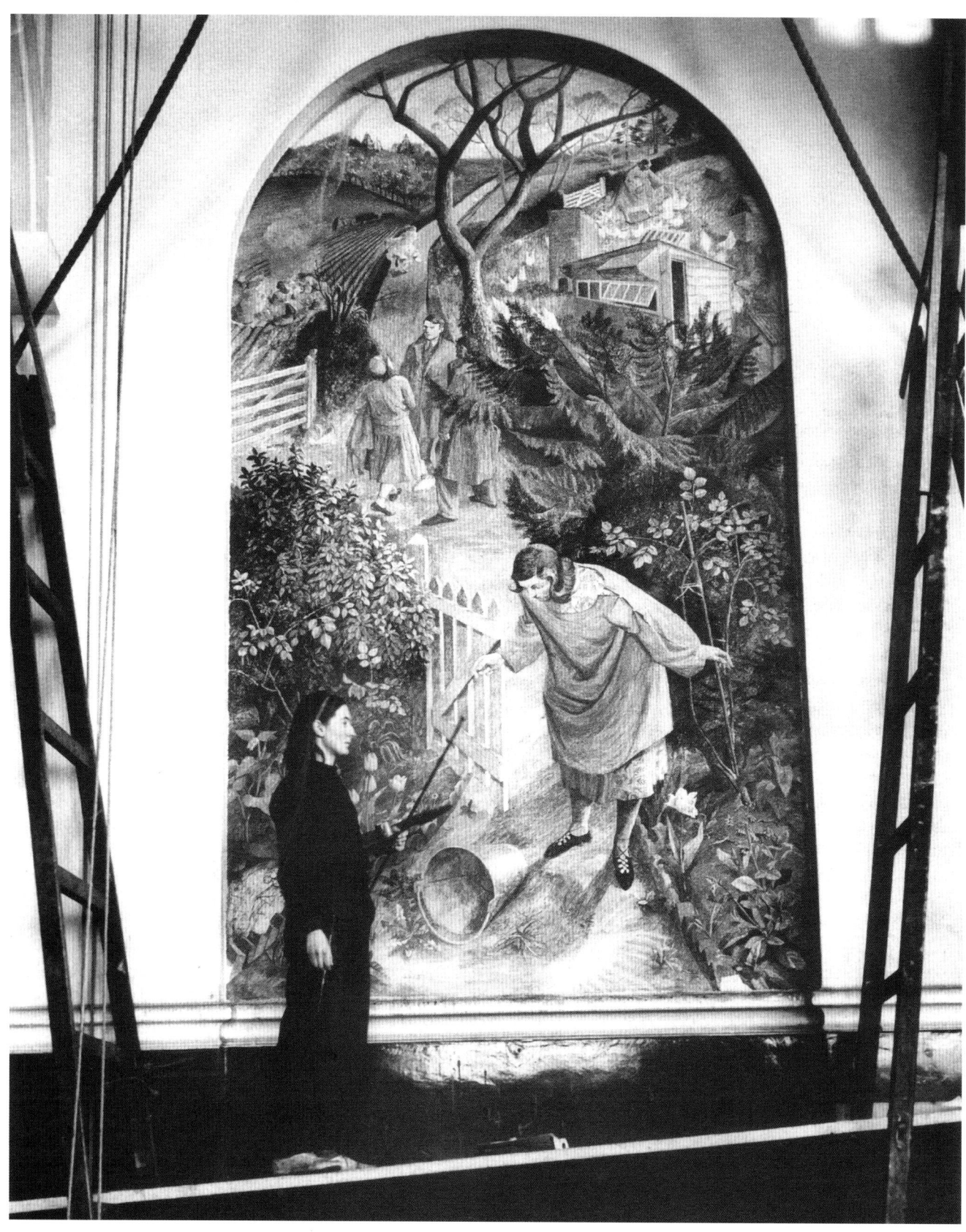

FIG 10 Evelyn Dunbar with her Brockley mural panel *The Country Girl and the Pail of Milk*.
1936 press photograph, staged for the inauguration.

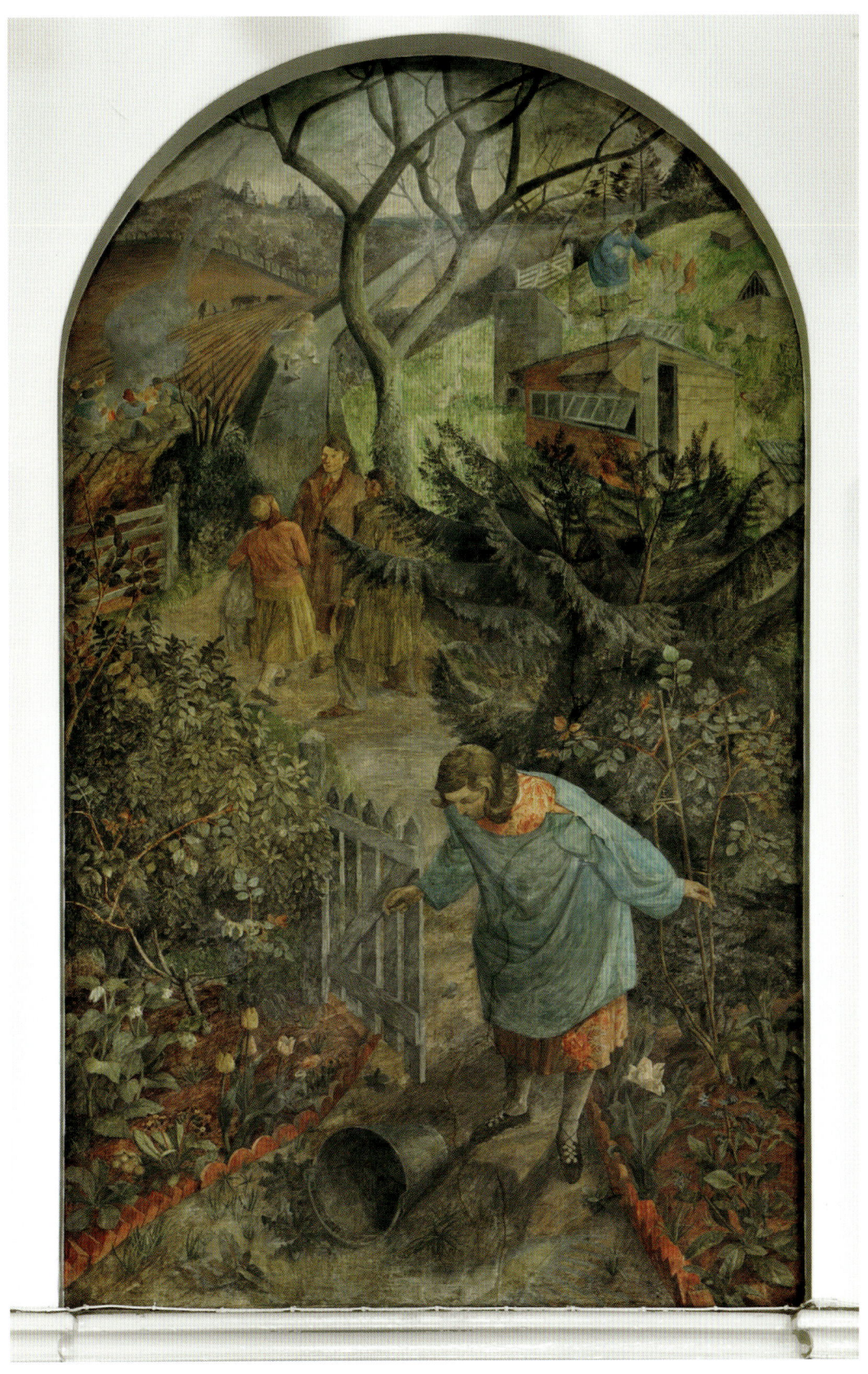

FIG 11 Brockley mural panel *The Country Girl and the Pail of Milk*, 1933, *in situ*.
Photo: Nigel Green

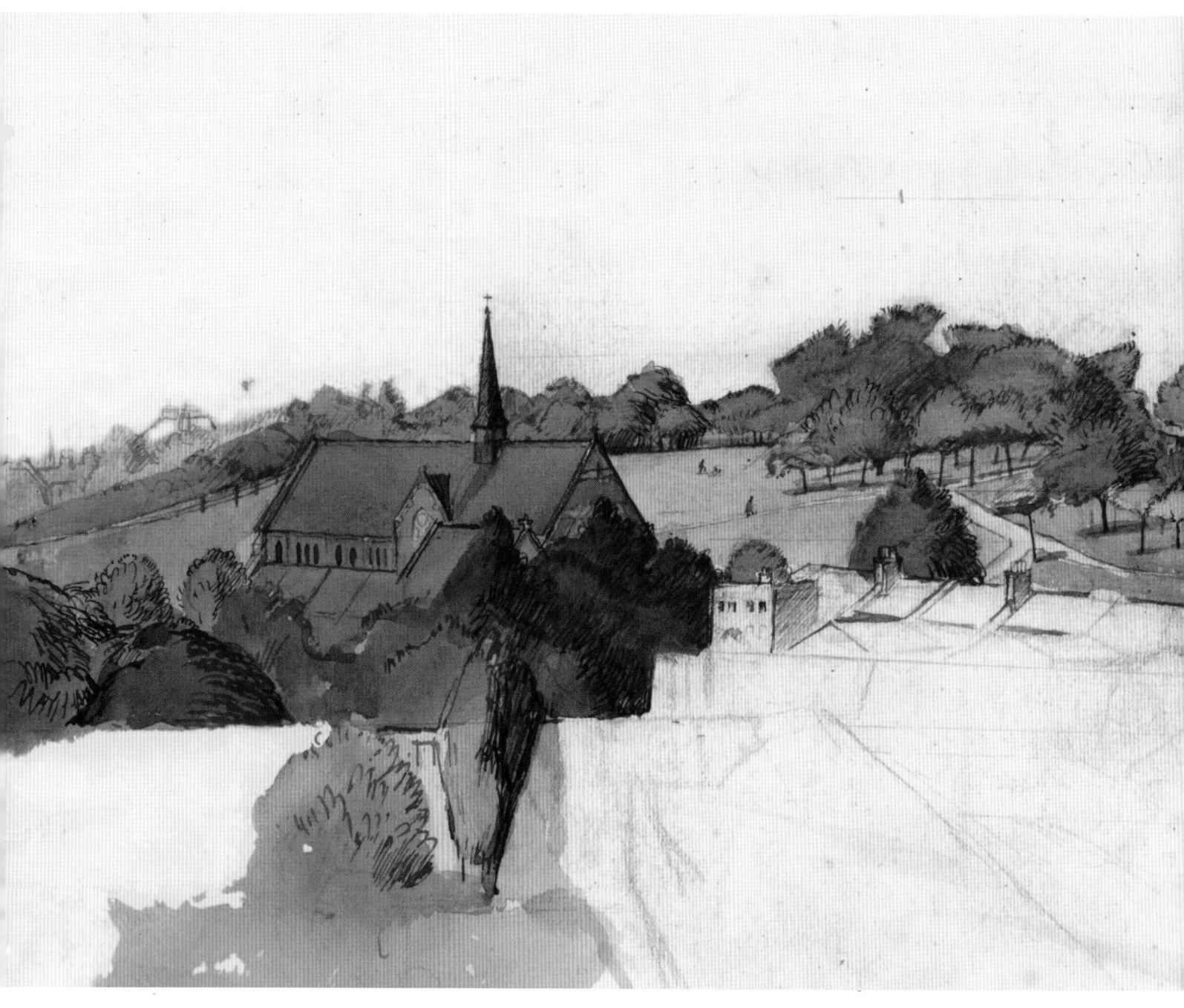

Detail of CAT 23

CAT 23 [HMO 429, 552 & 524]
Sketch for the background landscape of the Hilly Fields mural frieze at Brockley County School for Boys, 1934,
Watercolour on paper, 14 ¾ x 62 in. (37.5 x 158 cm).

This panoramic study shows Hilly Fields as seen from the top of the nearby Ladywell Institution water tower.
A related drawing is in the collection of the City Art Gallery of Carlisle.

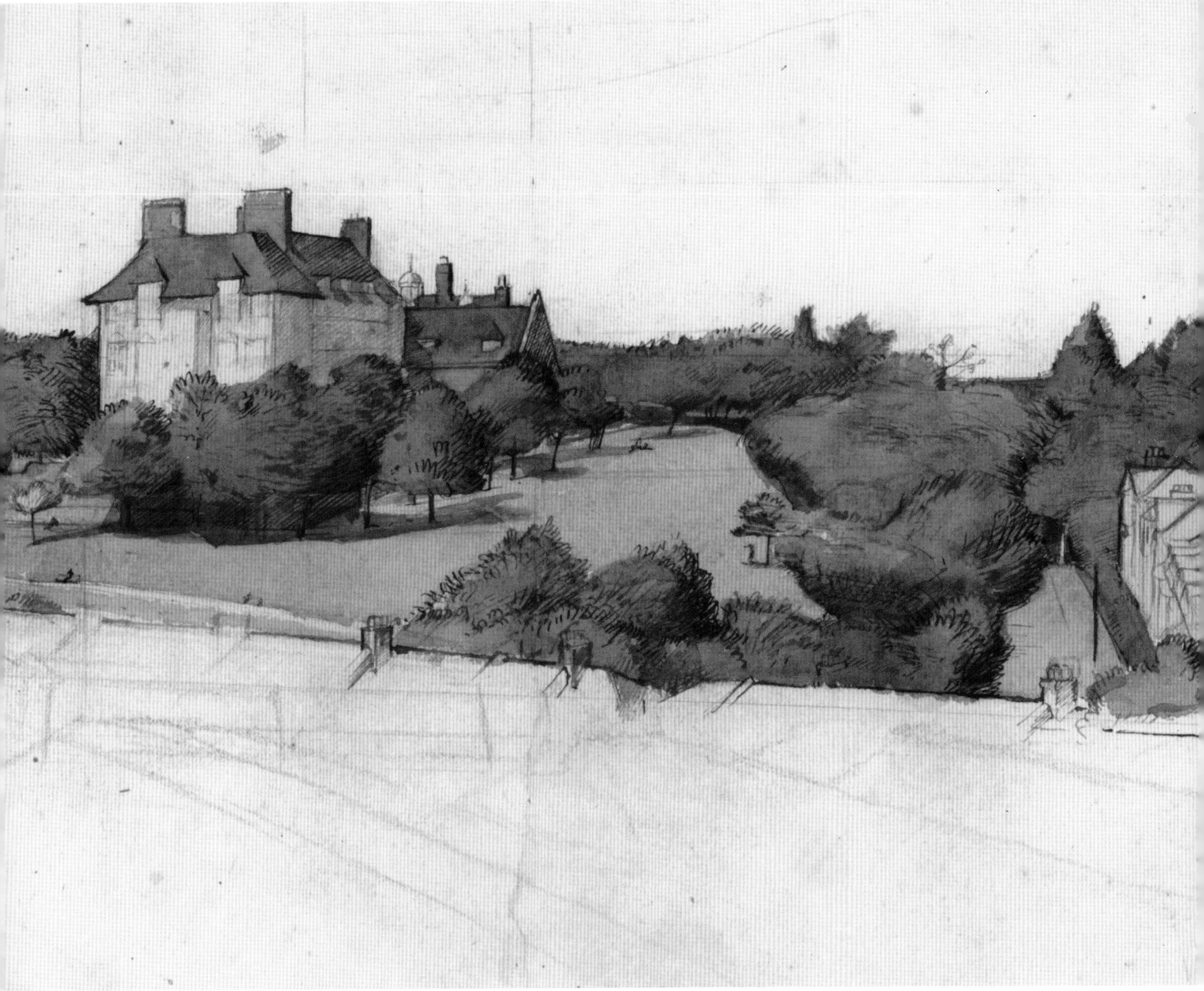

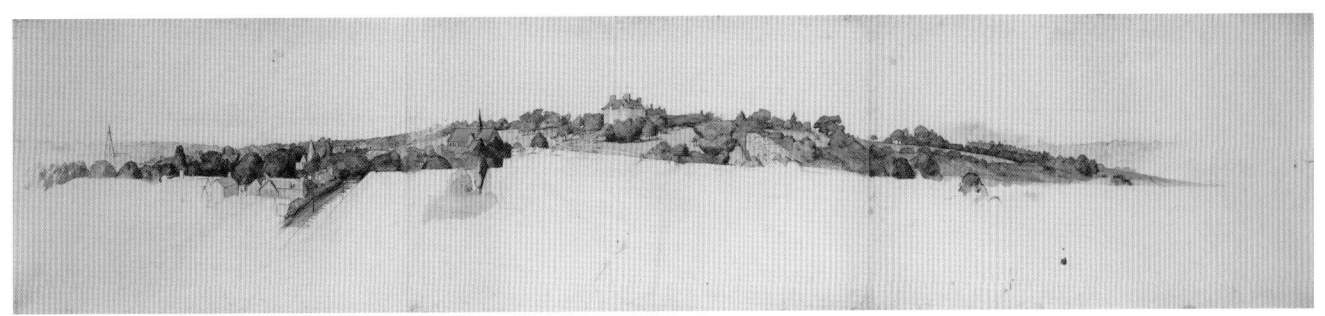

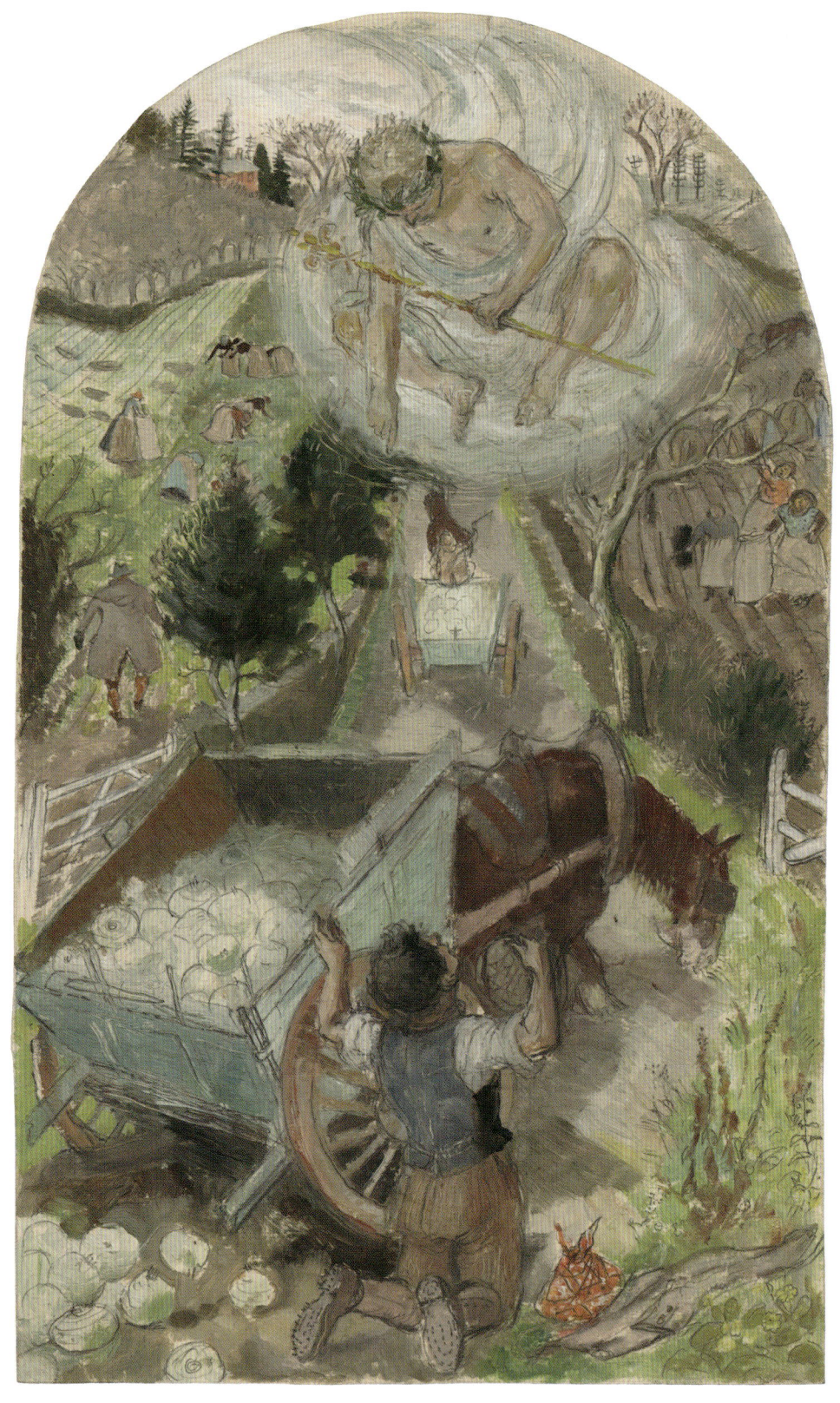

CAT 24 [HMO 308] *Hercules and the Waggoner*, spring 1933,
Pencil and oil on paper, 17 ¾ x 10 ½ in. (45.2 x 26.5 cm)
This sketch – as well as the one on the opposite page – was for a mural panel in the hall of Brockley County School for Boys. Both were probably prepared in case of a shortfall of artists to complete the scheme, but neither were in fact used.

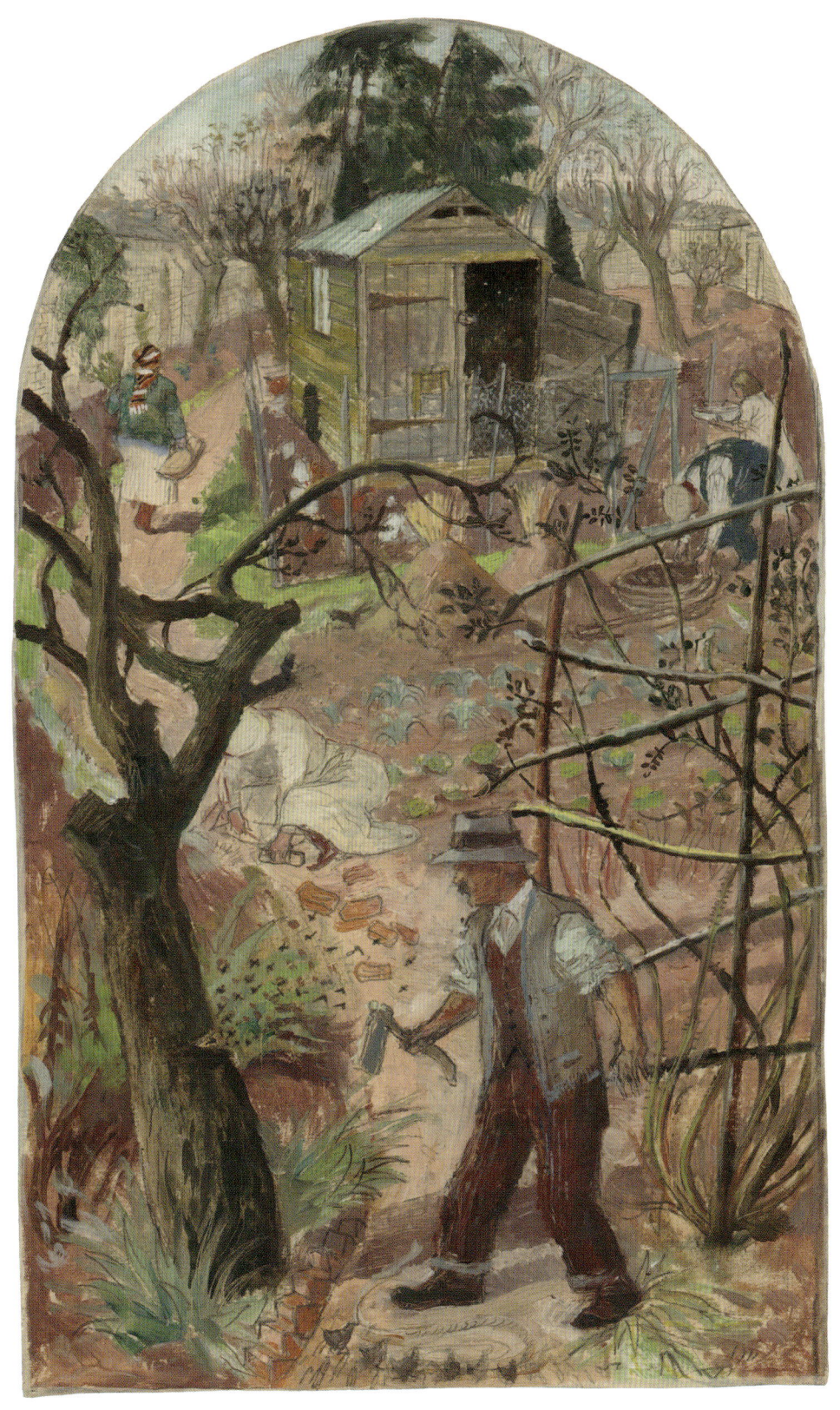

CAT 25 [HMO 309] *The Woodcutter and the Bees*, spring 1933,
Pencil and oil on paper, 17 ¾ x 10 ½ in. (45.2 x 26.5 cm)

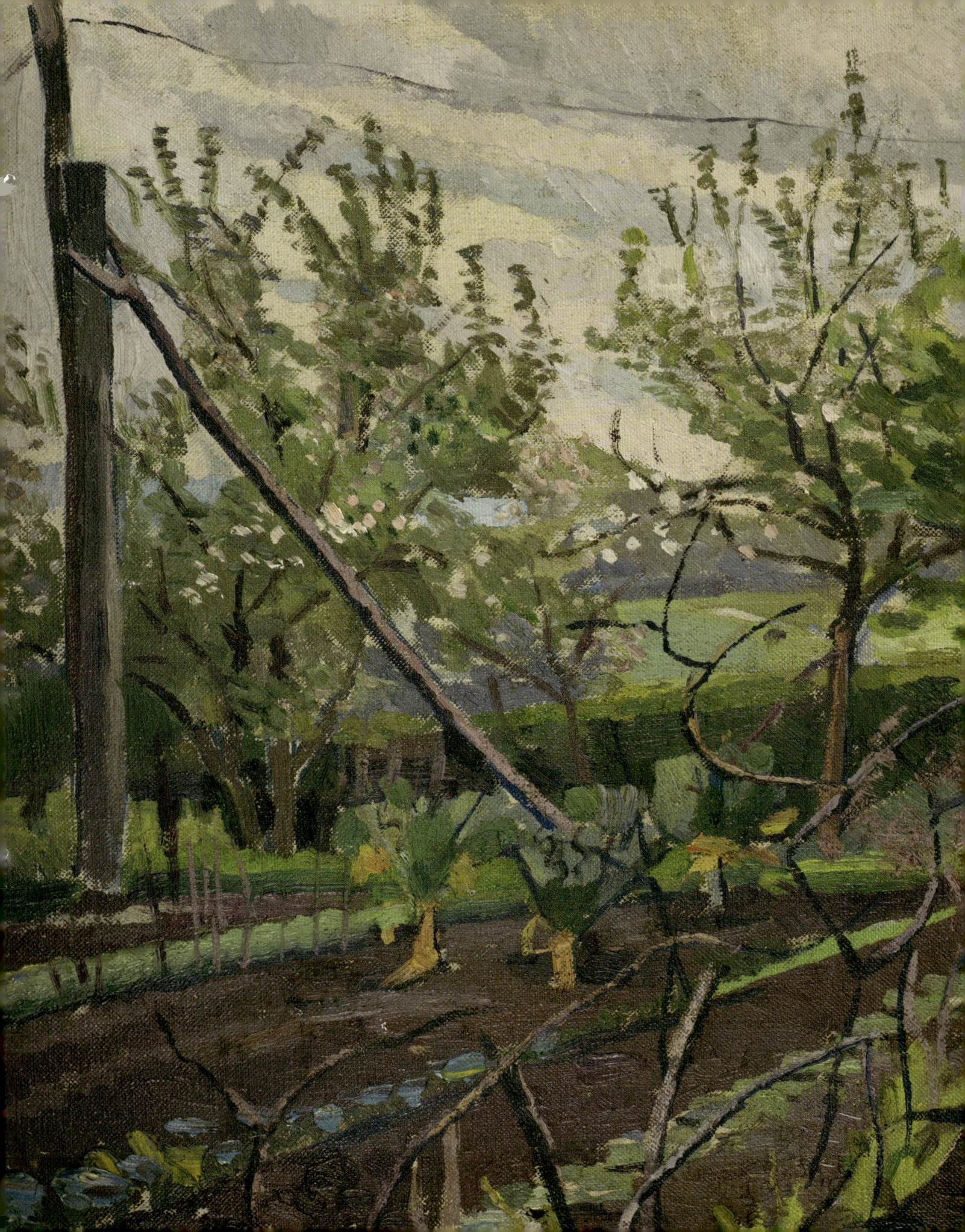

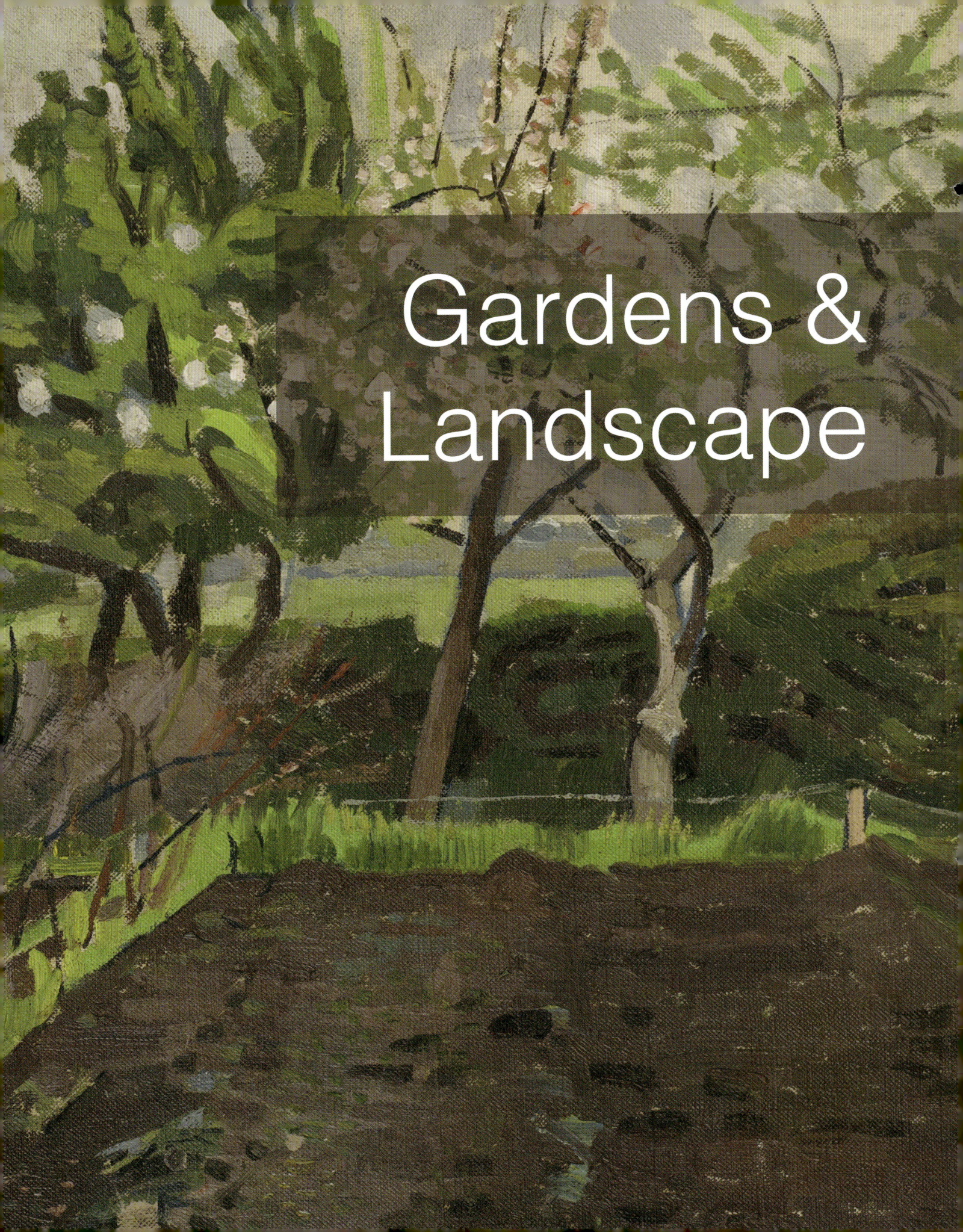

Gardens & Landscape

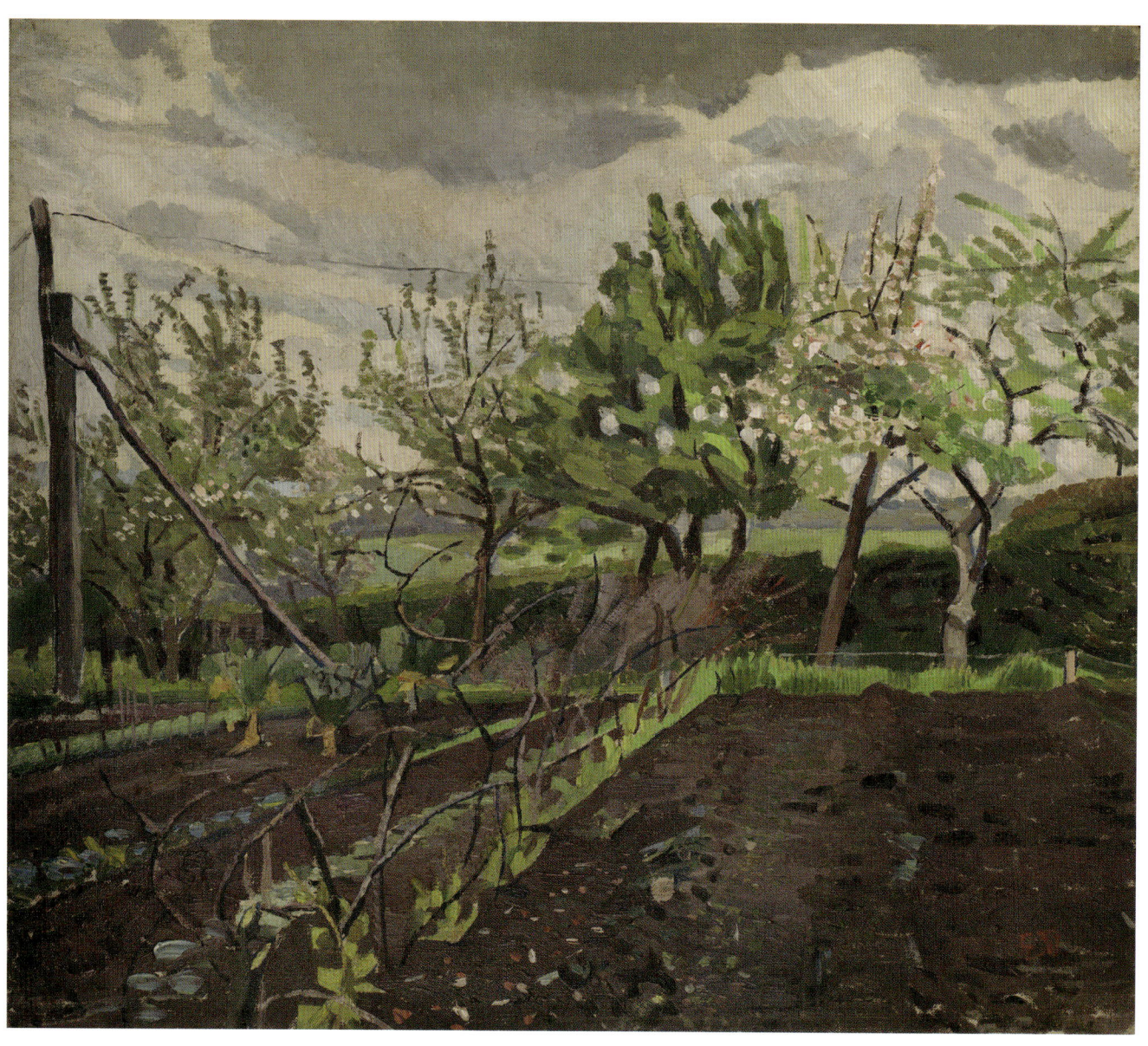

CAT 26 [HMO 794]
Vegetable garden at Strawberry Cottage, spring, signed 'ED', c.1938,
Oil on canvas, 18 ¼ x 20 ¼ in. (46.3 x 51.2cm)

Strawberry Cottage, Hurst Green (near Tunbridge Wells), was the occasional home of Dunbar's aunt Clara Cowling.

Gardens & Landscape

*The kiss of the sun for pardon
The song of the birds for mirth,
One is nearer God's heart in the garden
Than anywhere else on earth.*

Dorothy Gurney (1858-1932)

Evelyn Dunbar clearly shared Dorothy Gurney's vision and sentiments regarding gardens. In one of Dunbar's many letters to Mahoney she described how her 'little patch is beginning to form itself (with our help) into a lovely place, I think, and with all the new things, will be a perfect heaven of varied greys and greens and aromatic odours.' (September 1933). Painting and gardening were twin passions to her and in pursuit of both she exercised a strong degree of control laying out her garden with the same care and precision she exercised when laying out her palette.

Although born in Reading her formative years from the age of six, when the family moved to Rochester, were spent in Kent, 'the Garden of England' as it is often described. Gardens, hop-fields, orchards, the rich abundance of the Kentish landscape, is at the core of her work. While others might be moved by the Highland landscape of Scotland or the rugged beauty of the Alps, her heart remained firmly in 'the Garden of England'. Her identification with the homely man-made landscape of this corner of England was as much spiritual as visual and needed to be assisted by the hard graft of hedging, trenching, mulching, carting and pruning as well as celebrated in paint. One of her earliest exhibited paintings was entitled *Gardening*, (present whereabouts unknown) shown at the Goupil Gallery in 1931 and singled out by the critic of *The Scotsman* who described it as 'a most sensitive study of the Slade School type, of figures in a garden delicately drawn and thoroughly "felt".' (*The Scotsman*, 11 June 1931) Such a description could equally be applied to the study of *The Dunbar Family in the Garden at the Cedars* (CAT 2 and 3), the Brockley sketch for *The Woodcutter and the Bees* (CAT 25) or even the slightly later *Land Workers at Strood* (CAT 31) in the present exhibition. Her vision was always that of a comfortable rural middle-class domesticity as far removed from the peasant life that had inspired rural painters of the previous generation such as George Clausen (1852-1944) and Edward Stott (1859-1918) as from the urban scenes of Herkomer (1849-1914) or Mulready (1844-1904). Unlike her wartime paintings of the Women's Land Army the men and women – frequently members of her own family – who inhabit these landscapes and work these gardens are at home and comfortable with their surroundings.

Her acuity of observation is equally apparent in her landscape as in her figure subjects, trees are individual not generic, their deformations lovingly recorded: the apple trees growing in the orchard in the study of her mother gardening (CAT 27) are just as much portraits as *Sleeping Beauty* (CAT 12) the ten minute sketch of her father. In contrast to the immediacy of these oil sketches her large panoramic study of the landscape at Hilly Fields (CAT 23) spread over three sheets of paper has the awesome grasp of form that one associates more readily with eighteenth-century landscapists such as Francis Towne (1739/40-1816) and the Italian Giovanni Battista Lusieri (1754-1821) whose panoramas were so prized by the Grand Tourists. She had a countrywoman's eye for the nuances of landscape, of recession, cloud formations and weather which informs her slightest studies and gives authority to her major works, most particularly *A Land Girl and the Bail Bull* (FIG 19).

Peyton Skipwith

CAT 27 [HMO 785]
Florence Dunbar Tending the Garden, 1938-39,
Oil on panel, 17 ¾ x 9 in. (45.1 x 22.8 cm)

This painting depicts apple blossom time at The Cedars, with Florence Dunbar gardening in the distance: the sundial and several dead branches suggest the passing of time at a low point in the artist's career and personal life.

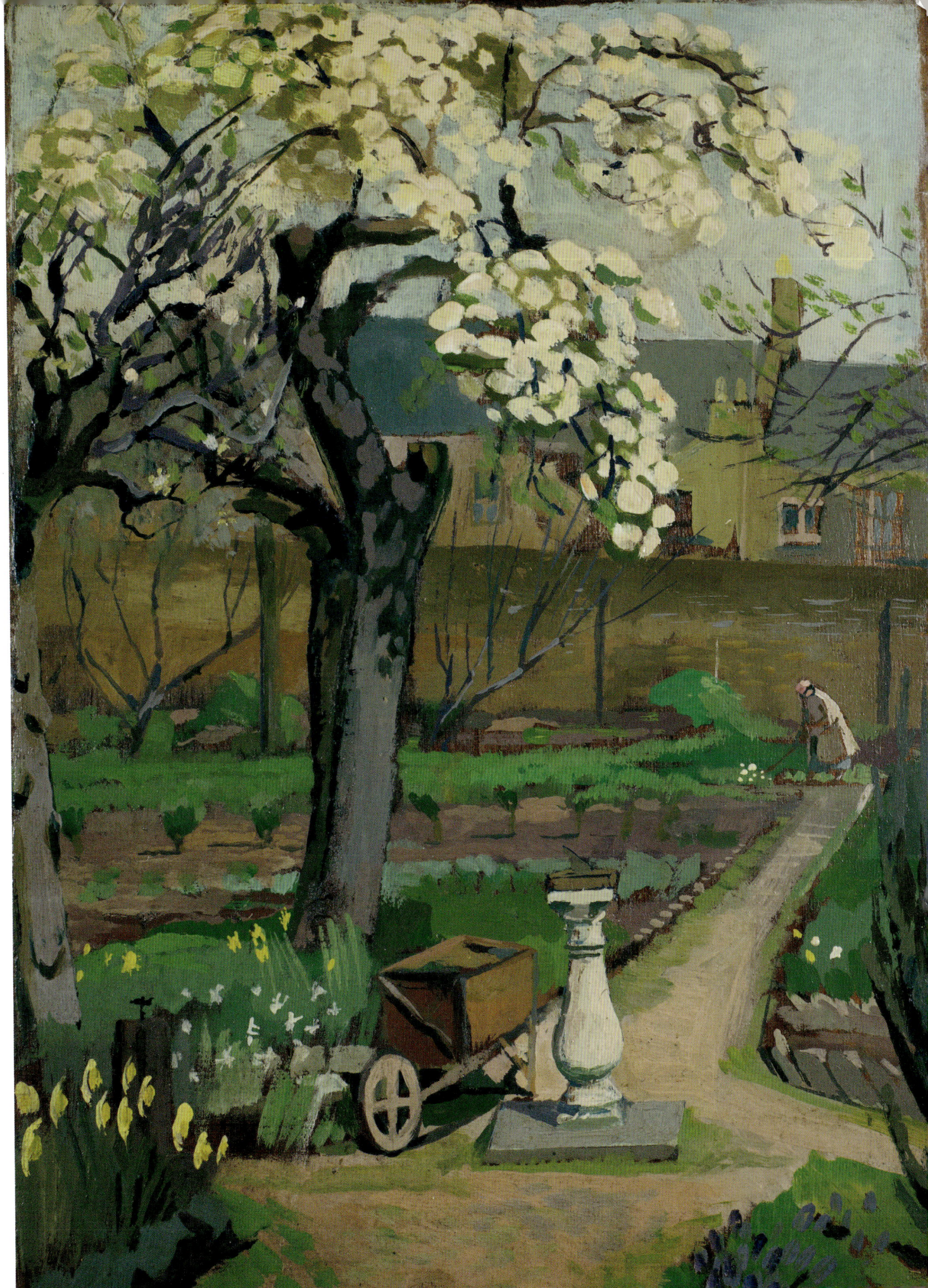

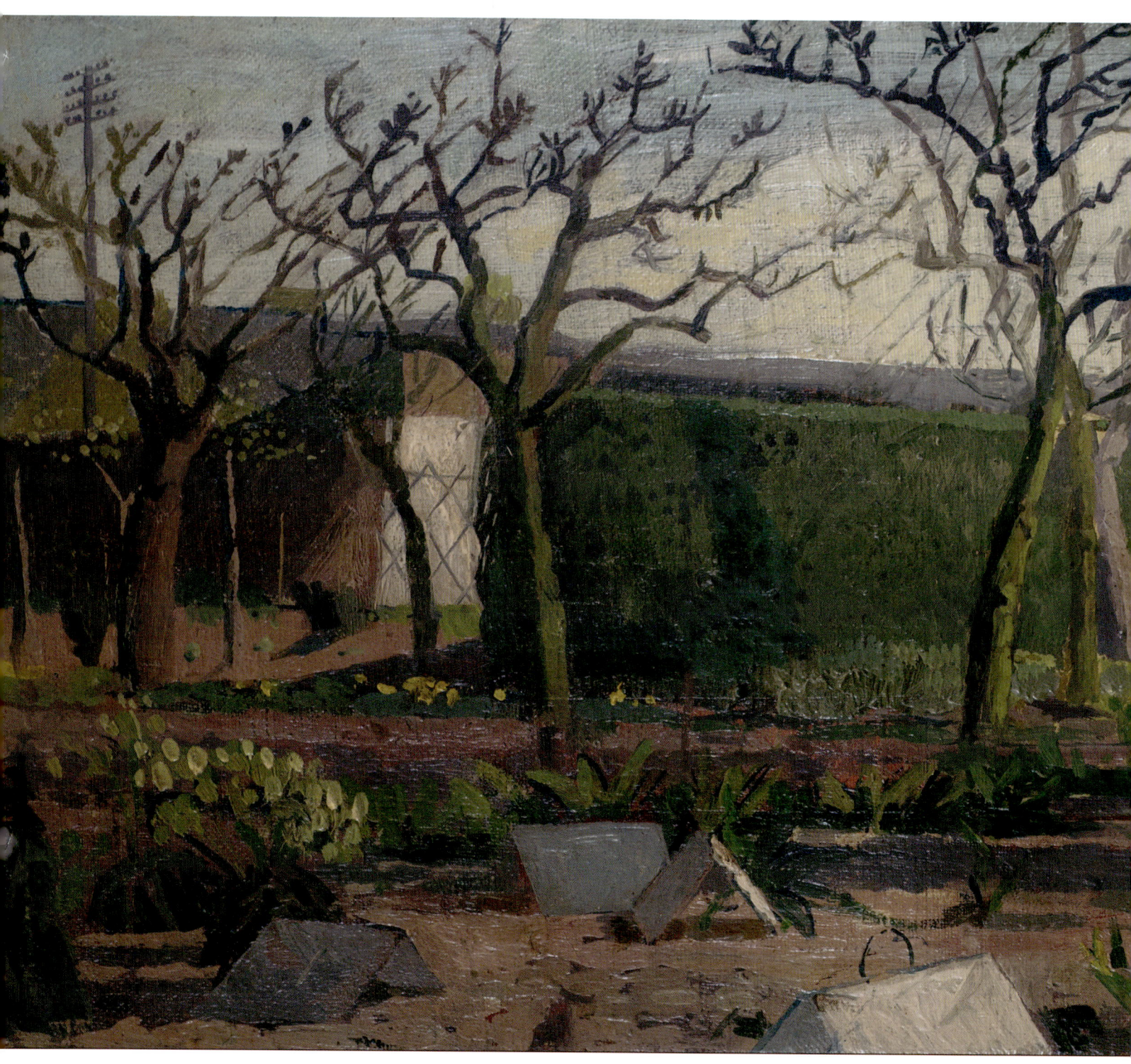

CAT 28 [HMO 778]
Early Spring, c.1936,
Oil on canvas, 7 ¾ x 17 ½ in. (19.7 x 44.5 cm)

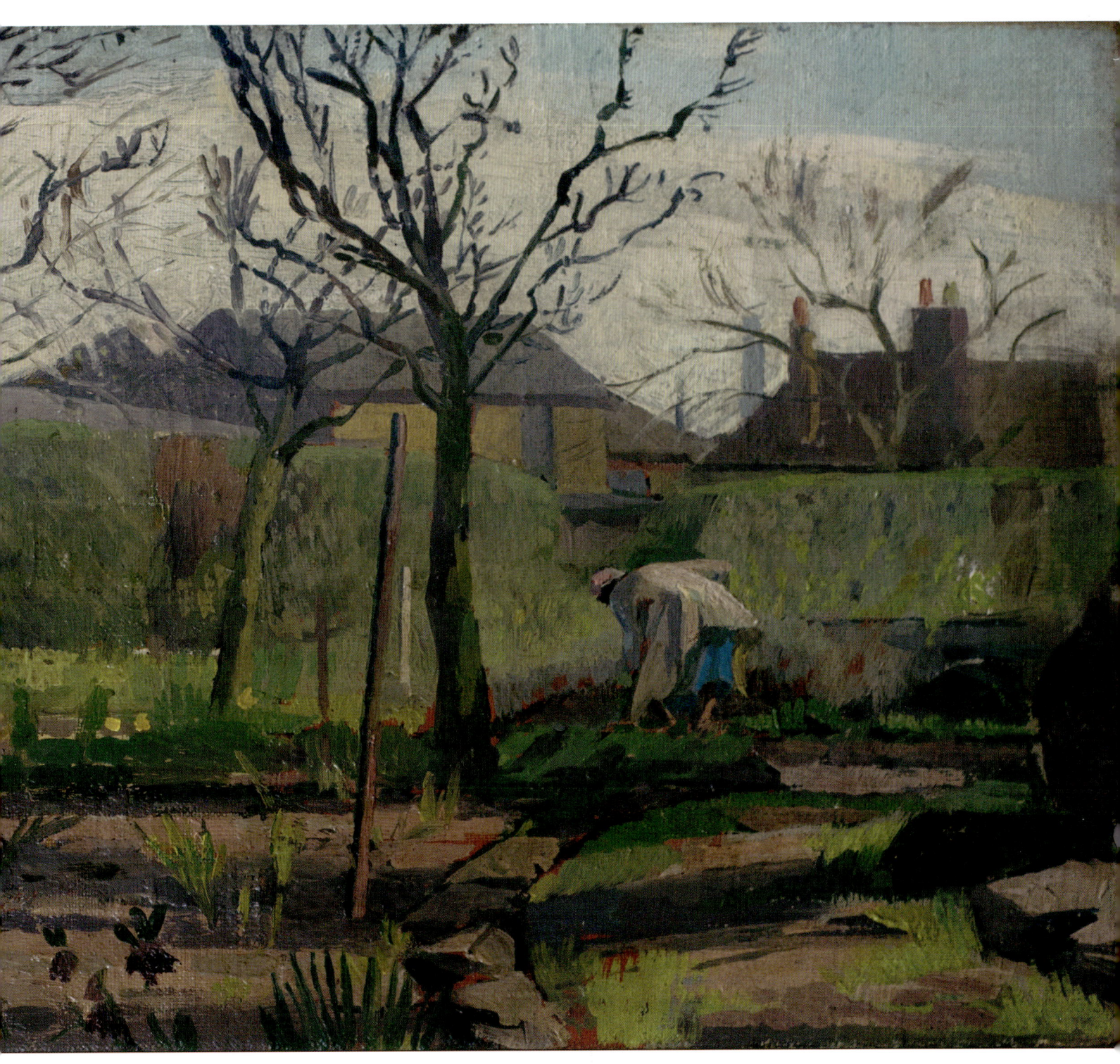

Early Spring can be compared with *Winter Garden* (FIG 2), now in Tate Britain. *Early Spring* depicts the garden at The Cedars with Florence Dunbar, the artist's mother, ar work.

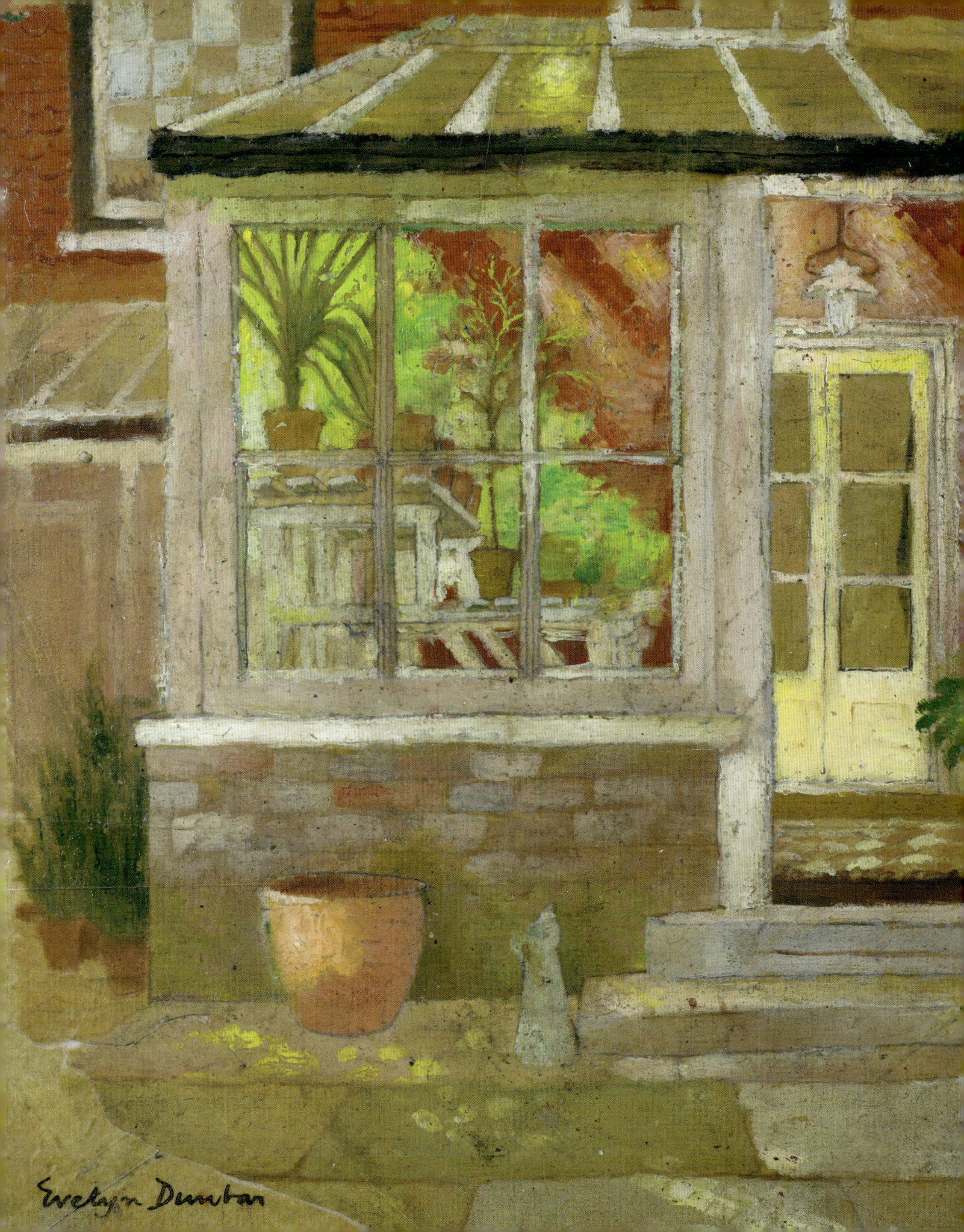

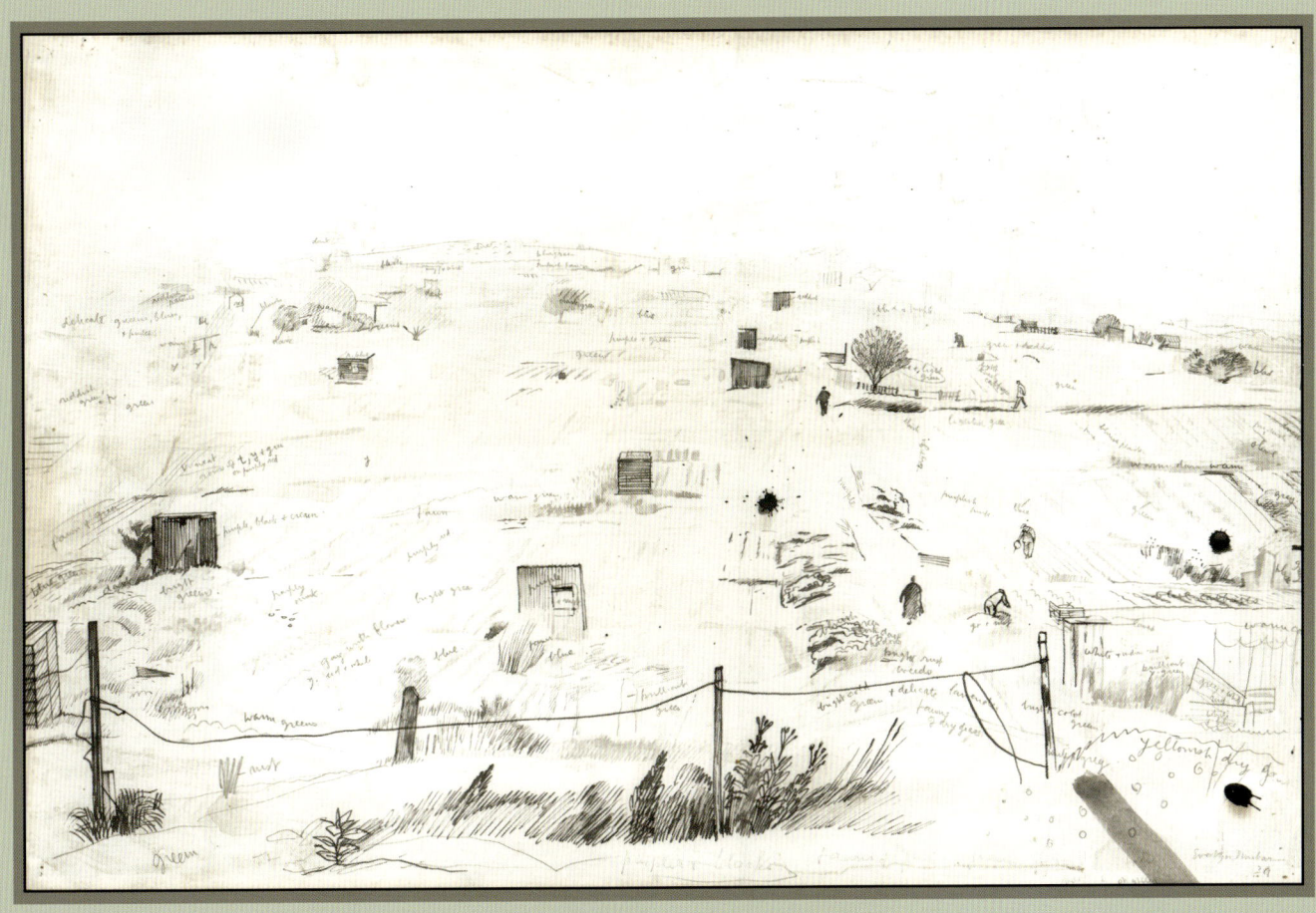

CAT 30 [HMO 774] A study of council allotments at Strood,
Signed and dated 'Evelyn Dunbar '39' and inscribed with colour notes,
Pencil and pen & ink on paper, 14 ¾ x 22 in. (37.6 x 56 cm)
Exhibited: The Blue Gallery, Dunbar's art gallery in Rochester in March 1939.

Dunbar returned to the Strood allotments as a war artist in 1940, hoping to undertake a more extensive version in oils of this pencil study for the War Artists' Advisory Committee. Having set up her easel, she was surprised and distressed at being chased away by allotment holders thinking she was a German spy: from the elevated position of the allotments there was a good view over the naval dockyard in nearby Chatham. She never went back.

CAT 29 [HMO 72] *The Garden Door,* studio stamp 'Evelyn Dunbar', c.1933,
Oil on tracing paper, 21¾ x 15½ in. (53.5 x 39.4 cm)

A study of the back door and porch at Steelands, Ticehurst, Sussex, home of Dunbar's aunt and uncle Clara and Stead Cowling.

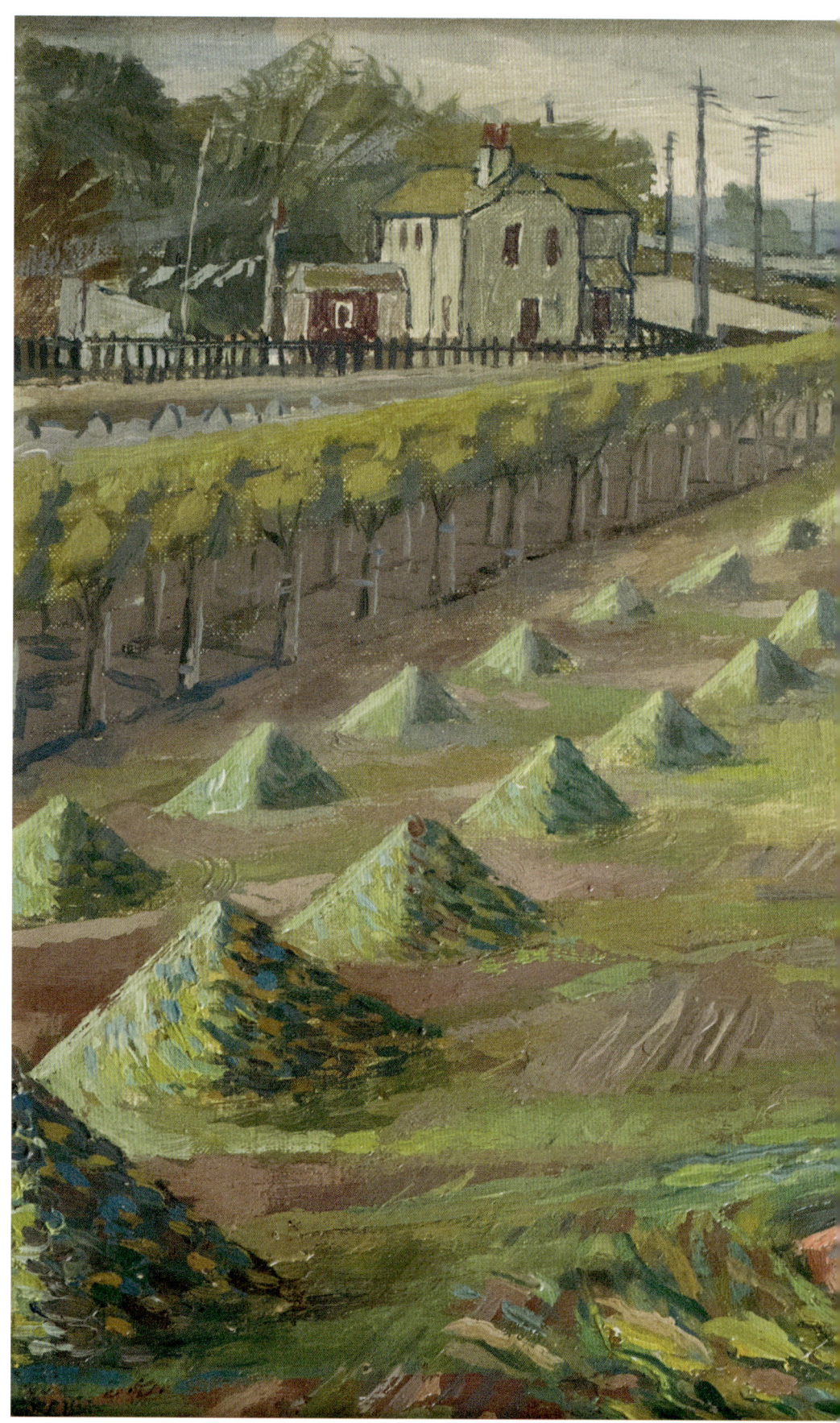

CAT 31 [HMO 762]
Land Workers at Strood, titled on frame. Also known as *Field Workers at Strood*. Predating World War II by some 18 months, this picture is curiously prophetic of some of the artist's wartime painting. 1938,
Oil on canvas, 8 ½ x 12 ½ in. (21.6 x 31.7 cm)
Exhibited: Wildenstein's, 1938, Royal Academy of Arts, 1943.

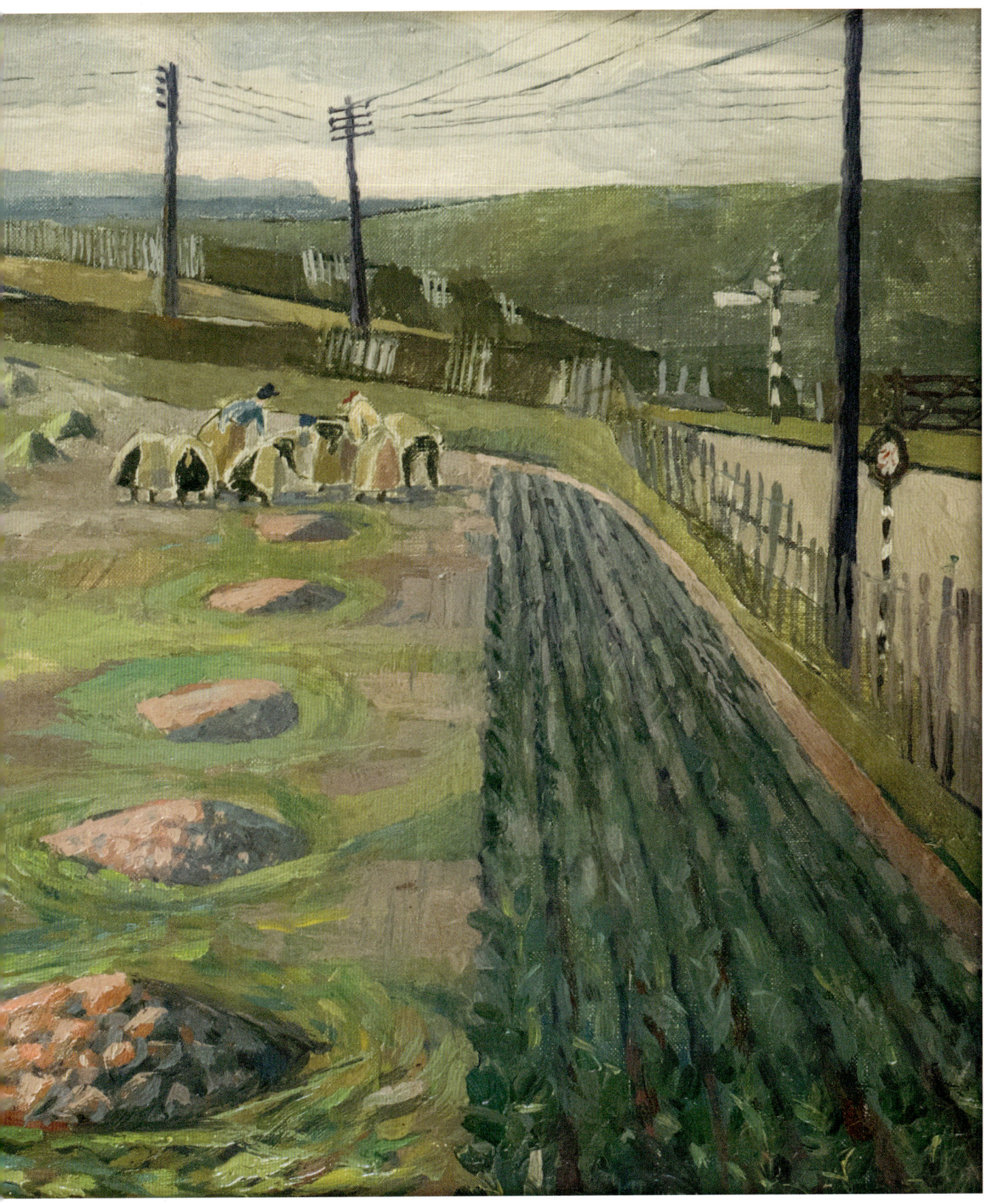

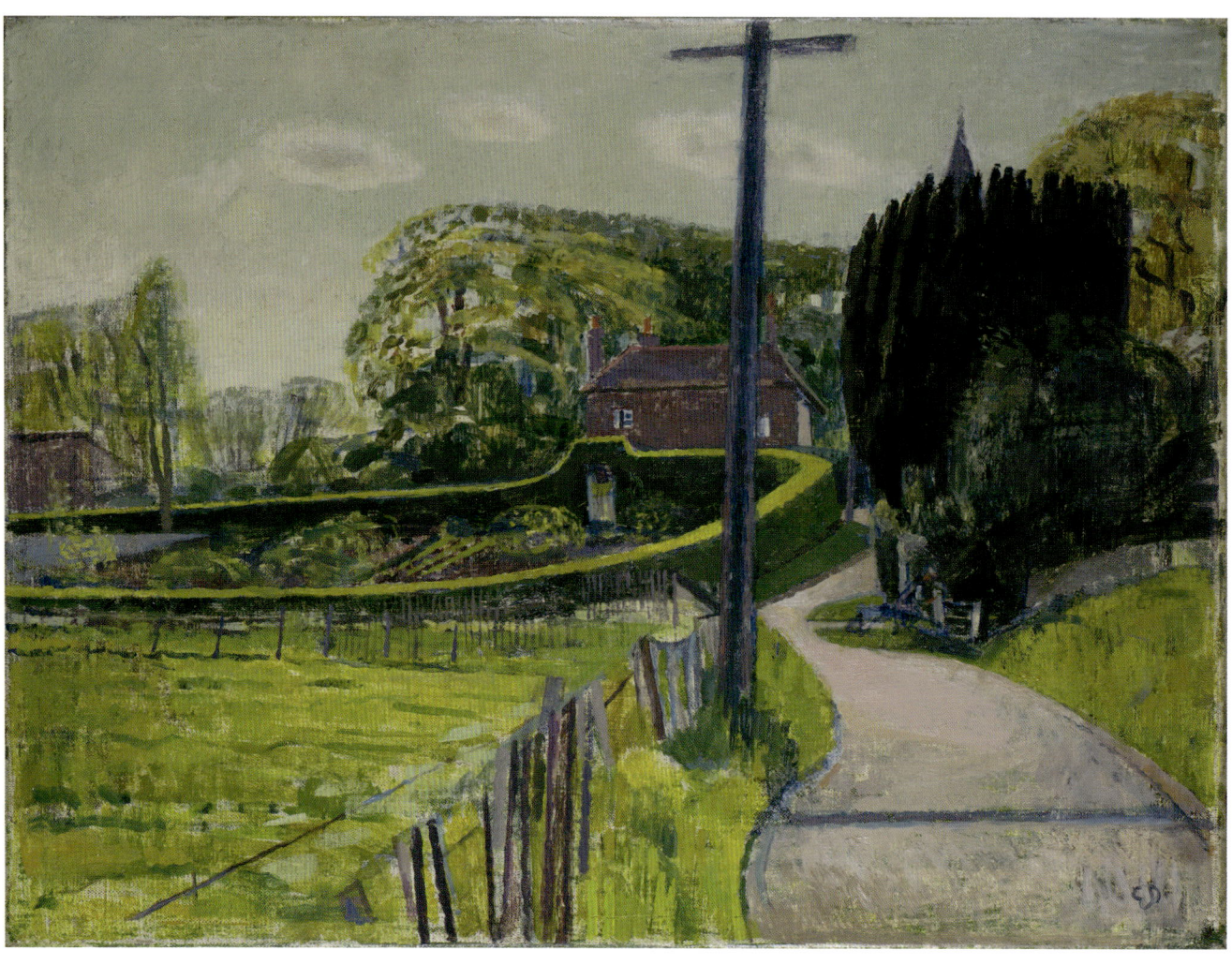

LEFT : CAT 32 [HMO 768] *Hinxhill*, c.1952,
Oil on canvas, 14 x 18 in. (35 x 45.7 cm)

Hinxhill is a tiny hamlet east of Ashford, Kent, supposedly named after Hengist, the 5th century AD Teutonic invader of Kent. The artist and her husband Roger Folley moved near here late in 1950, following Folley's appointment to the staff of Wye College. Signed 'ED', this is an early essay in the great series of Kentish landscapes that occupied Dunbar continually for the last 10 years of her life. As always, she finds a neat and organised vegetable garden irresistible.

CAT 33 [HMO 789]
Early autumn Kentish landscape with oast houses and ploughed fields. c.1956,
Oil on canvas, 13 ½ x 19 ¼ in. (34.3 x 48.9 cm)

CAT 34 *Sacking Potatoes,* 1948, oil on canvas, 12 ¼ x 18 in. (31.8 x 45.7 cm)
Private collection courtesy England & Co Gallery, London

Sacking Potatoes is probably Dunbar's design for the cover, including the spine and fold-in flaps, of *The Potato: A Survey of its History and of Factors Influencing its Yield, Nutritive Value and Storage*, a book by Roger Folley's friend Glynn Burton. It was never used.

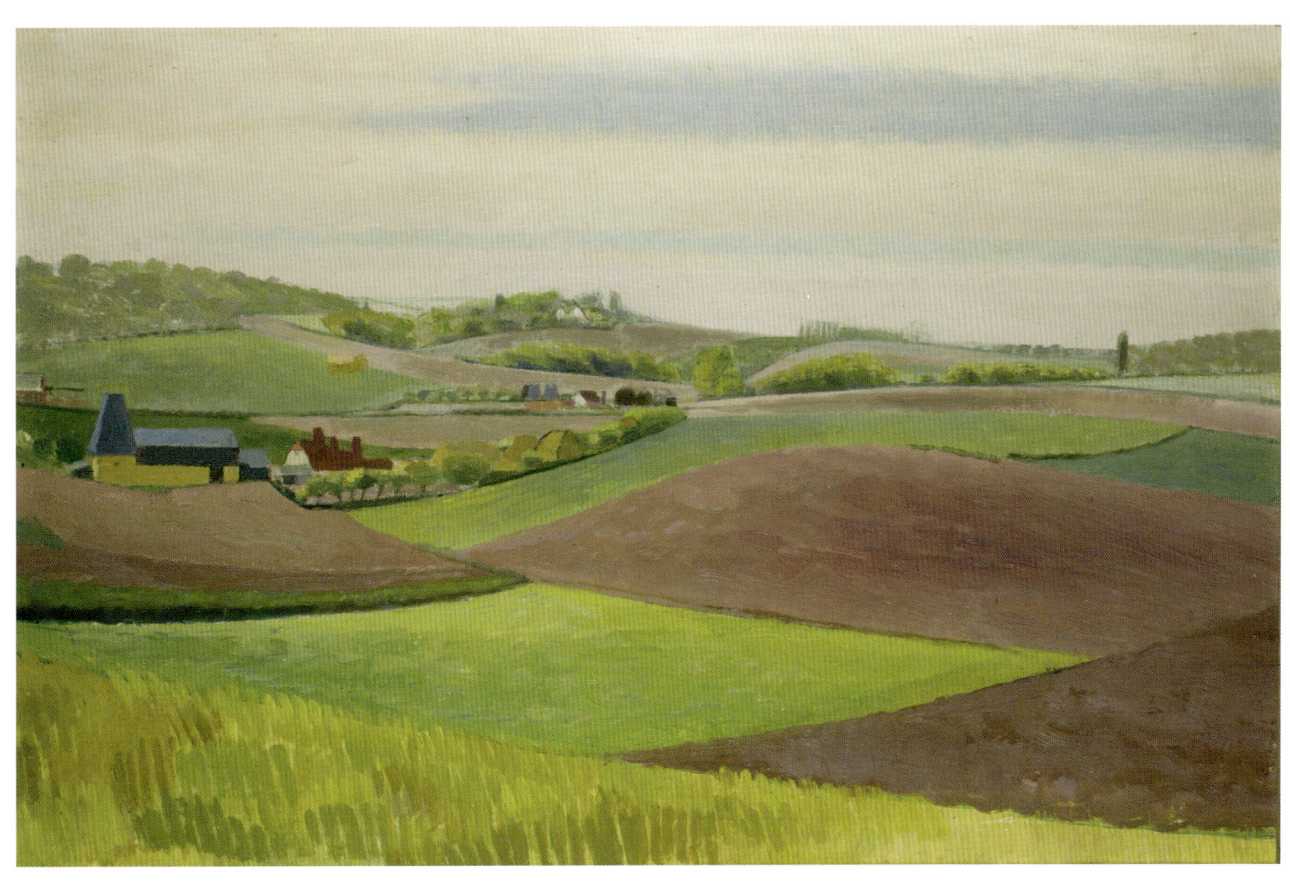

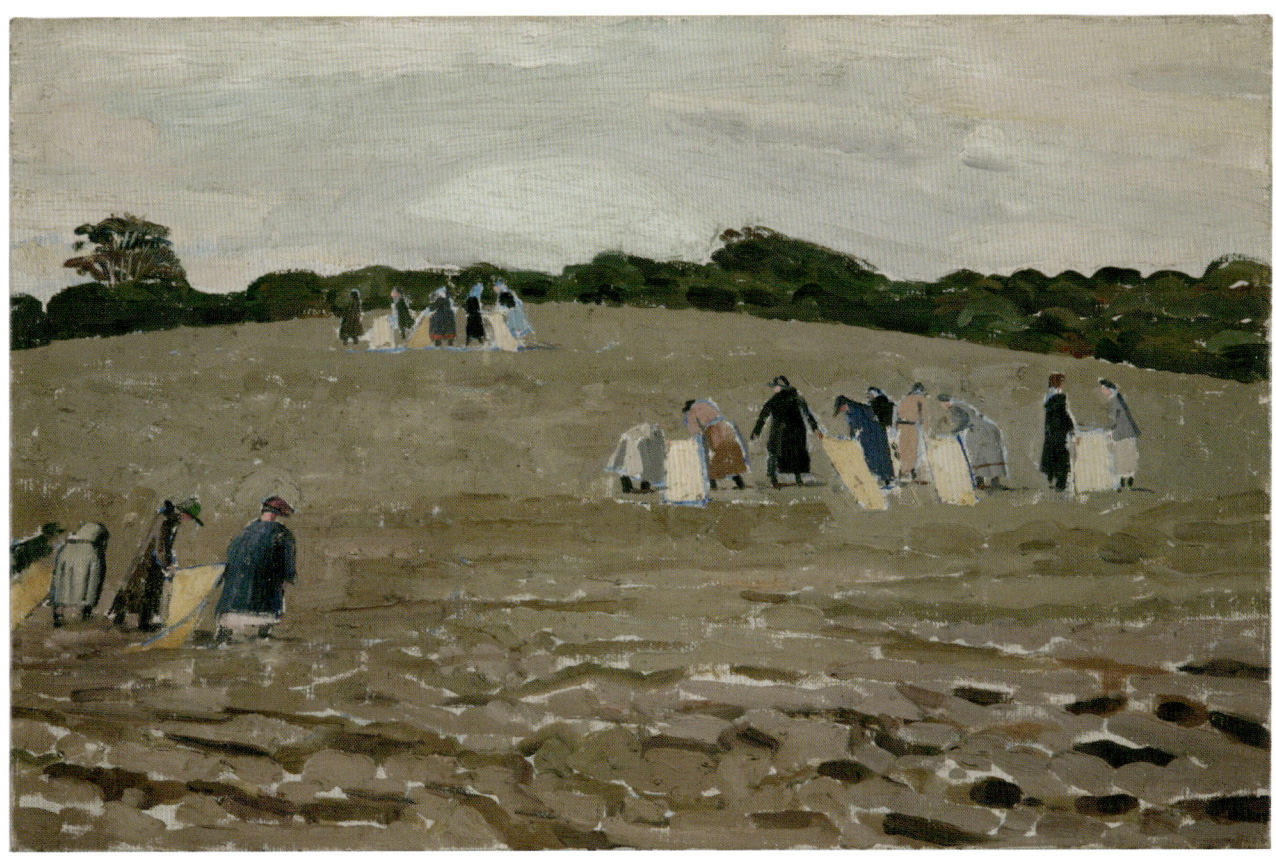

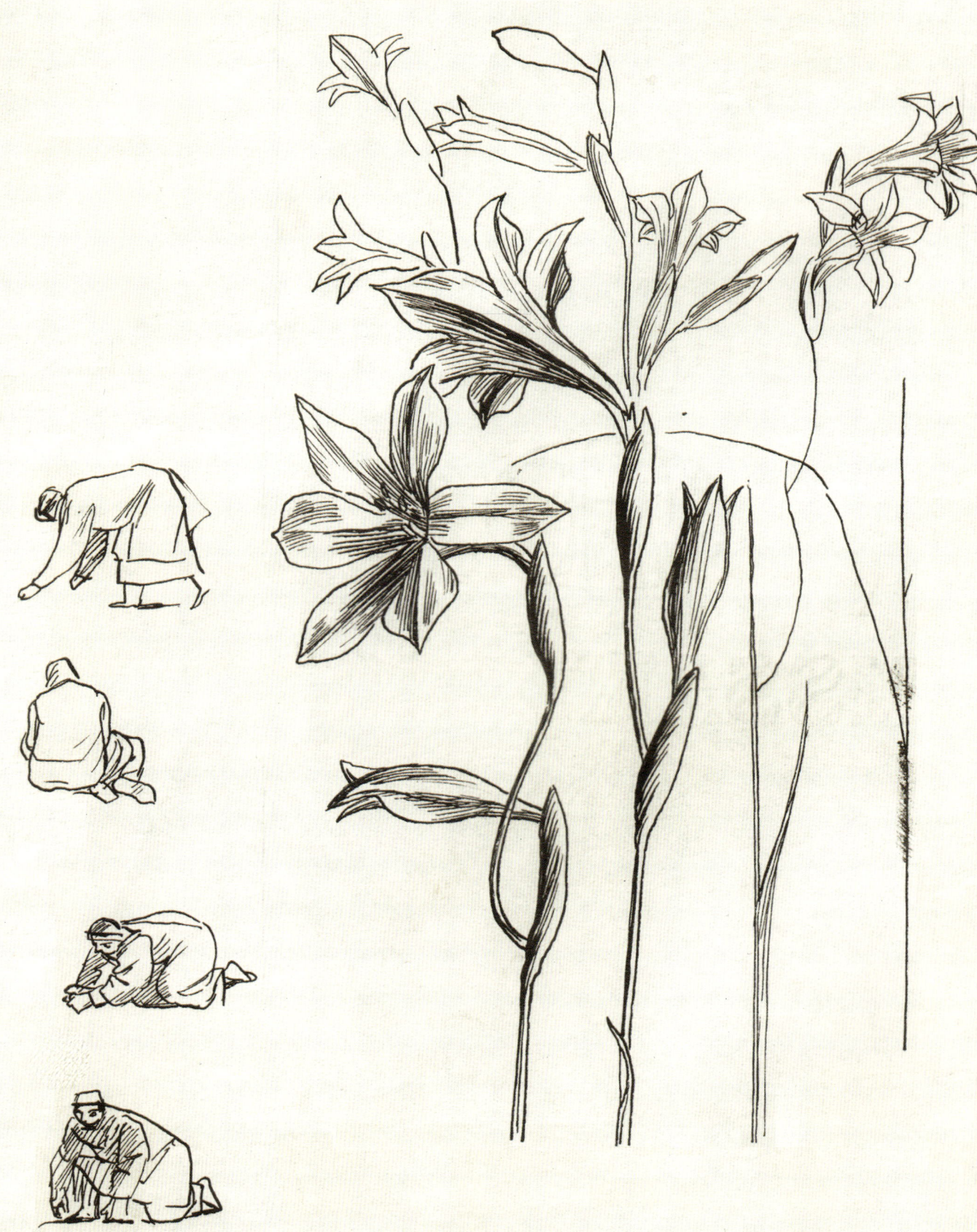

Gardeners' Choice

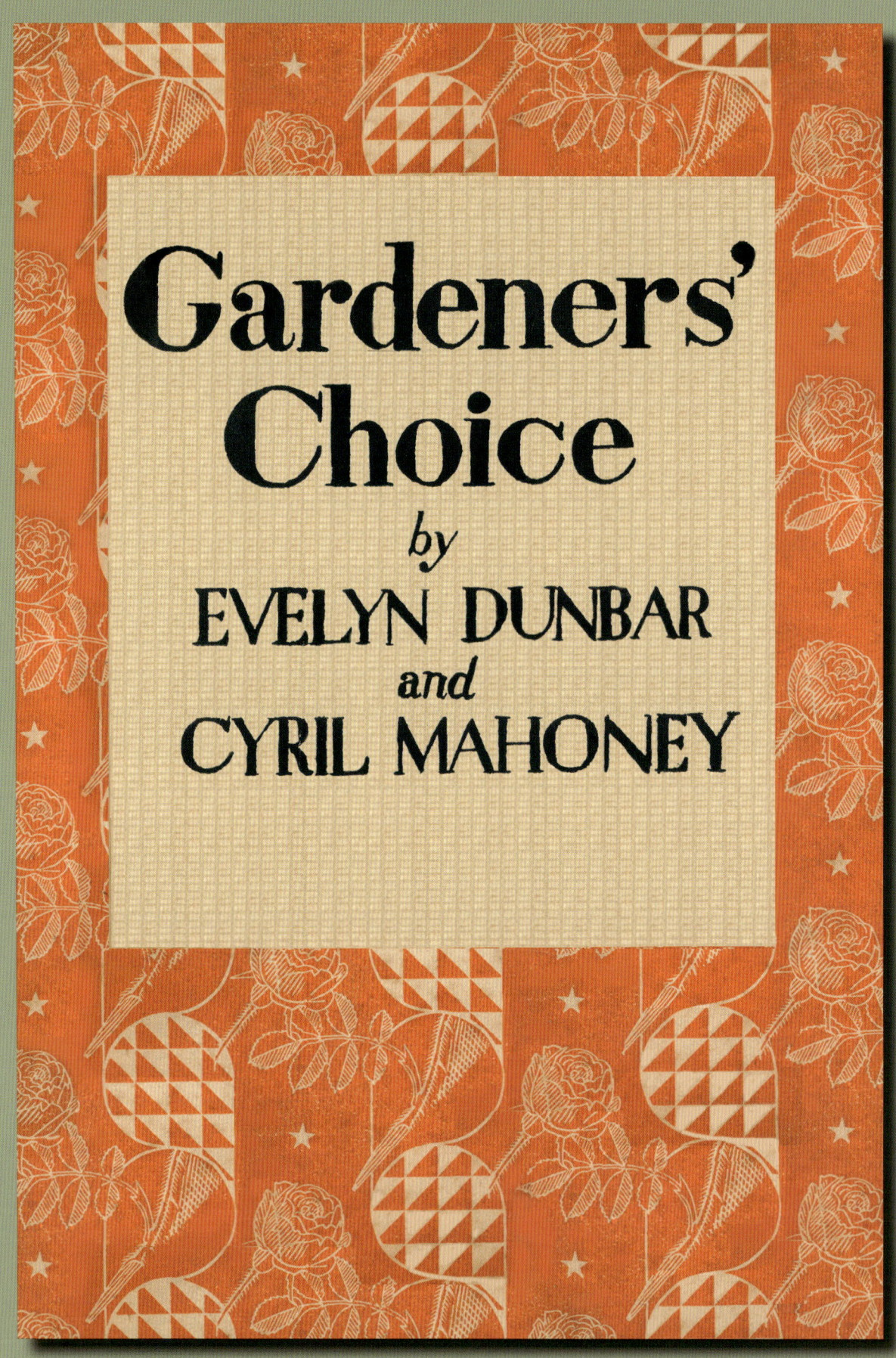

Gardeners' Choice

Following the completion of the Brockley murals Evelyn Dunbar looked for ways to earn some money, and was fortunate to be asked by Catherine Carswell, a Hampstead neighbour, to illustrate her and her husband's book *The Scots Week-End and Caledonian Vade-Mecum for Host, Guest and Wayfarer*, inspired by Francis Meynell's *The Week-End Book*. Following its publication by Routledge in the summer of 1936 she asked one of the partners, Mr Ragg, whether the firm had anything horticultural she could illustrate: his reply was negative unless 'you can suggest someone who could write something really new on gardening.' She passed this on to Charles Mahoney with the comment 'Now mate what about it.' (quoted Gill Clarke, p.54) Thus the seeds of *Gardeners' Choice* were sown.

Although her earlier children's book illustrations tended to be soapily pretty in a Margaret Tarrantish manner, for *The Scots Week-End Book* she honed a more incisive style of black pen and ink drawing, refining this further for *Gardeners' Choice* to create illustrations reminiscent of those in early herbals or eighteenth century chapbooks. That up to this stage she did not have a clearly defined style is born out by her wash illustration for *Wuthering Heights* (CAT 129) commissioned for an article by Kenneth Clark in the November 1936 issue of *Signature*, which, like some of Paul Nash's early work, is in a distinctly pre-raphaelite manner. However for *Gardeners' Choice* she reverted exclusively to pen and ink.

The division of labour between Dunbar and Mahoney in *Gardeners' Choice* is to all intents and purpose indistinguishable. The introductory chapter, 'Community of Plants', demonstrates their close collaboration: 'In this book we present a small selection of plants which our practical knowledge of gardening and our personal outlook have led us to make. In addition to our natural pleasure in beautiful plants and our experience in raising and cultivating them, we have gained a close intimacy through drawing and painting them.

FIG 12 Cover of *Gardeners' Choice* (Routledge, London, 1937)

We have observed them as artists as well as gardeners, and have necessarily been made aware not only of the garden value of a plant and the intrinsic beauty of its flower, but of proportions, forms and contrasts, of the subtle relations of the leaf to the bloom, or the plant to its neighbour. These observations have bred in us an animate point of view which is the inspiration of our experimental gardening and the basis of our writing.' This fusion of authorship applies as much to drawings as to text. Gill Clarke in her 2006 book, *Evelyn Dunbar: War and Country,* suggested that Dunbar did the vignettes with Mahoney 'drawing the main large plates', (GC p.58) but with the evidence before us in this exhibition of Dunbar's drawings of the cyclamen, eryngiums and snake's head fritillary (CAT 45, 42, 43) – respectively reproduced on pages 55, 81 and 89 in *Gardeners' Choice* – such a distinction no longer holds good.

Looking at the ten studies of *Gladiolus tristis* presented here (CAT 46-55) it is instructive to note how obsessively Dunbar drew and redrew each plate to achieve the clarity and precision she and Mahoney were seeking. It is also interesting to realise that, despite such claims in 'Community of Plants' (p.7) as: With one of us *Hieraceum aurantiacum*... has behaved most meekly for years... With the other it has shown signs of becoming a menace to a small garden', Mahoney did not have a garden of his own until he and his brother bought Oak Cottage at Wrotham in 1937, the year *Gardeners' Choice* was published. It is possible that he grew some plants in his mother's small back garden at Anerley on the Kentish-London border but most of the plants discussed were probably grown at The Cedars, and in the sheet of sketches (CAT 56-58) we get several vignettes of Mahoney seated in the garden there drawing diligently.

P.S.

CAT 35 [HMO 363] Studies for the cover of *Gardeners' Choice*, 1936-37, Pencil and pen & ink on paper, 22 x 15 in. (55.7 x 38 cm)

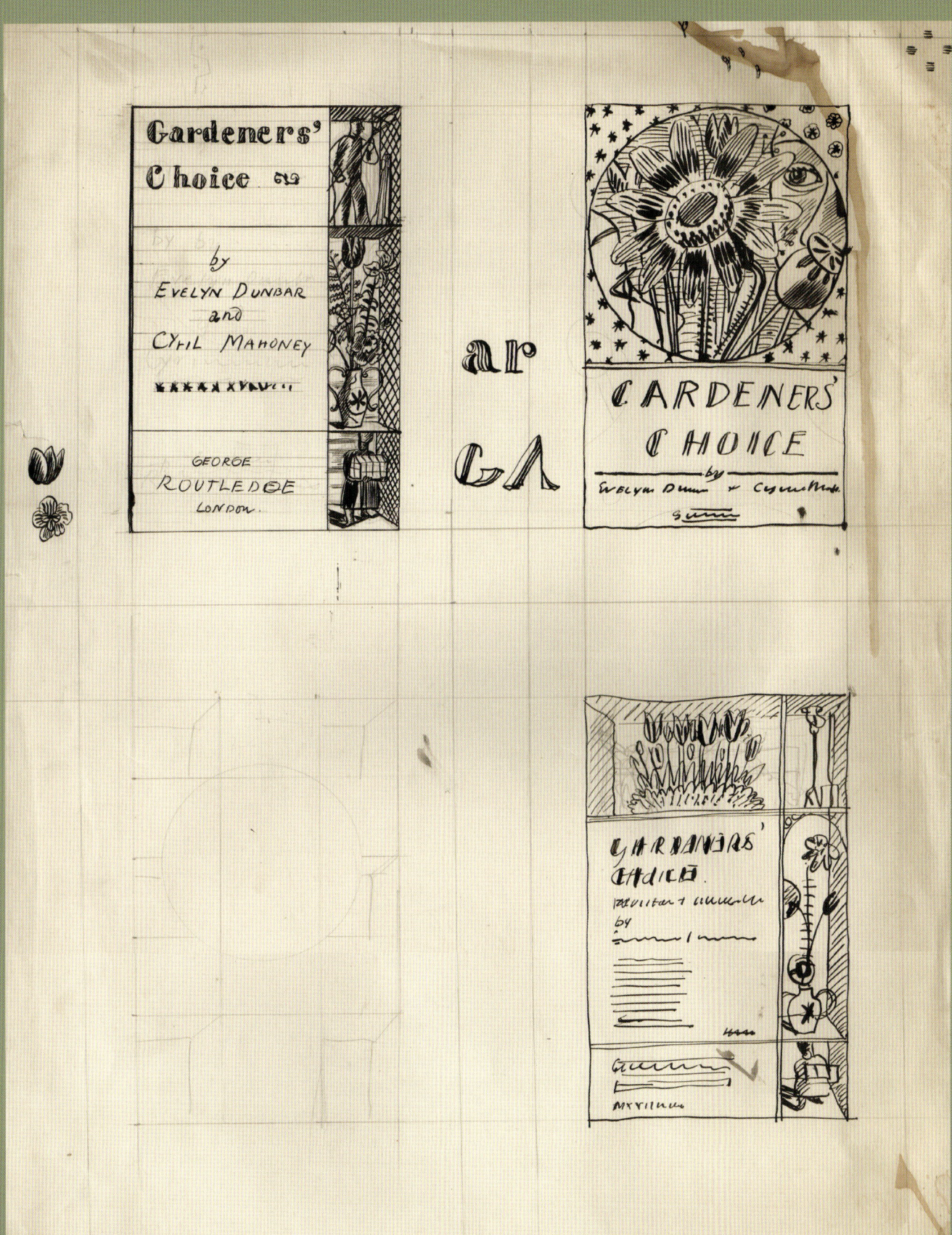

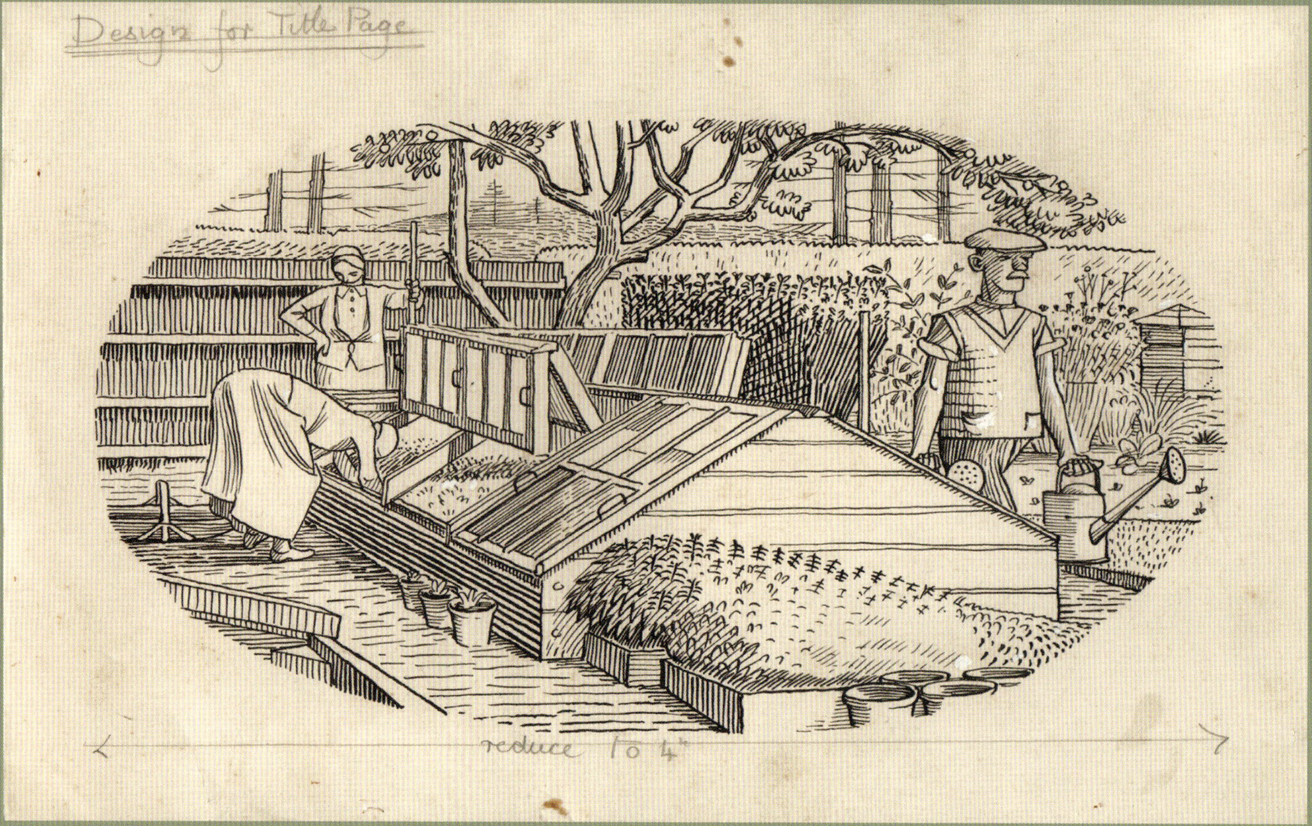

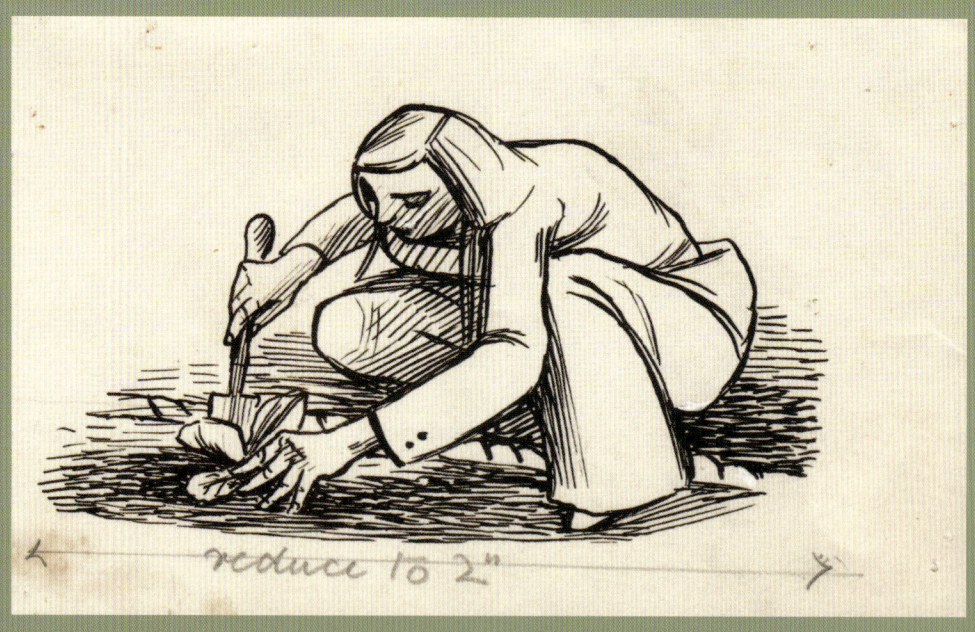

CAT 36 [HMO 239] Vignette for title page of *Gardeners' Choice*, 1937,
Inscribed with printer's instructions,
Pencil and pen & ink on paper, 7 ½ x 13 ¼ in. (18.8 x 33.8 cm)

CAT 37 [HMO 253] Vignette for page 49 of *Gardeners' Choice*, 1937,
Inscribed with printer's instructions,
Pencil and pen & ink on paper, 3 ¾ x 6 ½ in. (9.5 x 16.4 cm)

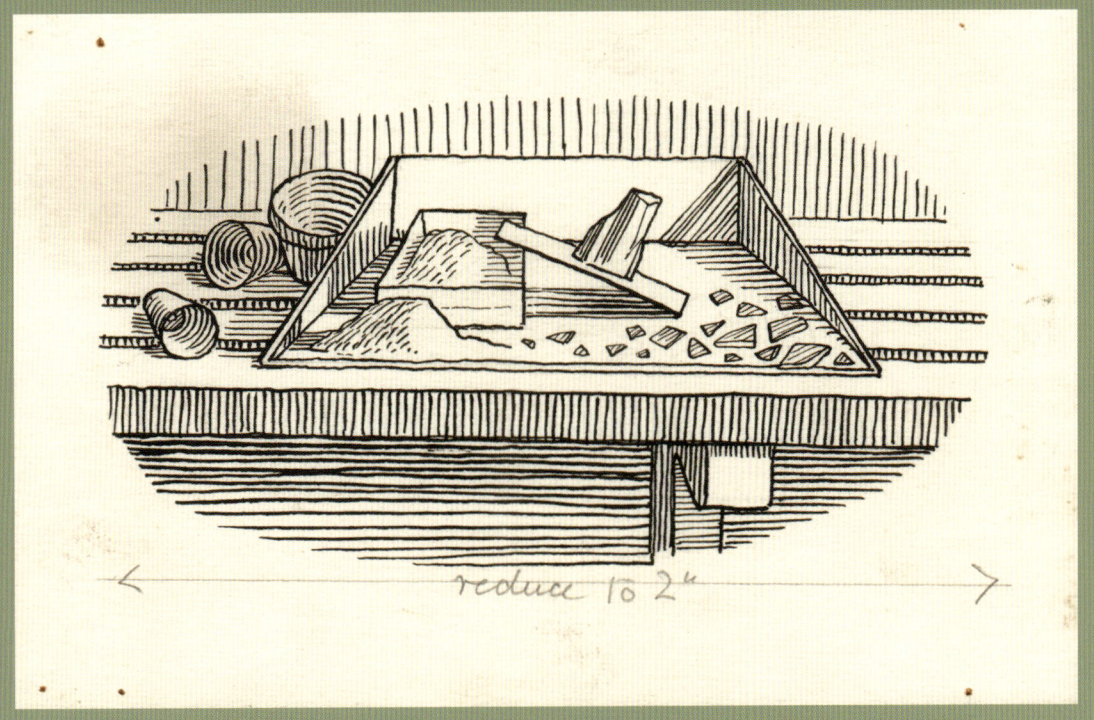

CAT 38 [HMO 254] Vignette for pages viii and 168 of *Gardeners' Choice*, 1937,
Inscribed with printer's instructions,
Pencil and pen & ink on paper, 4 ½ x 8 in. (11.5 x 19.8 cm)

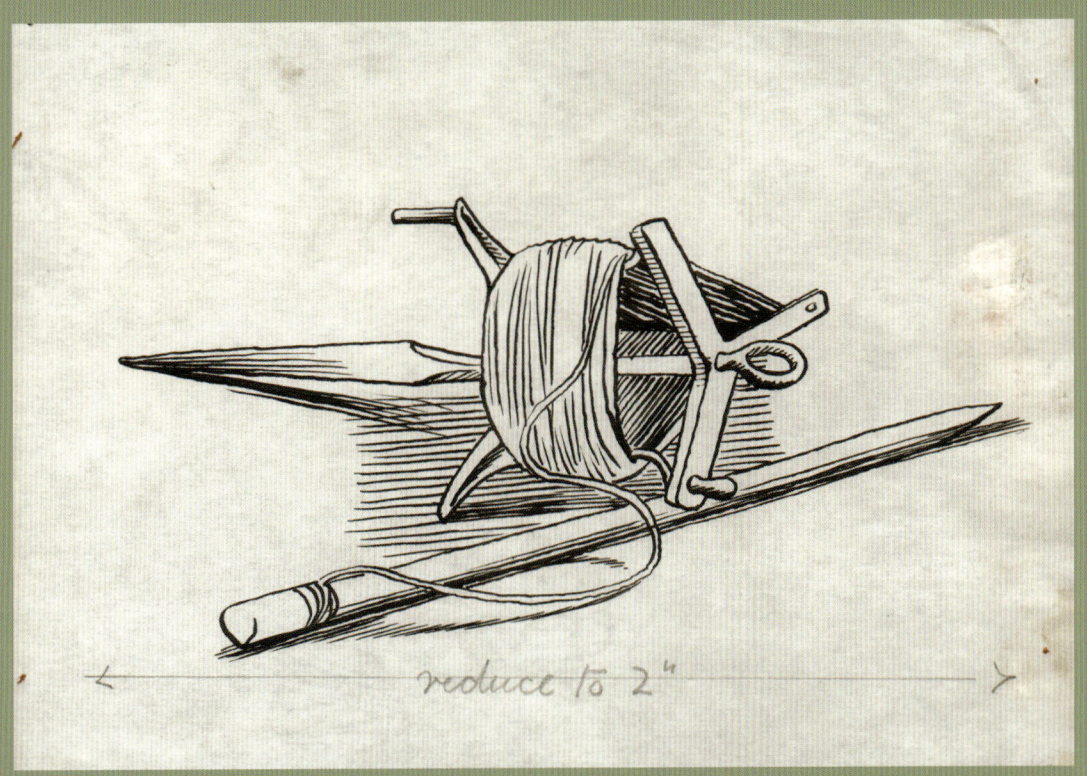

CAT 39 [HMO 245] Vignette for pages 71 and 222 of *Gardeners' Choice*, 1937,
Inscribed with printer's instructions,
Pencil and pen & ink on paper, 5 ¼ x 7 in. (13.6 x 17.8 cm)

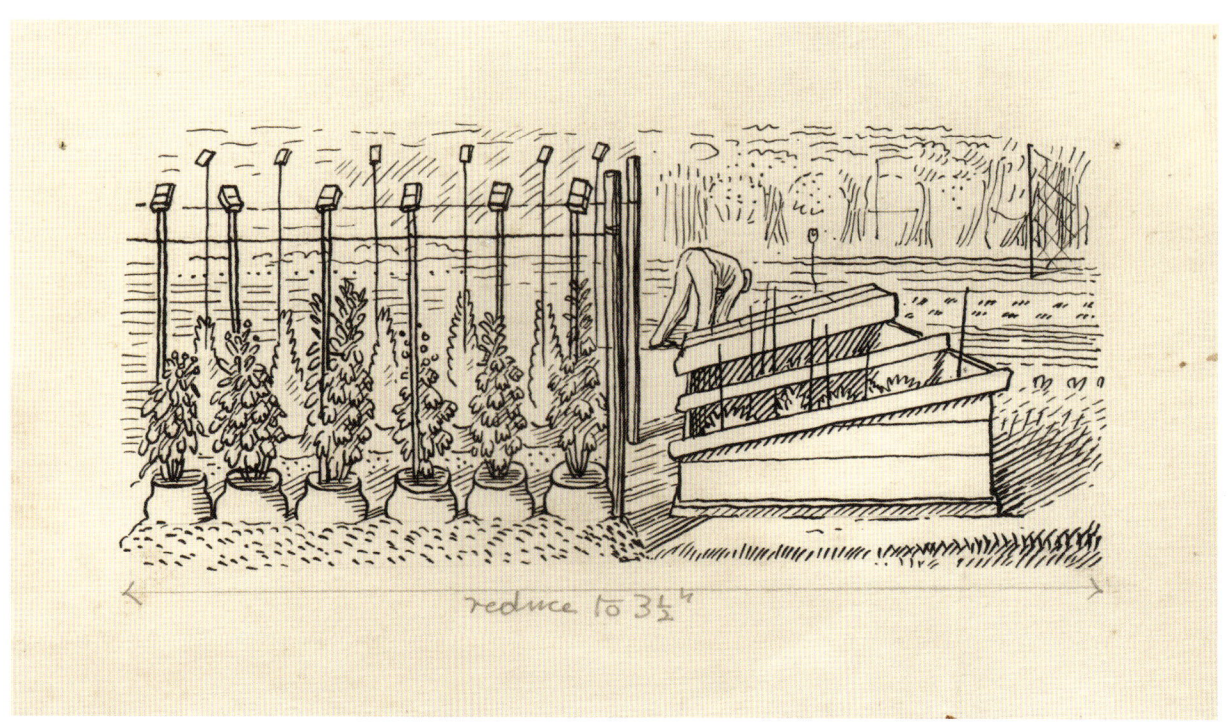

CAT 40 [HMO 251] Vignette for page 199 of *Gardeners' Choice*, 1937,
Inscribed with printer's instructions, pencil and pen & ink on paper, 5 ¼ x 9 in. (13.5 x 22.8 cm)

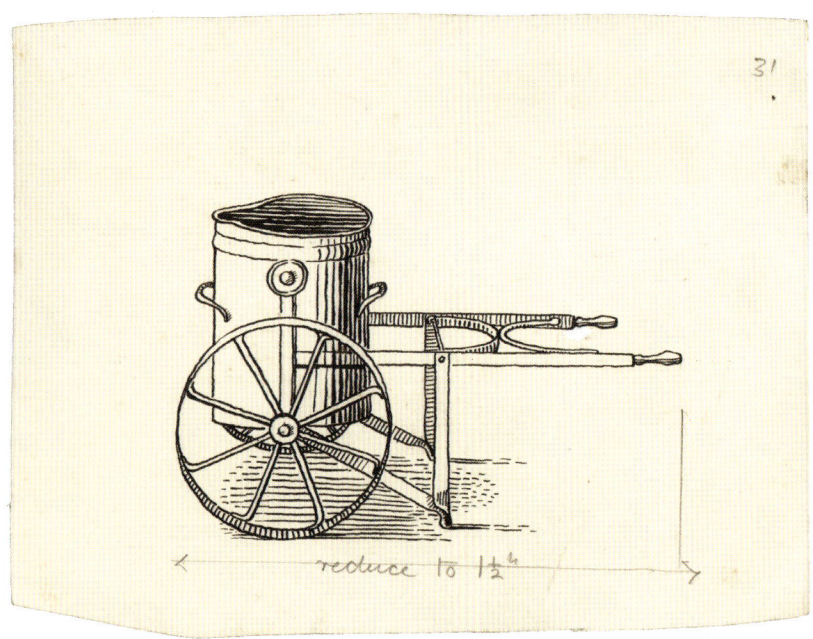

CAT 41 [HMO 244] Vignette for page 199 of *Gardeners' Choice*, 1937,
Inscribed with printer's instructions,
Pencil and pen & ink on paper, 15 ½ x 7 ¼ in. (14.4 x 18.3 cm)

CAT 42 [HMO 25] Study of *Eryngium agavifolium* for page 81 of *Gardeners' Choice*, 1936,
Pen and ink on paper, 21¼ x 14½ in. (54 x 37.2 cm)

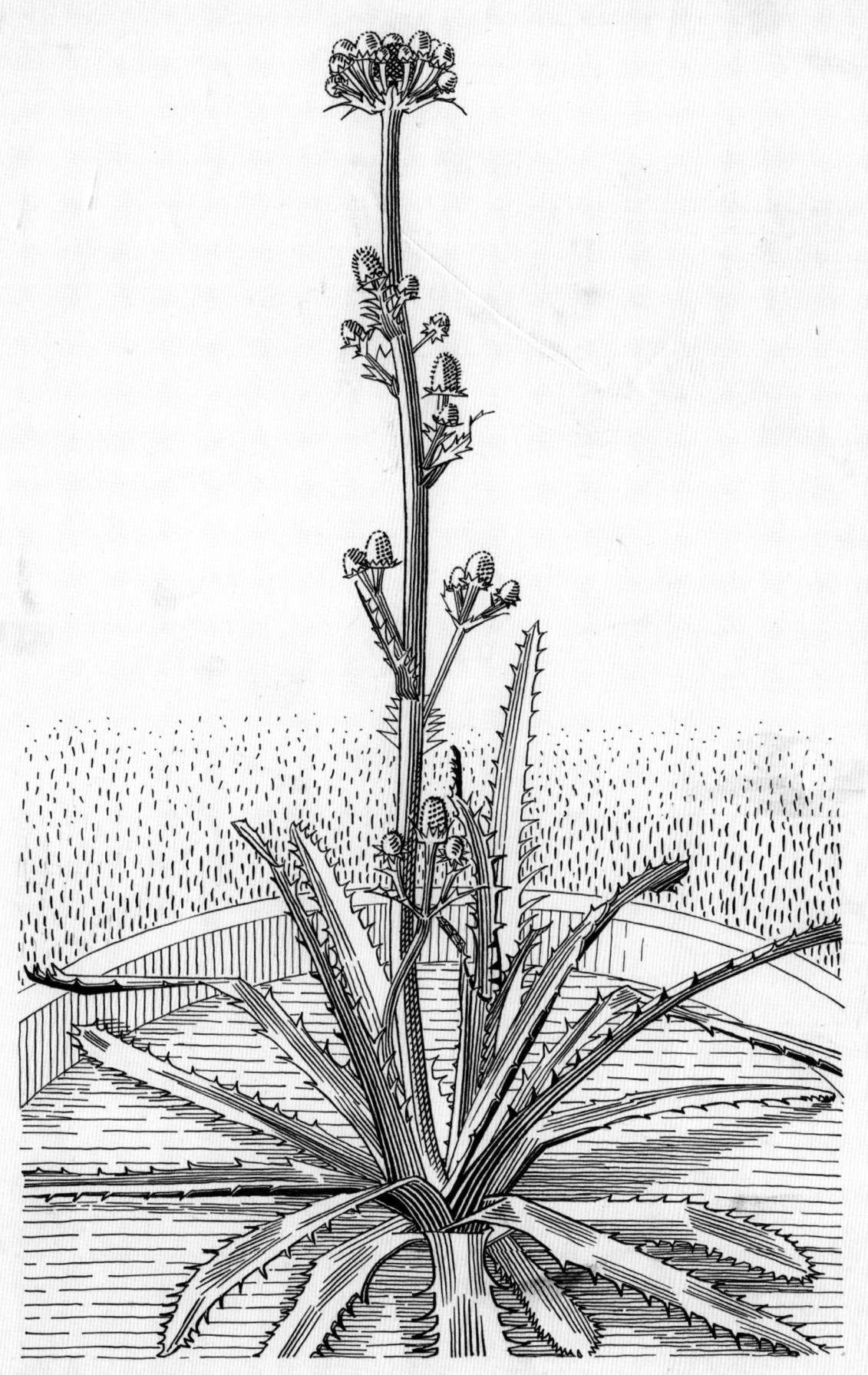

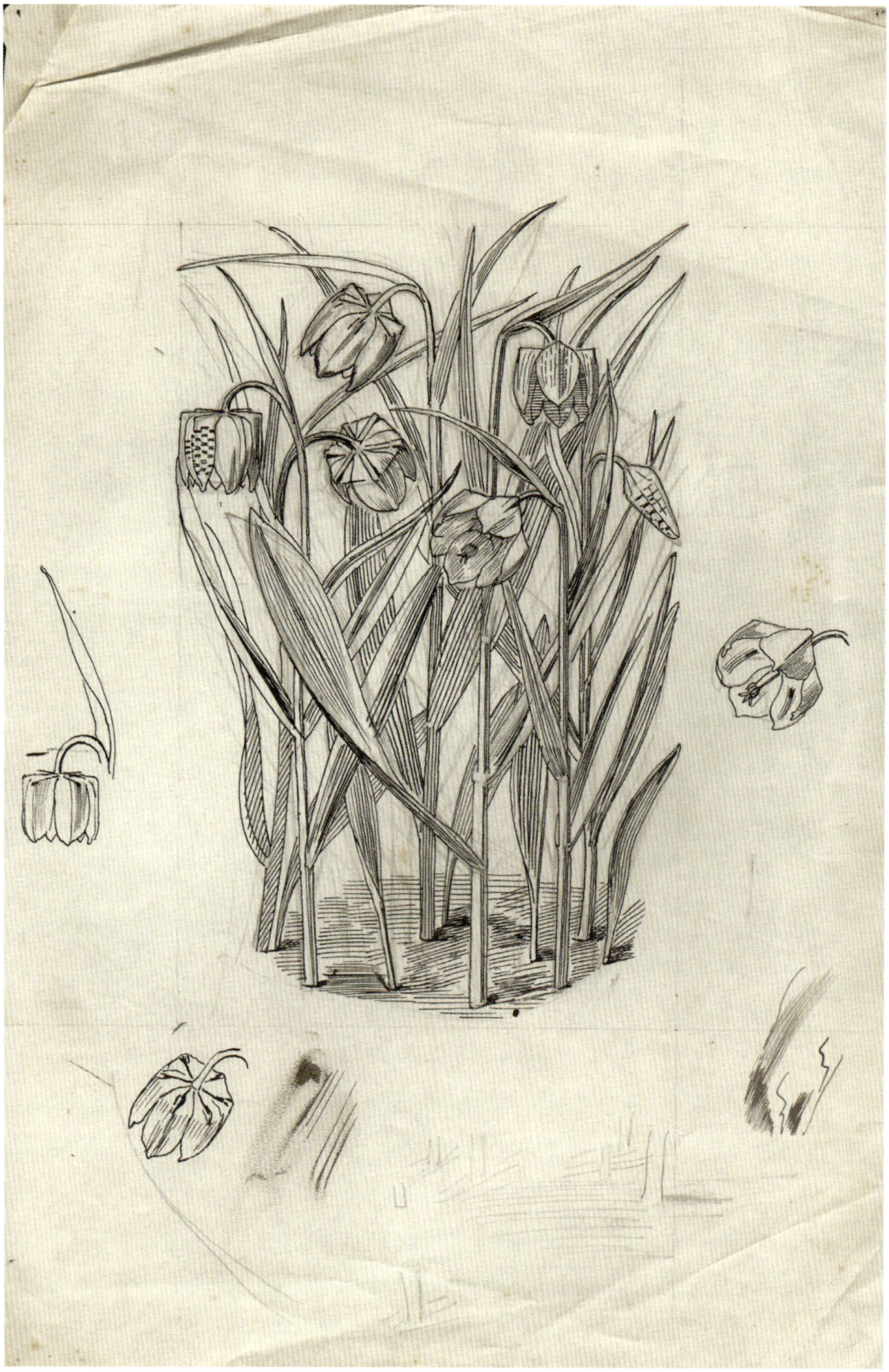

CAT 43 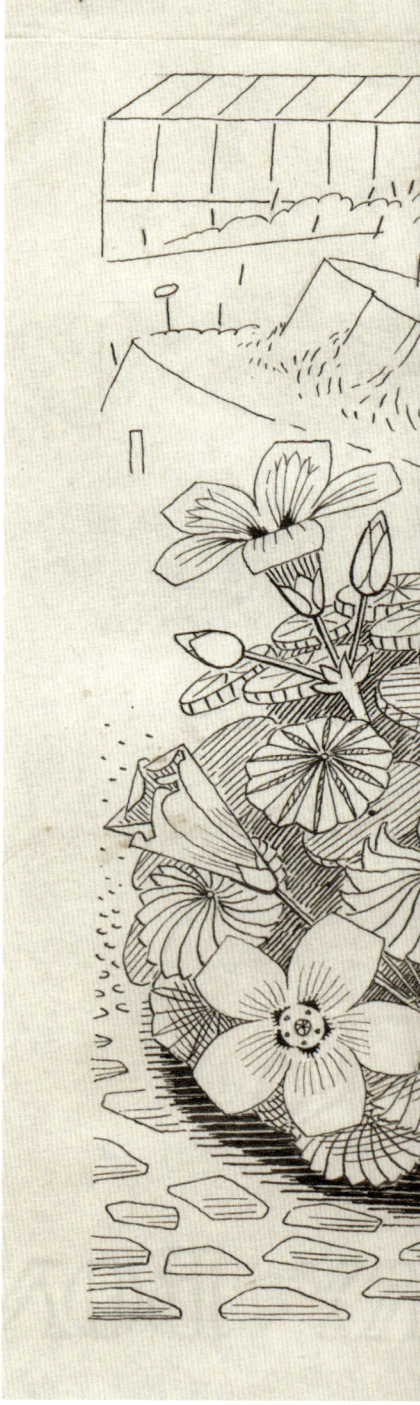 CAT 44

CAT 43 [HMO 214] Study of *Fritillaria meleagris* (Snake's Head Fritillary) for page 89 of *Gardeners' Choice*, 1937,
Pencil and pen & ink on paper, 12 ¾ x 8 in. (32.4 x 20.3 cm)

CAT 44 [HMO 240] Study of *Oxalis adenophylla* for page 129 of *Gardeners' Choice*, 1937,
Inscribed with printer's instructions, pen & ink on paper, 12 ¾ x 8 in. (32.3 x 20.2 cm)

CAT 45 [HMO 260] Studies of *Cyclamen coüm* (upper drawing, in flower) and for *C. neapolitanum* (lower drawing, sprouting corm) for page 55 of *Gardeners' Choice*, 1936,
Pen & ink on paper, 10 x 8 in. (25.3 x 20.3 cm)

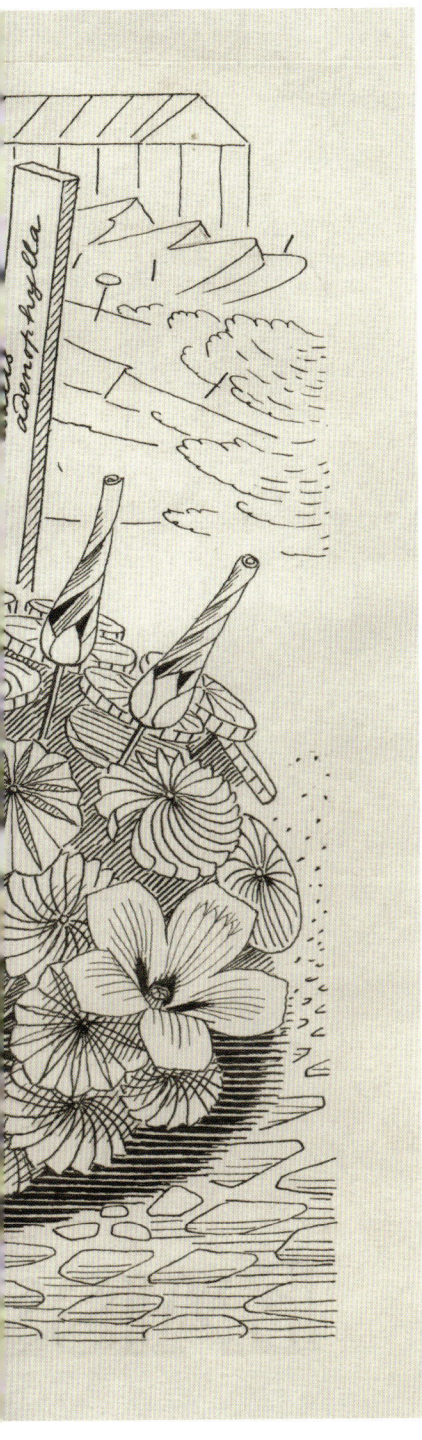

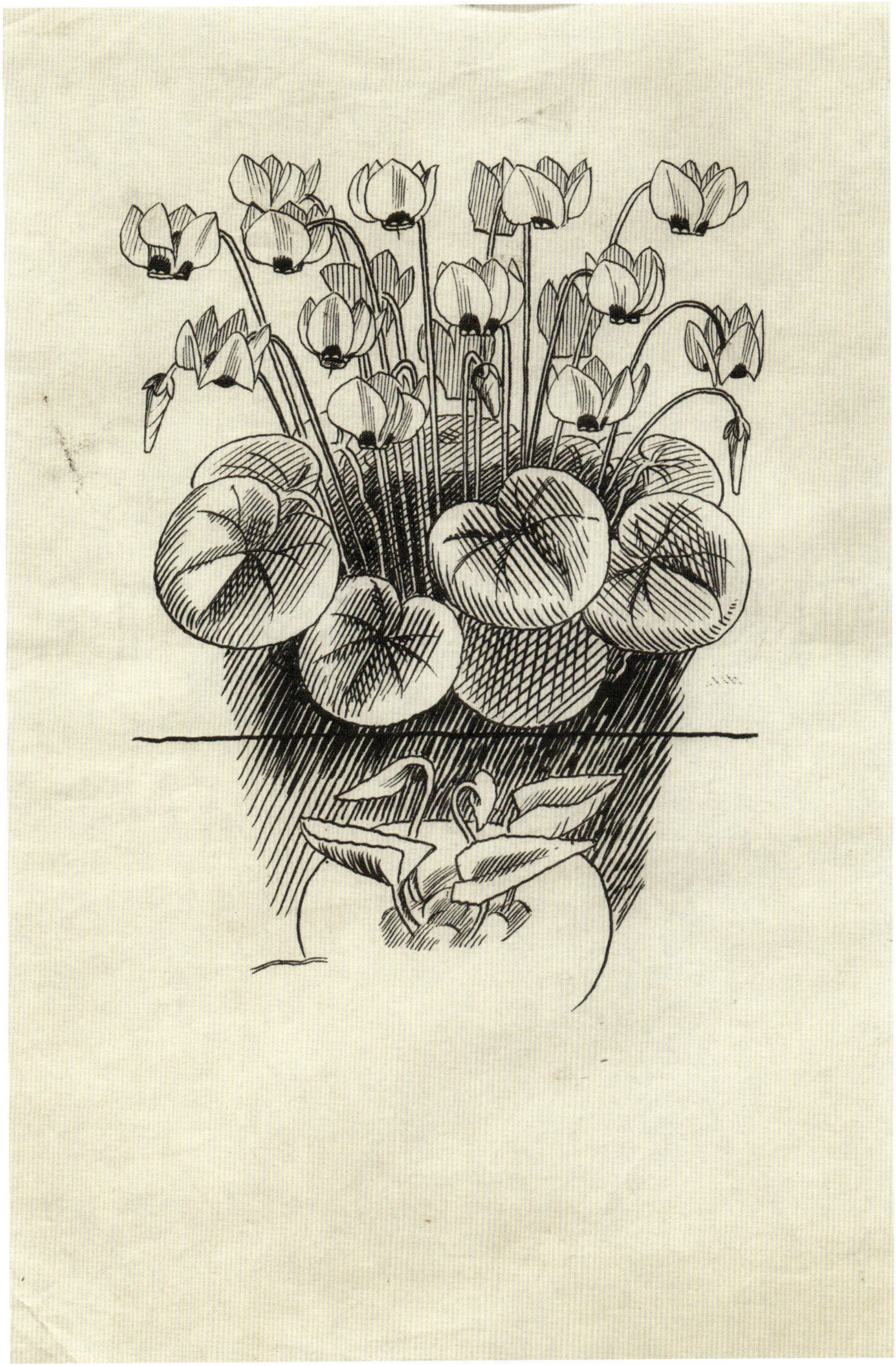

CAT 45

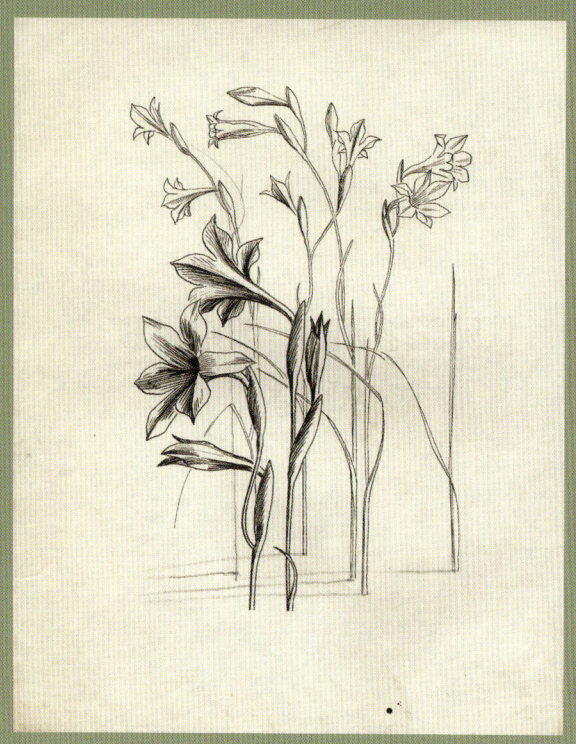
CAT 46

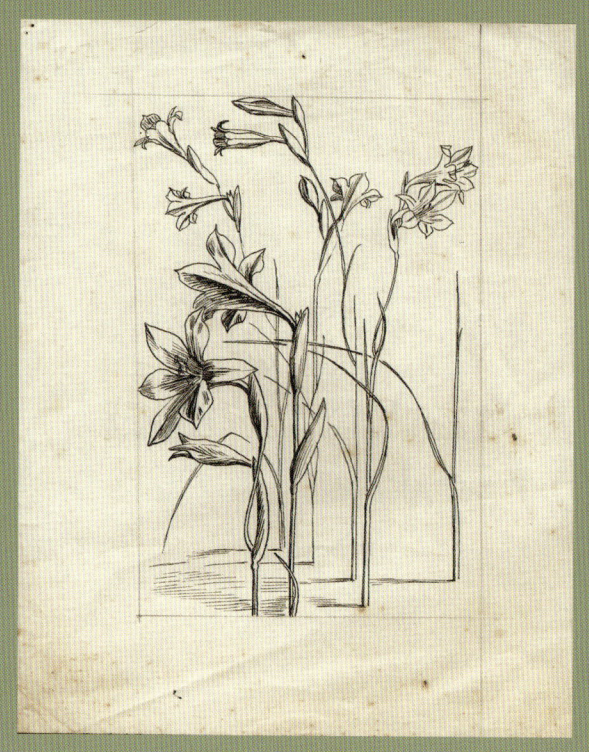
CAT 47

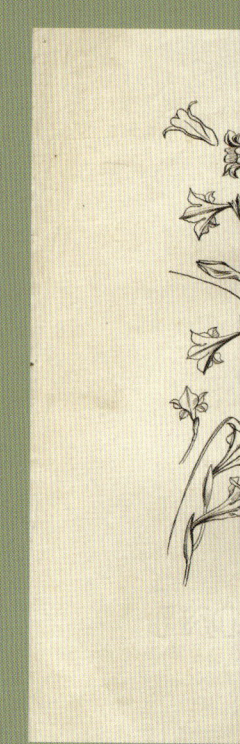
CAT 48

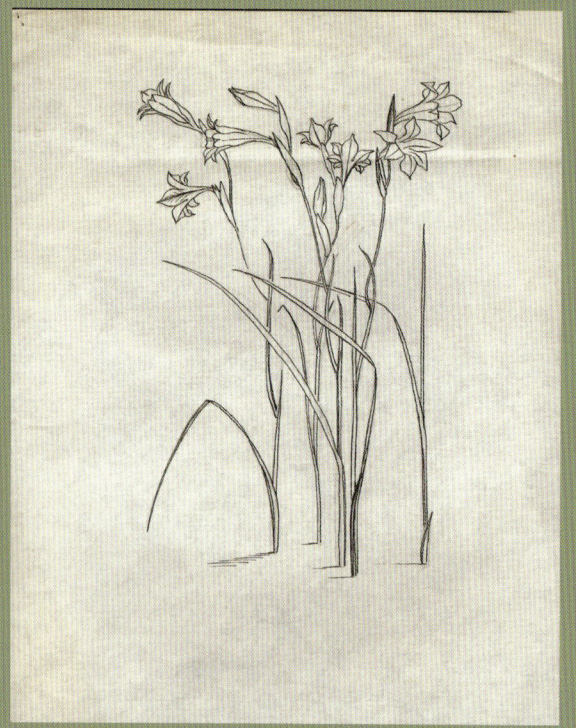
CAT 51

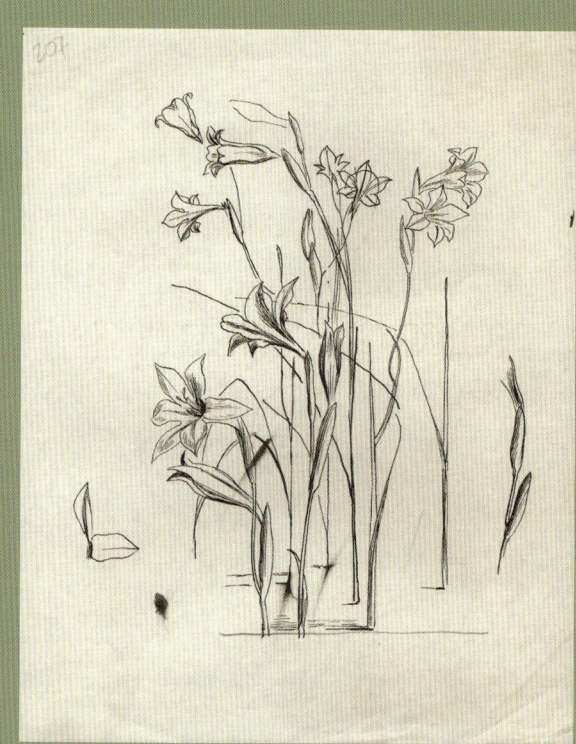
CAT 52

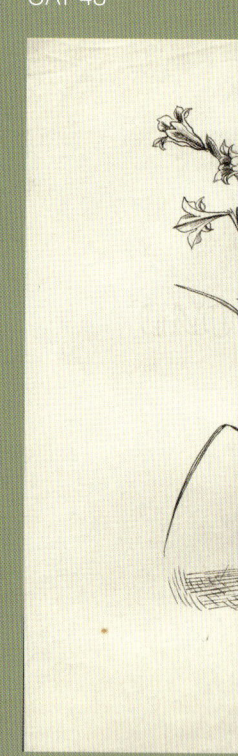
CAT 53

CAT 46 - 55 [HMO 36]   Studies of *Gladiolus tristis* for page 103 of *Gardeners' Choice*, c.1936, Pen and ink on paper, Variously 10 x 8 in. (25.4 x 20.3 cm) and 12¾ x 8 in. (32.4 x 20.3 cm)

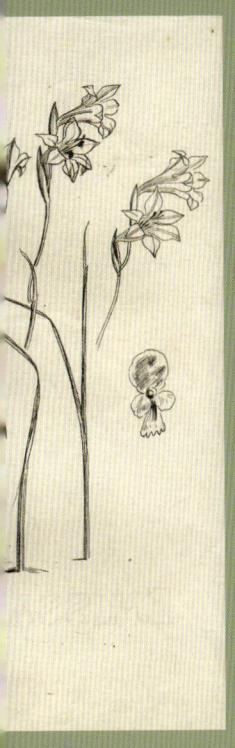
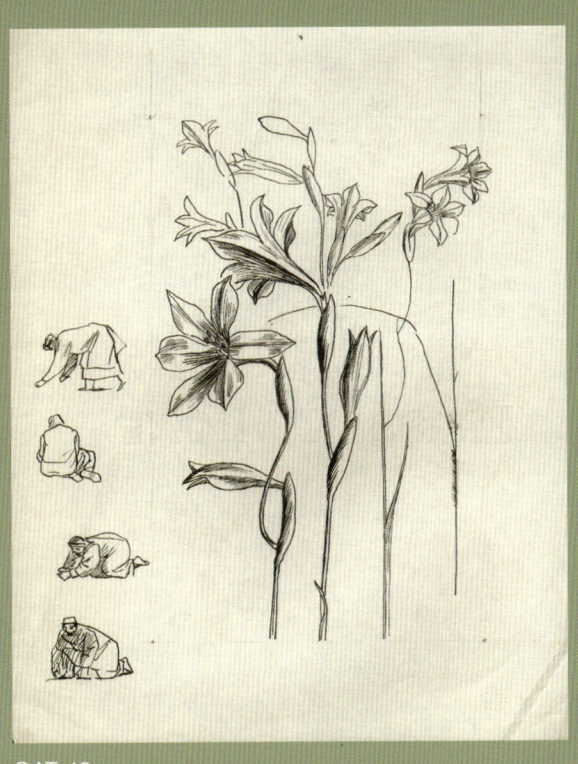
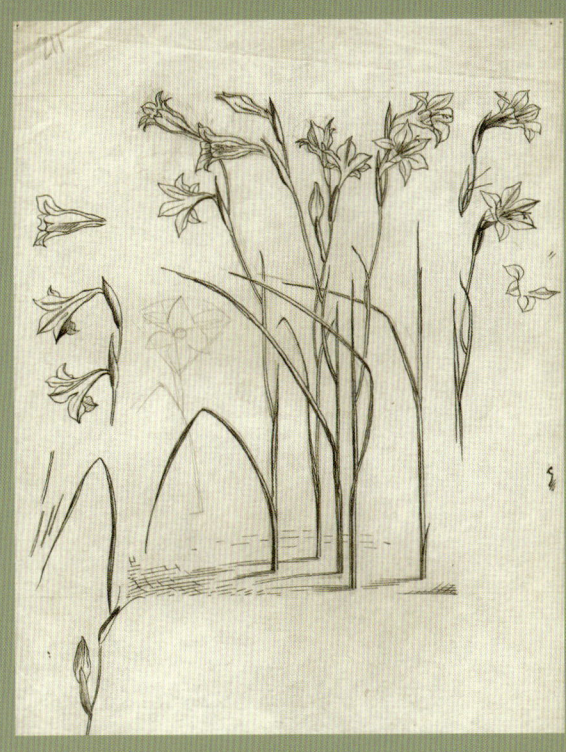

CAT 49

CAT 50

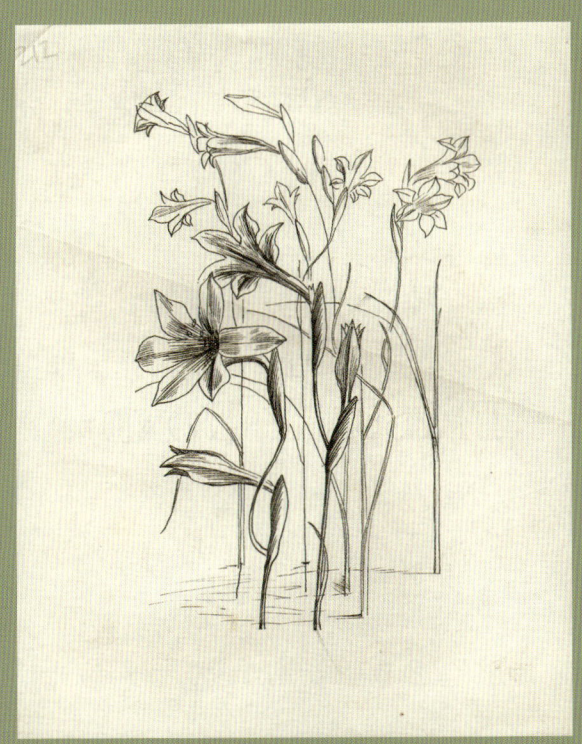
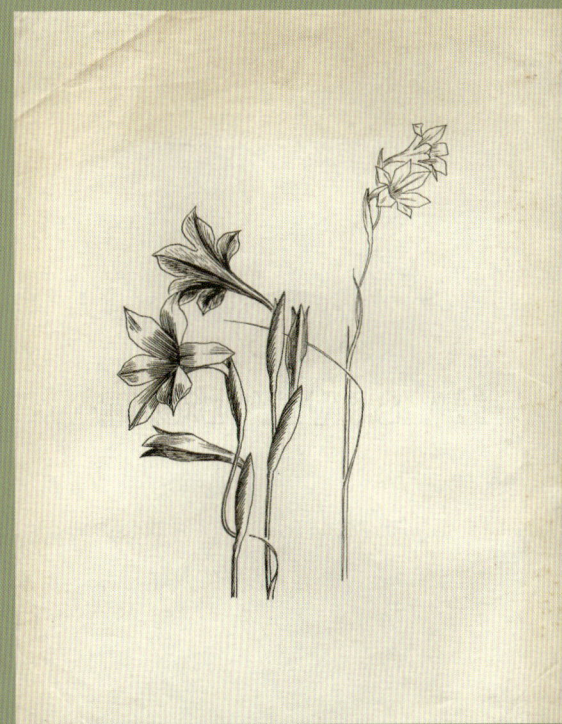

CAT 54

CAT 55

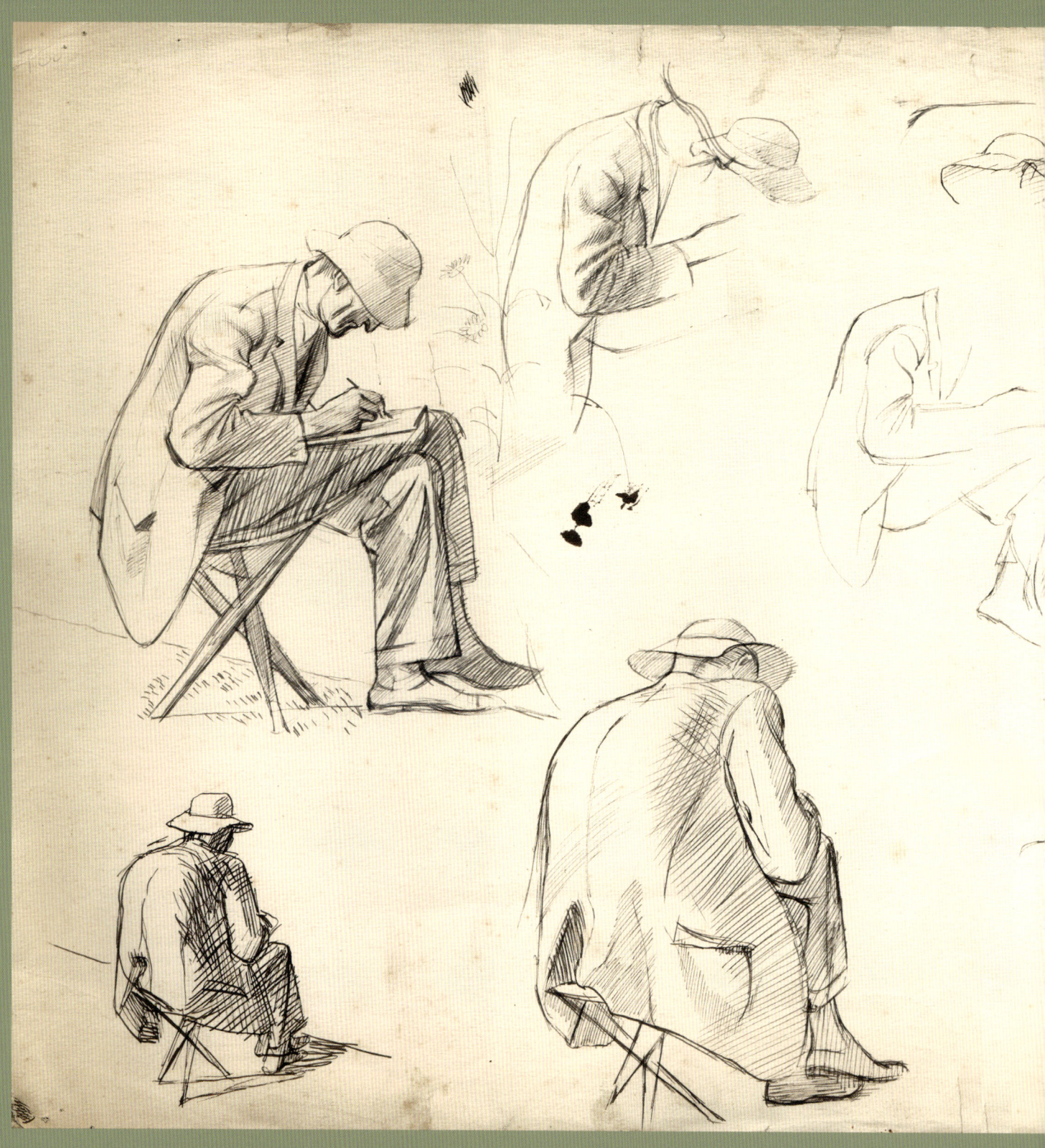

CAT 56 [HMO 700] Studies of Charles Mahoney sketching, c.1936,
Pen & ink on paper, 15 1/4 x 22 in. (38.5 x 56 cm)

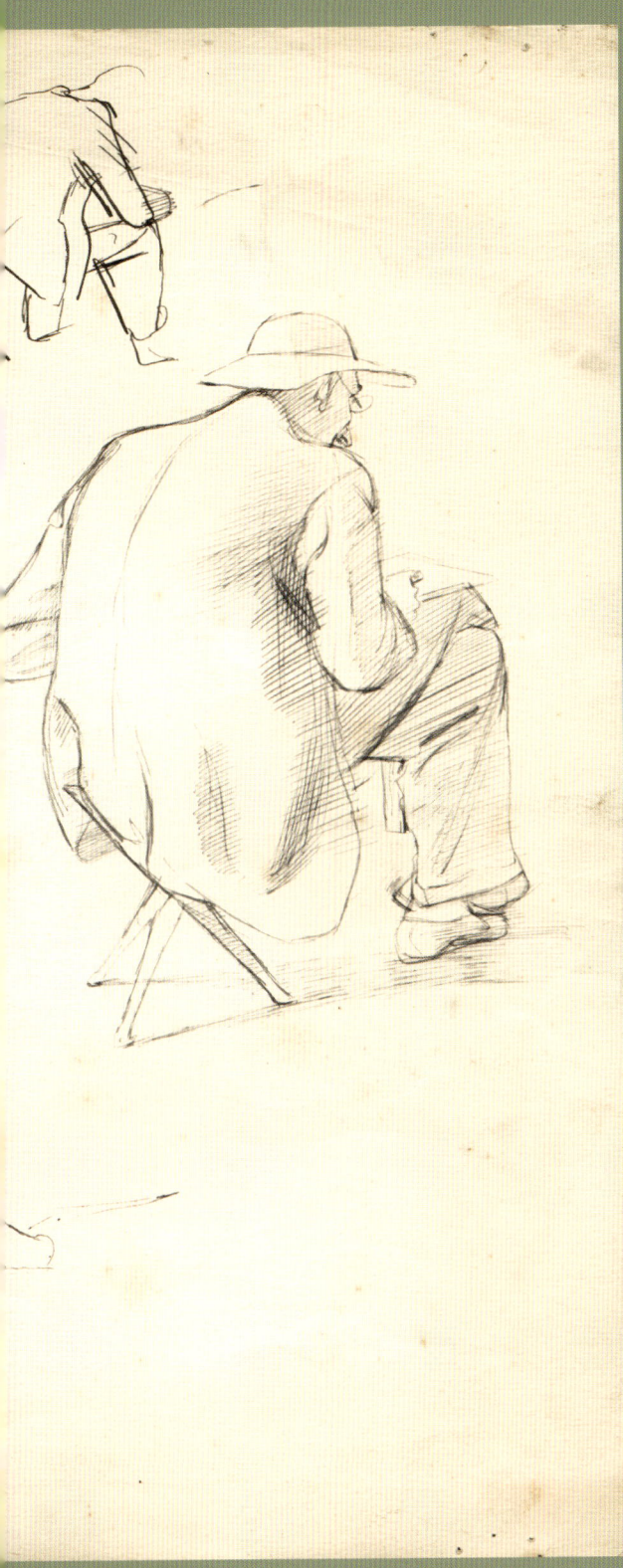

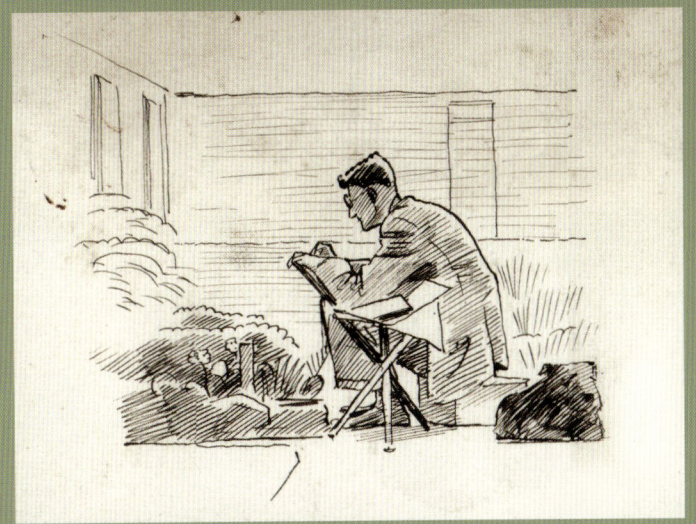

CAT 57 [HMO 632a] Study of Charles Mahoney drawing plants in the garden of The Cedars in preparation for *Gardeners' Choice*, 1936.
Pencil and pen & ink on paper, 3 ½ x 4 ¾ in. (8.5 x 12 cm)

Beside Mahoney is the Dunbar family dog, Paul (last seen as a puppy in Cat. 13), possibly considering that this modest prominence some 80 years later is no more than his due.

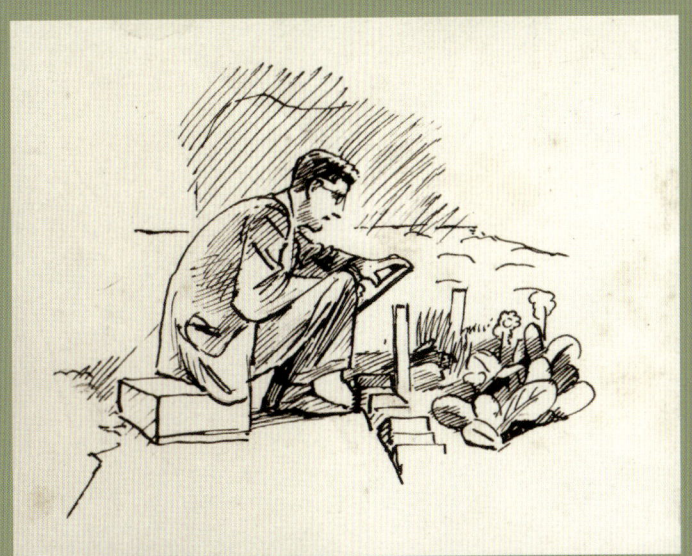

CAT 58 [HMO 632b] Study of Charles Mahoney drawing plants in the garden of The Cedars, in preparation for *Gardeners' Choice*, 1936,
Pencil and pen & ink on paper, 4 ¾ x 5 ½ in. (12 x 14 cm)

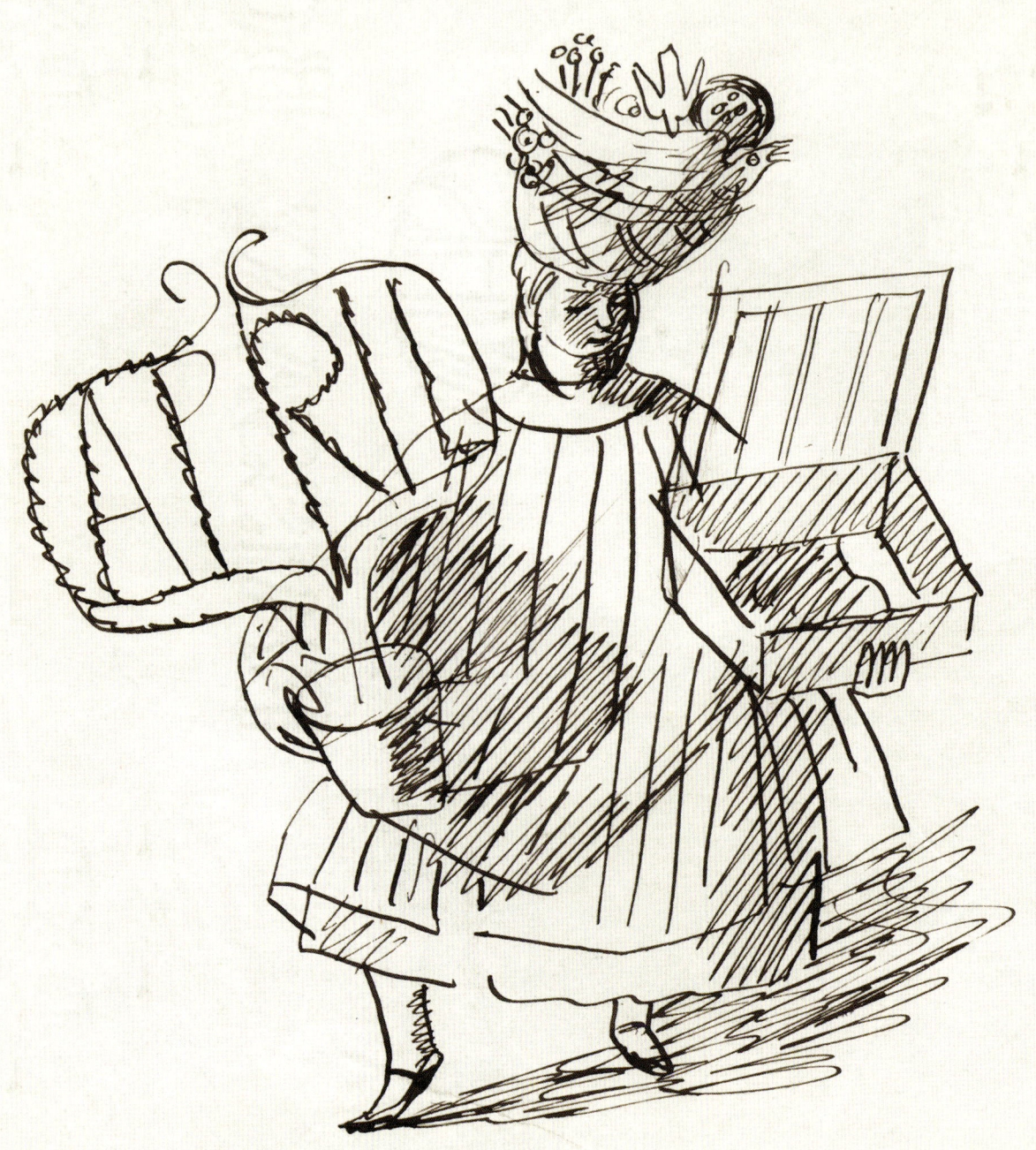

Gardener's Diary 1938 & Related Paintings

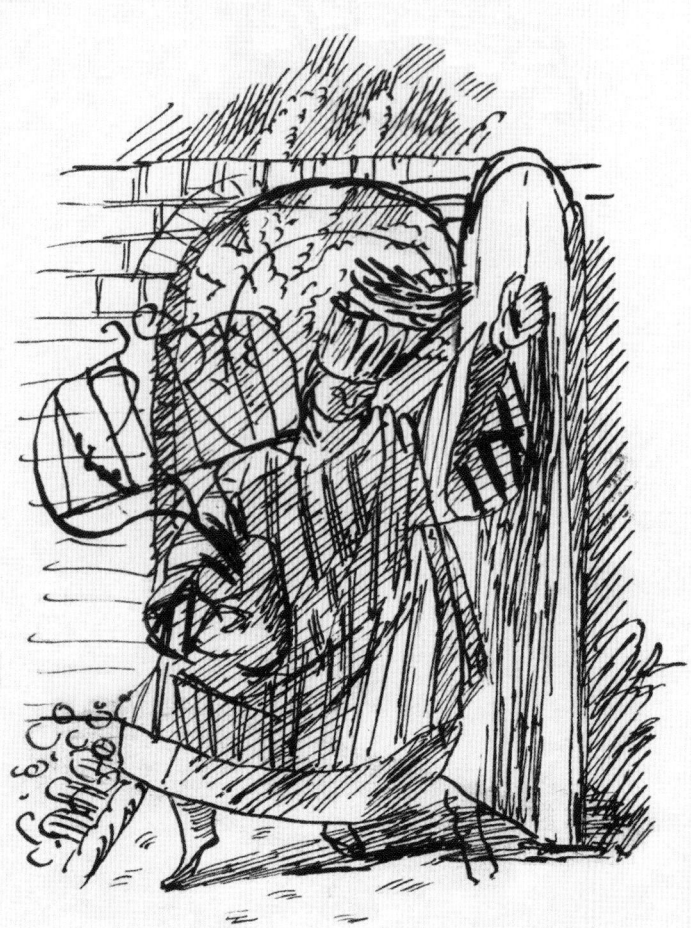

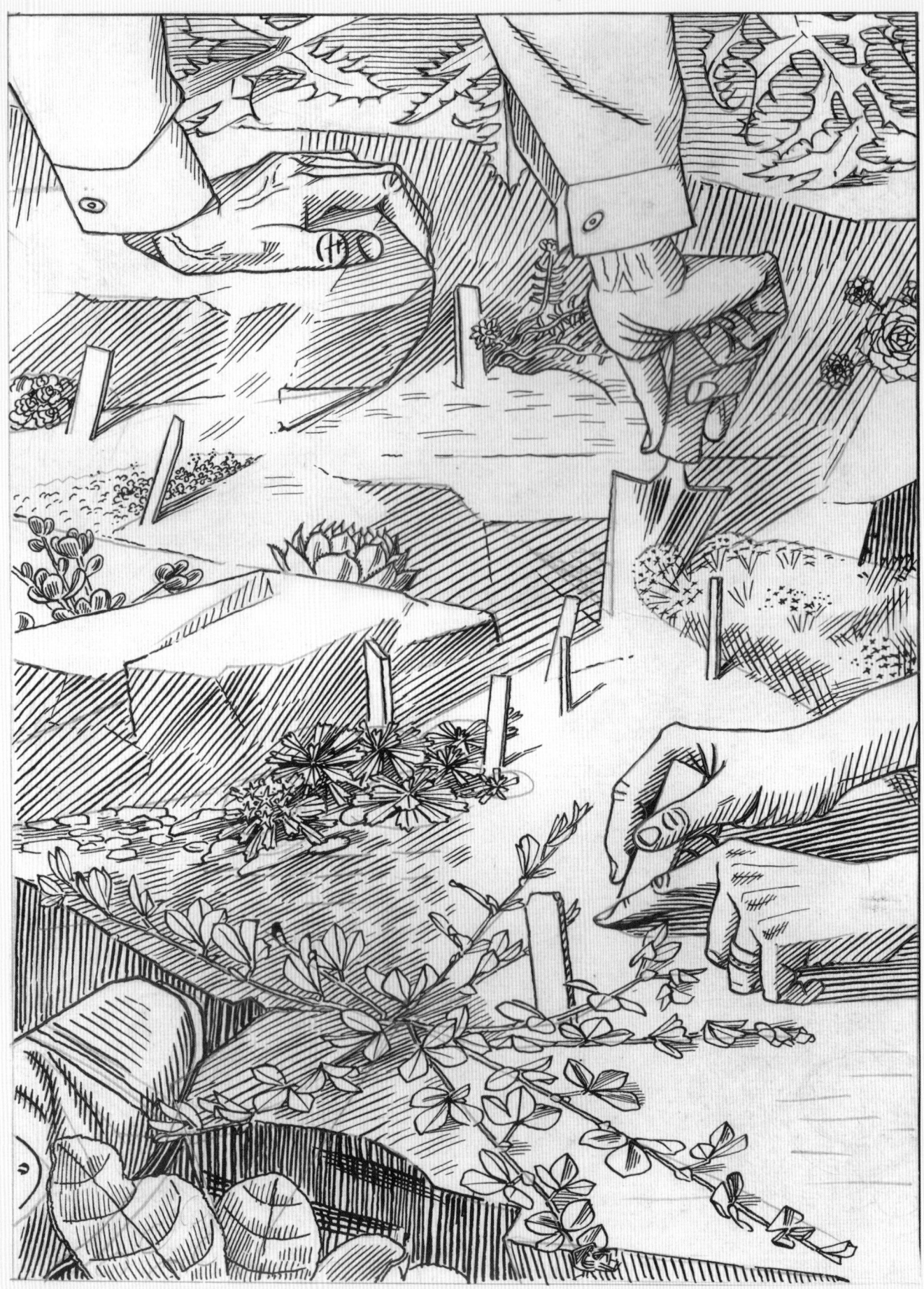

Gardener's Diary 1938 & Related Paintings

Noel Carrington, Dunbar's Hampstead landlord, was keen to promote the work of those artists he admired. In 1937 as editor at *Country Life Ltd.* – a separate publishing entity from the eponymous magazine – he commissioned Ravilious to illustrate *The Country Life Cookery Book* and Edward Bawden *The Gardener's Diary*. These were followed in 1938 by *High Street*, again illustrated by Ravilious, with text by J.M. Richards, and a further *Gardener's Diary* illustrated by Evelyn Dunbar. Although the two diaries are similar in format they are very different in content – the 1937 one has a running frieze of flowers and plants along the top of each weekly double page, balanced at the bottom by quotes from William Cobbett's *English Gardener* of 1827: within each week the *Diary* provided upright columns for daily entries and notes, while a considerable space was allowed for comments on the weather. Bawden's end-papers depicted a cut rose in a vase with his own half-drawn sketch pinned neatly to the drawing board beside it.

For 1938 the brief must have changed quite radically, perhaps in response to comments received on the previous year's production, as the emphasis changed from the depiction of individual plants to the physical attributes of gardeners and gardening, with quotes ranging from the *Book of Job* to authors as varied as Charles Lamb and Thomas Hardy. The decision to depict the months through the personification of their attributes was probably a joint decision between Dunbar and Carrington, but chimes with the otherworldly quality she had exploited so successfully at Brockley in her mural *The Country Girl and the Pail of Milk*. Bawden's running frieze of plants and flowers at the top of each page was replaced by discreet depictions of fruits and seeds in the top right-hand corner while Dunbar's tailpieces consisted of simple outline depictions of gardeners – male and female. There were only a dozen vignettes of these toiling figures and the delightful sheet of studies (CAT 60) shows several of them in embryonic form, most particularly the rear view of one of the Dunbar's gardeners bent double with rake or hoe in hand. This figure makes five appearances in all, being repeated as the tailpiece

CAT 59 [HMO 417] Study for the frontispiece of *Gardener's Diary 1938*, 1937,
Pencil and pen & ink on paper 22 x 15 in. (55.5 x 38 cm)

The upper hands and shoes can be taken to be Charles Mahoney's, the hands on the right with wedding ring to be Dunbar's, who until their relationship broke up in 1937/38 thought seriously of marriage to him.

to various weeks in January, March, April, May and December. Apart from the figure of a weary gardener carrying two full watering cans, who appears just twice – in June and July – there is little correlation between the seasons and the activity depicted; Dunbar took the opportunity through a studied awkwardness to emphasise the fact that physical labour is the gardener's lot throughout the year. A lighter mood is reflected in her depictions of the months each of which takes human form: female in the gentler months – *February* (CAT 65) with crocus flowers and daffodil shoots in her hat, and *April* (CAT 69) jauntily wearing a bird's-nest hat and carrying attributes of topiary and a garden frame. *August* is definitely a male month with its abundance of cabbages and onions, as is November, the season for bonfires and general clearance. The figure of *April* – expressive of lightheartedness – became almost a *leitmotif* in her work recurring in odd drawings and doodles, as well as in one of her most beautiful oil paintings.

Dunbar was not one to waste a good idea or design. These personifications of the months also recur as the principal motifs in *An English Calendar* (CAT 71), the large (6 foot square) decoration she painted the same year and later presented to Wye College (on the closure of Wye in 2005 it passed into the collection of its parent body Imperial College). Personation of the Seasons and the Virtues is deeply rooted in our psyche from the Green Man of northern climes to classical sculptures of ancient Greece and Rome. Dunbar delighted in personifying abstract conceptions returning to this device in *The Days of the Week* (CAT 72) and in her projected *Faith, Hope and Charity* (CAT 109) as well as transforming *April* into the heavily muffled figure in her wartime painting *Putting on Anti-Gas Protective Clothing* (FIG 4).

P.S.

CAT 60 [HMO 200]
Studies for gardening vignettes, drawn on variously for *Gardeners' Choice,* 1936-37, and *Gardener's Diary 1938*, 1937,
Pencil and pen & ink on paper 22 x 15 in. (55.5 x 38 cm)

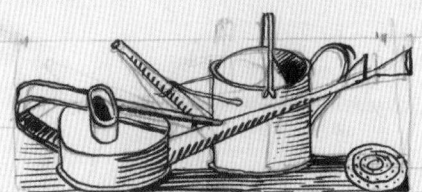 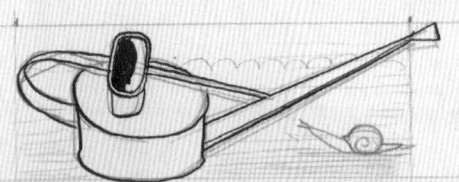

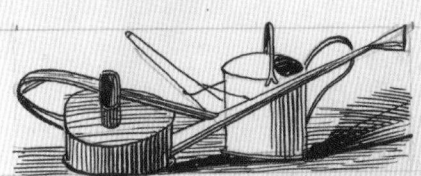 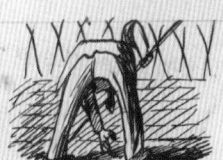 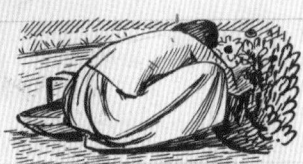 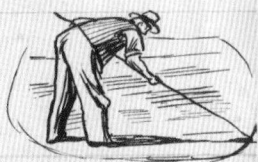

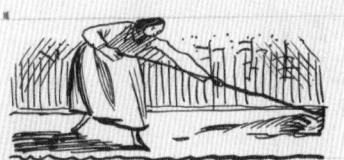 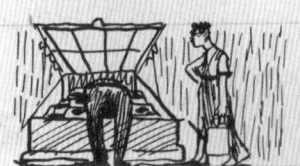 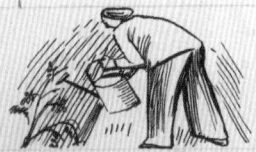

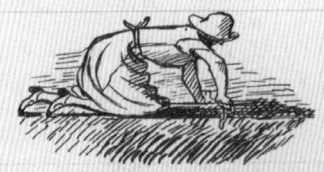 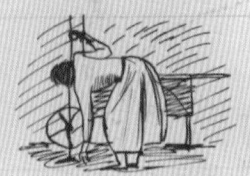 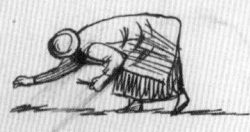

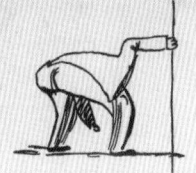 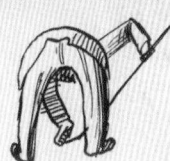

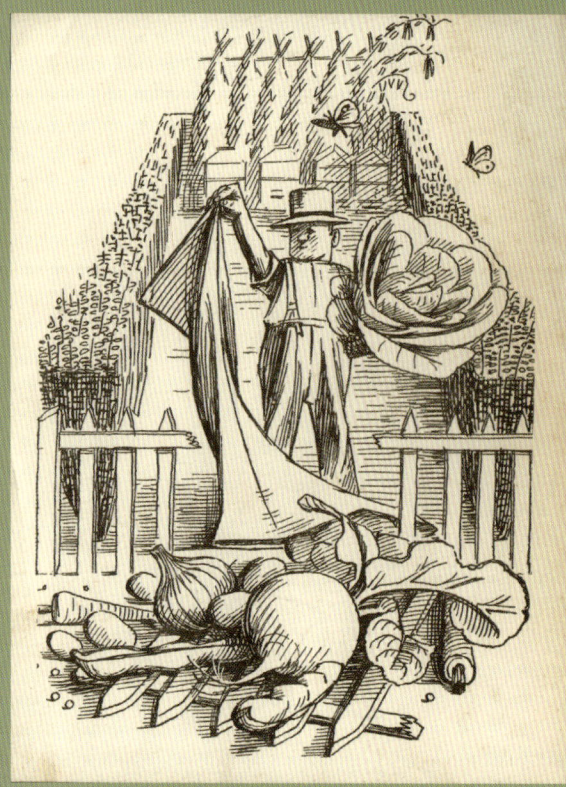

CAT 61 [HMO 57] Recto-Verso: Galley proof of preliminary prospectus for *Gardener's Diary 1938*, 1937, Printed document 6 ¾ x 9 ¾ in. (17.2 x 24.7 cm)
A slightly different design was eventually used. The title page drawing illustrated above was chosen to represent July. (See CAT 62)

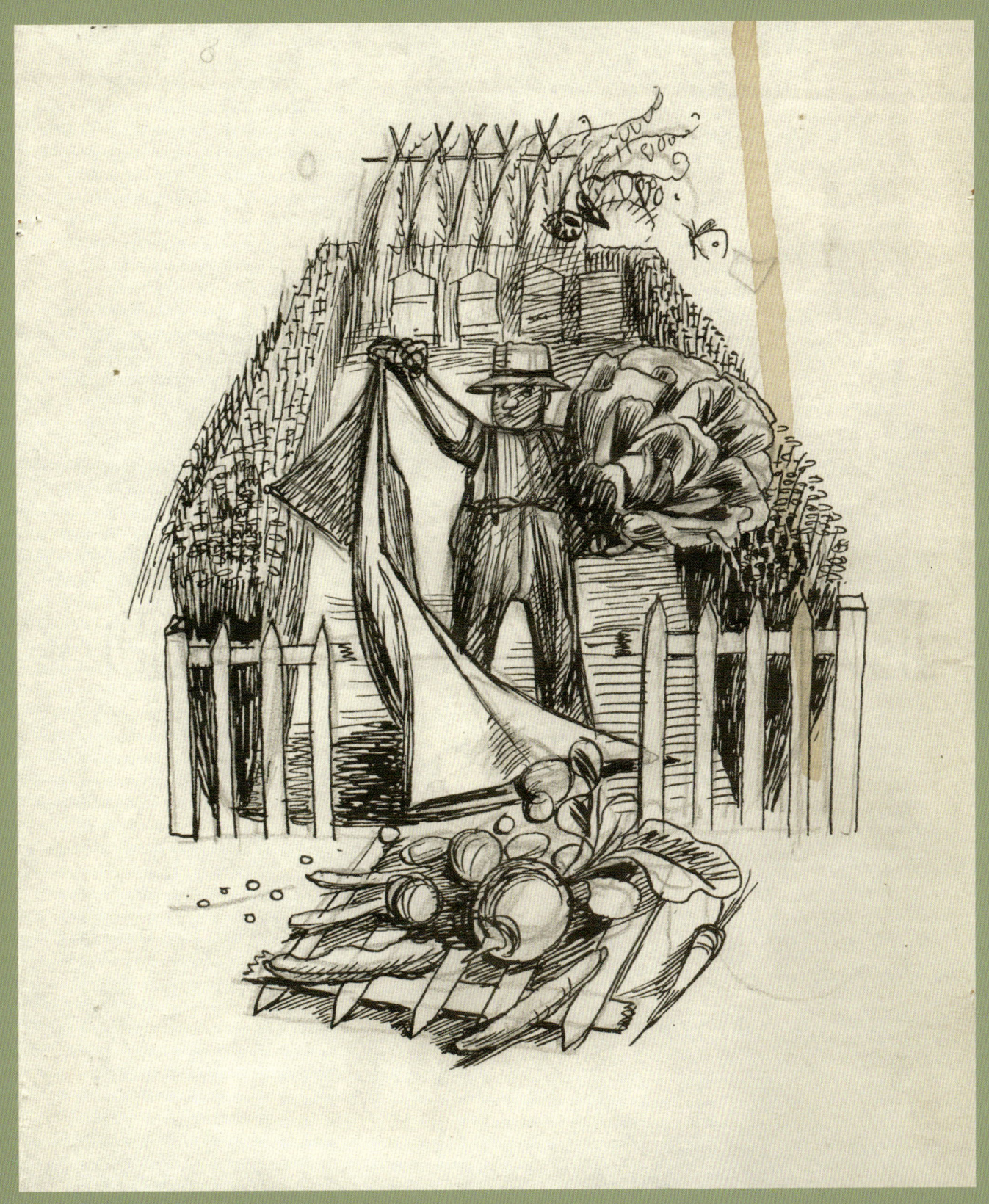

CAT 62 [HMO 84] *July*, preparatory drawing for *Gardener's Diary 1938*, 1937,
Pencil and pen & ink on paper, 10 x 8 in. (25.3 x 20.3 cm)

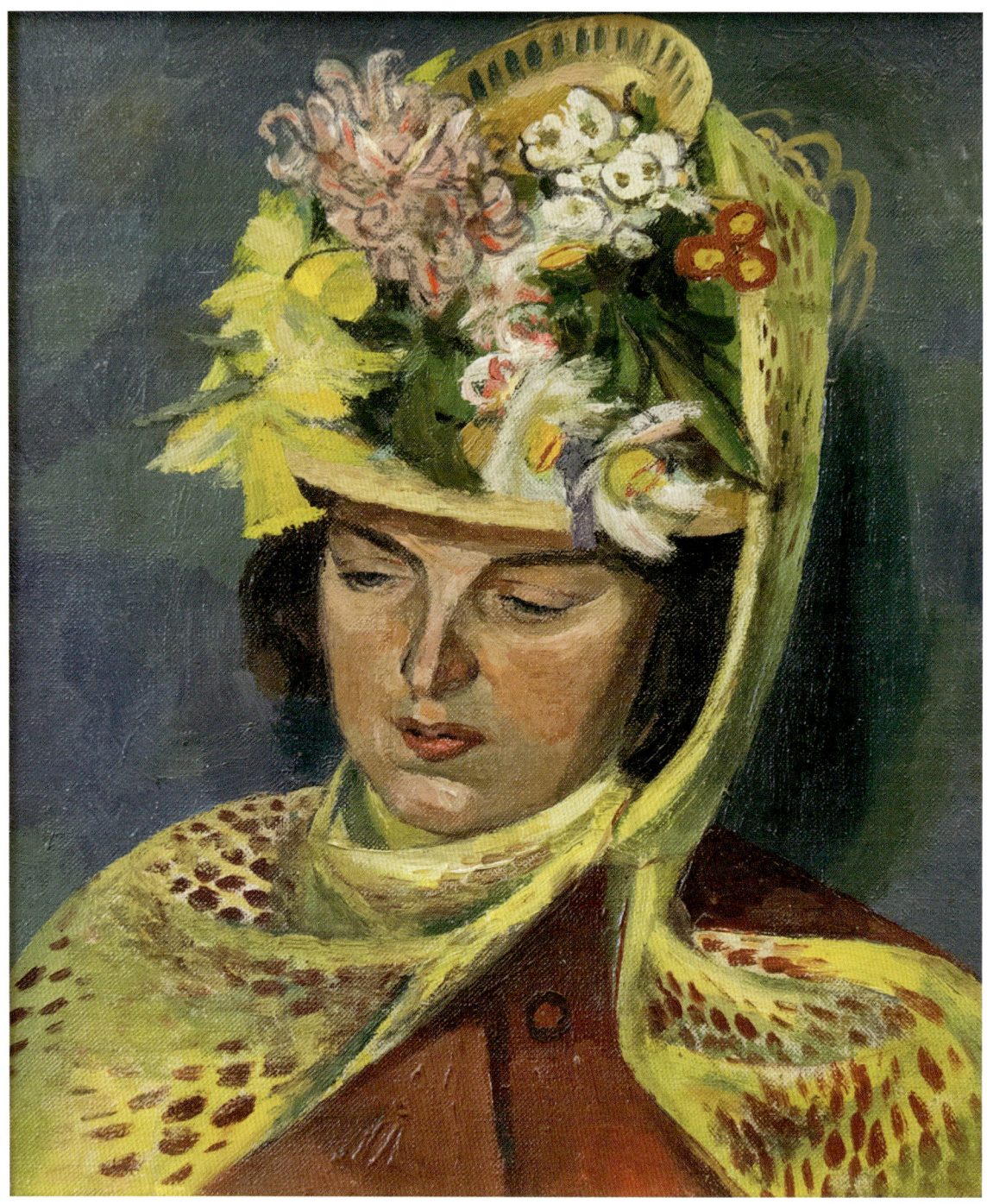

CAT 63 [HMO 750] *Spring*, c.1932,
Oil on canvas, 11 ½ x 9 ½ in. (29.2 x 24.1 cm)

An early example of the artist's delight in the personification of the months and seasons. The model was probably the artist's cousin Vera Swain.

CAT 64 [HMO 203] Studies for endpapers for *Gardener's Diary 1938*, 1937,
Pencil and pen & ink on paper 22 x 15 in. (56 x 38.3 cm)

Dunbar's models are her mother Florence and her sister Marjorie.

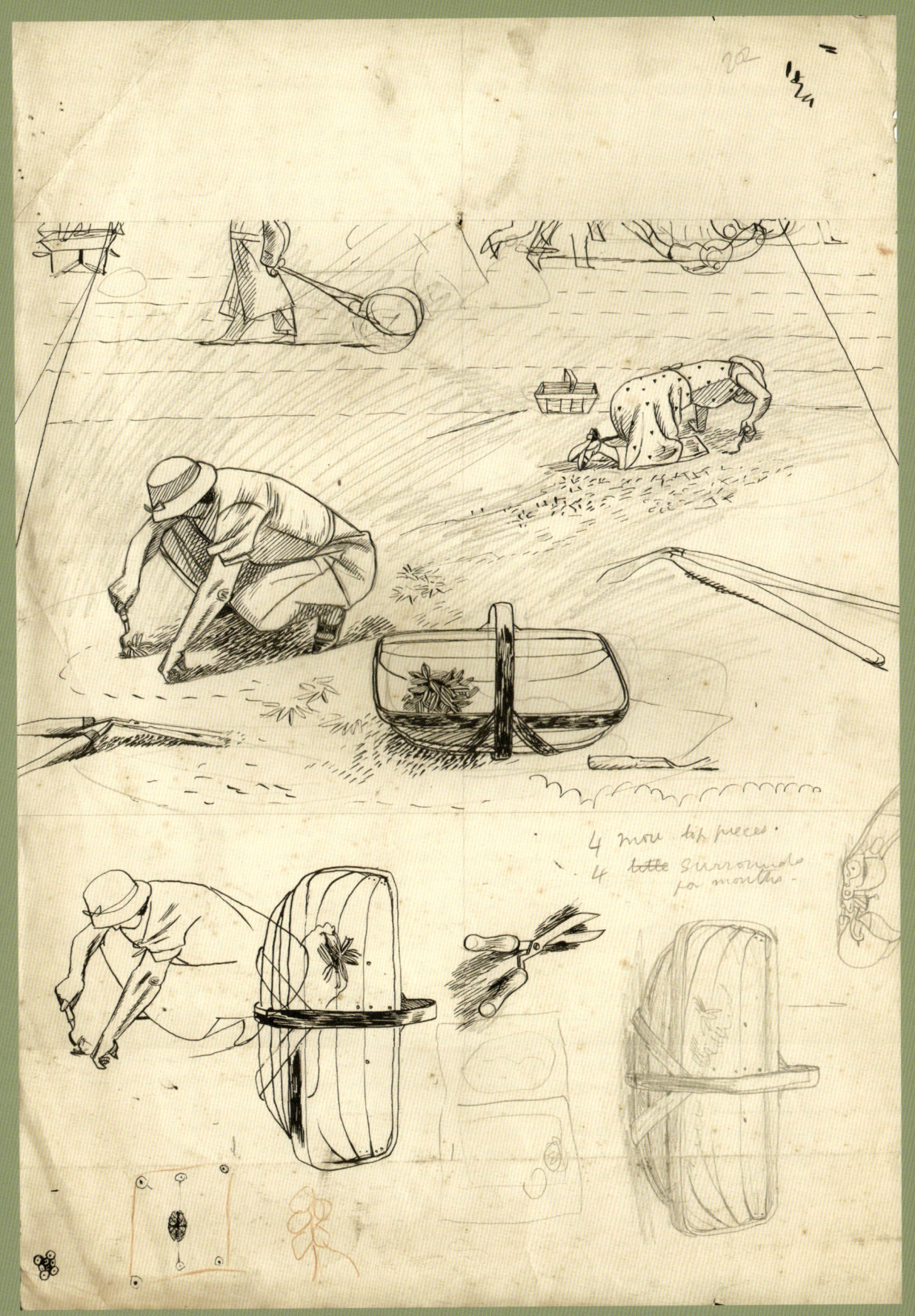

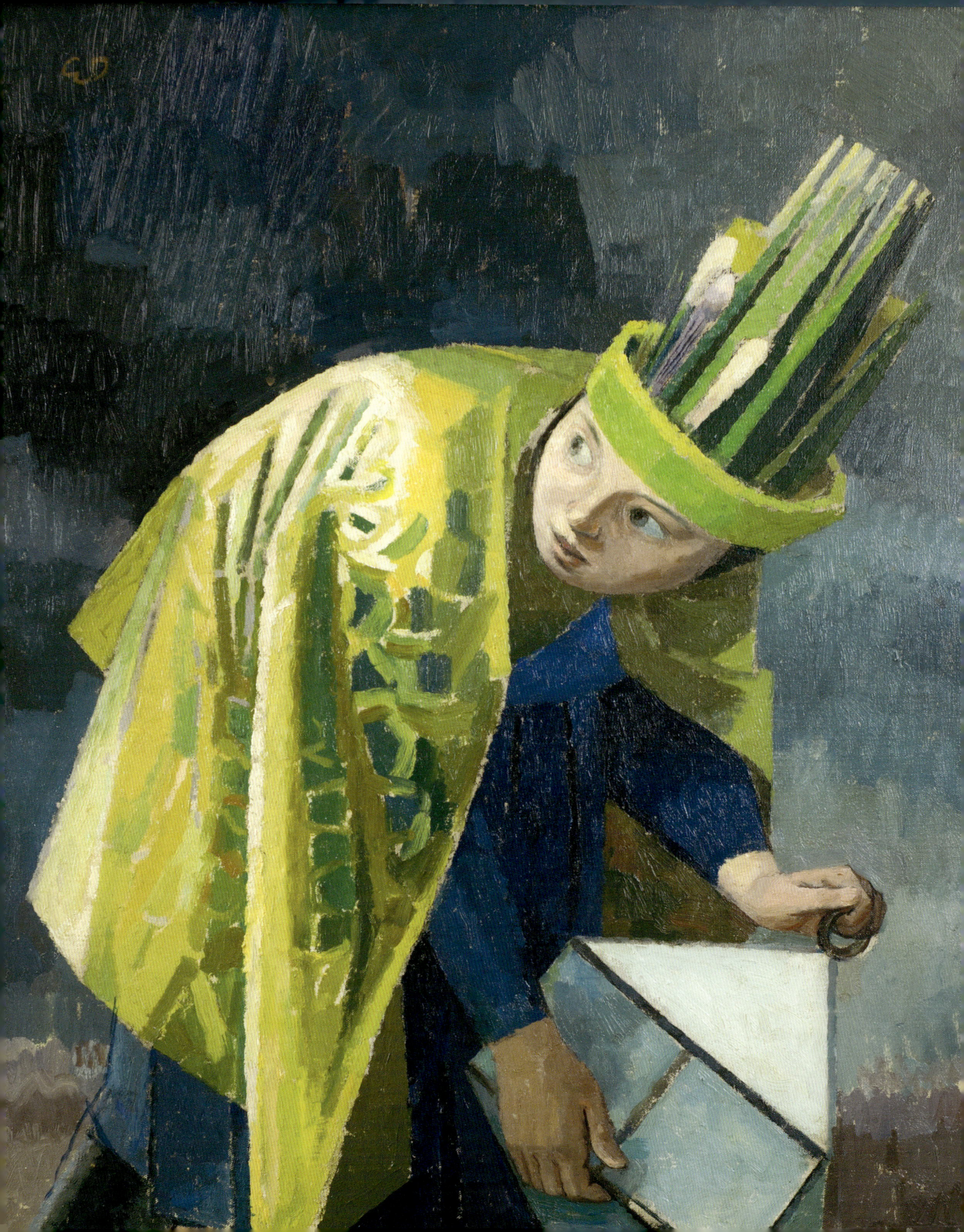

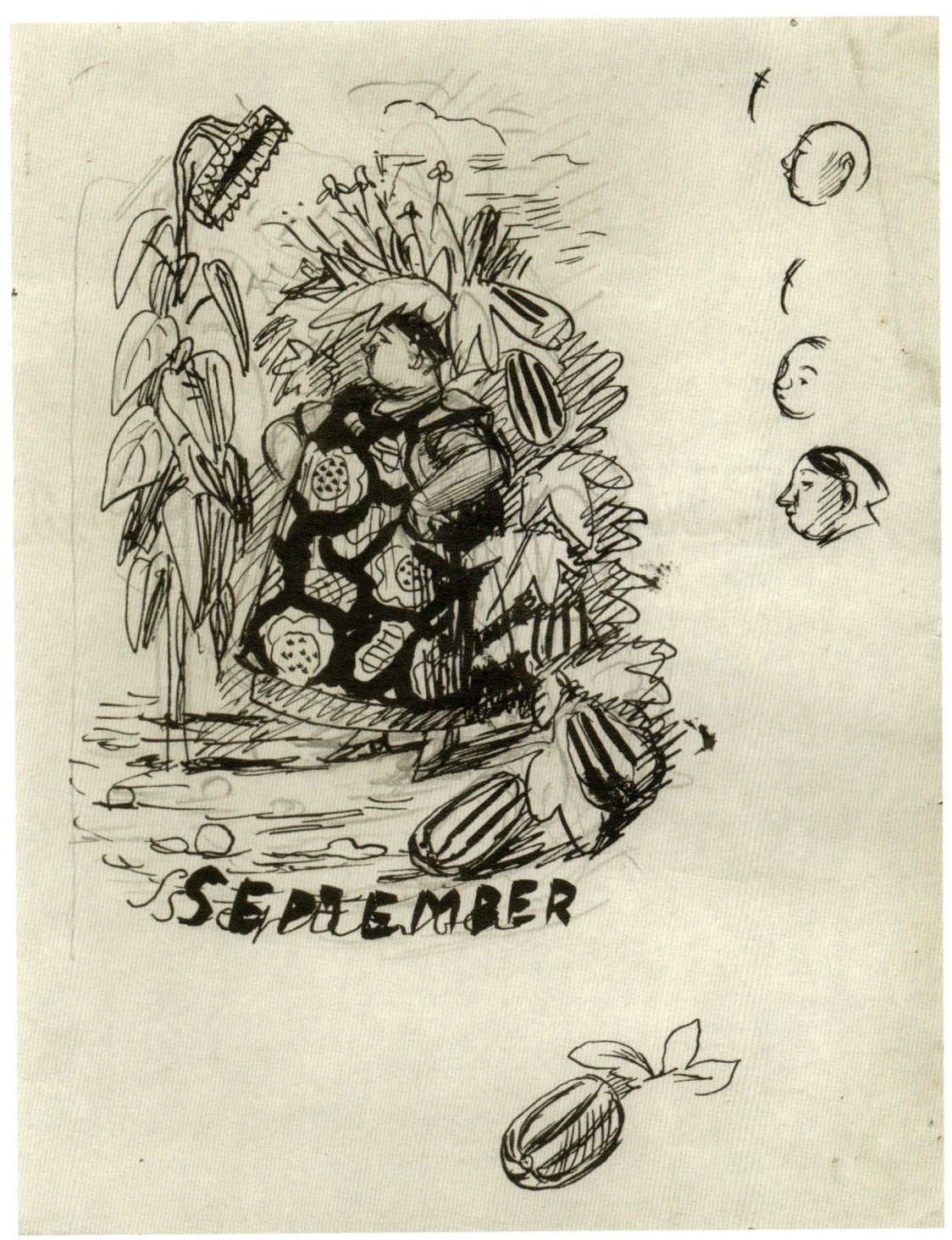

CAT 66 [HMO 232] *September*, preparatory drawing for *Gardener's Diary 1938*, 1937, Pencil and pen & ink on paper, 10 x 8 in. (25.3 x 20.3 cm)

CAT 65 [HMO 764] *February*, c.1937-38, signed 'ED', Oil on canvas, 23 ½ x 19 ½ in. (59 x 49.5 cm)

This image originates from the artist's drawing of February for *Gardener's Diary 1938*.

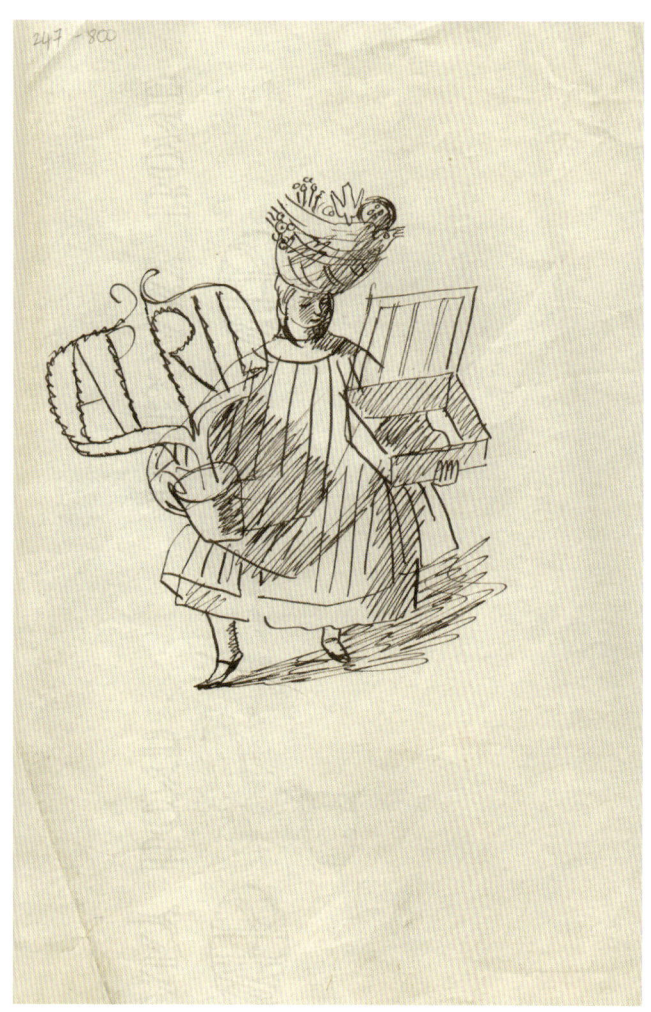
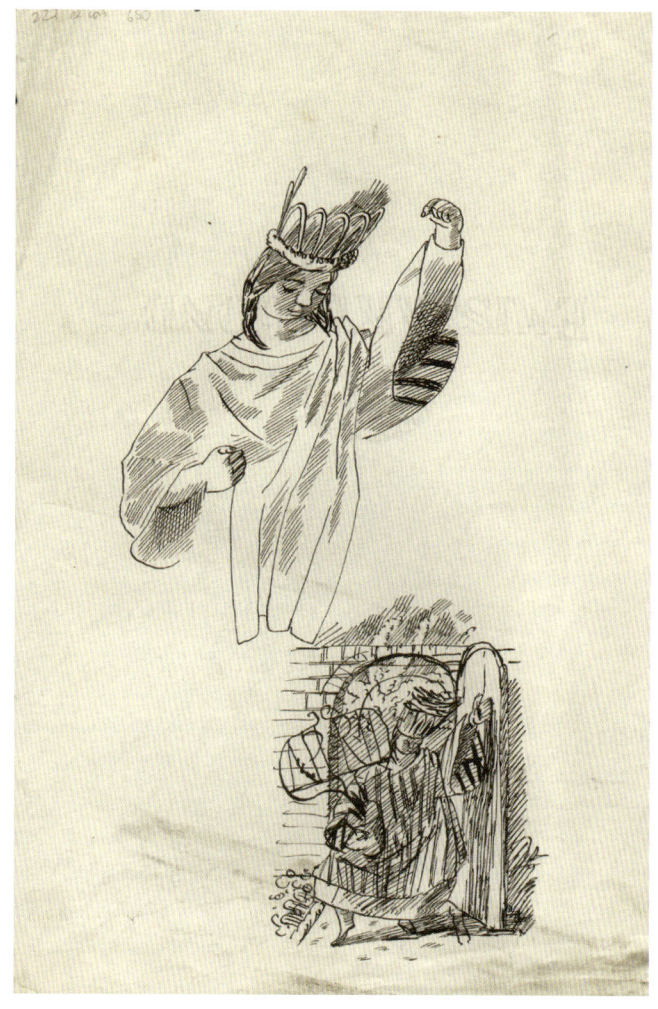

CAT 67 [HMO 247]
Study for *April* for *Gardener's Diary 1938*, 1937,
Pen & ink on paper, 12 ¾ x 8 in. (32.4 x 20.2 cm)

CAT 68 [HMO 228]
Study for *April* for *Gardener's Diary 1938*, 1937,
Pen & ink on paper, 12 ¾ x 8 in. (32.4 x 20.2 cm)

In 1937-38 Dunbar selected three of the twelve line drawings with which she had illustrated her *Gardener's Diary 1938* and worked them up into oils. (The other two were *February* (CAT 65) and *August*.)
1937-1940 was a troubled period in the artist's life and *April* may be a reflection of this. A psychological interpretation would emphasise the significance of the cuckoo invading the greenfinches' nest in the most fantastic hat in all Dunbar's work, while enclosure of the figure of *April* inside a box, a practice of Dunbar's at the time (cf. *Joseph's Dream*) implies a deep need for security and protection.

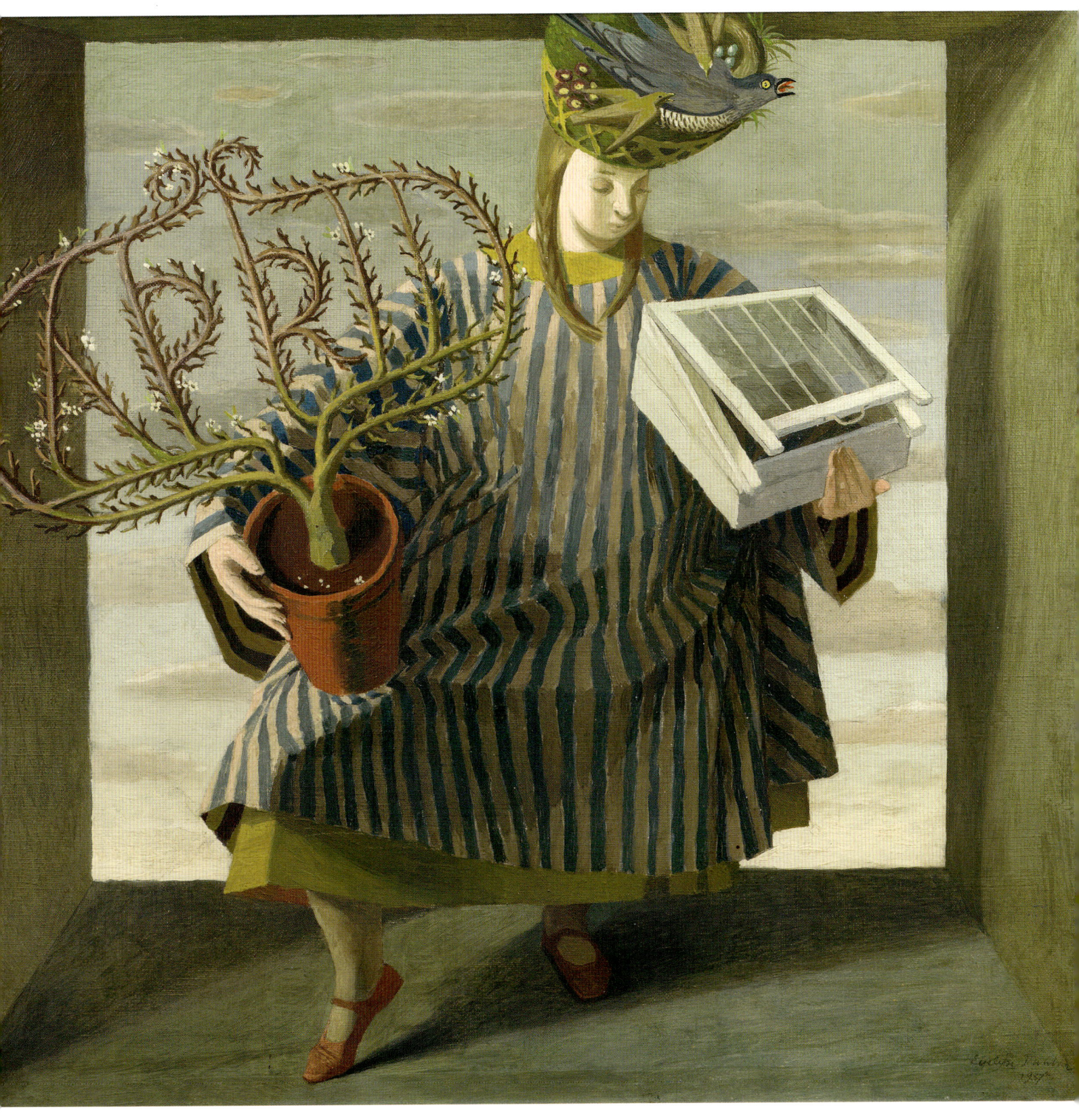

CAT 69 *April*, signed and dated 1937,
Oil on canvas, 19 ½ x 20 in. (49 x 51 cm) Private collection
Photograph: Richard Valencia © Christopher Campbell-Howes

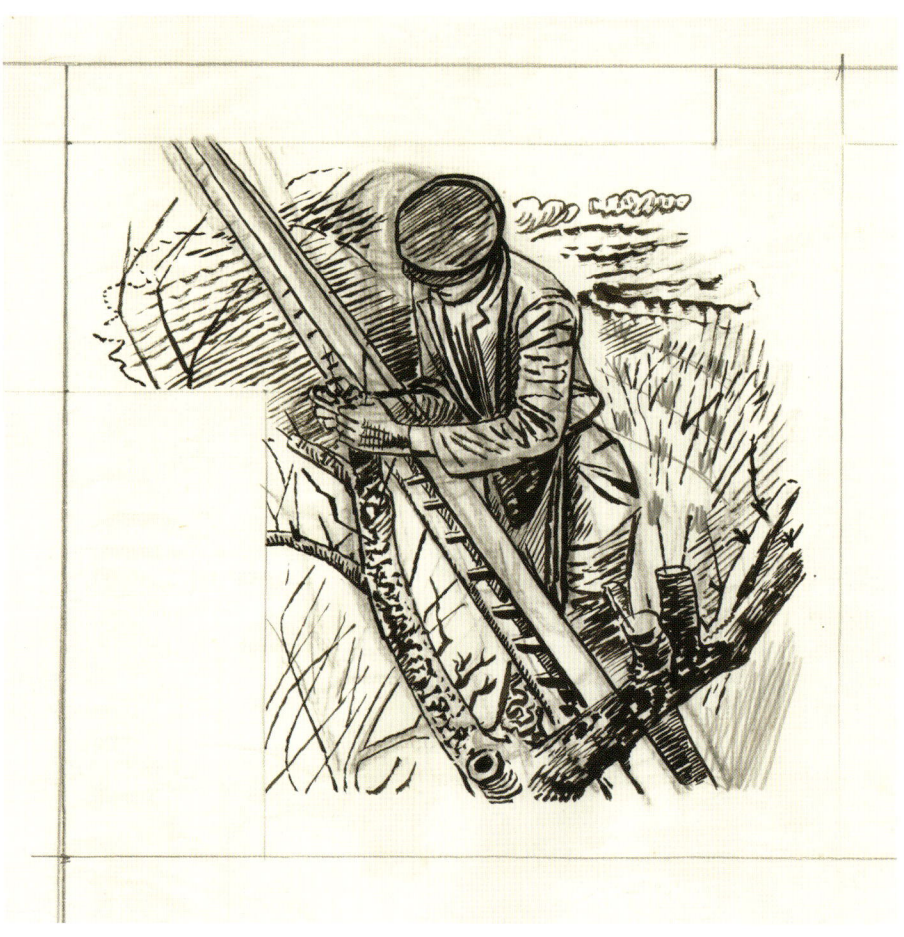

CAT 70 [HMO 360]
Man on a pruning ladder, perhaps intended for *Gardener's Diary 1938*, 1937,
Pencil and pen & ink on paper, 15 x 20 in. (38 x 50.5 cm)

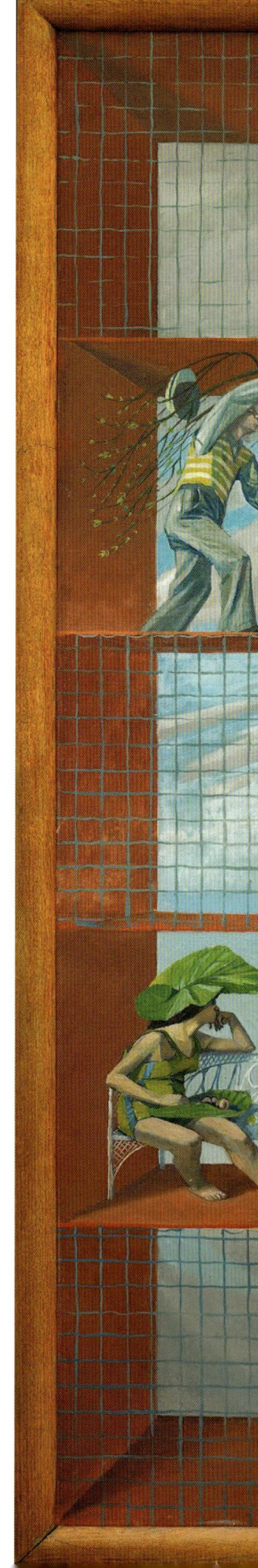

CAT 71 *An English Calendar*, 1938,
Oil on canvas, 72 x 72 in. (183 x 183 cm)
Exhibited: Wildenstein's 1938
Collection: Archives Imperial College London
Photograph: Richard Valencia © Christopher Campbell-Howes

Overleaf:
CAT 72 *The Days of the Week*, inscribed on stretcher 'Design for mural'. c.1939,
Oil on canvas, 18 x 30 in. (45.8 x 76.2 cm)

This painting shows Monday (carrying bundles of washing) on the left, through to Sunday (attending to things of the mind) on the right.

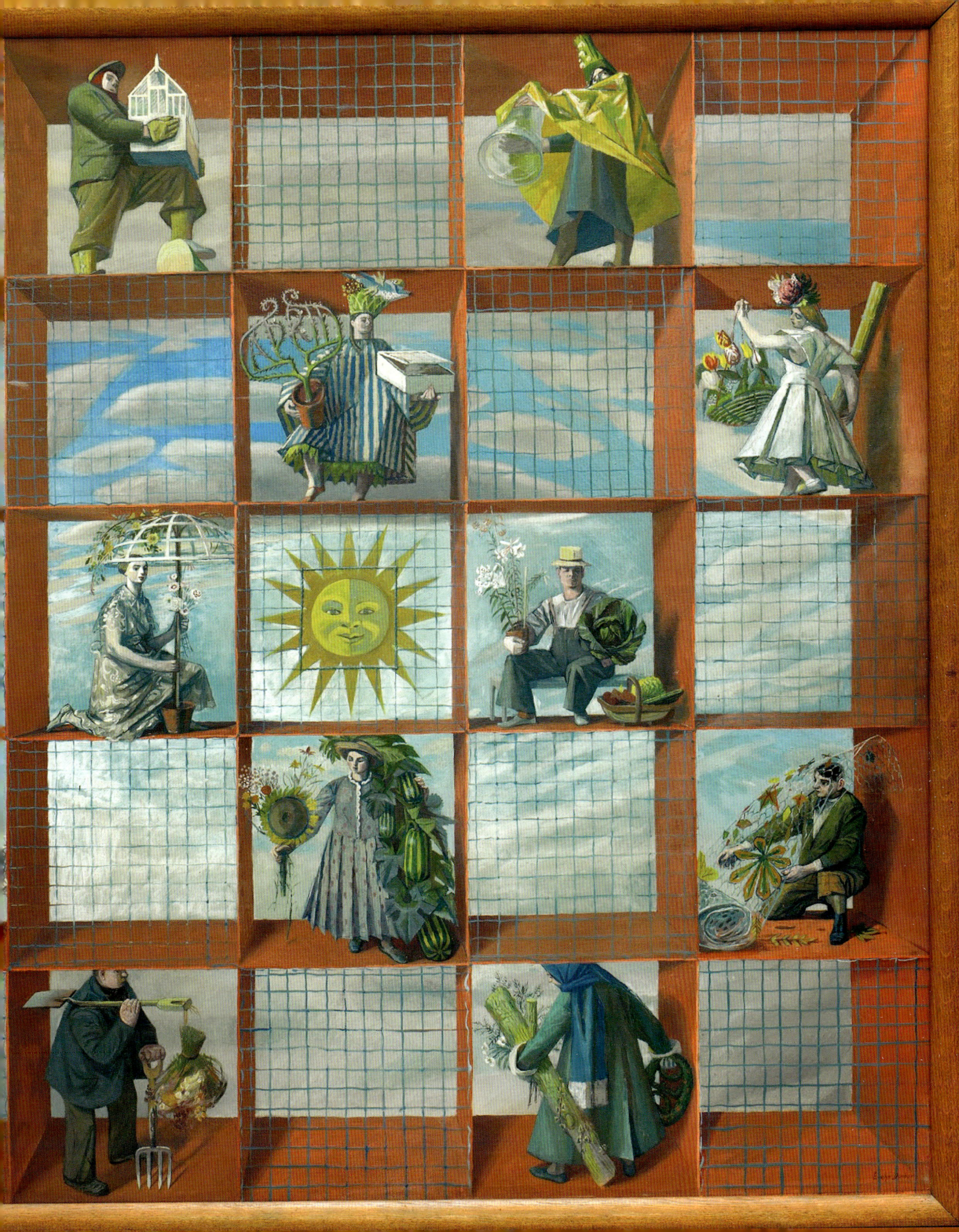

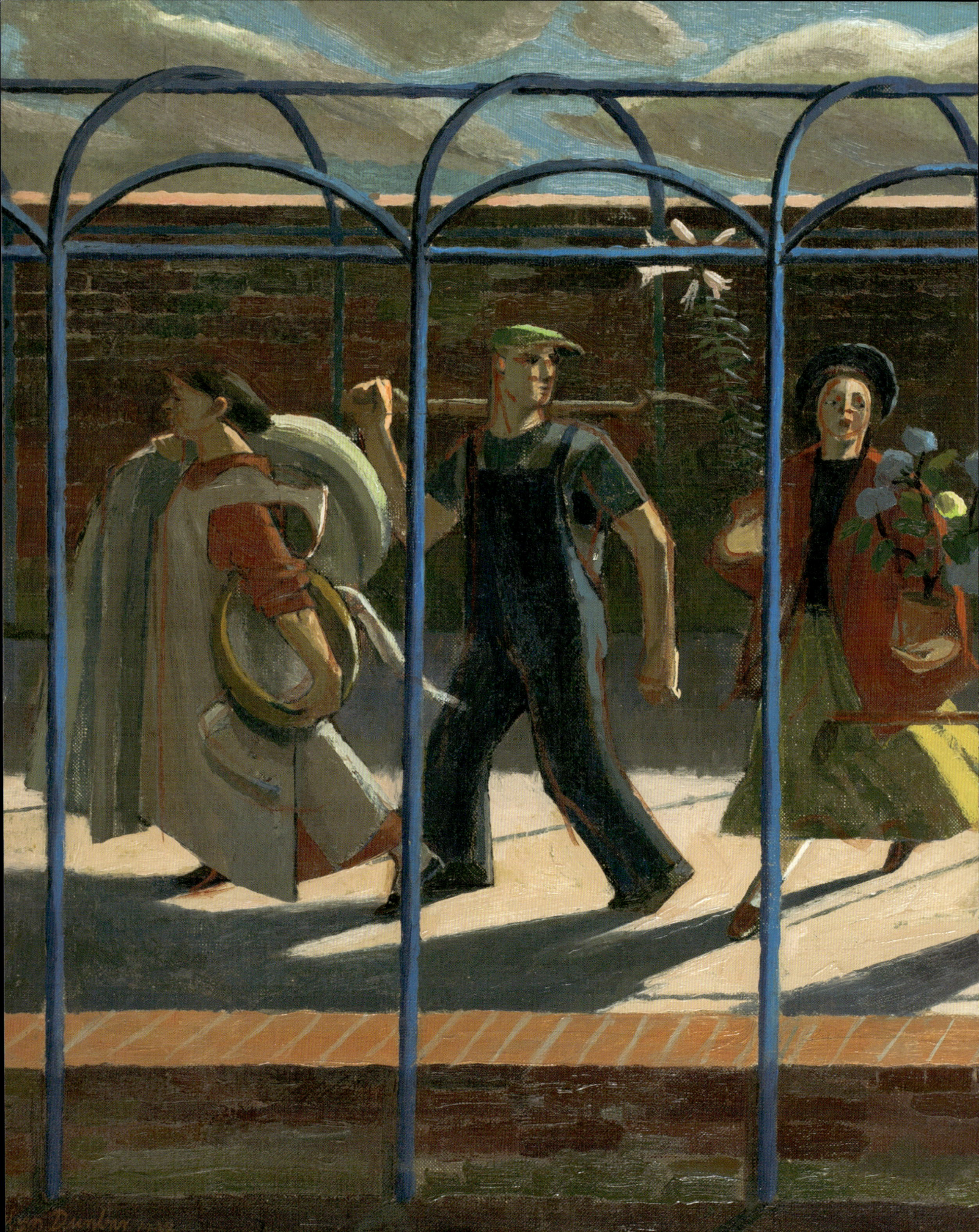

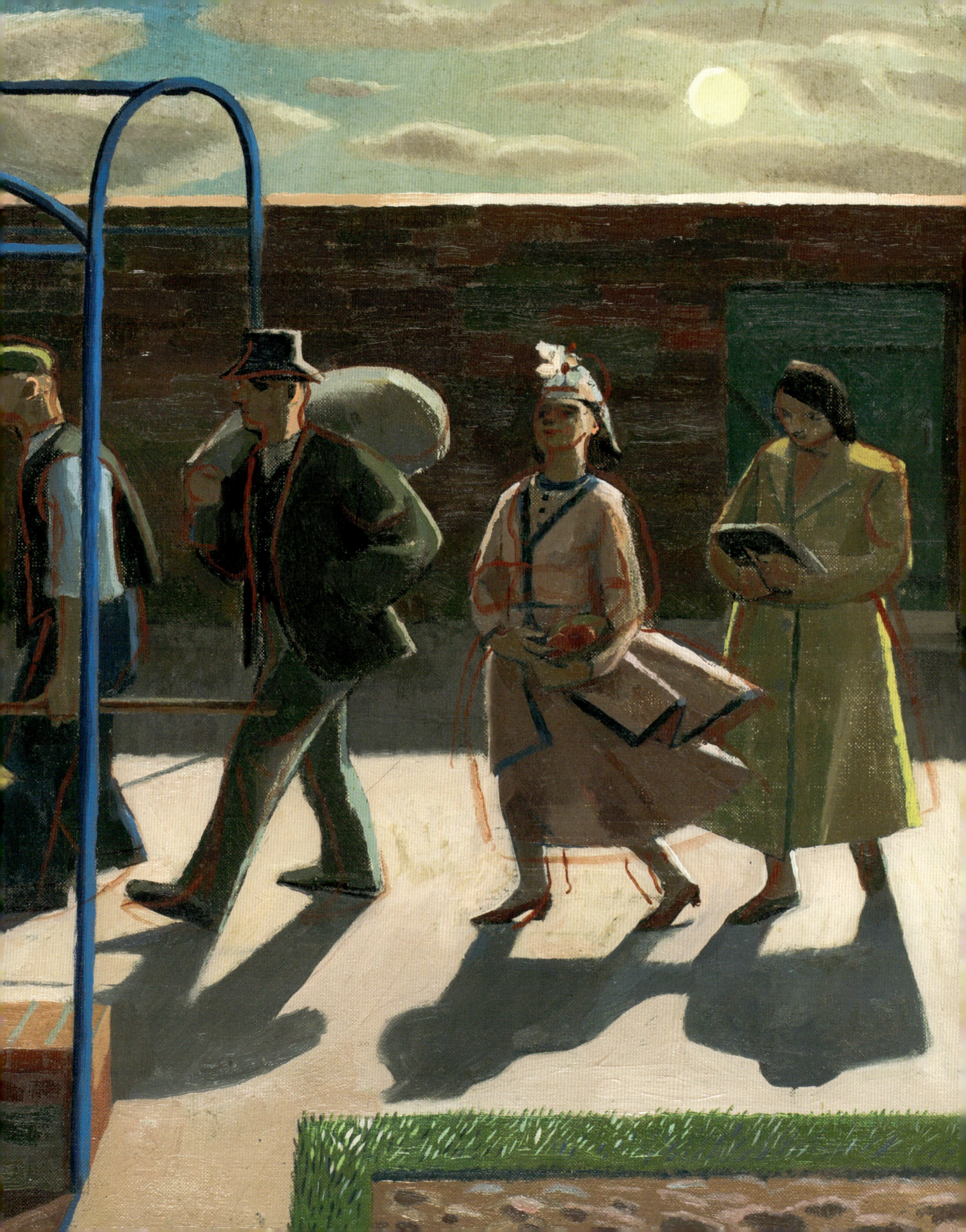

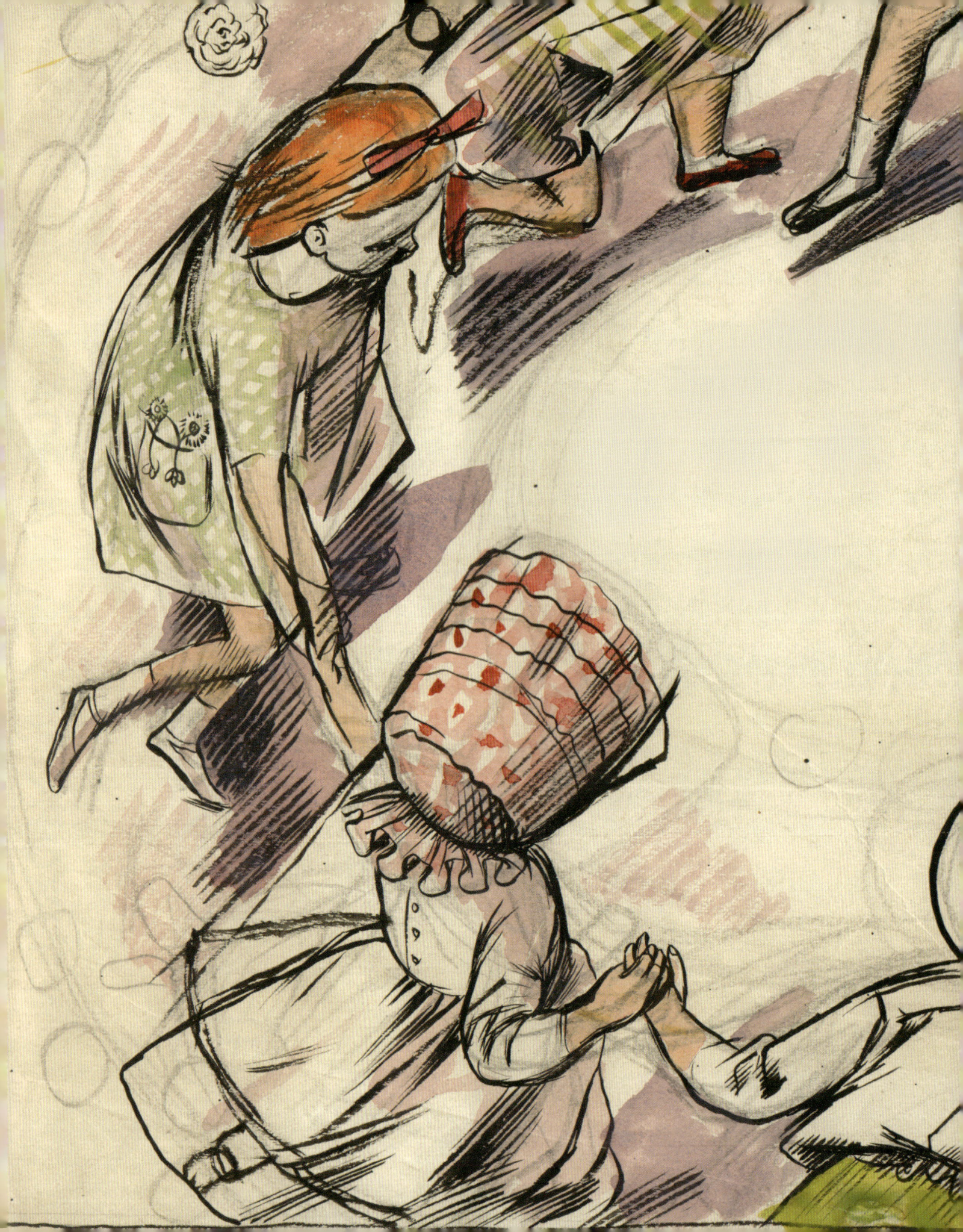

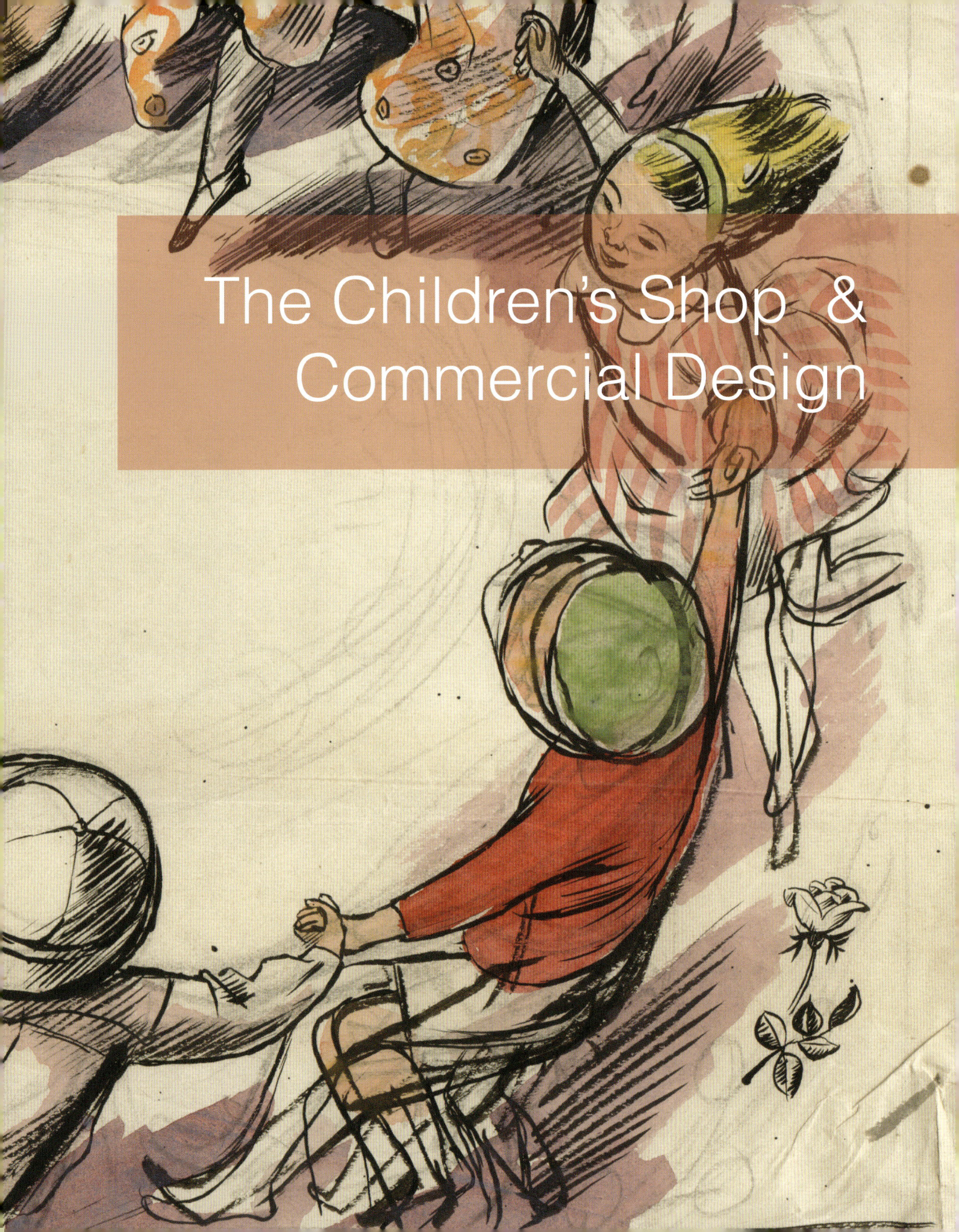

The Children's Shop & Commercial Design

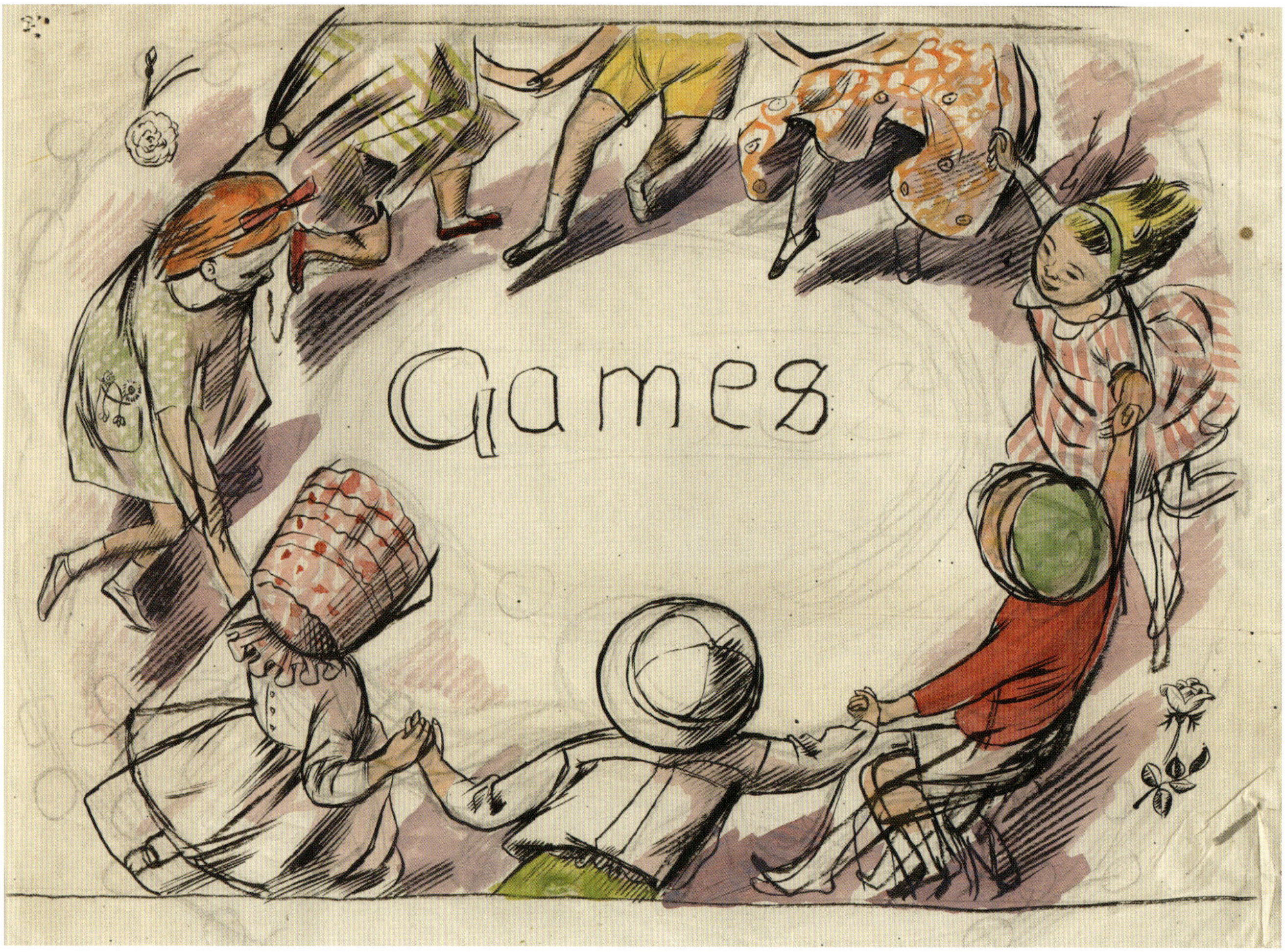

CAT 73 [HMO 113] Games, inscribed verso, c.1952,
Pencil, pen & ink and watercolour on paper, 8 x 10 ¼ in. (20.5 x 26 cm)

Dunbar's two older sisters, Jessie and Marjorie, ran The Children's Shop, selling children's clothes, at 38, High Street, Rochester.

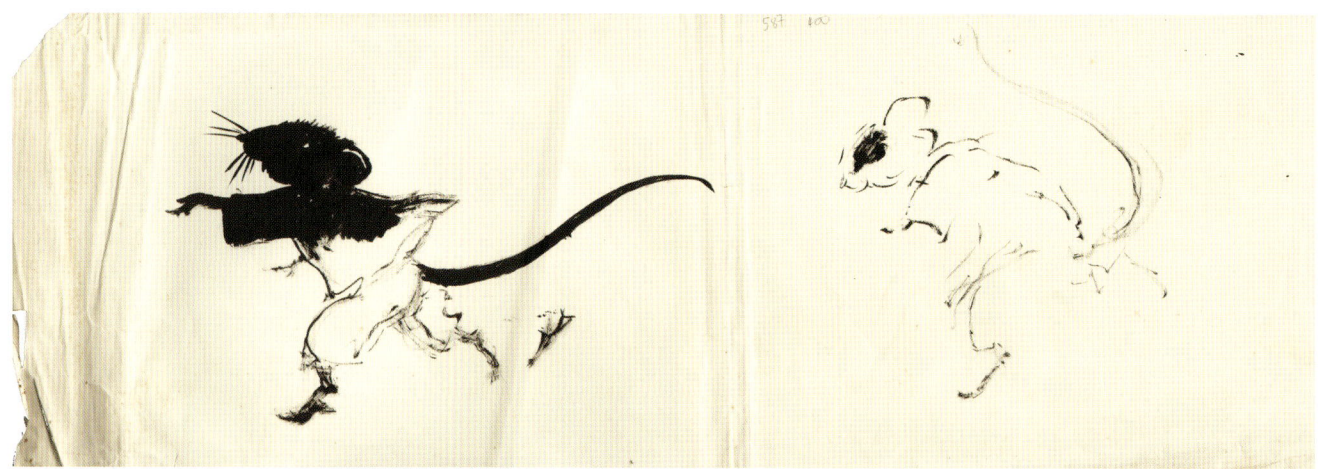

CAT 74 [HMO 587] Study of two running mice, probably a design associated with The Children's Shop,
Ink on paper, 11 x 30 in. (28 x 76 cm)

The Children's Shop & Commercial Design

There was clearly a strong entrepreneurial streak in the Dunbar family. In December 1938 an article in *The Chatham News* proclaimed that 'Although today there are half-a-dozen flourishing businesses associated under the name Dunbar, the family was unknown in Strood when the twentieth century was born.' William, Evelyn's father, had come south from Scotland some time in the latter years of the nineteenth century, first to Reading and then briefly to Bournemouth before finally setting up in business as a bespoke tailor and draper in Rochester, Kent, 'the archaeologist's and the historian's heaven' as Richard Church described it. During the interwar years as the Dunbar children grew to maturity the name became ubiquitous in Rochester High Street: Evelyn's brother Ronald branched out into radios and bicycles while two of her sisters, Jessie and Marjorie, opened The Children's Shop. For several years the living accommodation above this shop at 244 High Street was also the family home until William bought The Cedars across the Medway at Strood.

Jessie and Marjorie were only one year apart in age, they never married and were like twins living for each other happy in themselves, delighting in their work dressing small children, and firm in their in their adherence to the Christian Science faith in which their mother had reared them. They established The Children's Shop soon after the end of World War I and Evelyn, though still in her early 'teens was happy to help. Even when her commitments at the Royal College of Art and Brockley shifted the focus of her activity to London, she continued to assist designing headed notepaper (CAT 79) and other stationery (CAT 77), lettering publicity panels and painting the delightful signboard for the shop with its frolicking mice and sparrows (CAT 76).

In 1938, some eighteen years after opening The Children's Shop, the two sisters expanded their business interests when they took over a well-established haberdashery further down the High Street, including, according to a notice in *The Chatham News*, its stock of rare silks: they renamed it The Fancy Shop. Their brother Ronald's business had by then expanded to such an extent that he took over Strood Hall and in December that year advertised a Home Comfort Exhibition and a Miniature Radiolympia with: 'TELEVISION, FREE DEMONSTRATION DAILY: FURNITURE, a representative selection of the most up-to-date and attractive styles for Bedroom, Dining Room and Sitting Room: CHILDREN'S WEAR and TOYS: Knitting Wools, ART NEEDLEWORK and Fancy Goods'. The *gros point* panel *Opportunity* (CAT 75) embroidered in wools from The Fancy Shop and copied from a 1936 painting by Evelyn might well have been one of the pieces of Art Needlework included in this display.

With the opening of The Fancy Shop at 168 High Street Evelyn took over the first floor to show paintings and items of antique furniture; she named her department the Blue Gallery and in March 1939 staged an ambitious exhibition of work by friends including Charles Mahoney, Allan Gwynne-Jones, Kenneth Rowntree and Edward Bawden as well as sculpture by Bainbridge Copnall. However, with war looming on the horizon, times were not propitious and the gallery soon closed and Evelyn found employment as an Official War Artist. The Christian Science Reading Room took over the vacant space in The Children's Shop under the care of Jessie and Marjorie.

P.S.

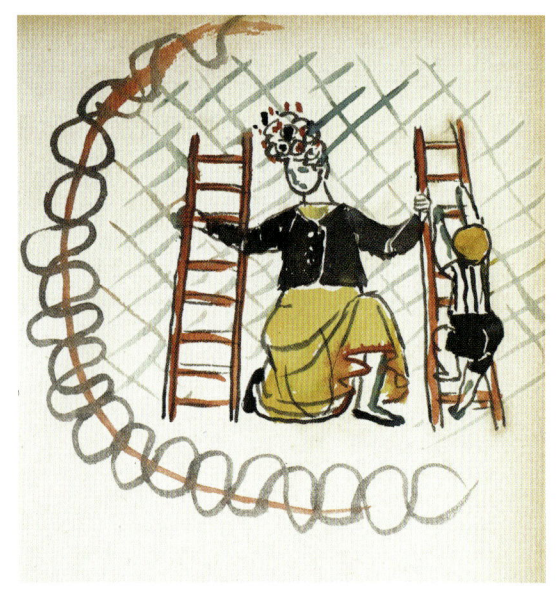

FIG 13
Drawing from one of Dunbar's sketchbooks

CAT 75 [HMO 796]
Opportunity. 1938,
Needlework in wool with silk highlights, backed and sleeved,
27 x 18 ½ in. (68.6 x 47 cm)

Canvas work (needlework in American terminology) allows for a huge variety of pictorial effects through the use of different stitches (here tent stitches with cross stitches with additional highlights on the face in silk). After Evelyn's 1936 painting of the same title, for the Dunbars' commercial exhibition, December 1938. The wools would have been available from her sisters' newly-acquired Rochester haberdashery, The Fancy Shop.

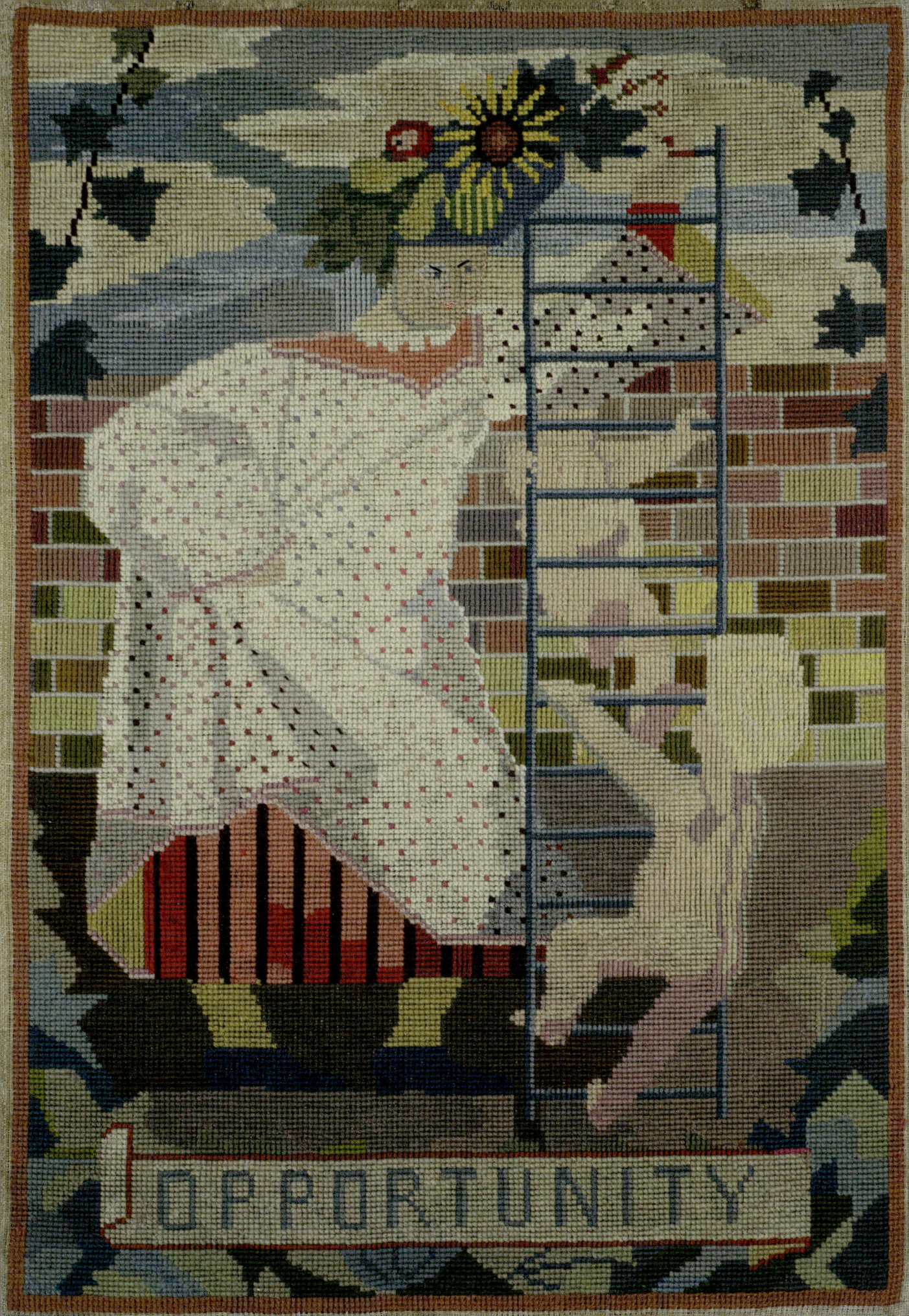

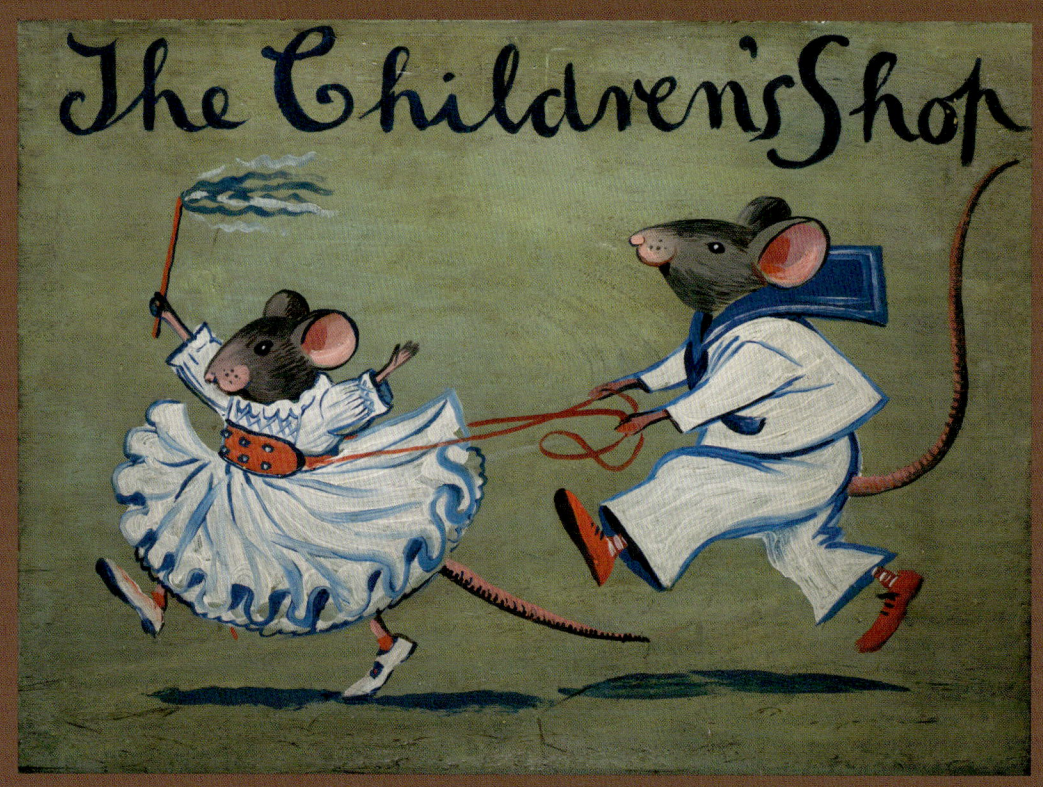

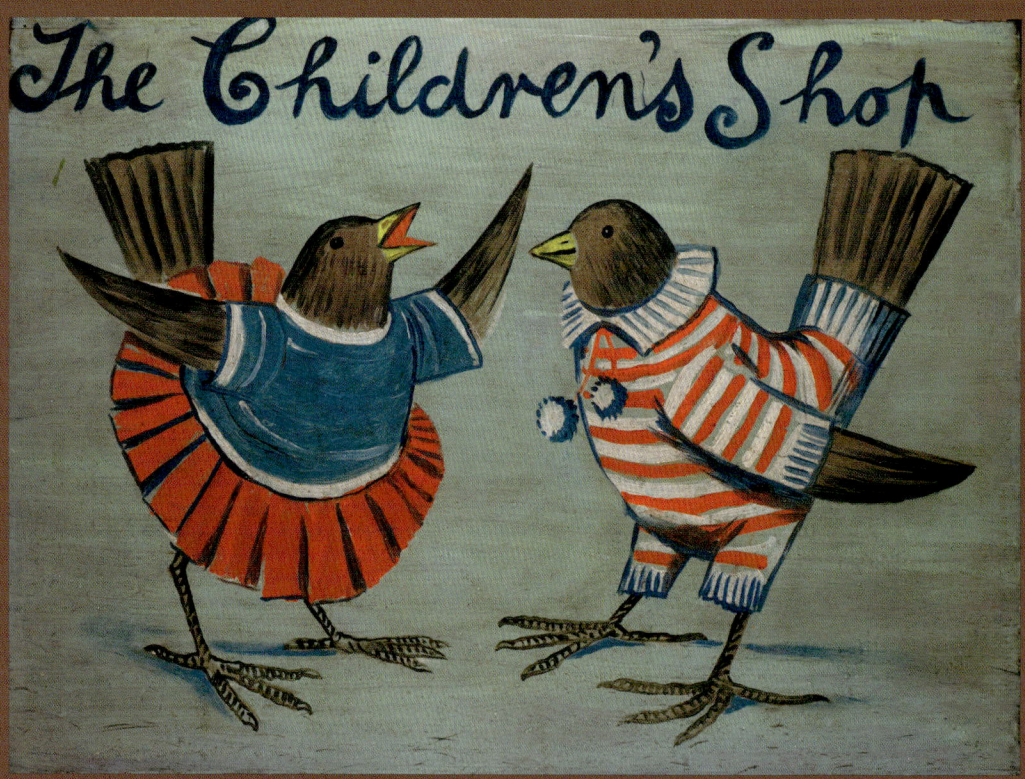

CAT 76 [HMO 749] *The Children's Shop*: mice (recto), birds (verso), 1938,
Oil on wood, 18 ½ x 23 ¾ in. (46.6 x 60.1 cm)

This panel was painted to advertise Jessie and Marjorie's Rochester High Street shops as part of an exhibition in 1938. It was designed to be suspended from above, like an inn-sign.

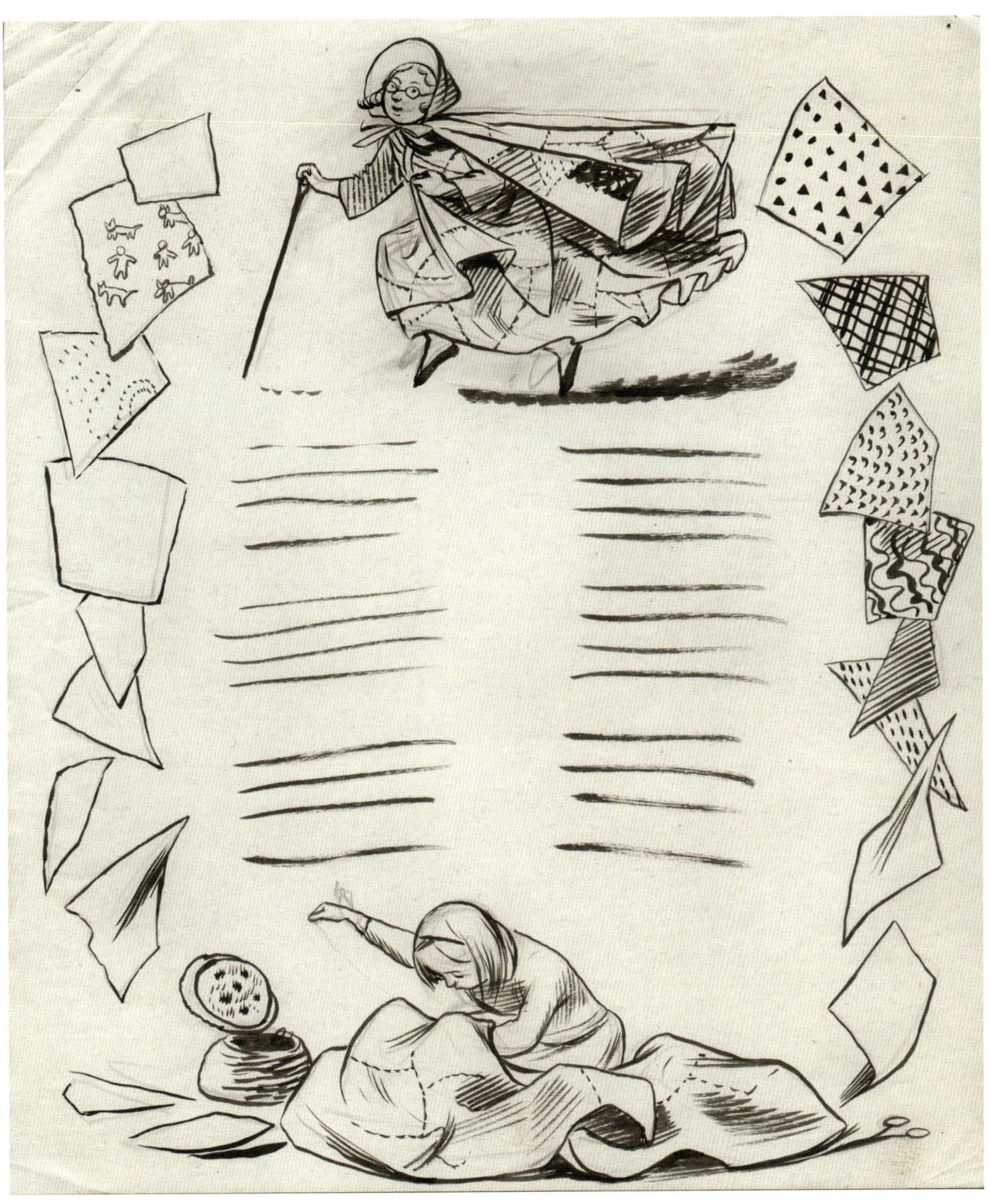

CAT 77 [HMO 374] Design for a Children's Shop verse, c.1938,
Pencil and pen & ink on paper, 10 x 8 in. (25 x 20.5 cm)

The sets of parallel lines represent space for the verses Jessie and/or Marjorie occasionally composed about children and their clothes. (See CAT 78)

Roses of Britain are blooming again
Fragrant and fresh after soft Summer rain;
And Babies of Britain, those sweetest of roses,
With satiny cheeks, and wee button noses,
And petal-pink ears, and eyes heaven-blue,
Make Summer unfading and hope ever new!

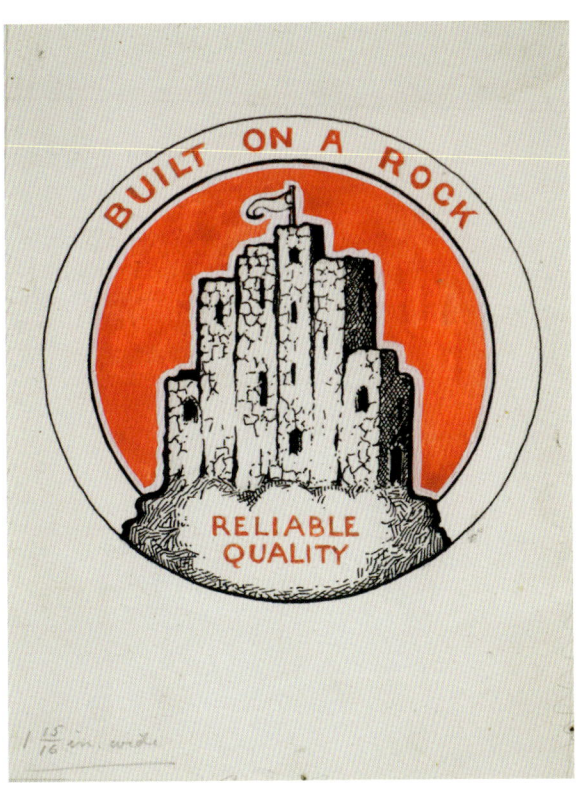

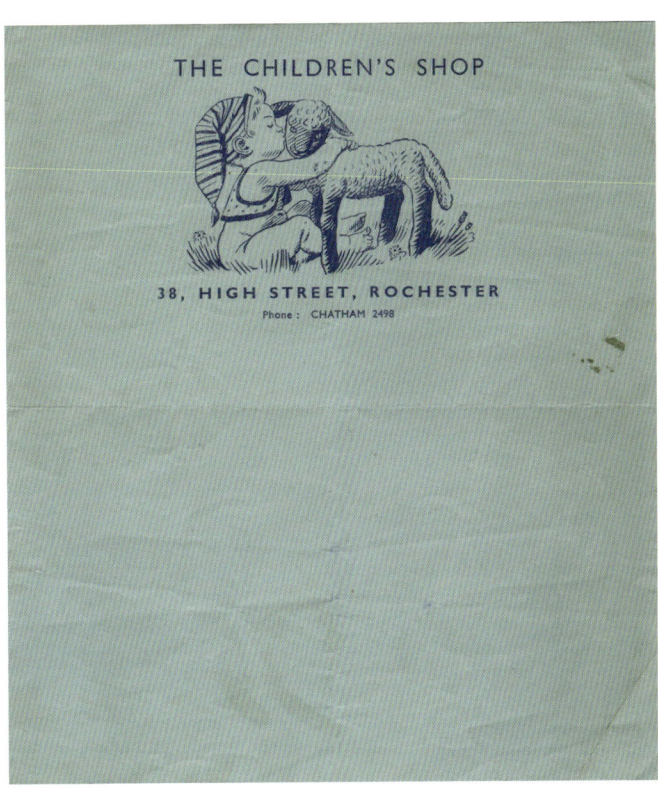

CAT 79
Built on a Rock, logogram for one of Alec Dunbar's sometimes ephemeral business enterprises, c.1937
Watercolour on paper, 5½ x 4 in. (14 x 10 cm)

The fortress slightly resembles Rochester Castle, which the Dunbar family knew well.

CAT 80 [HMO 375]
Headed notepaper, with design by Dunbar, for The Children's Shop, c.1952,
Printed in blue ink on blue paper,
8 x 6 ¾ in. (20.2 x 17.1 cm)

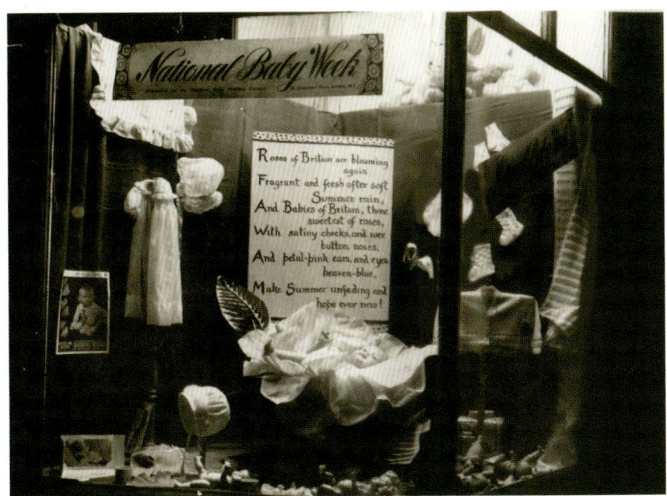

FIG 14 Shop window of The Children's Shop on Rochester High Street.

CAT 78 [HMO 783]
Roses of Britain. No date,
Oil on canvas, 29 ½ x 20 in. (75 x 51 cm)

Shop window display for the artist's sisters' The Children's Shop on Rochester High Street. Design and lettering by Dunbar.

OLD MOTHER HUBBARD

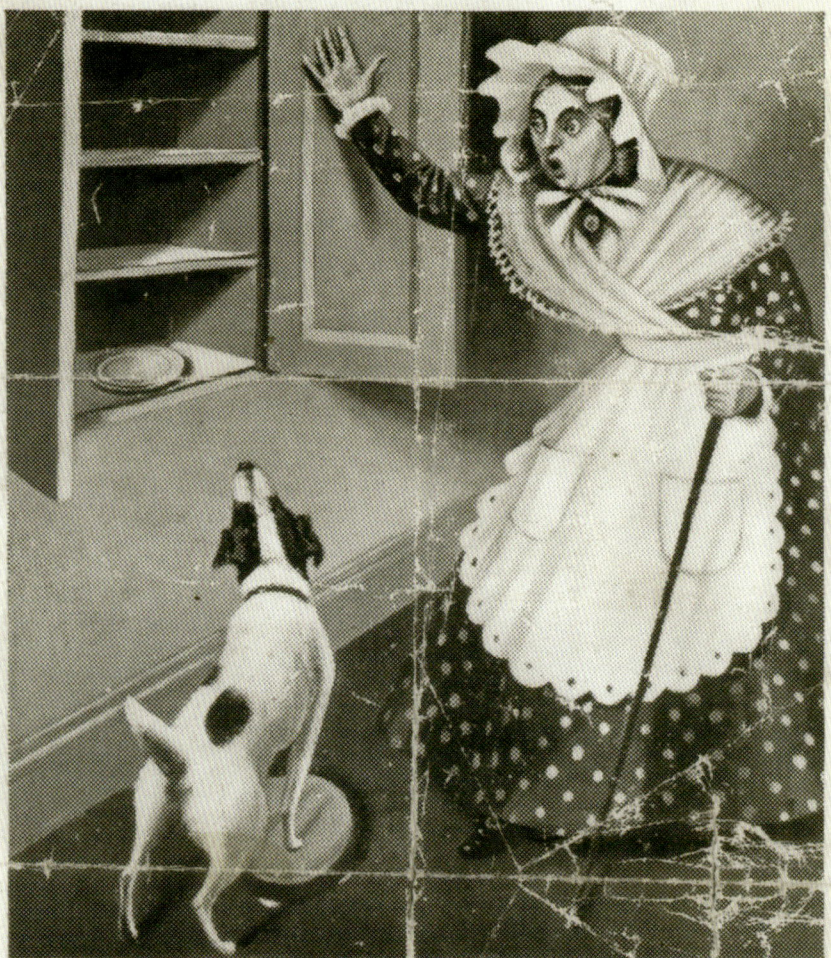

FEW store cupboards in Britain are today without their emergency stock of canned, bottled or preserved foods. None should be, for total war makes "iron rations" necessary for civilians as for fighting men. Thanks to the great strides in the science of food conservation, the housewife now enjoys an increasingly wide choice of nourishing and palatable foods that will keep for long periods. Although she is using many home methods (runner beans in salt, eggs in "water glass" and other chemicals, and fruit and vegetables either bottled in presence of sulphur dioxide as a preservative or in vacuum jars) it is on the canning industry that she largely relies. Canning in its turn relies largely on the chemist and the chemical industry to maintain its high standards of pure and wholesome food. This involves incessant research for example, into the acidity of different foodstuffs, special linings for the containers and how to preserve both the vitamins and the appearance of canned foods. At home great strides are being made in the *drying* ~~digging~~ of vegetables. The necessity of war has given urgency to food conservation. Chemistry is also showing how, by dehydration and other methods, our ships can carry to the British housewife the greatest possible amount of nutriment in the shape of meat, milk, eggs and vegetables in the smallest possible bulk. When the story of the war-time feeding of Britain can be told, the chemist will be found to have no mean share in the great credit that must go to British farms and the British merchant navy.

No. X in the "Services of an Industry" series

issued by

IMPERIAL CHEMICAL INDUSTRIES LTD.

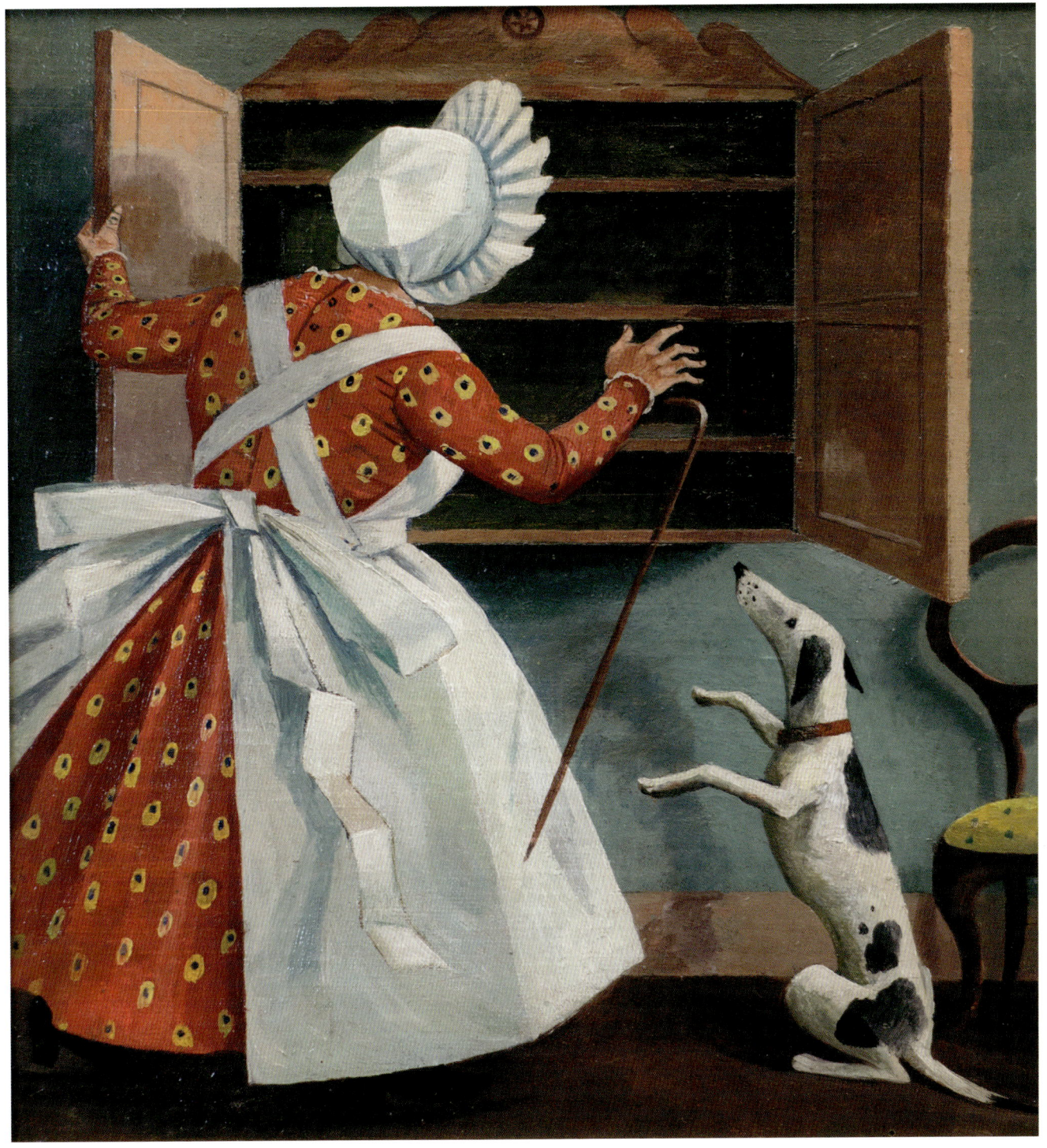

CAT 81 [HMO 798] *Old Mother Hubbard* may also be known as *A Children's Picture*, c.1946, Oil on canvas, 12 x 11¼ in. (30.2 x 28.7 cm)

Having identified bare cupboards with agriculture unimproved by ICI products (Fig. 15), Dunbar returned to the theme with this rather gentler Old Mother Hubbard, perhaps intended as a decoration for her sisters' The Children's Shop.

FIG 15
Submission proof (with Dunbar's correction) for a wartime ICI advertisement featuring an alternative version of *Old Mother Hubbard*. Printed document, date stamped 17 SEP 1943

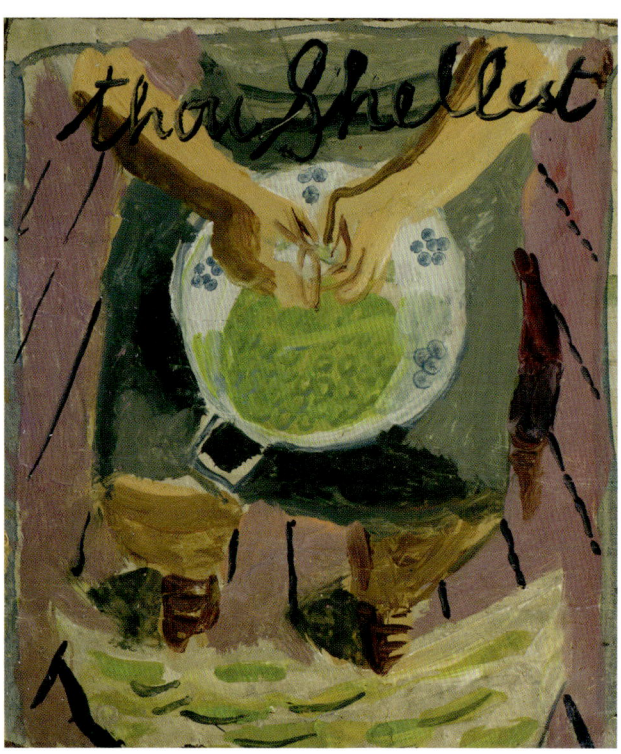 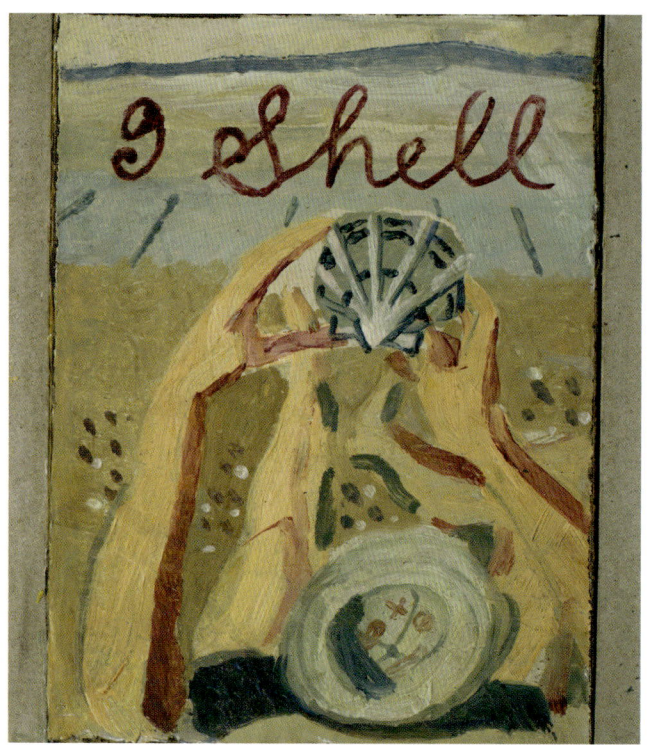

CAT 82 [HMO 751]
Thou Shellest, proposed design for Shell petrol, c.1937, Oil on board, 7¾ x 6½ in. (19.5 x 16.7 cm)

Dunbar was possibly commissioned in the 1930s to produce original commercial publicity material, as Freedman, Ravilious and others were, but nothing further is known of her designs for Shell.

CAT 83 [HMO 751]
I Shell, Sketch for design for Shell petrol. c.1937, Oil on board, 7¾ x 6½ in. (19.5 x 16.7 cm)

Viewed from above a figure wearing a hat sitting on the beach, is shown holding a scallop shell. The presentation of the shell (the company's logo) is designed to give the impression of a driver seated at the wheel.

CAT 84 [HMO 751]
Go Shell, proposed design for Shell petrol. c.1937, Oil on board, 12 x 8¼ in. (31 x 21 cm)

There is no record of Dunbar being commissioned by Shell to produce original publicity material.

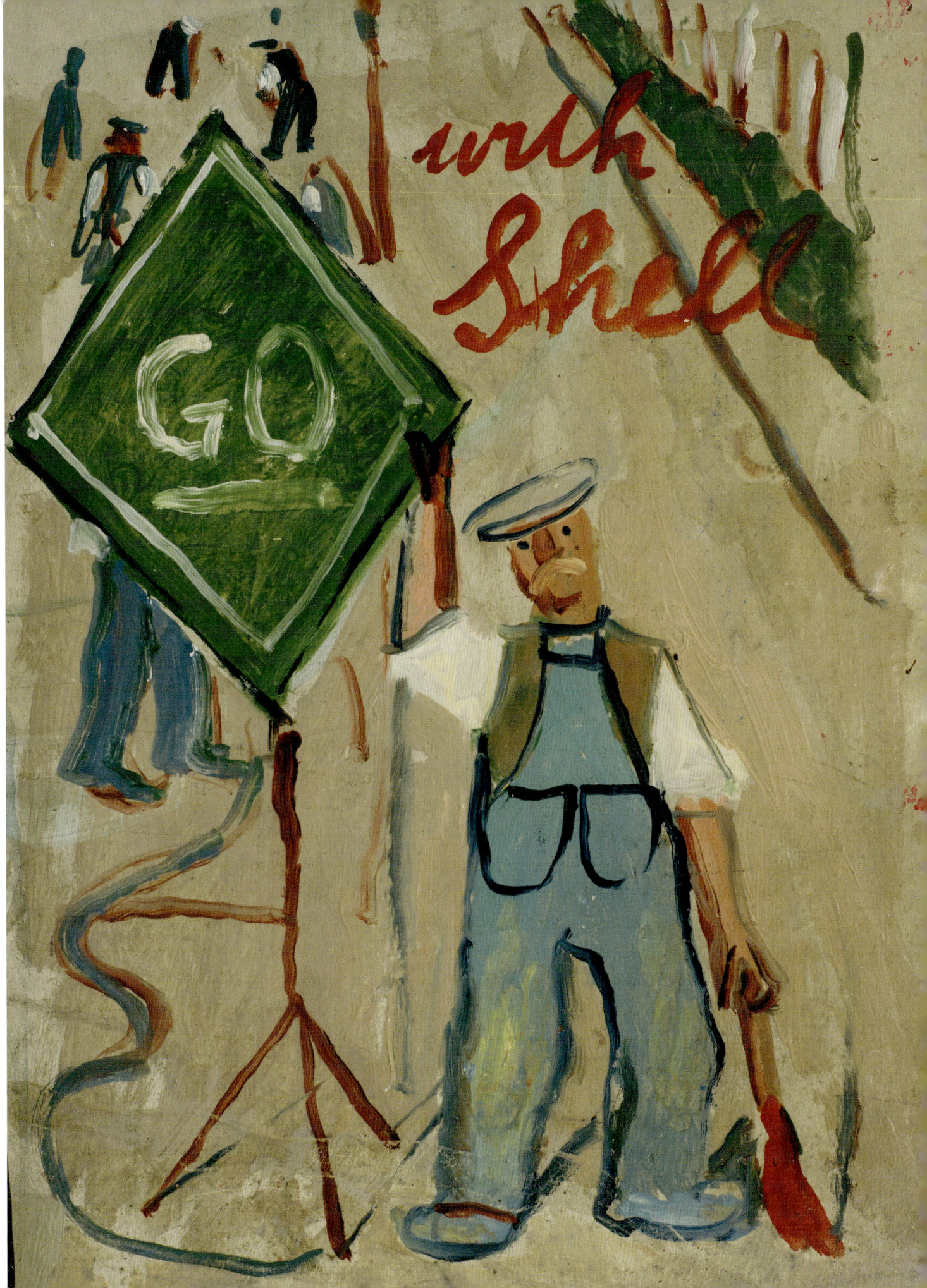

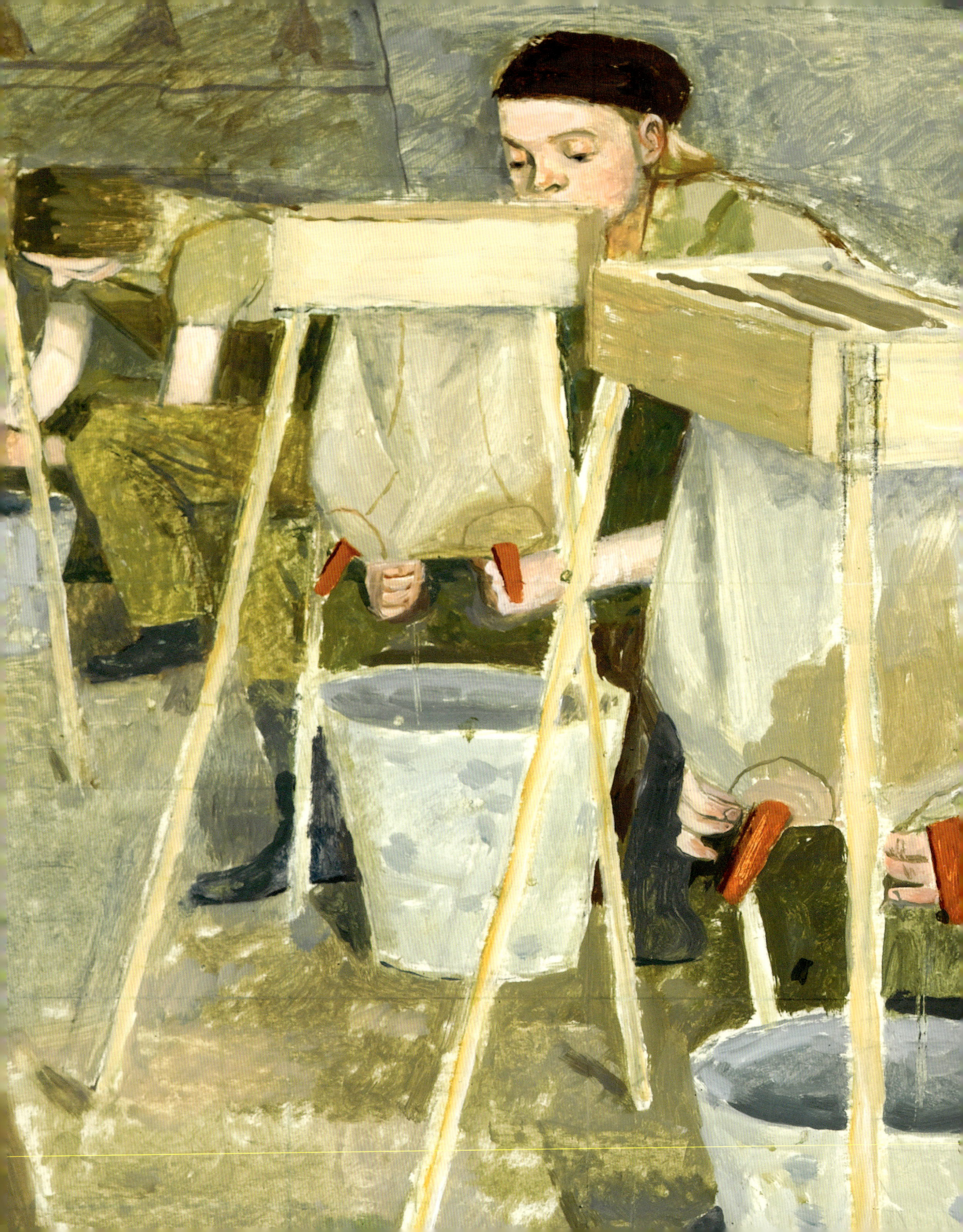

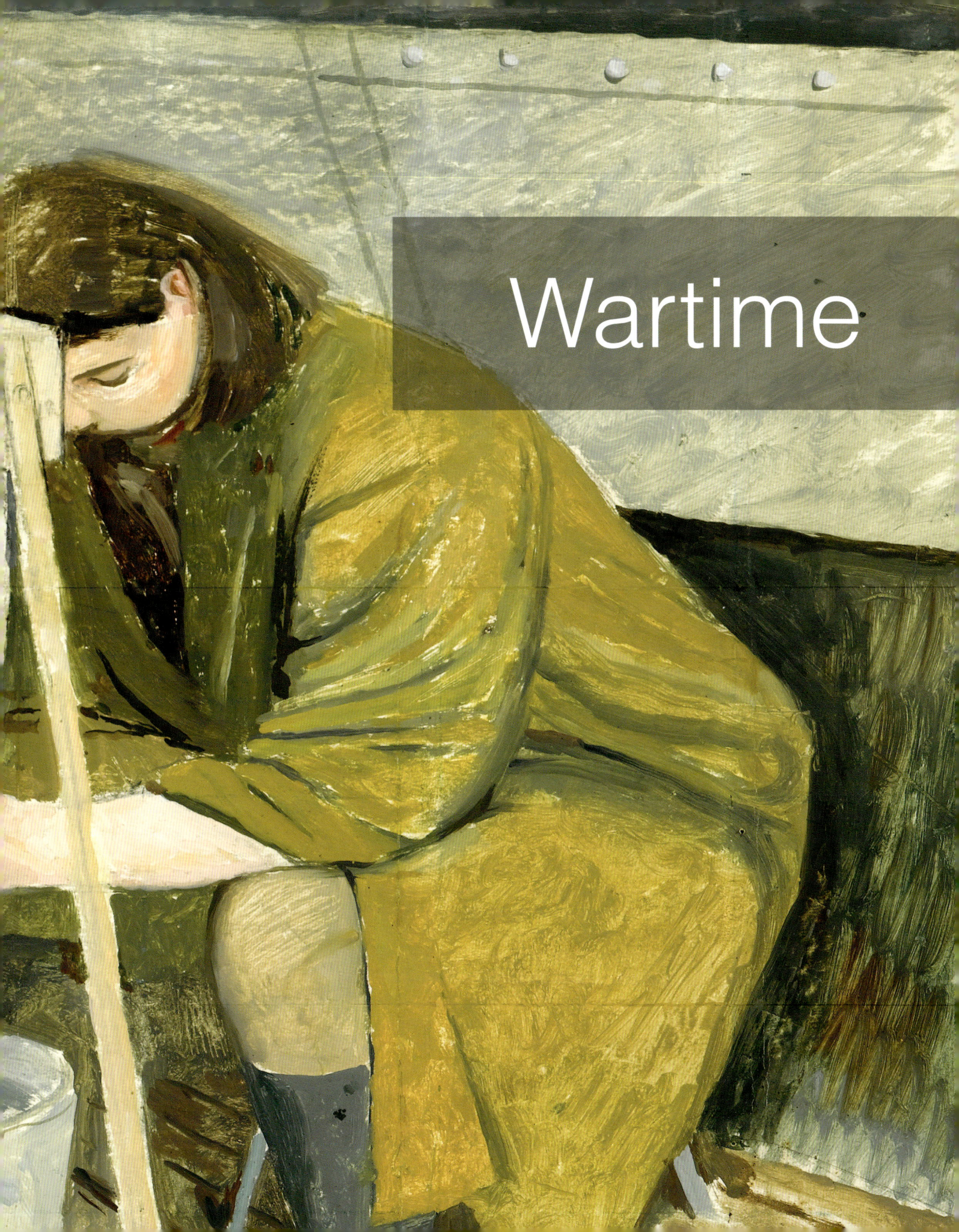

Wartime

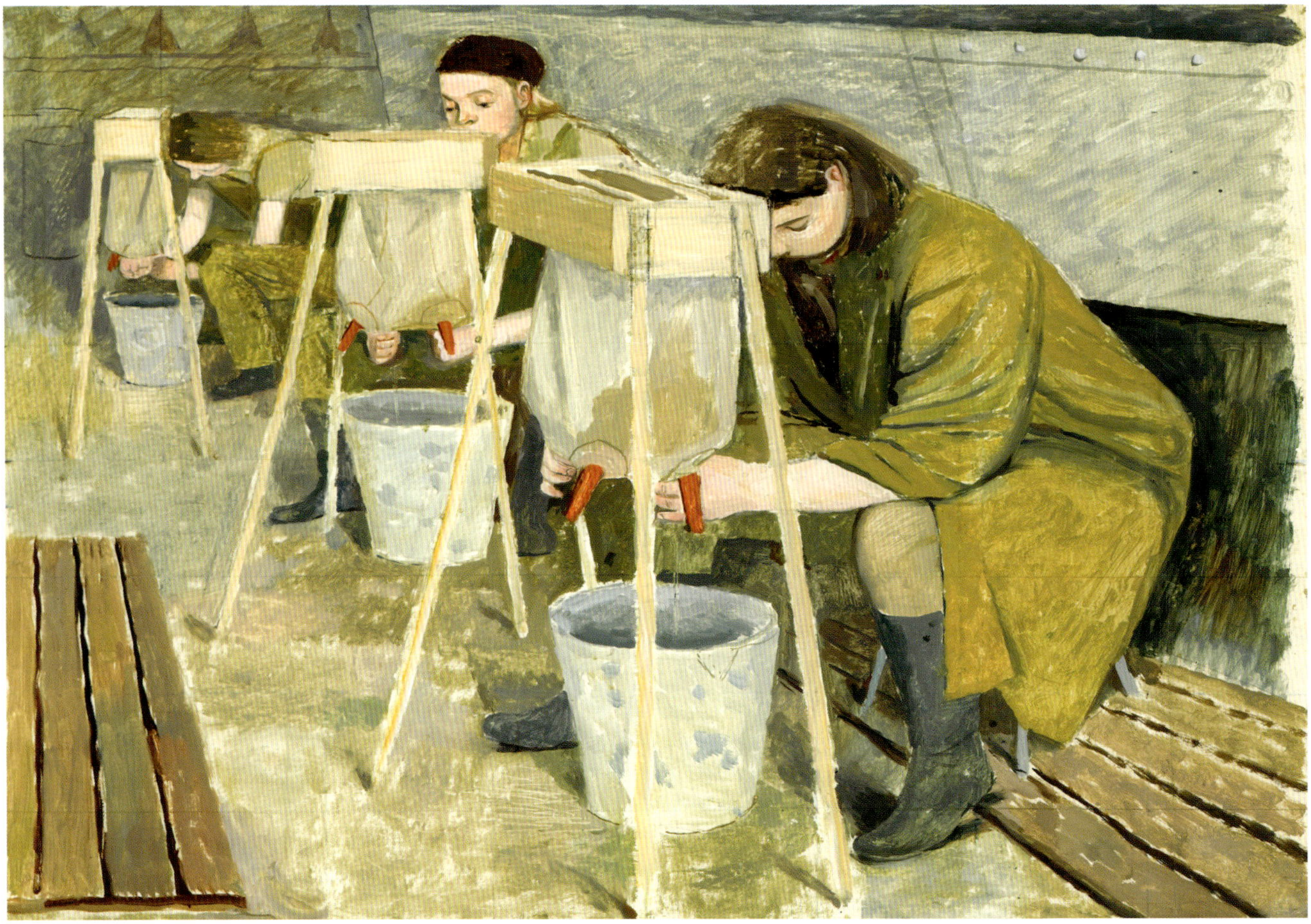

CAT 85 *Milking Practice with Artificial Udders*, 1940,
Oil on paper, 22 x 30 in. (55.8 x 76.2 cm)

This sketch is a study for, and almost identical to, the finished painting in the Imperial War Museums collection (FIG 6). Painted at about the time Dunbar was considering *A Book of Farmcraft*, this study in the dairy of Sparsholt Farm Institute shows three novice Land Girls coming to grips with a Heath Robinson contraption, current at the time, for learning how to milk. The Land Girl in the middle has assumed the recommended posture.

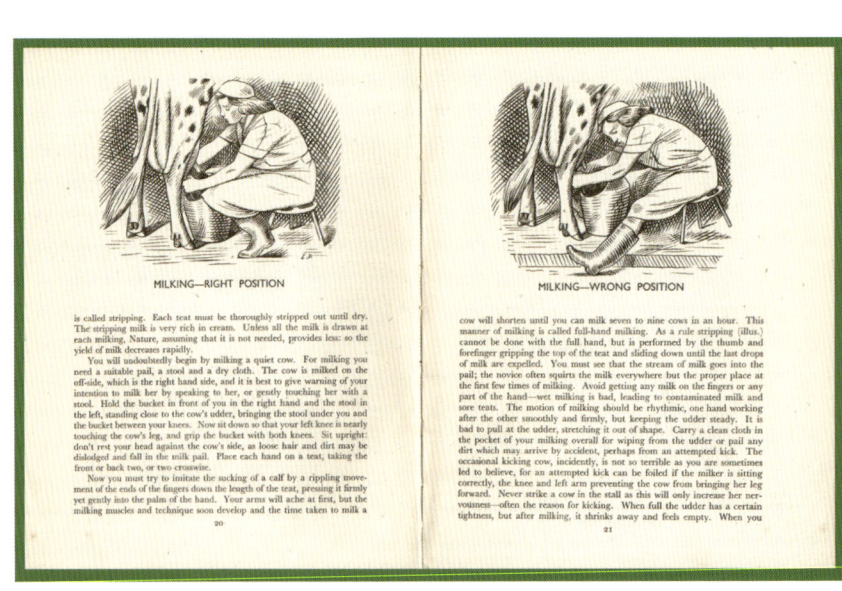

FIG 16
A Book of Farmcraft (Text: Michael Greenhill. Illustrations: Evelyn Dunbar), Longmans, Green & Co., London, was published in 1942. Greenhill was Instructor in Agriculture at Sparsholt Farm Institute, Winchester. *A Book of Farmcraft* was conceived partly as an introductory primer for the Women's Land Army.

Wartime

The Country Girl and the Pail of Milk at Brockley (FIG 11) was a strangely prescient subject in view of Evelyn Dunbar's later work as a war artist. Her career had gone into the doldrums at the end of the 1930s, but the war gave her the opportunity to create paintings and illustrations for which her skills seemed especially well suited, moving out of the garden and into the productive landscape peopled by dungareed volunteers of the Women's Land Army. In addition, she recorded other subjects on 'the home front', such as the fish queue in the high street of Strood (FIG 18), or the knitting circle in a comfortable middle class house (FIG 7).

In these varied subjects, Dunbar's keen observation and skill in drawing and composition paid off in paintings of relatively large scale. They were criticized at the time for being insufficiently dramatic, but that does not diminish their value today, when we have become equally interested in the experiences of non-combatants. Two things stand out from these paintings. One is the didactic quality of many of them, which can be related to the illustrations Dunbar made at Sparsholt Farm Institute for use in Michael Greenhill's *A Book of Farmcraft*, 1942 (FIG 16). From Hesiod to Thomas Tusser, there has been a tradition of using verbal art to convey practical rural wisdom, but the visual element was now added, helping land girls avoid elementary mistakes. *Milking Practice with Artificial Udders*, 1940 (CAT 85), the final version of which is in the Imperial War Museum, shows intense concentration yet has an edge of comedy. The physical and psychological demands of farm work are perhaps most apparent in *A Land Girl and the Bail Bull*, 1945 (Tate, London) (FIG 19), a work that required early rising to catch the atmosphere and action involved, described by her as 'a delicate and dangerous job'. It is a complex composition,and we can see how, in the preparatory drawings (CAT 92-93), the academic method worked to good effect. The study for *Potato Sorting, Berwick* (FIG 20) is in some ways more interesting than the finished work because of the sense of movement in the overlaid outlines of the figures.

Men Stooking and Girls Learning to Stook (CAT 100) is unusual in technique for Dunbar, with a pointilliste treatment of the newly cut field more like Ravilious than her usual work. The catalogue of actions depicted makes the whole process easily understandable, successfully holding the disparate composition together. She did not underestimate the difficulties involved, writing in October 1943, when the terms under which her appointment as a War Artist might be continued were under discussion. 'Anyone who paints a figure composition knows that it takes often much longer than 10 days.' The Advisory Committee acknowledged her need for more time.

The drawings for *Joseph's Dream* (CAT 104-106) also give us the chance to see Dunbar's process at work in a different kind of subject, as they move from what is essentially illustration to become the basis for a haunting metaphysical painting, a foretaste of her more imaginative post-war work.

A.P.

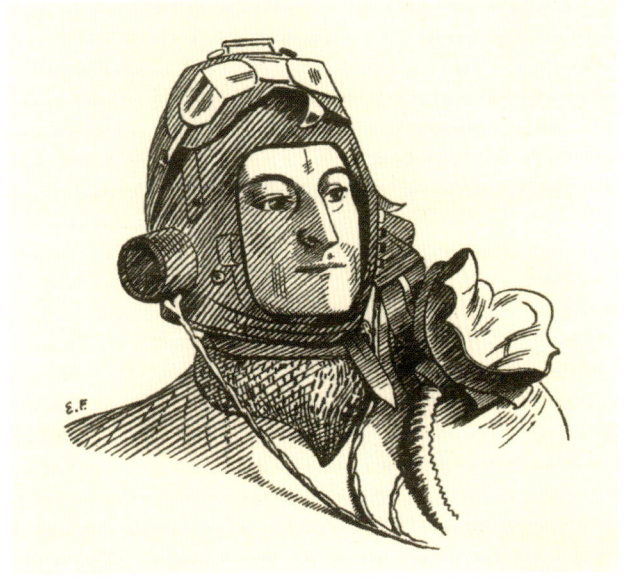

FIG 17
Evelyn Dunbar's Christmas card for 1944.
Private collection.

CAT 86 [HMO 280]
Portrait of Flying Officer Roger Folley, RAFVR.
Signed and dated 'Evelyn Dunbar Jan '44'.
Pencil and black chalk on paper,
17 ¾ x 17 in. (45 x 43 cm)

Dunbar met Roger Folley, a horticultural economist, at Sparsholt Farm Institute, where he worked before the war. They were married in 1942. Folley, on leave from France when this was drawn, served in the RAF as a Navigator.

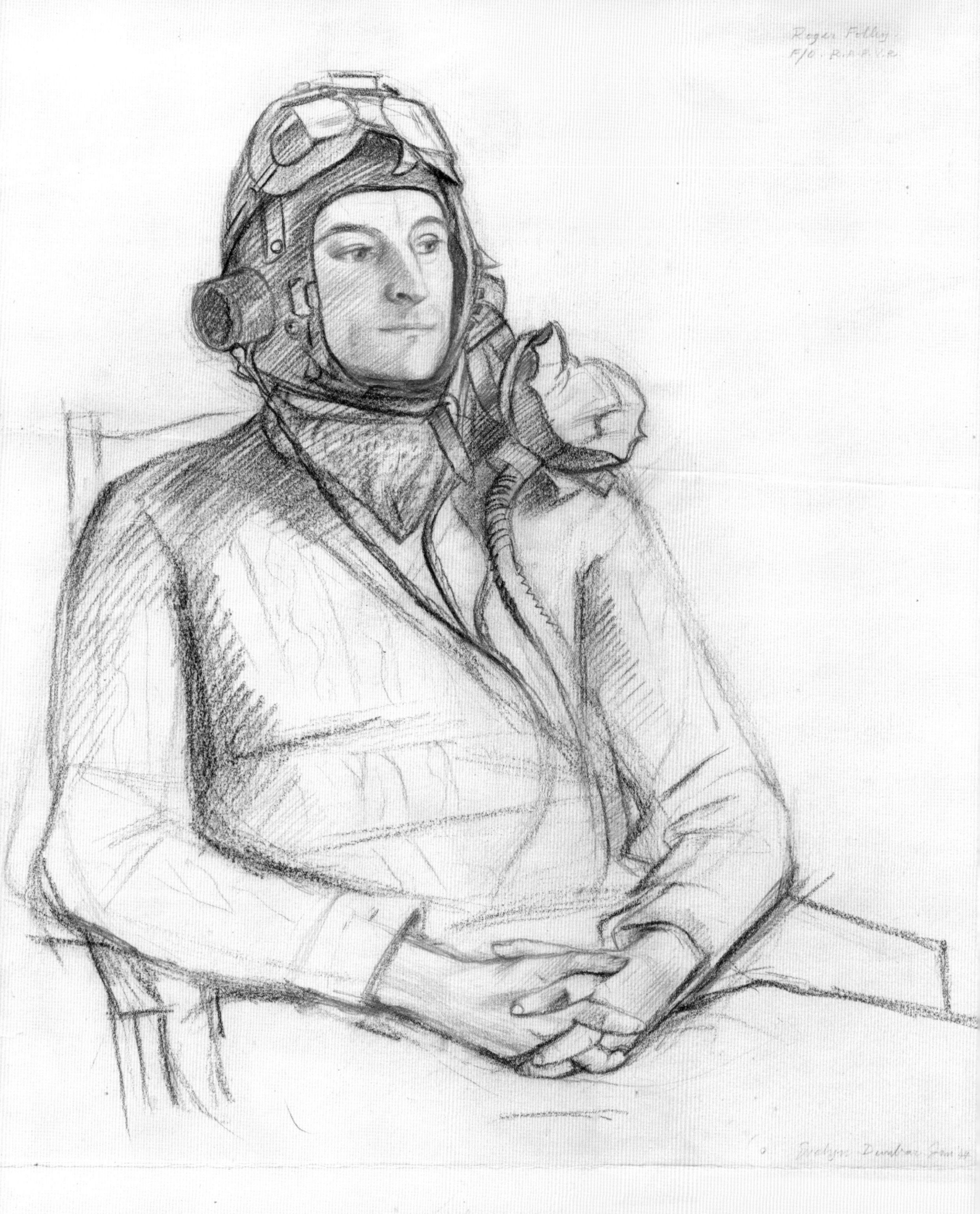

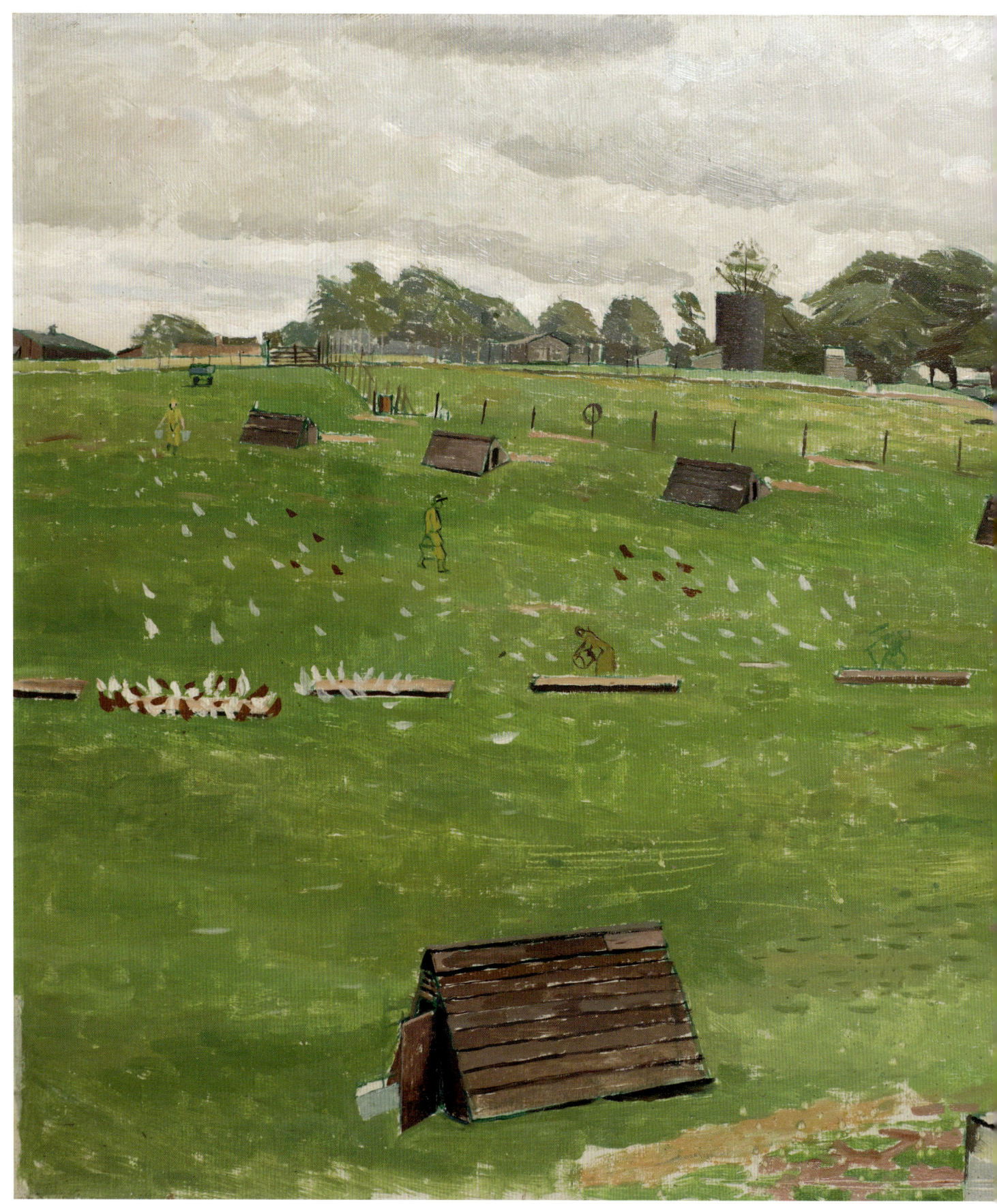

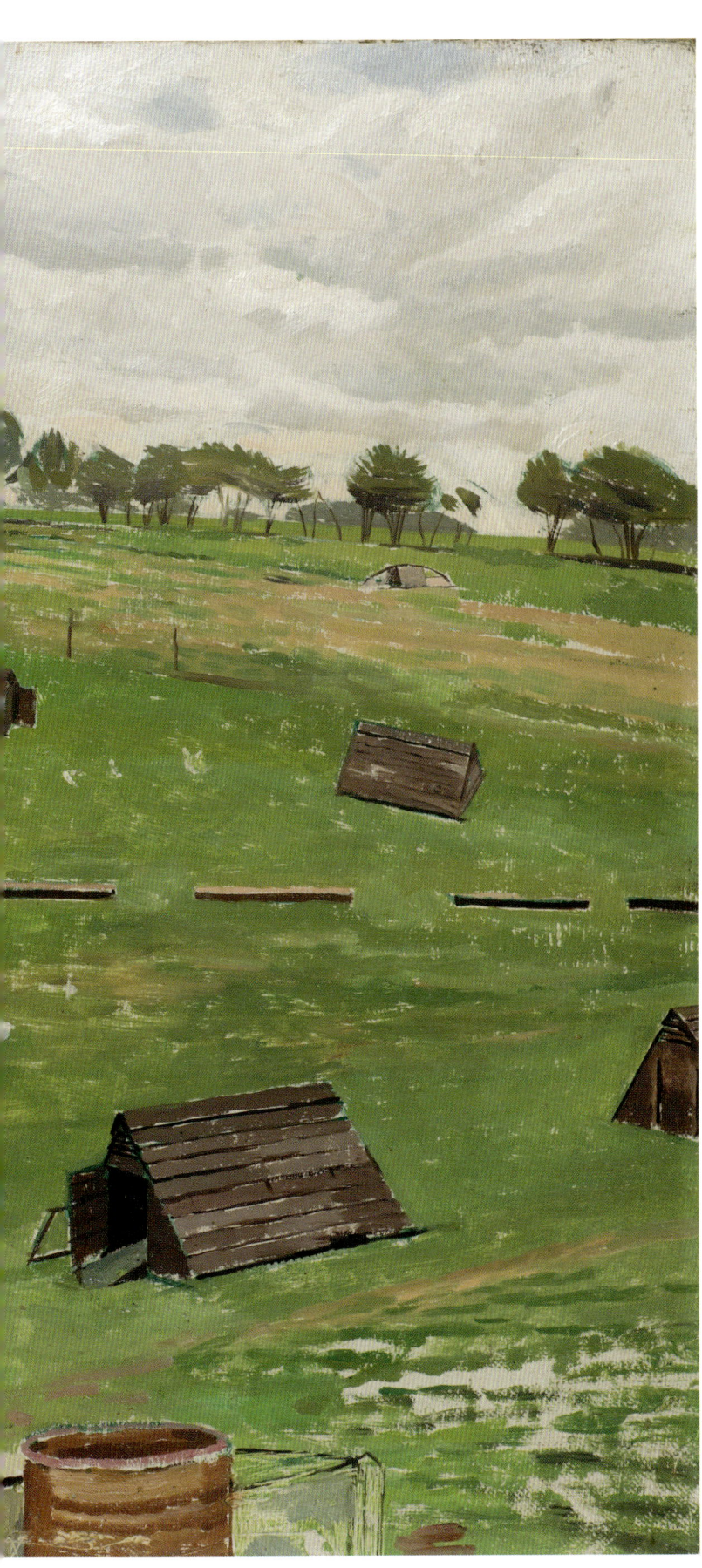

CAT 87 [HMO 781]
Night Arks at Sparsholt, 1940,
Oil on canvas, 18 x 24 in. (45.7 x 61 cm)

Night arks are fox-proof poultry roosts. The Sparsholt flocks are being fed by uniformed Land Girls. This painting was never submitted to the War Artists' Advisory Council possibly on account of the lack of prominence given to the Land Girls.

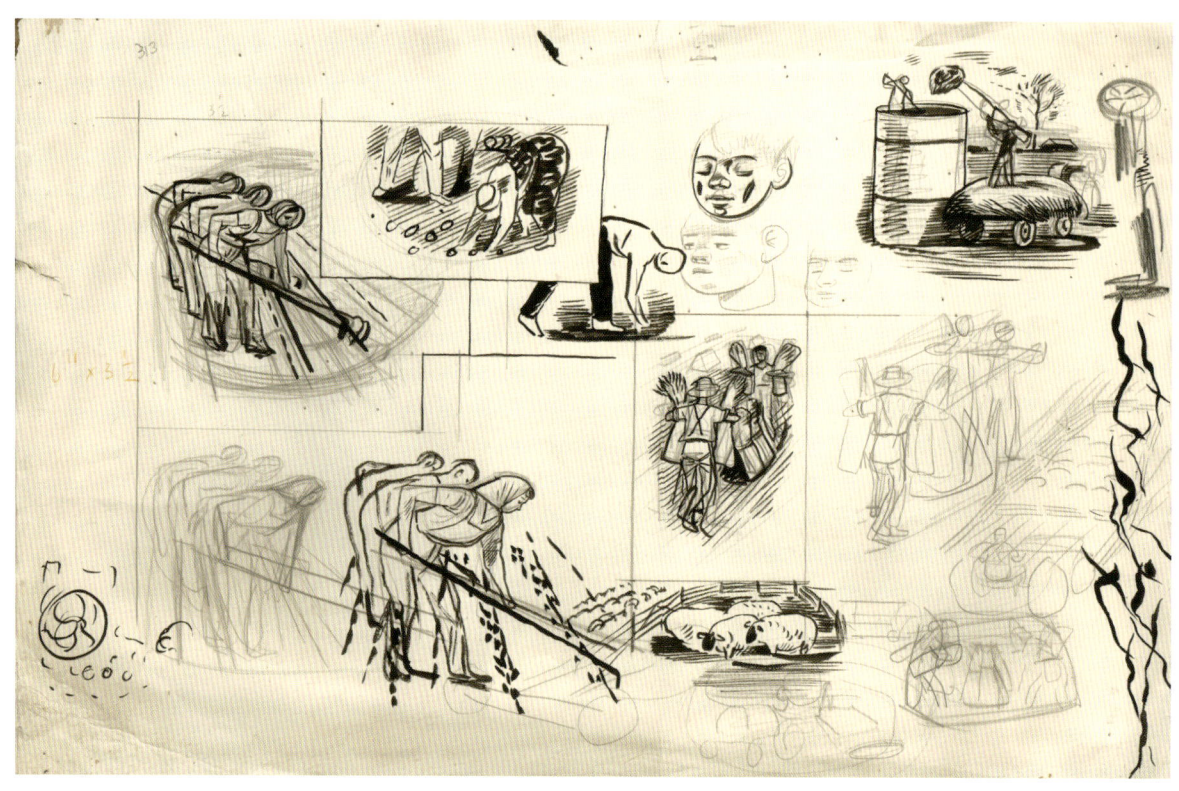

CAT 88 [HMO 313] Studies for various Women's Land Army activities, 1943,
Pencil and pen & ink on paper, 15 x 22 in. (38 x 55.5 cm)

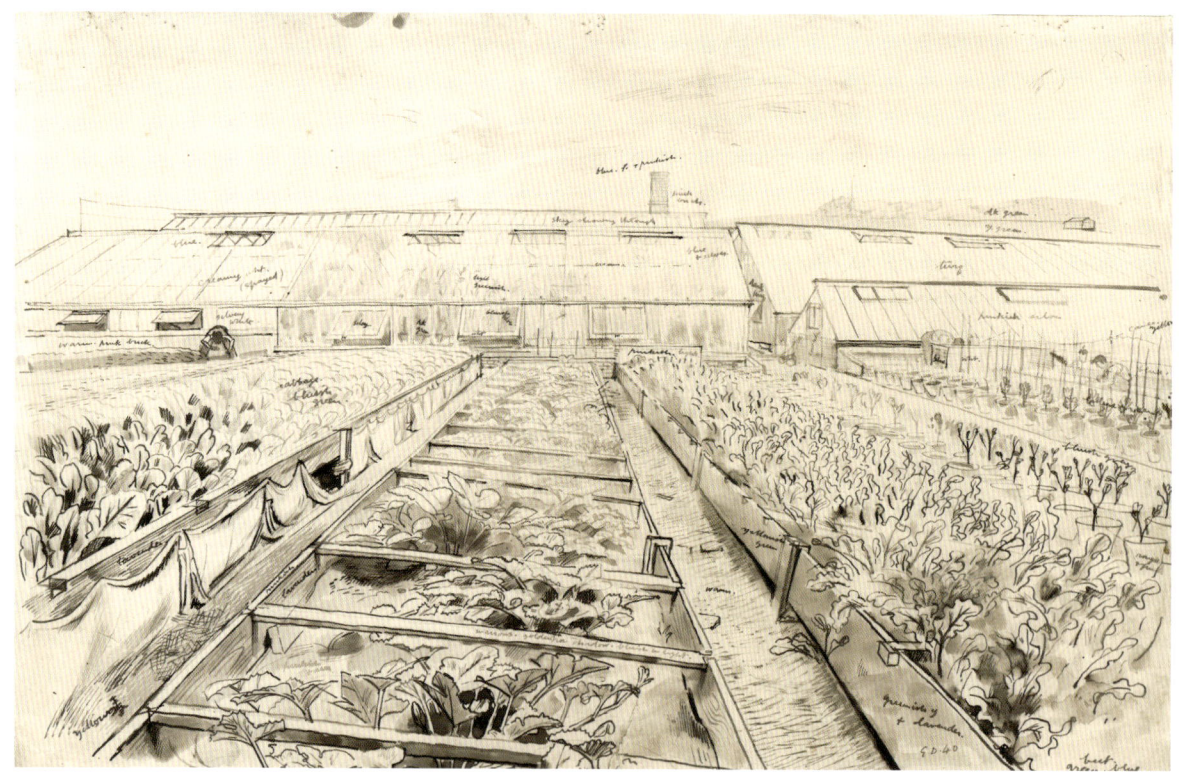

CAT 89 [HMO 425] Study for vegetable cultivation at Sparsholt Farm Institute, 1940,
Signed with initials and dated: 'E.D 40', inscribed with colour notes
Pen & ink on paper, 15 x 22 in. (38 x 56 cm)

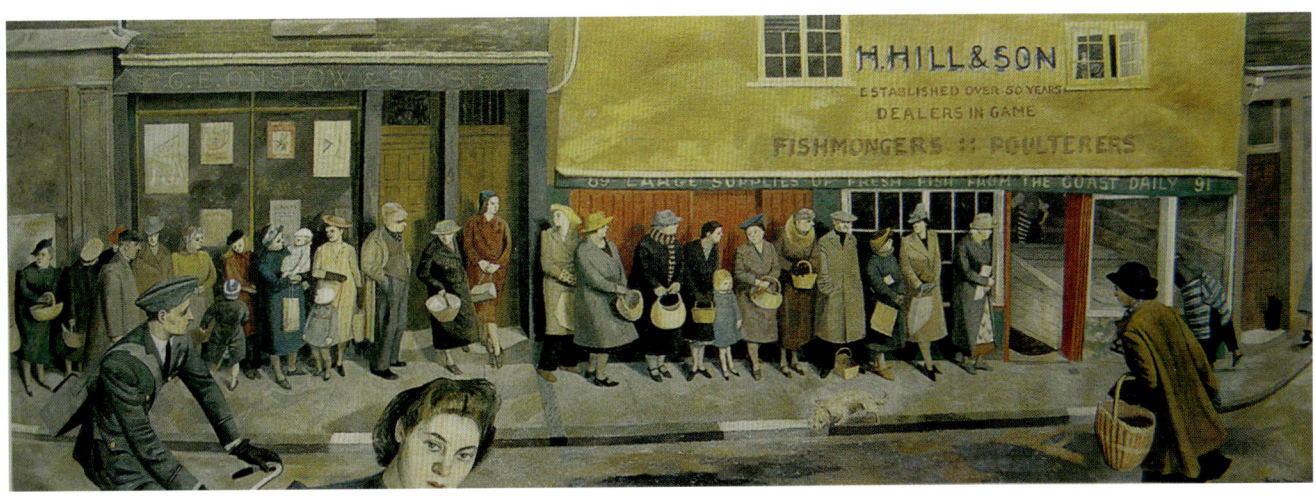

FIG 18 *The Queue at the Fish Shop*, 1942, 24 ½ x 71 ½ in. (62 x 182 cm)
Collection: IWM (Imperial War Museums)

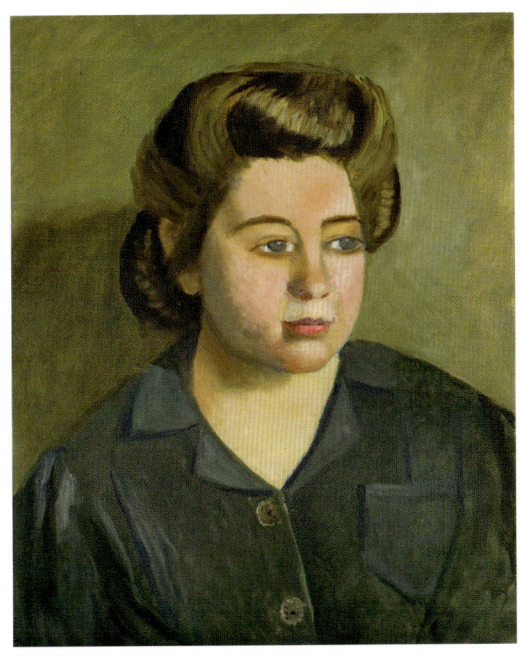

CAT 90 [HMO 773]
Study for an unidentified WAAF (Women's Auxiliary Air Force) member, painted at RAF South Cerney, Gloucestershire, in July 1944. Oil on canvas, 18 x 14 in. (45.7 x 35.6 cm)

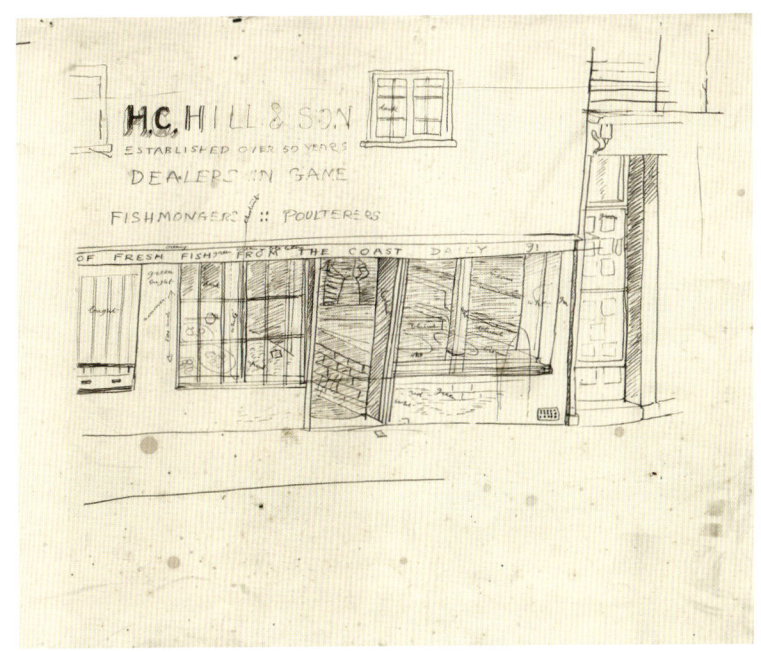

CAT 91 [HMO 584]
Study for the background to *The Queue at the Fish Shop*, 1942, Pen & ink on paper, 15 x 22 in. (38 x 56 cm)

Inscribed with colour notes. Hill's fish shop in Strood High Street, reduced from its actual height and elongated laterally to accommodate the queue eventually to be painted in front of it.

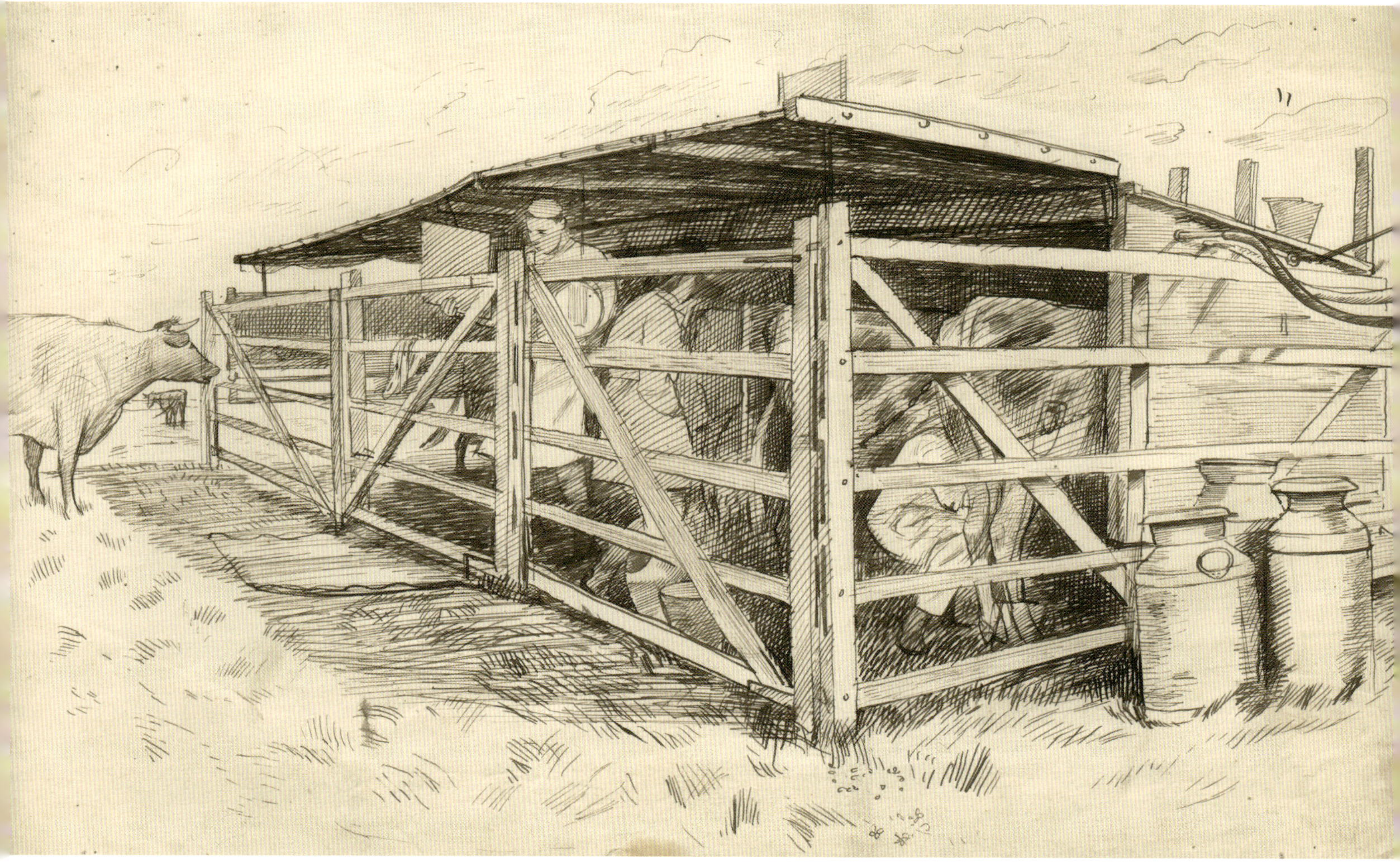

CAT 92

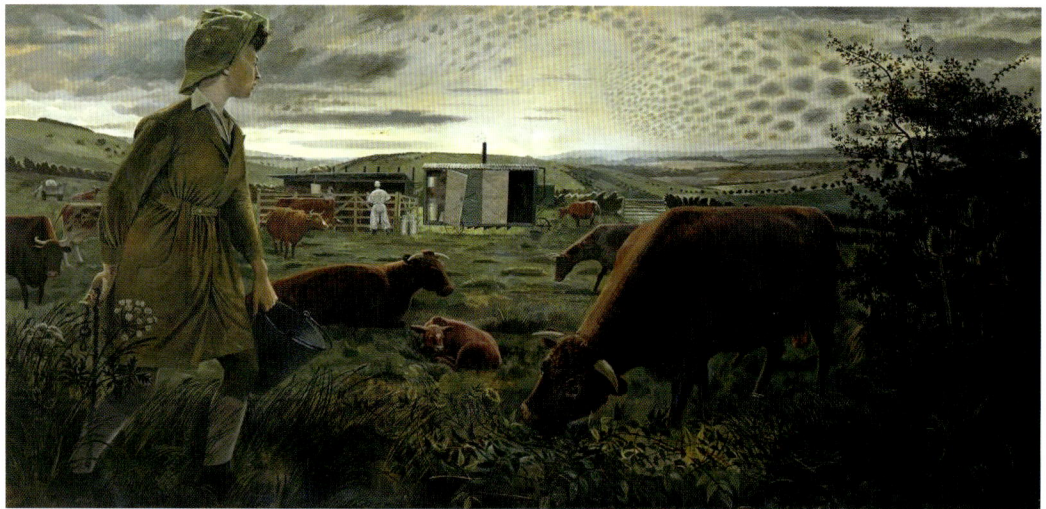

FIG 19 *A Land Girl and the Bail Bull*, 1945, oil on canvas, 36 x 72 in. (91.4 x 182.9 cm)
Collection: © Tate, London 2015

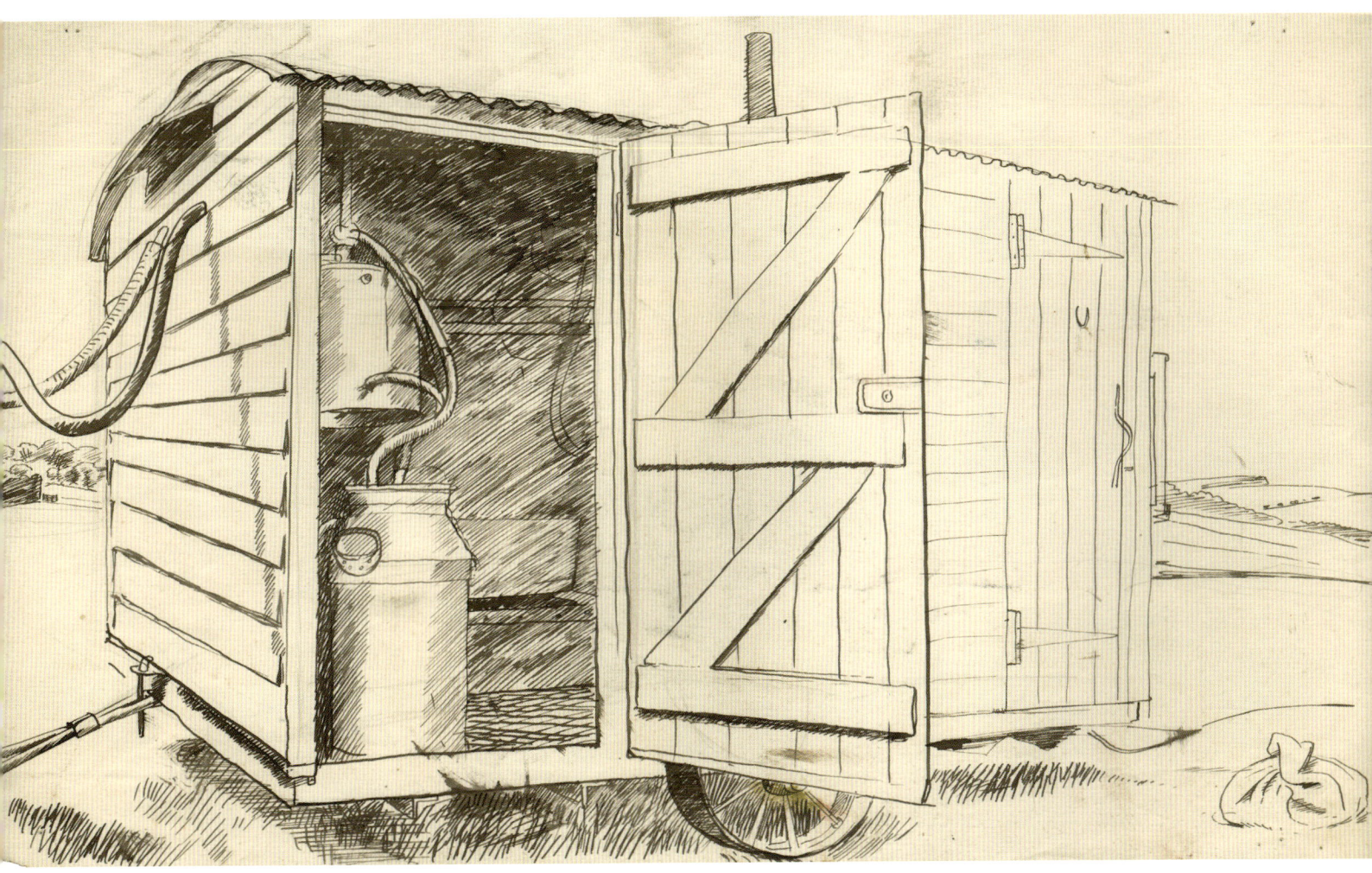

CAT 93

CAT 92 [HMO 39] Study at Sparsholt Farm Institute for *A Land Girl and the Bail Bull*, 1944,
Pen & ink on paper, 13 x 21 in. (33 x 53 cm)

Part of the 'bail' is the set of temporary milking stalls erected in the field to avoid having to drive the herd to the dairy. A white-coated figure records the milk yield on a board, Land Girls are urging cows into the stalls and fitting milking apparatus.

CAT 93 [HMO 40] Study at Sparsholt Farm Institute for *A Land Girl and the Bail Bull*, 1944,
Pen & ink on paper, 13 x 21 in. (33 x 53 cm)

'Bail' was originally an Australian term for a movable wooden halter or series of halters in which to tether cows in order to milk them in the field rather than drive them to the dairy. Its meaning was extended to include the wheeled shed housing the milking pump engines.

Overleaf: CAT 94 *Singling Turnips*, 1943,
Oil on canvas, 20 x 30 in. (50.8 x 76.2 cm)
Private collection courtesy England & Co Gallery, London

This study of teams of Land Girls thinning turnips was painted in the spring of 1943. The setting is a farm in Berwickshire, close to where the artist's husband Roger Folley was undergoing night-fighter navigation training at RAF Charter Hall. Curiously, the order of singling is in direct contradiction to that illustrated by Dunbar in *A Book of Farmcraft*.

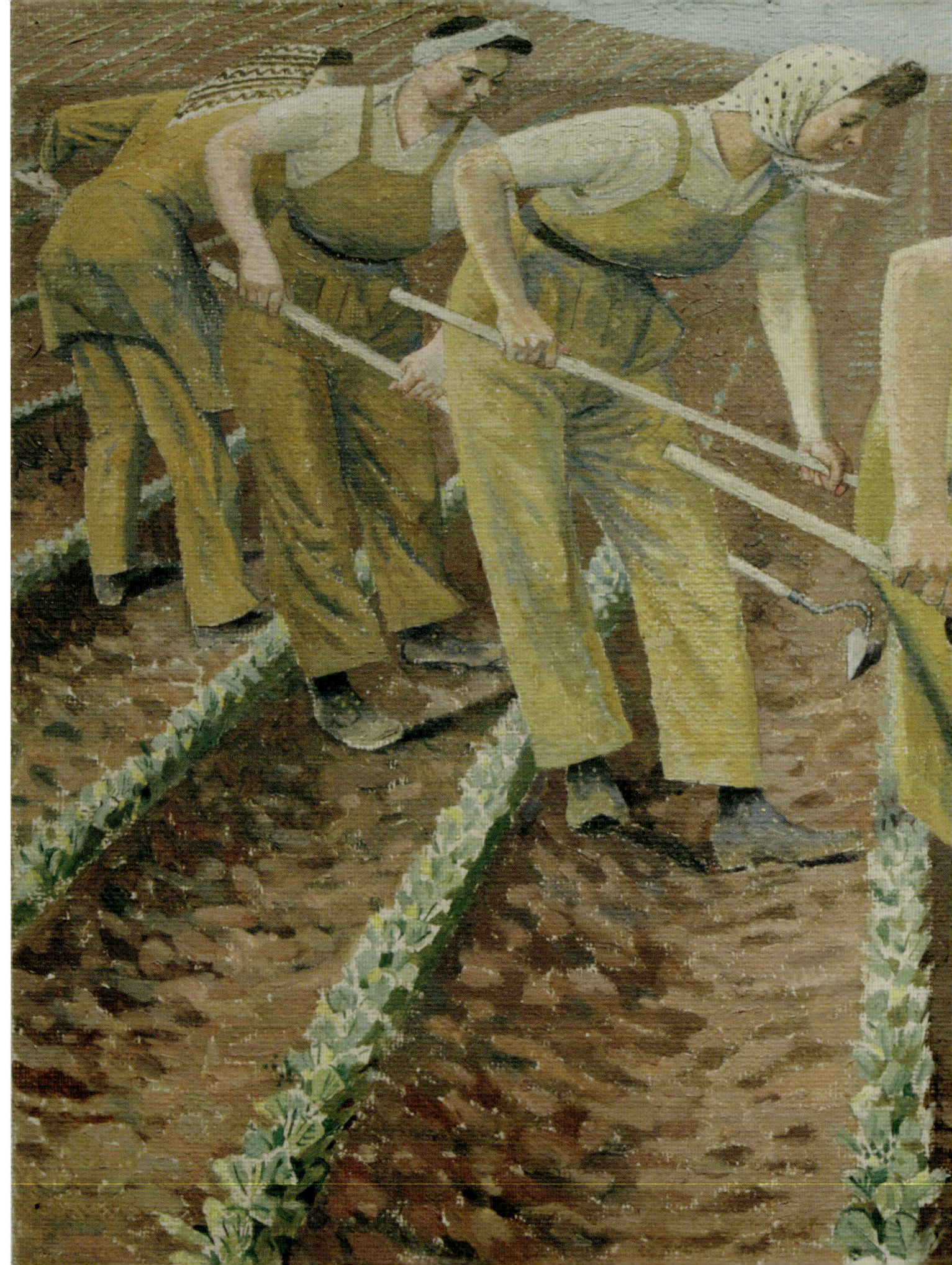

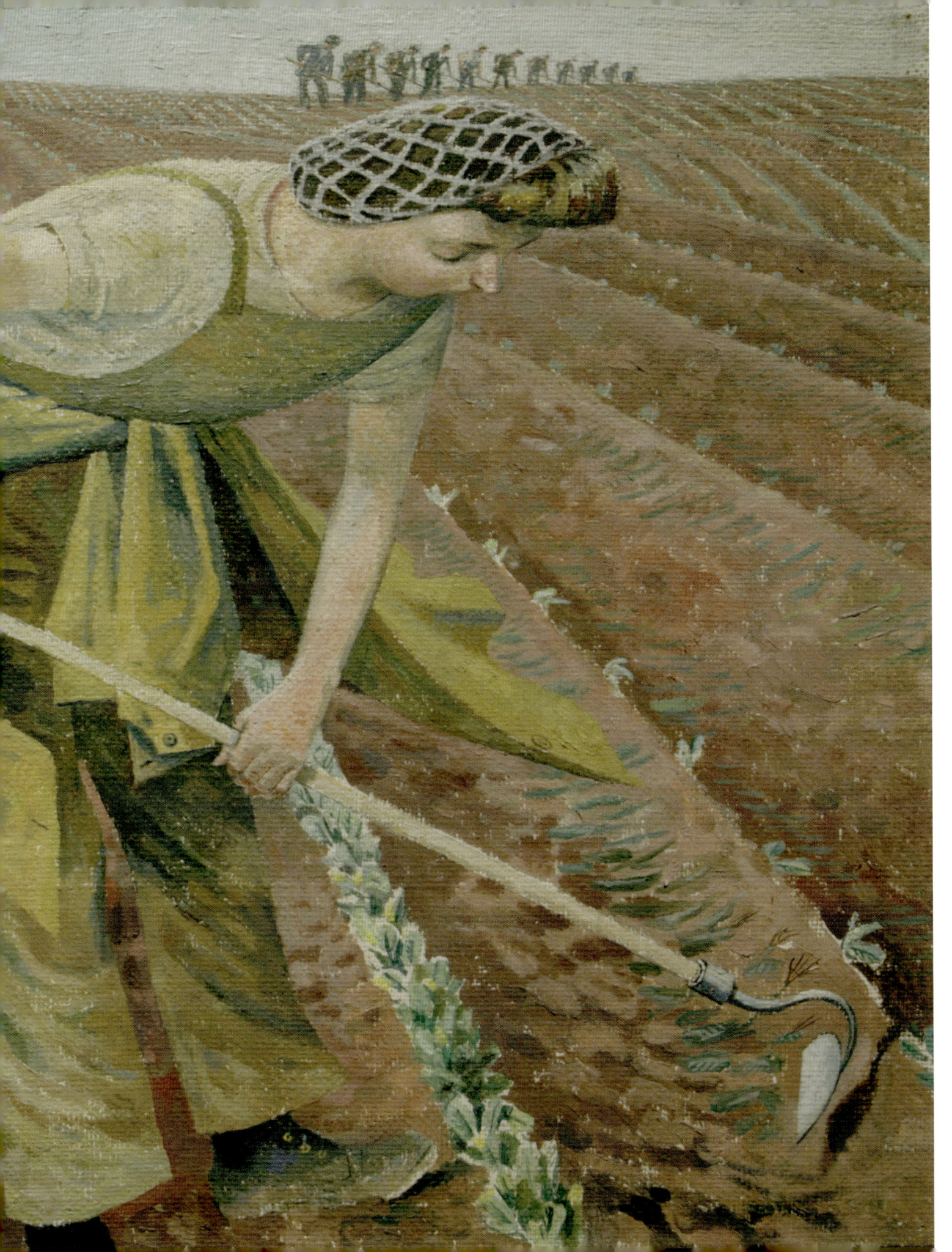

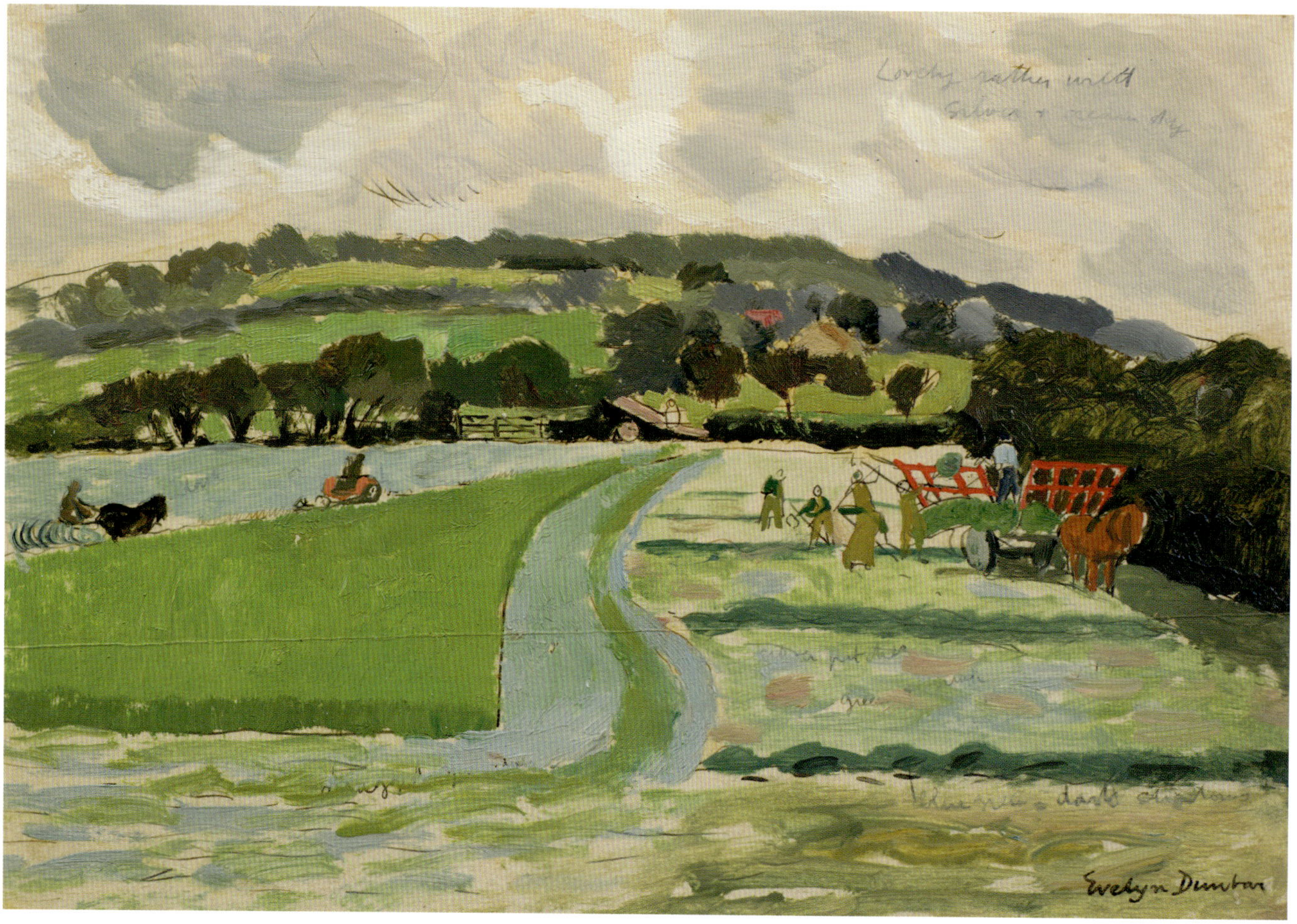

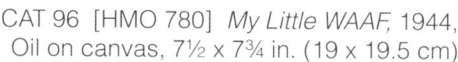

CAT 95 [HMO 558] Study for haymaking with Land Girls in training at Sparsholt Farm Institute,
Inscribed with colour notes. Studio stamp "Evelyn Dunbar". 1940,
Oil on canvas, 9 x 12½ in. (23 x 31 cm)

The completed version of this, if one ever existed, was not submitted to the War Artists' Advisory Committee because too little prominence was given to the Land Girls.

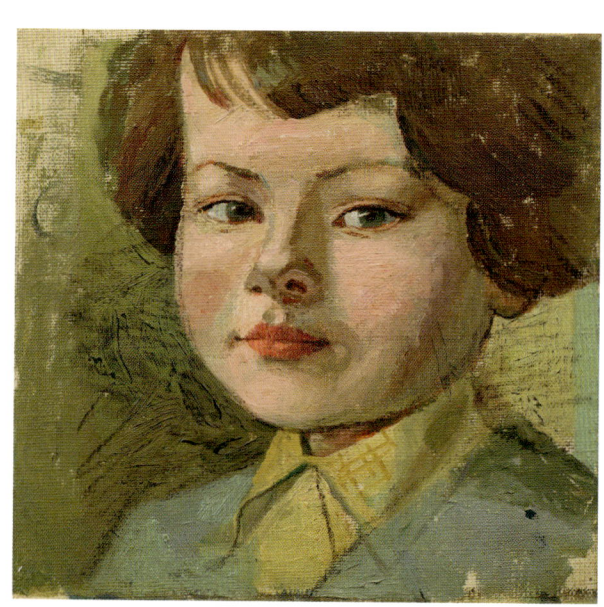

CAT 96 [HMO 780] *My Little WAAF*, 1944,
Oil on canvas, 7½ x 7¾ in. (19 x 19.5 cm)

'My little WAAF' was how Dunbar referred to a particularly baby-faced member of the Women's Auxiliary Air Force, a service whose activities she was sent to paint at RAF South Cerney, Gloucestershire, in July 1944. Her identity is unknown.

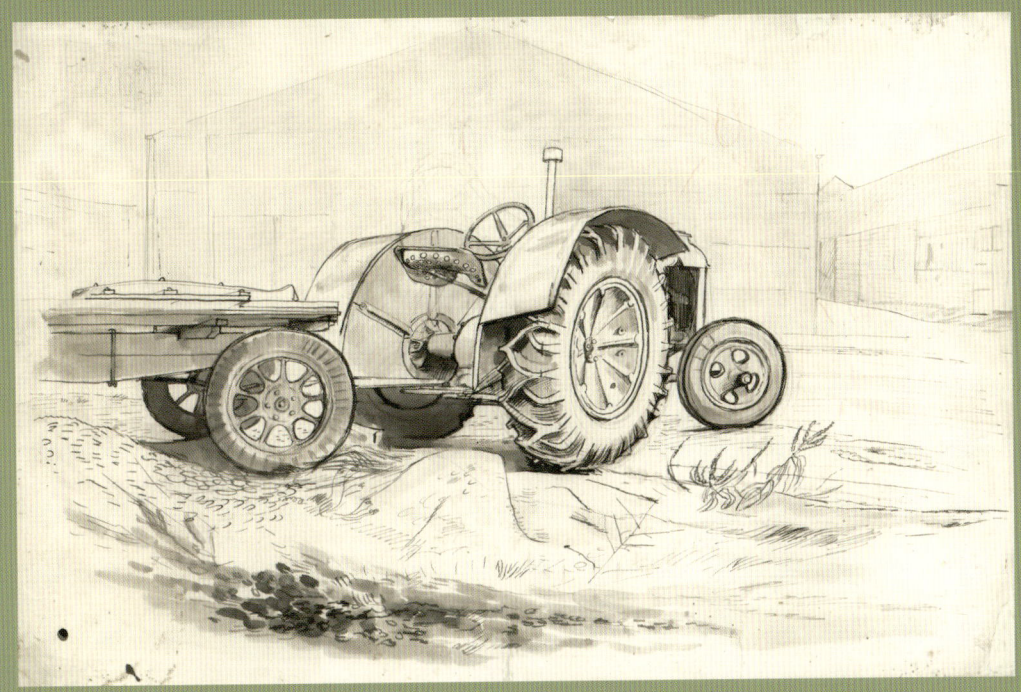

CAT 97 [HMO 281] Study of tractor at Sparsholt Farm Institute, 1940.
Pen & ink and wash on paper. 15 x 22 in. (38 x 56 cm)

Sparsholt, near Winchester, was a training centre for recruits to the Women's Land Army. Posted to Sparsholt as a war artist in the summer of 1940, Dunbar recorded many of her war images there.

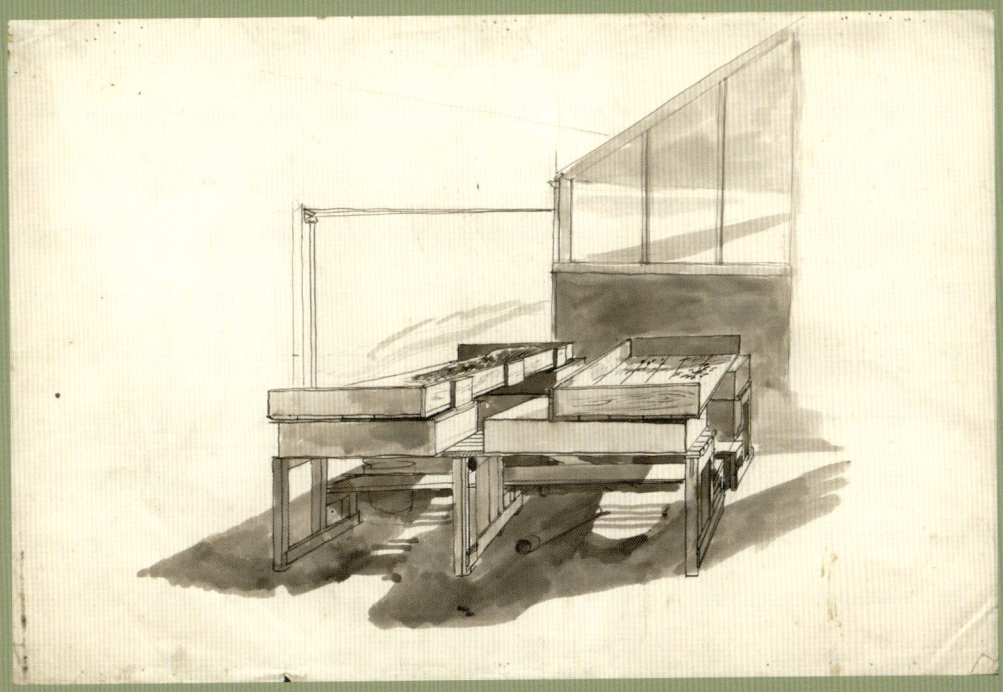

CAT 98 [HMO 562] Seed potato trays at Sparsholt Farm Institute, the Hampshire training centre for Women's Land Army recruits. 1940,
Pencil, pen & ink and wash on paper, 15 x 22 in. (38 x 56 cm)

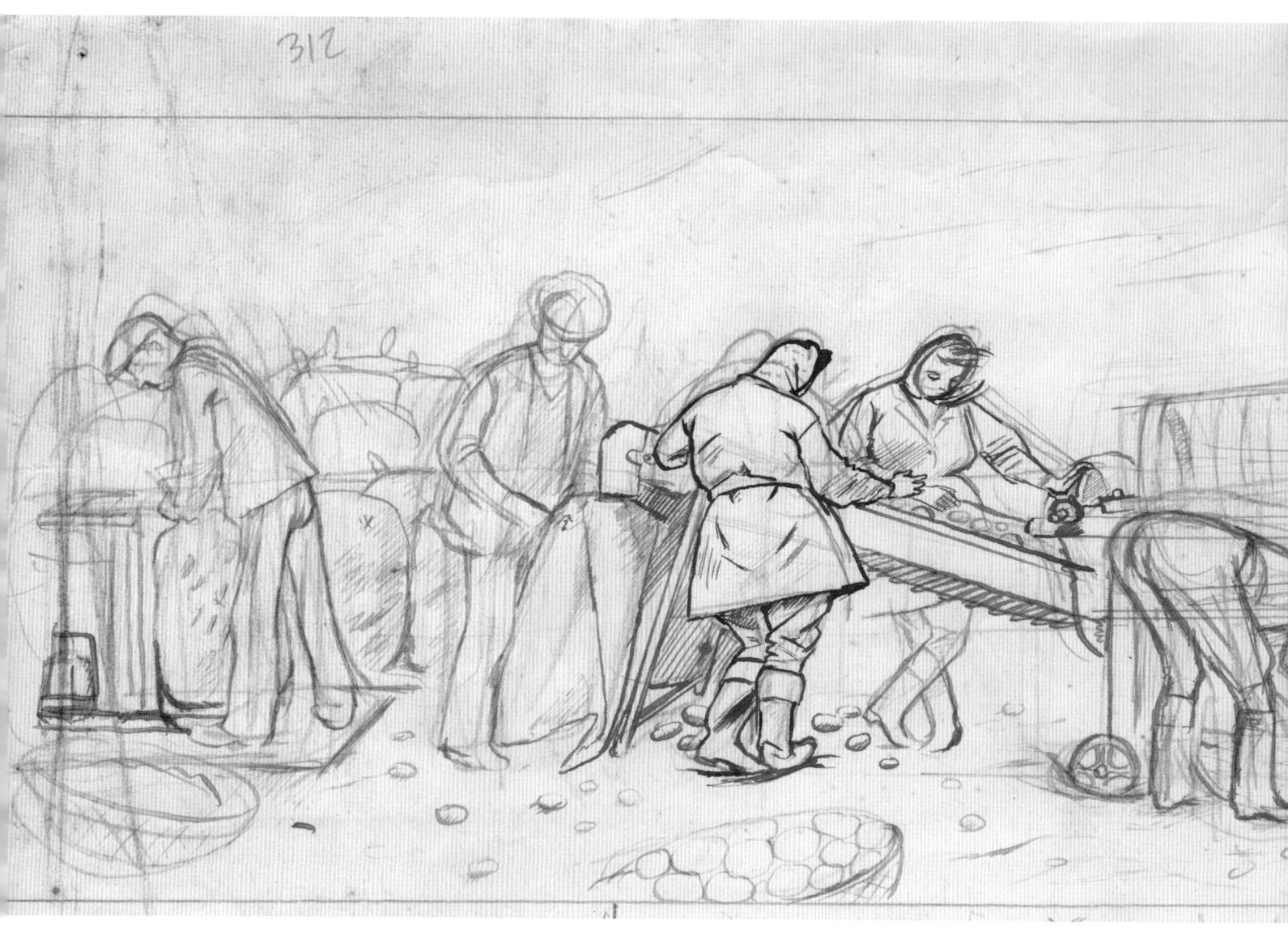

CAT 99 [HMO 312] Top half of sketch for *Potato Sorting, Berwick*, 1943
Pencil and pen & ink on paper, 14 x 19 ½ in. (35 x 49 cm)

A sketch for one of the four paintings for the War Artists' Advisory Committee which Dunbar completed in the summer of 1943 while in the Scottish Borders. The farm is probably Edington Mains, between Berwick on Tweed and Greenlaw, not far from RAF Charter Hall where her husband Roger Folley was undergoing his final training as a night fighter navigator.

FIG 20 *Potato Sorting, Berwick*, 1943,
Oil on canvas, 12 x 30 in. (30.7 x 76.2 cm)
Collection: Manchester Art Gallery

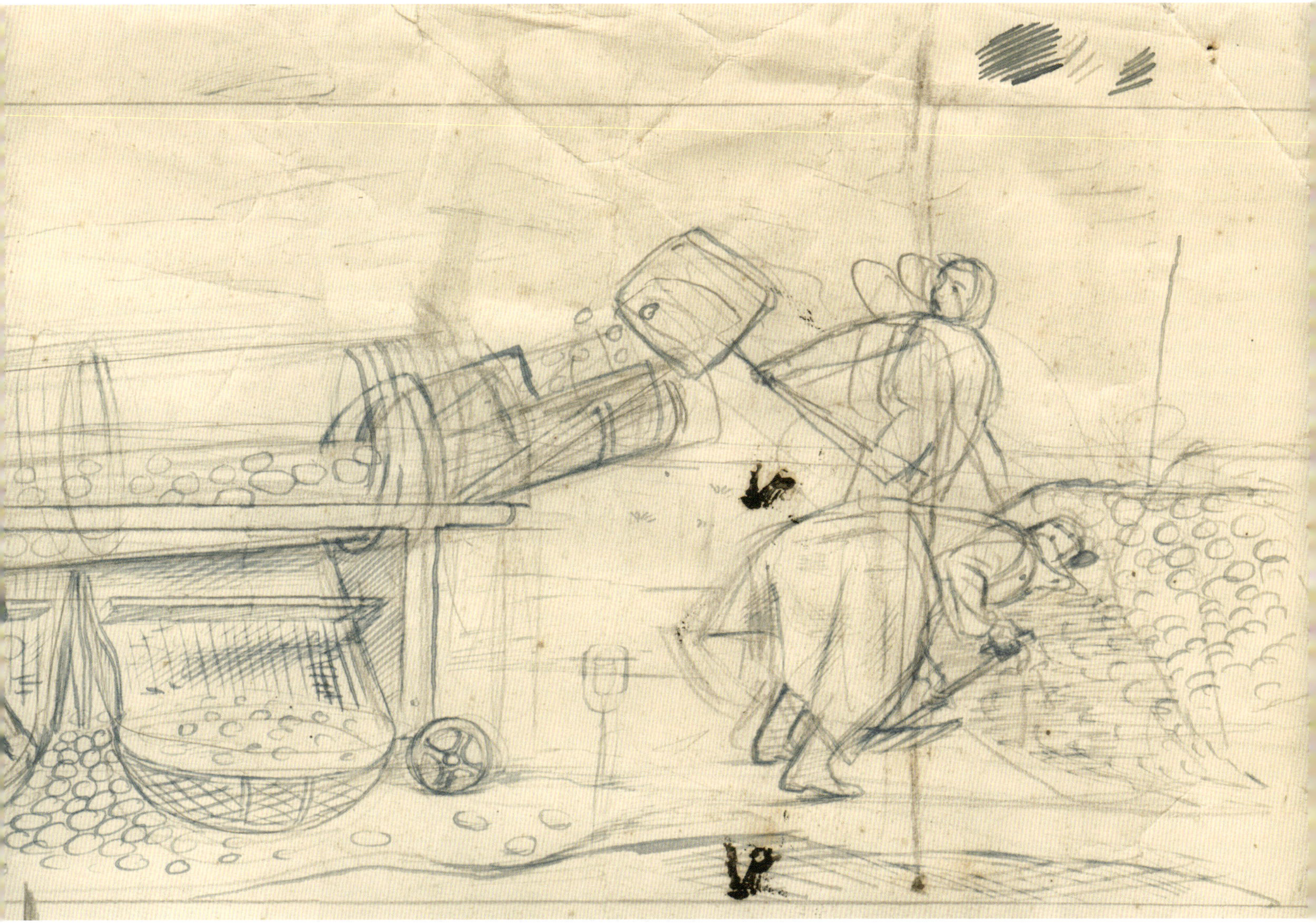

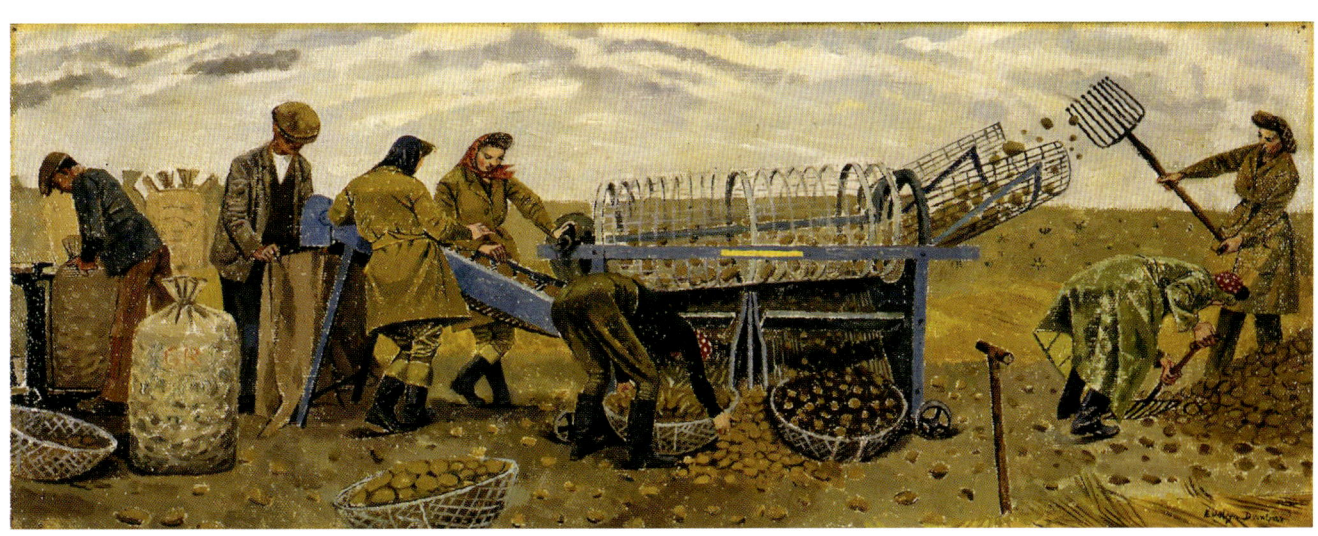

145

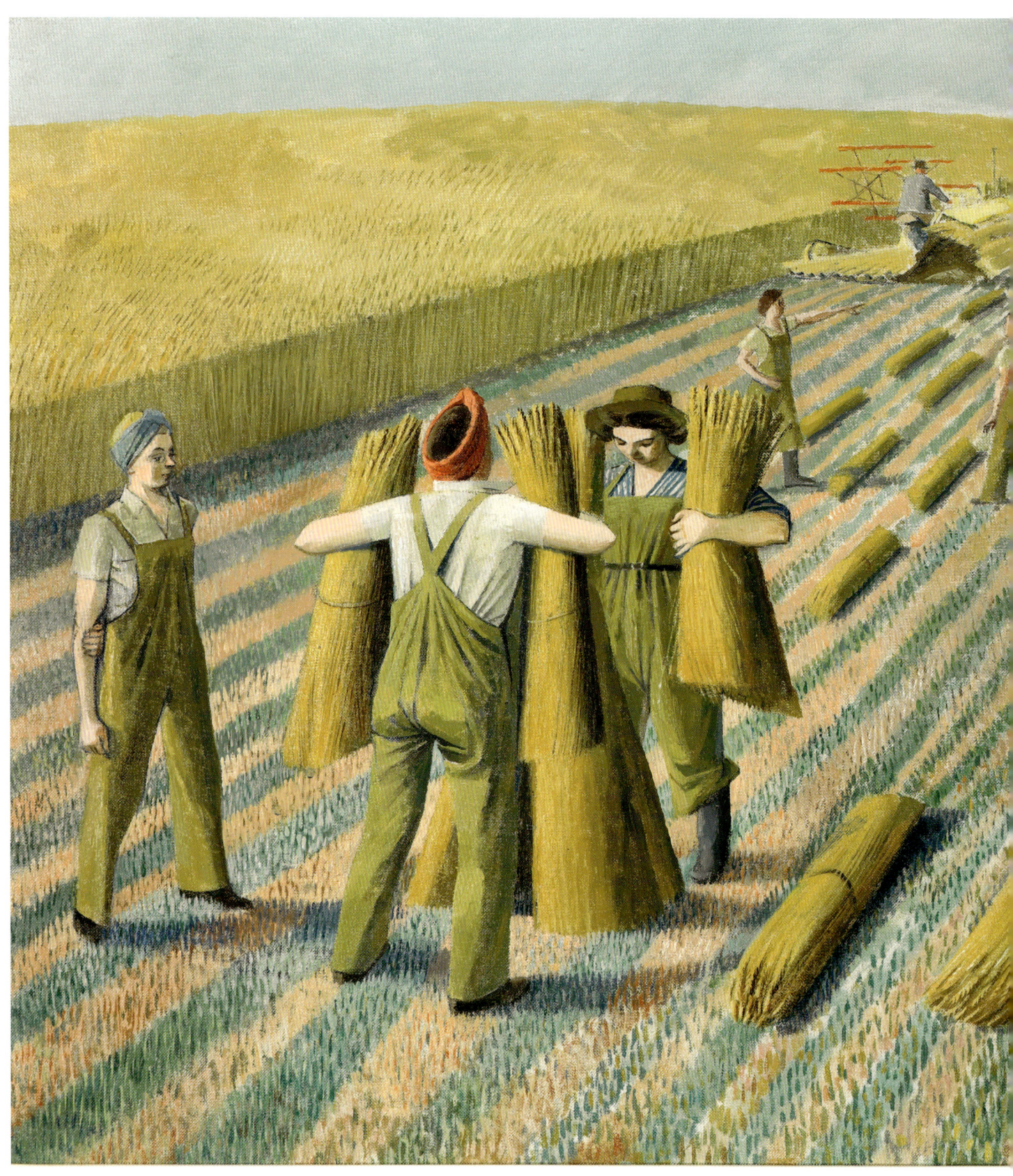

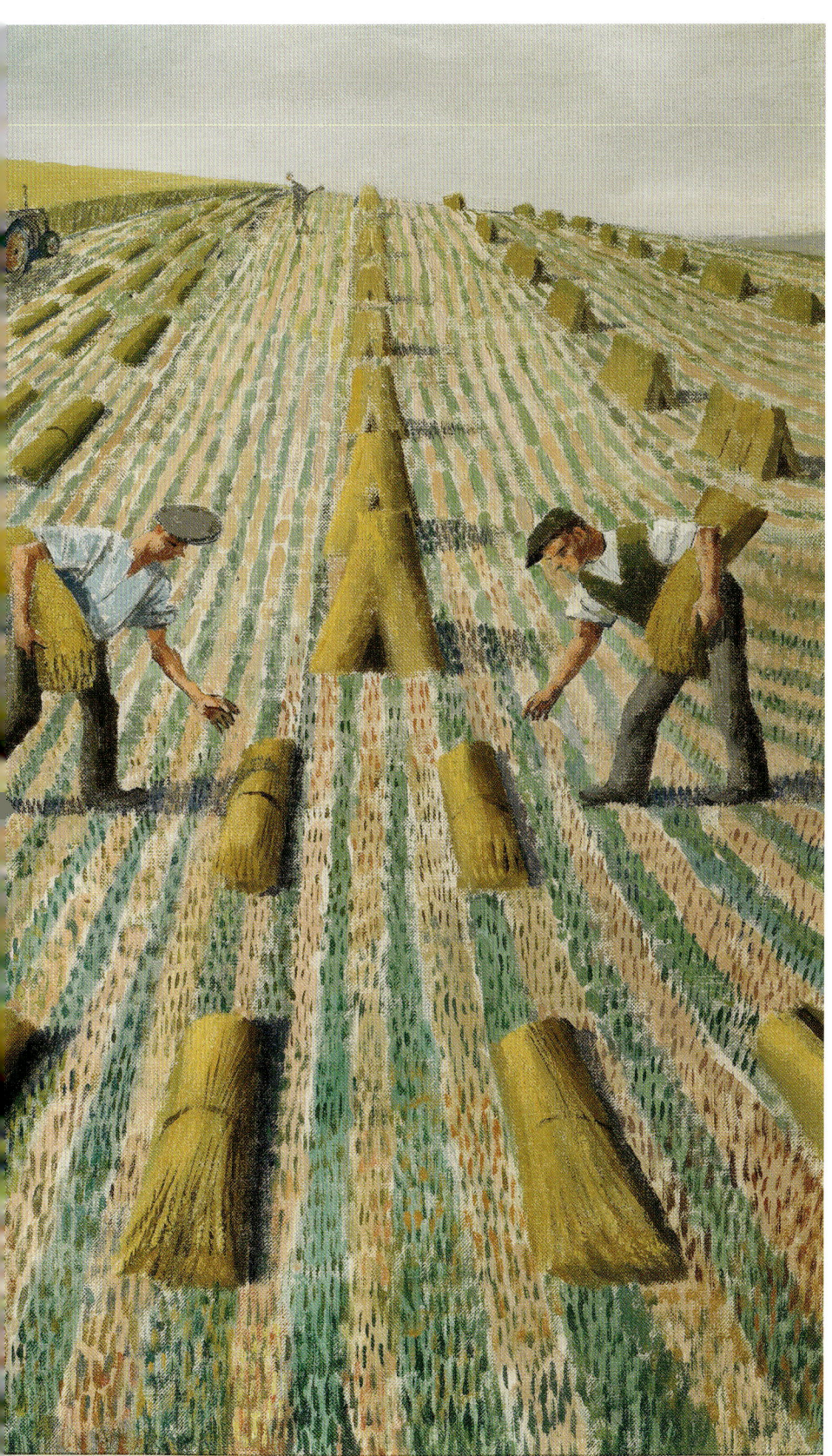

CAT 100
Men Stooking and Girls Learning to Stook,
Oil on canvas, 29 ½ x 19 in. (75 x 49 cm)

Painted in the long, hot summer of 1940, when so often the skies of southern England were criss-crossed with vapour trails from RAF Spitfires and Hurricanes defending the homeland from Hitler's Luftwaffe in the Battle of Britain. Dunbar's magnificent canvas is a great reassurance: the harvest is on the way to being in, the wheatfield is limitless, like the Creator's generosity. The Land Girls of the Women's Land Army are marching with the men, so to speak, and have turned the task of stooking into a military operation, mirroring the men on the right. Note the man in the distance with a shotgun, maybe hoping to supplement his meat ration with a unwary rabbit. Note also the way the Land Girl on the left, who appears to be giving the orders, has tucked her left hand behind her back into the crook of her right elbow in a definitely non-military pose, a touch of a gentle feminist subversion often observable in Dunbar's war paintings. Strangely this painting was not accepted by the War Artists' Advisory Committee.

Provenance: Margaret Iliffe, née Goodwin
Private collection
Photograph: Richard Valencia
© Christopher Campbell-Howes

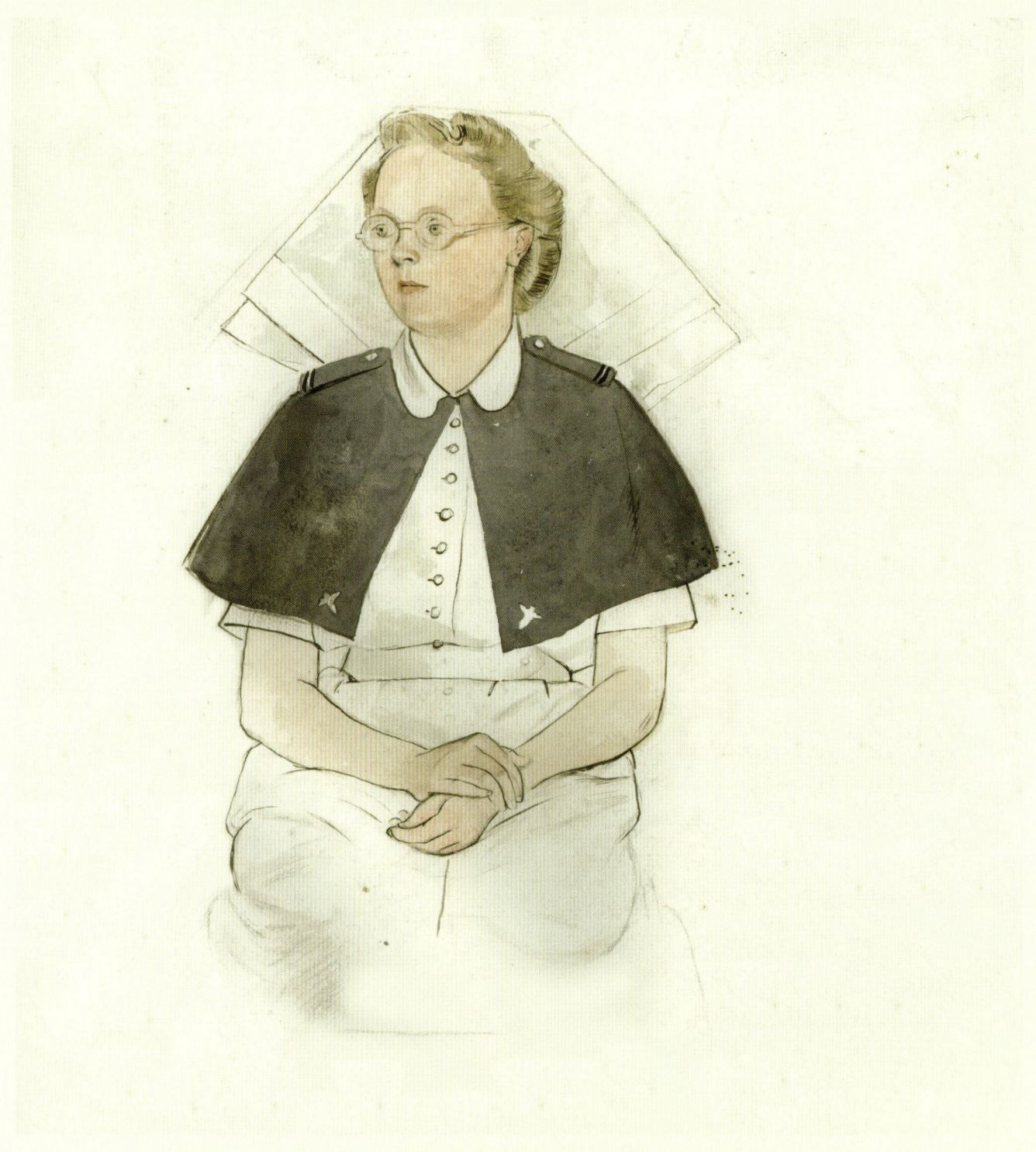

CAT 101 [HMO 55] Senior Sister PMRAF Nursing Service, 1944,
Labelled on verso 'RAF South Cerney 1944' in Roger Folley's handwriting,
Pencil and watercolour on paper, 22½ x 15½ in. (58 x 39.5 cm)

We do not know the identity of this Senior Sister, and it may be that while she was at RAF South Cerney recording the activities of women's uniformed services Dunbar was directed not to name her subjects. All that we know is that her subject is wearing a white ward dress underneath an RAF blue tippet adorned at the points with the Rod of Aesculapius, the classical healing wand emblem of medical services, and shoulder boards showing her rank and status. One of the artist's rare watercolours for the War Artists' Advisory Committee, it was never submitted.

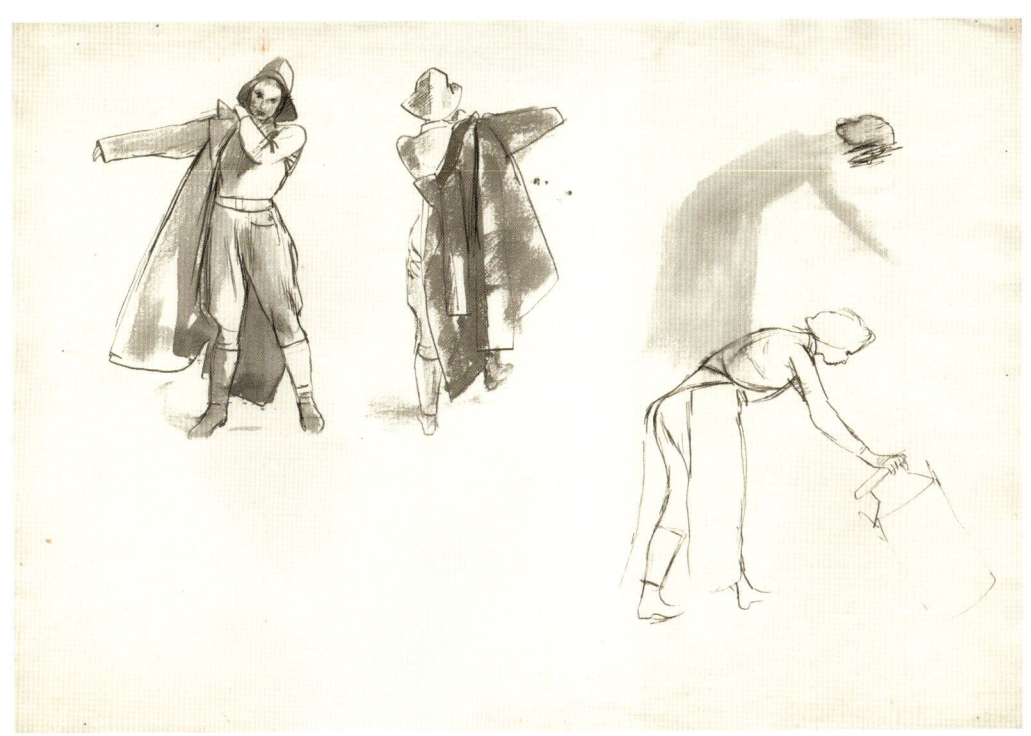

CAT 102 [HMO 709] Study of Land Girls in training
Pen & ink and wash, 15 ¼ x 22 ½ in. (39 x 57.5 cm)

Trainees at Sparsholt Farm Institute putting on wet weather gear and rolling a milk churn.

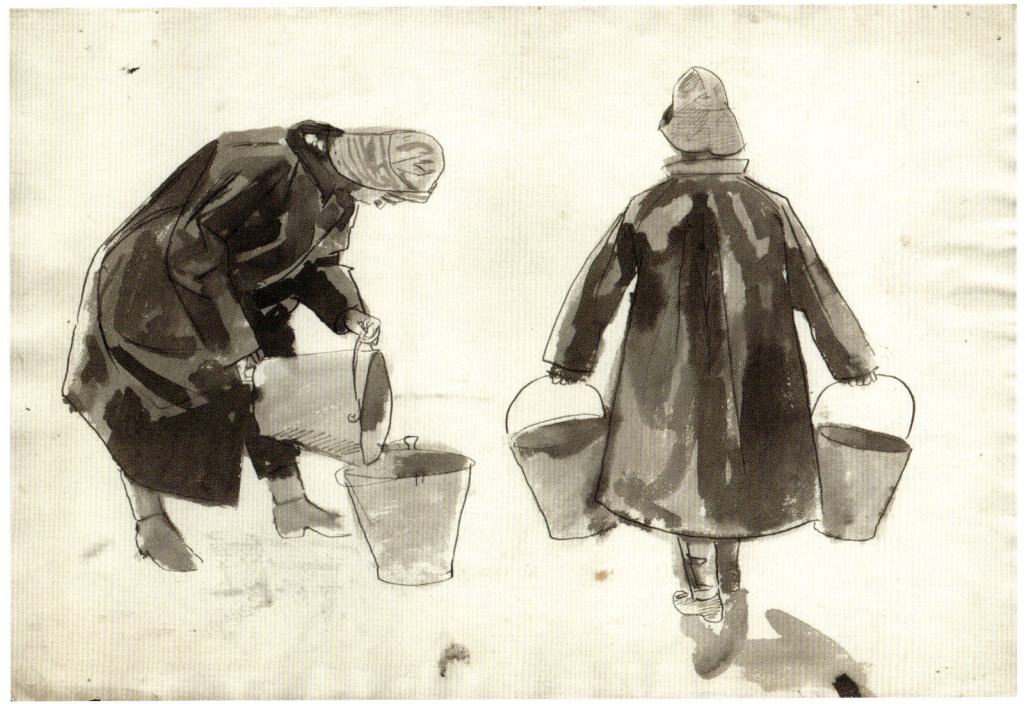

CAT 103 [HMO 52] Study of two trainee Land Girls, c.1940,
Pen & ink and wash on paper, 15 ¼ x 22 ½ in. (39 x 57.5 cm)

This study depicts two Land Girls with oilskins and sou'westers filling and carrying pig-swill or hen-mash pails, probably at Sparsholt Farm Institute, Winchester.

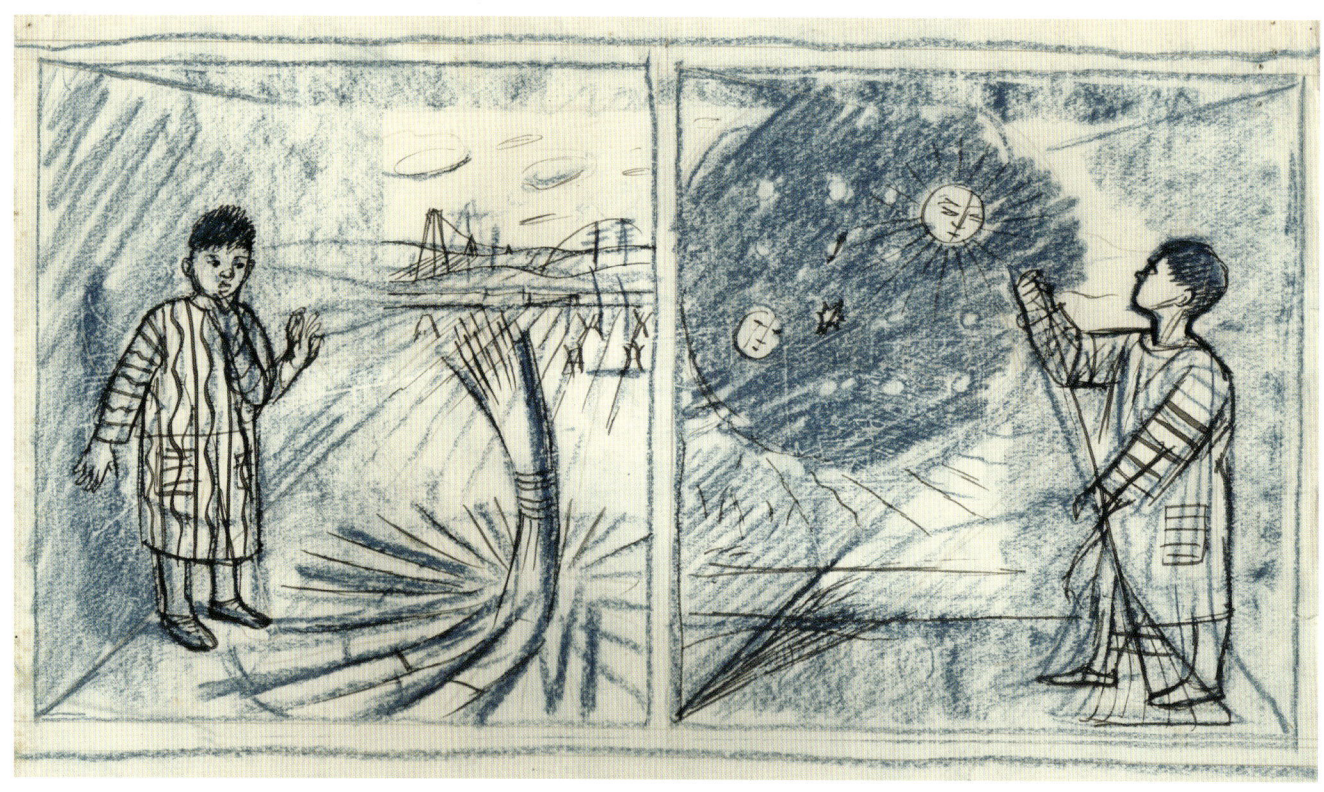

CAT 104 [HMO 122] An early study for *Joseph's Dream*, 1938,
Pencil, pen & ink and blue chalk on paper, 10 ½ x 15 in. (26.5 x 38.2 cm)

The story of Joseph and his dreams, as told in Genesis, chapter 37ff., was Dunbar's inspiration for several paintings illustrating his life. The left panel of the diptych shows sheaves of corn bowing down in homage before Joseph. The right panel depicts the sun, moon and stars, representing Joseph's parents and brothers, doing the same.

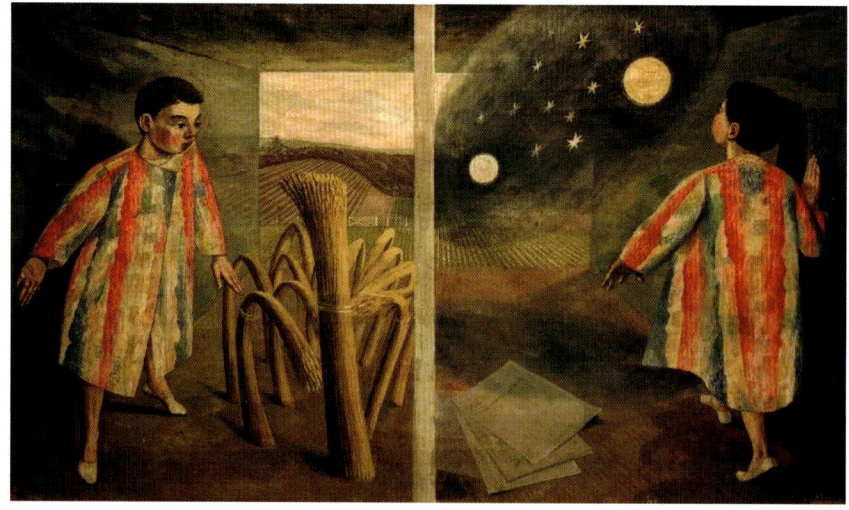

FIG 21 *Joseph's Dream*, 1938-42, oil on canvas, 18 x 30 in. (46 x 76 cm)
Collection of Original Works for Children, Cambridgeshire Education Department

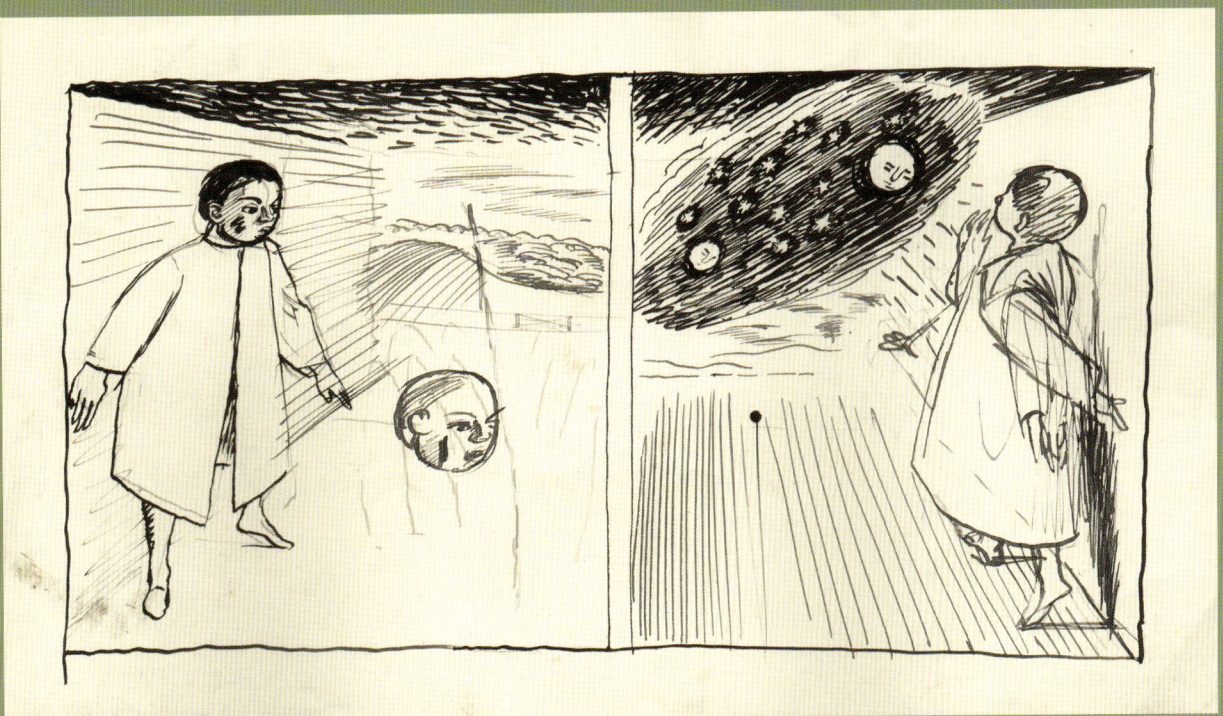

CAT 105 [HMO 279a] Preliminary study for the diptych *Joseph's Dream*, 1938,
Pen & ink on paper, 15 x 22 in. (38 x 55.5 cm)

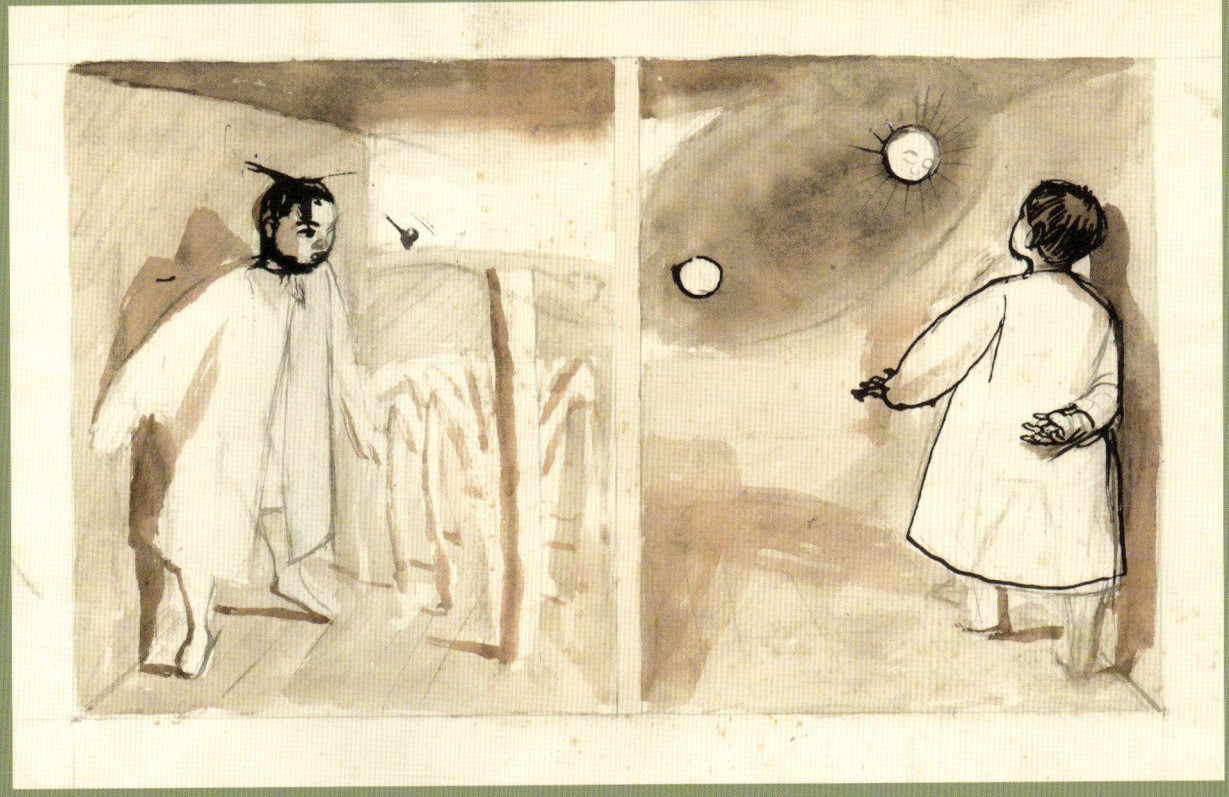

CAT 106 [HMO 279b] Preliminary study for the diptych *Joseph's Dream*, 1938,
Pencil, pen & ink and wash on paper, 15 x 22 in. (38 x 55.5 cm)

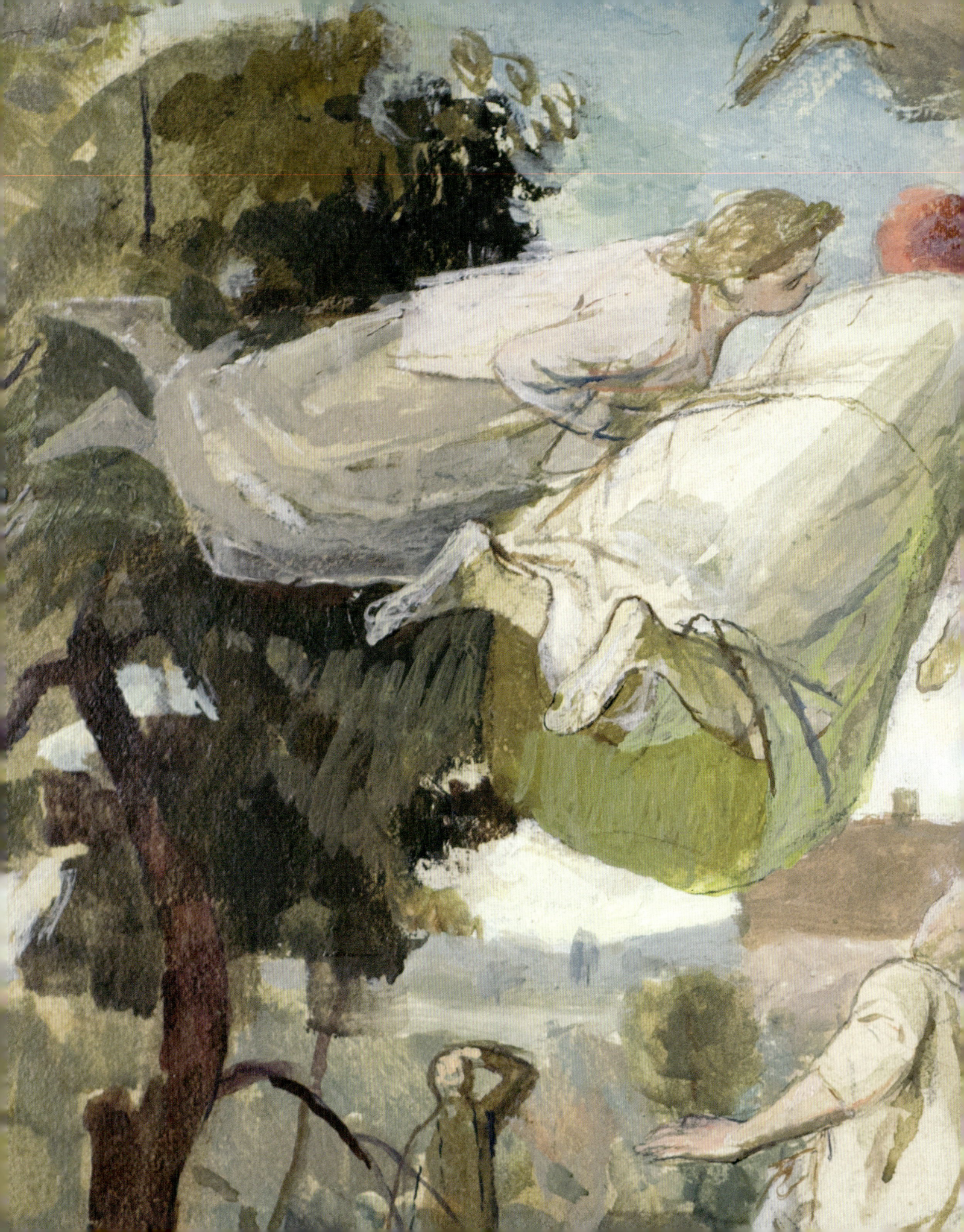

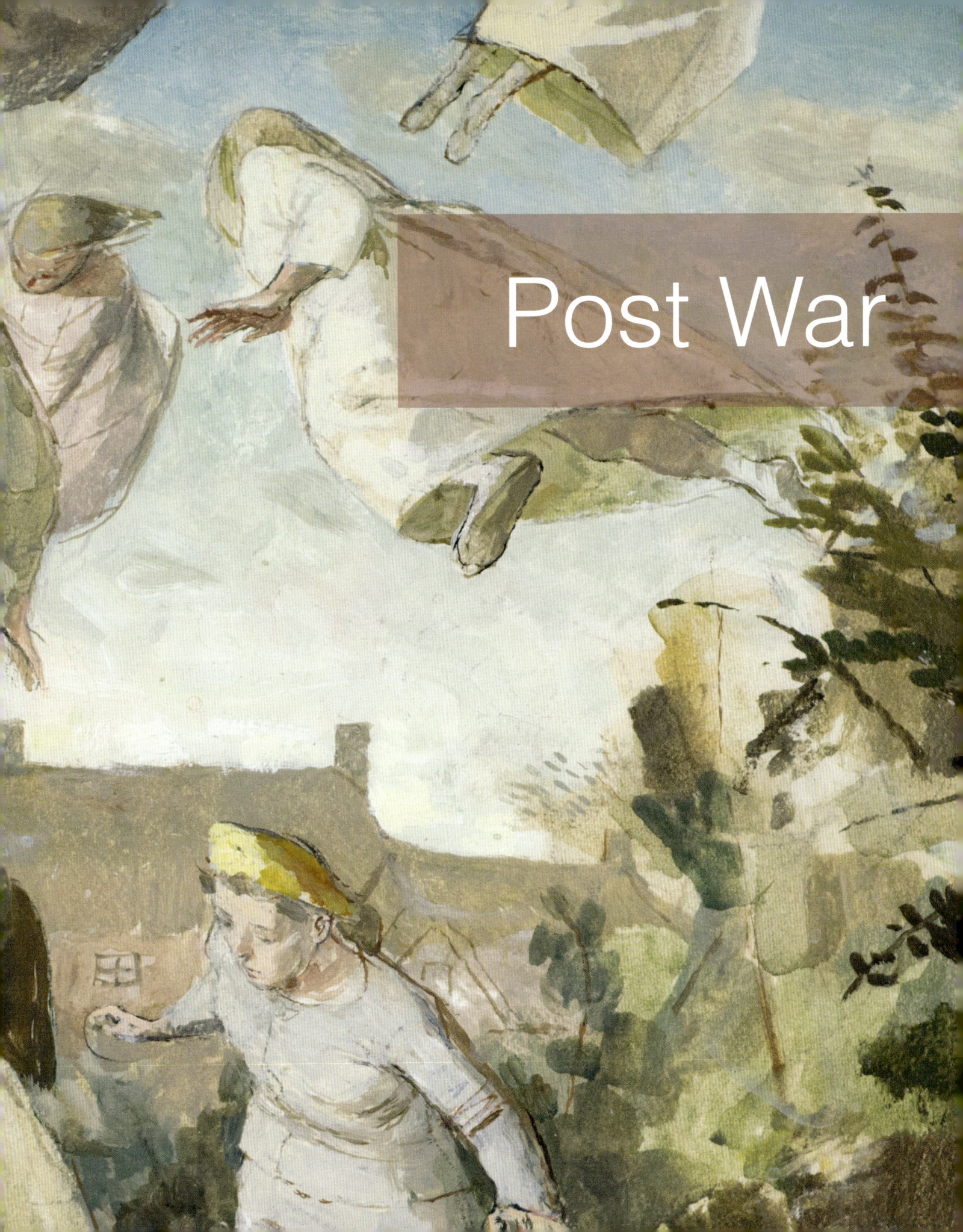
Post War

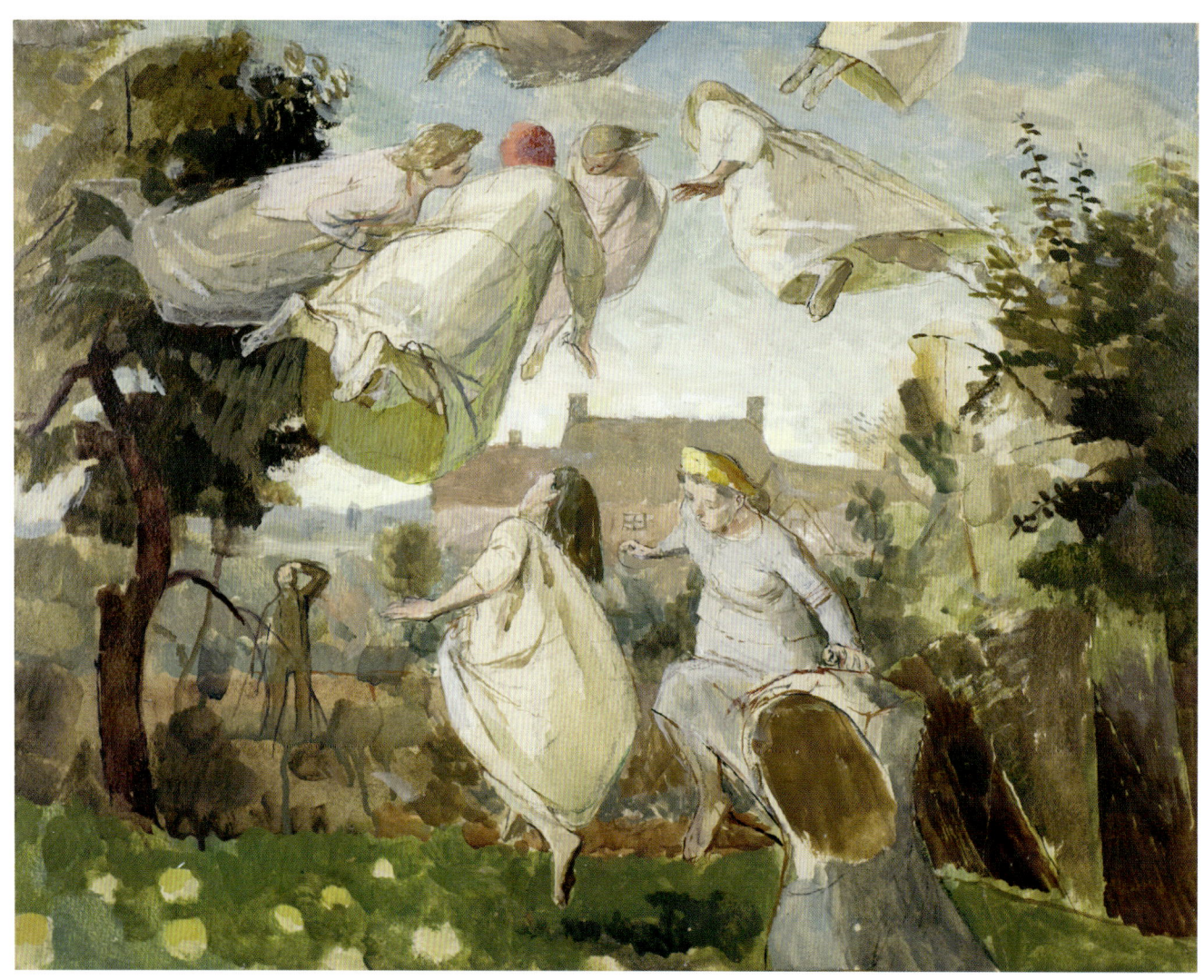

CAT 107 [HMO 765] Oil sketch for *Flying Applepickers*, 1945-46,
Oil on paper, 15 x 16 in. (38.2 x 40.7 cm)

This cheerful fantasy arose from discussion between Dunbar and her then next-door neighbour, her sister-in-law Joan Duckworth, about the most effective way to harvest the immense crops of apples in their gardens. The setting is Long Compton, the Warwickshire village to which Dunbar and her husband Roger Folley moved in late 1945. The whereabouts of the finished painting is unknown.

Post War

At the end of the war, Dunbar was still only 38 years old. Married in 1942 to Roger Folley, she was able to spend time with him at last, setting up home firstly in Warwickshire, then in Oxfordshire, finally in Kent. In a manner similar to Stanley Spencer, to whose work her *Joseph's Dream* (FIG 21) was not unexpectedly compared, she had worked in a personal and mystical mode as well as in a more objective observational one. Dunbar's *Portrait of a Retired Schoolmistress* (CAT 110) is compelling in its directness, with the sitter's determined gaze, solid figure and floral patterned overall. The black line between the shoulders forms the base for an equilateral triangle to the crown of the head. Her self-portrait (CAT 113) has the quality found in some of Spencer's of being caught off guard in the act of painting, as the awkward positioning of the legs seems to suggest.

In *Flying Applepickers* (CAT 107), the theme of levitation, used at Brockley in the soffits of the balcony, returns. Is it a metaphor of liberation after the years of pre-war unhappiness in love, followed by the privations and war? No doubt this theme of weightless bodies emanates from the spiritual seeking of a Christian Scientist, but it is also delightfully comic, with more tenderness than is found in most of Spencer's comparable works of supernatural events in Cookham High Street. Such compositions were falling out of fashion in the post-war world, but this did not prevent Dunbar from working on a series of allegorical and deliberately mysterious paintings that continue the pastoral romantic tradition in which she was trained, as her companion painter at Brockley, Mildred Eldridge, was to do with her cycle, *The Dance of Life*, painted for the Orthopaedic Hospital at Gobowen in the Welsh Marches. They shared a belief that humans are most complete when close to the rhythms of the natural world, to which Eldridge brought a more mistrustful view of 'civilisation'. These are themes of urgent contemporary relevance and far from sentimental.

Several of Dunbar's major late works remain to be relocated and revealed. *Autumn and the Poet* (CAT 114) has the look of a post-war painting in its brushwork and slightly distorted drawing (with a hint of John Minton, perhaps), which pulls away from the more purely classical pre-war works. The iconography of poet and his fecund pin-headed muse, characterized as a season but more representative of nature as a whole, continues the celebratory quality of Dunbar's painting of the numinous landscape as shaped by man, very different from Minton's more sinister evocations. Lines in the composition tie the surface together in a root two rectangle, while leading the eye into the distance by a double perspective.

Dunbar's last mural commission, *Alpha and Omega* (CAT 111), painted for the library at Bletchley Park Training College, fortunately survives, although not *in situ*. The many studies that came with the two paintings to Oxford Brookes University show Dunbar's range of experiment in finding an appropriate iconography for a modern dress allegory. Both panels have the unforced otherworldly quality that Dunbar found early on and which stayed with her to the sadly early end.

A.P.

CAT 108 [HMO 173]
Studies for *Mercatora*, an allegorical painting (whereabouts unknown) based on map projections and navigation.
Pencil, pen & ink and gouache on paper 15 x 22 in. (38 x 56 cm)

CAT 109 [HMO 699]
Studies for *Faith, Hope and Charity*, an unrealised allegorical painting.
Pencil and pen & ink on paper, 15 x 22 in. (38.2 x 56 cm)

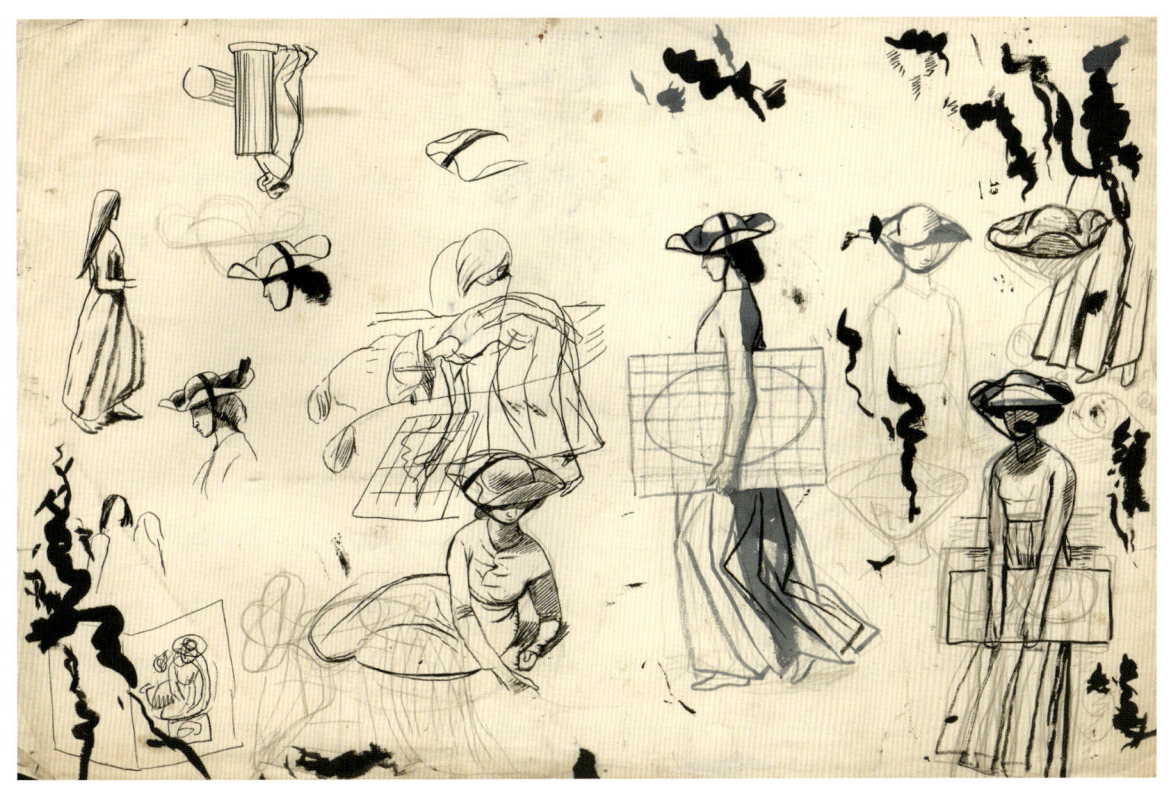

CAT 108

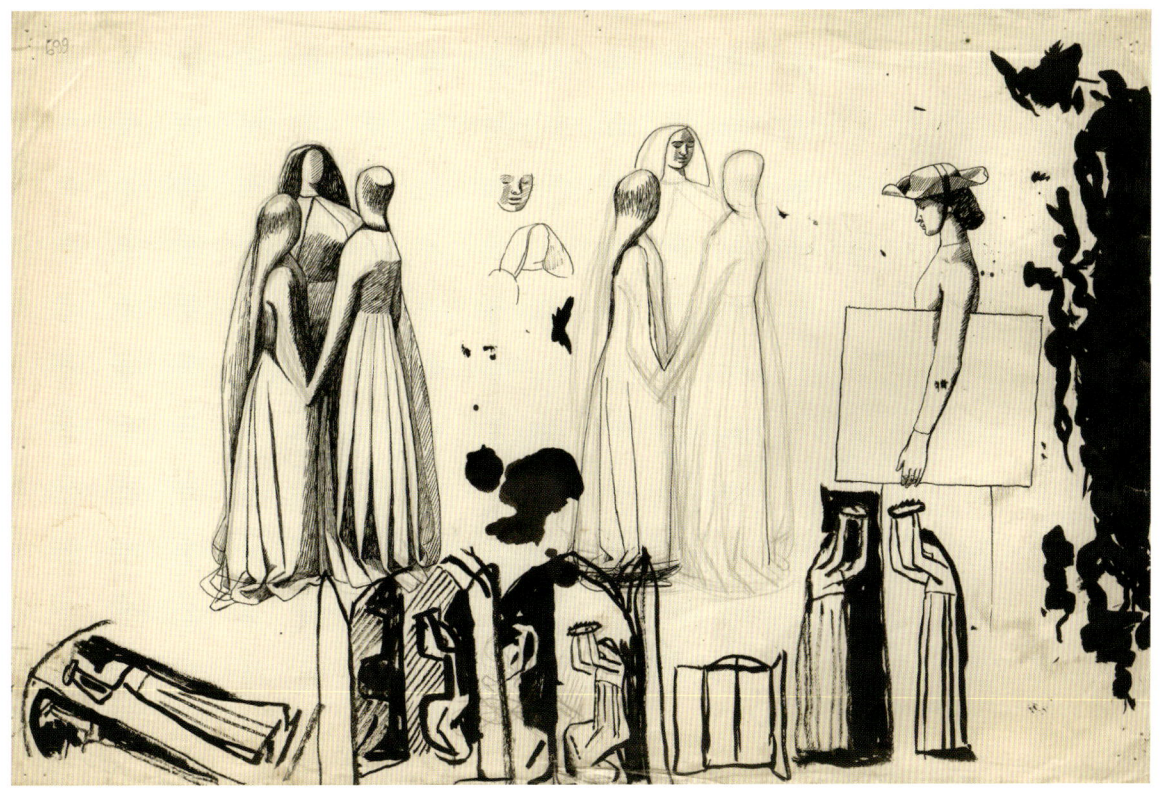

CAT 109

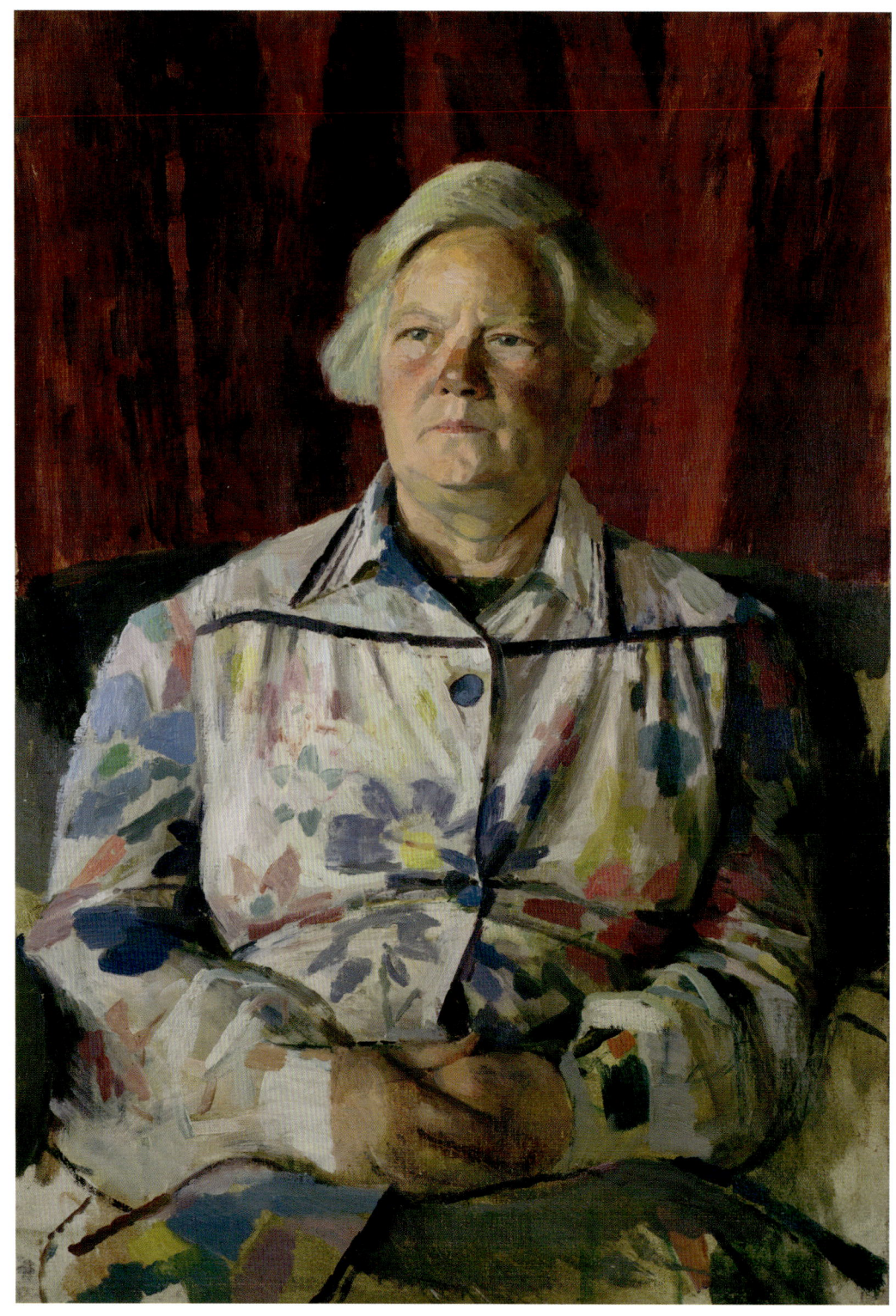

CAT 110 [HMO 782] Portrait of a Retired Schoolmistress. Inscribed verso by Dunbar's father-in-law, E.W. Folley, 'The Old Schoolmistress (by Evelyn Dunbar unfinished)', c.1955, oil on canvas, 30 x 20 in. (76 x 51 cm)

This portrait was commissioned by E.W. Folley, himself a retired headmaster in Colne (Lancs.), probably for presentation to a retiring colleague. For unknown reasons it was never presented.

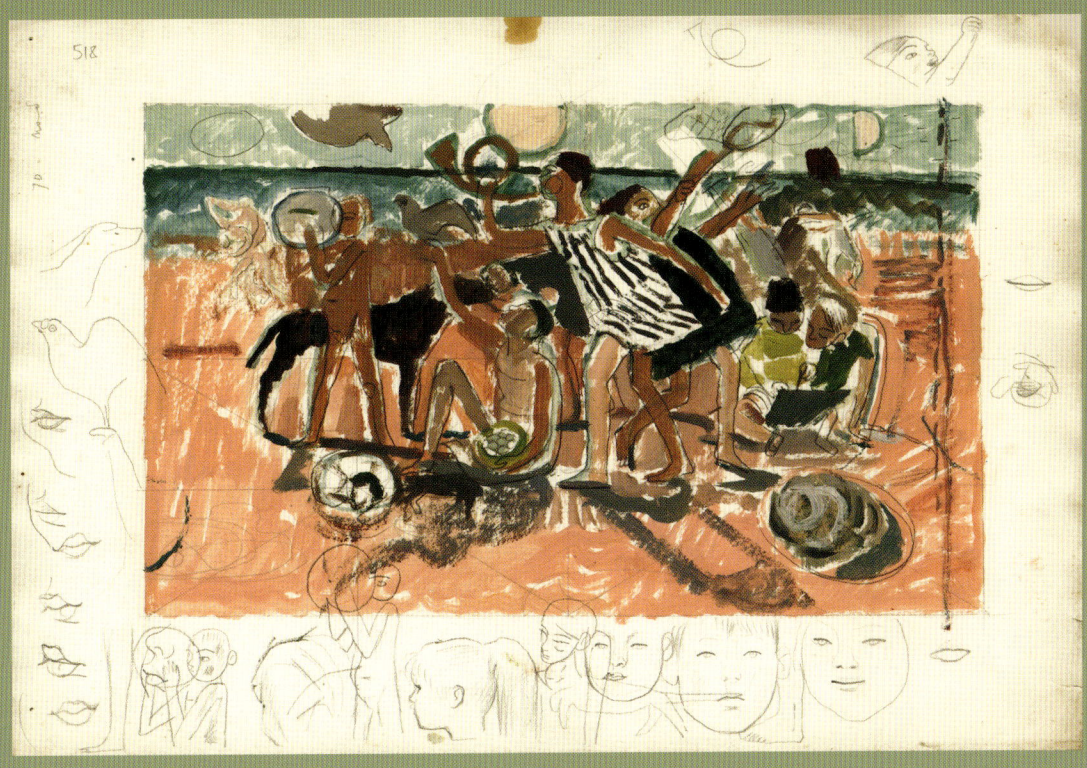

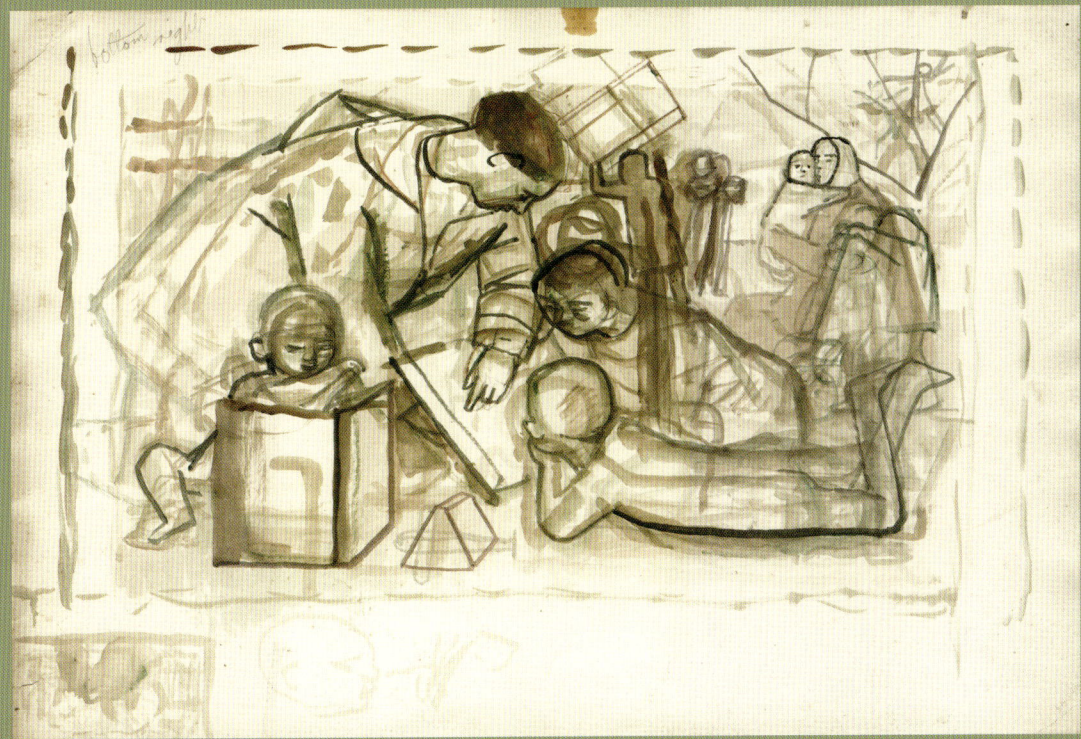

CAT 111 [HMO 518] Recto: Study for *Alpha*. The shape of the Greek letter Alpha, from the college motto Alpha and Omega, is reflected in the shape of the horn. Verso: Study for the second panel, featuring a teacher instructing children.
Pencil and gouache on paper,   15 ½ x 22 ½ in. (39.5 x 56.8 cm)

These studies are for two panels commissioned for the library at Bletchley Park Teacher Training College in 1957.

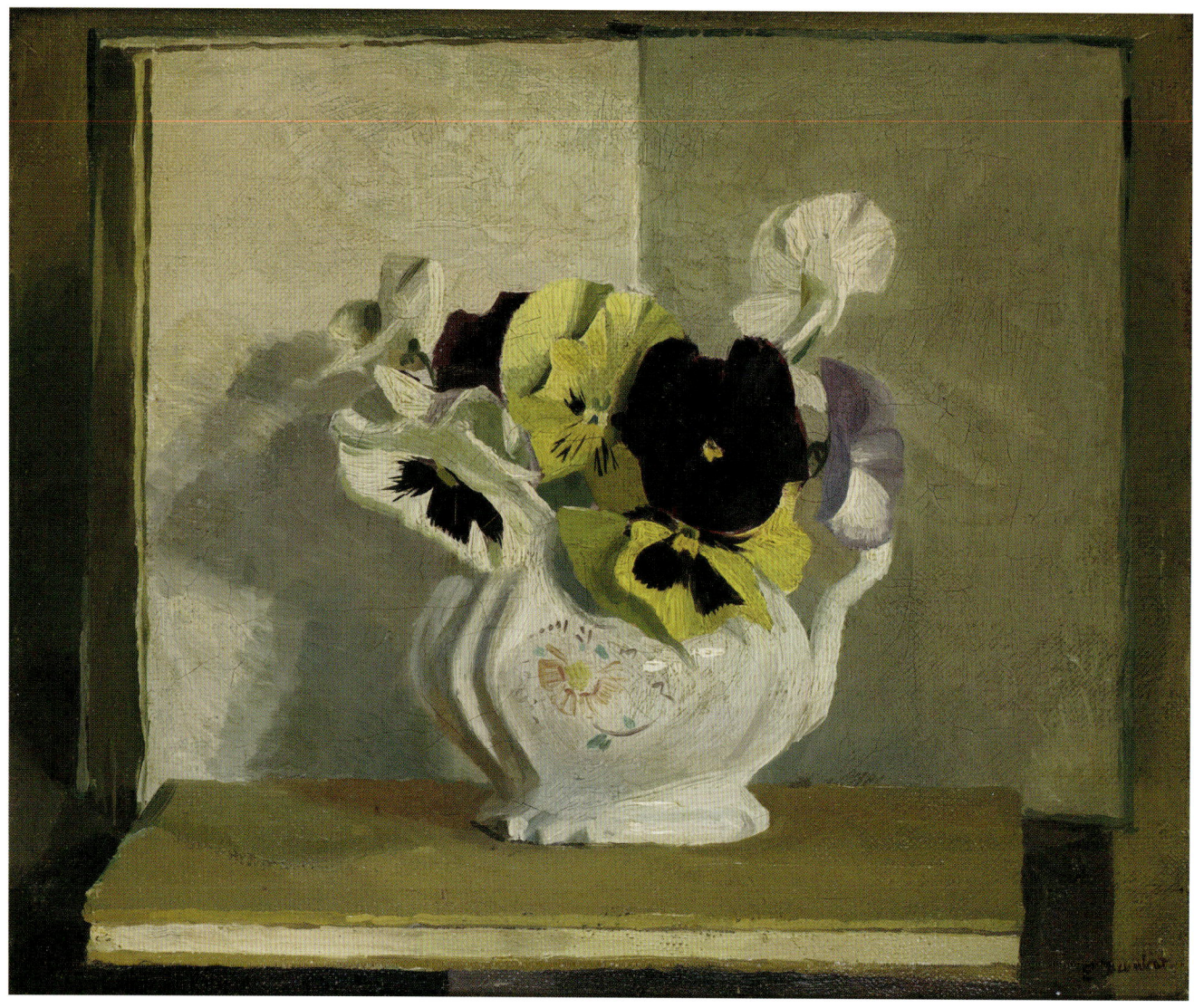

CAT 112 [HMO 1013] *Pansies and Violas*. Signed 'E.Dunbar', winter 1945-46,
Oil on canvas, 9 ½ x 13 in. (24 x 33 cm)

Dunbar's still lifes are extremely rare. There are only five known examples in her entire oeuvre. *Pansies and Violas* was painted in the spring of 1946, while the artist and her husband (who classed it among her most striking work) were living in Long Compton, Warwickshire. It can be thought of as an *in memoriam* tribute to Dunbar's mother Florence, who died in 1944, and who painted floral still lifes almost exclusively.

CAT 113 [HMO 766] Self-portrait. Signed 'ED', 1958,
Oil on canvas, 20 x 12 in. (49.5 x 29.4 cm)
Collection: Christopher Campbell-Howes.

Painted in her studio at Staple Farm, near Wye, Kent, this was the last self-portrait Dunbar undertook.

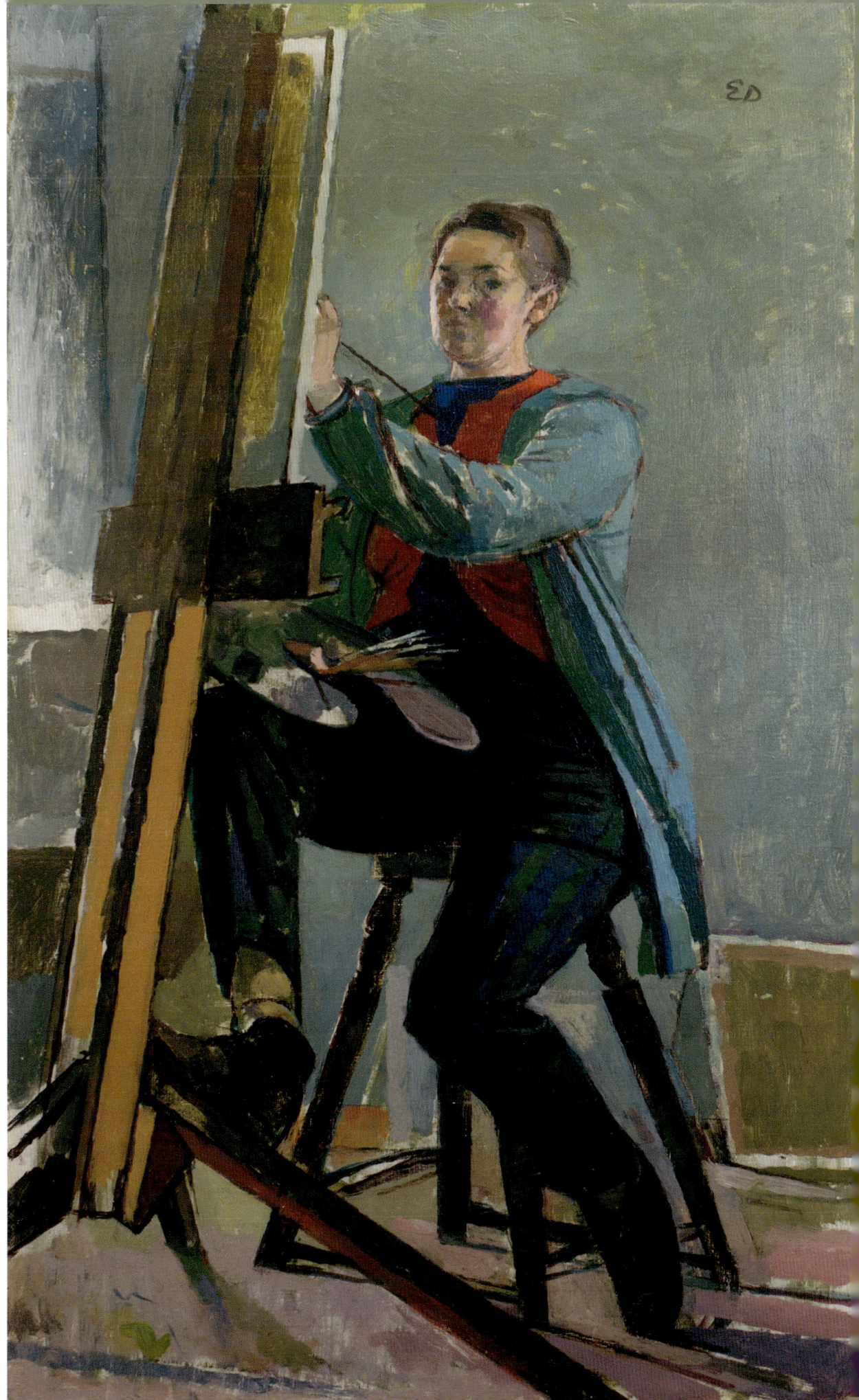

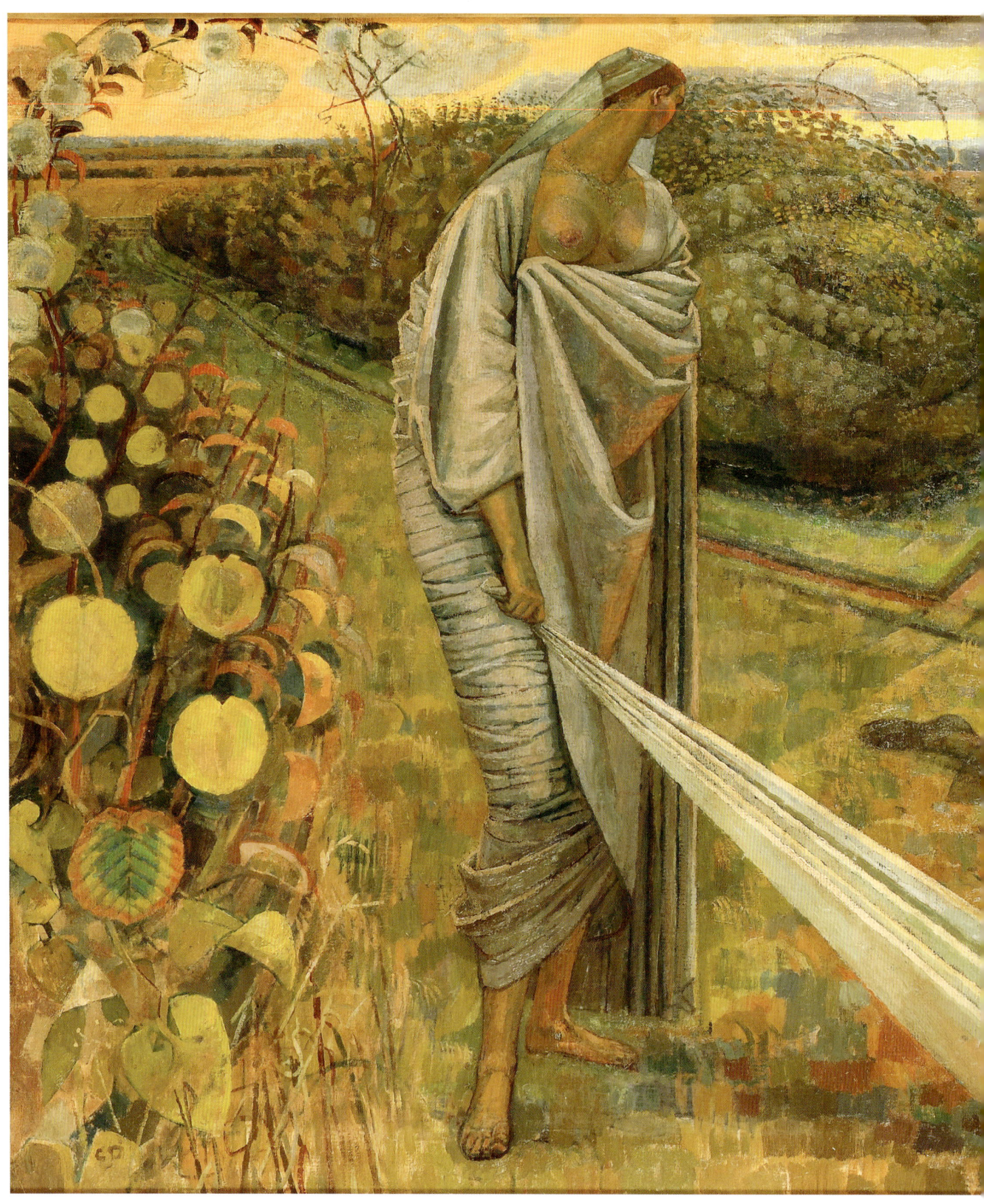

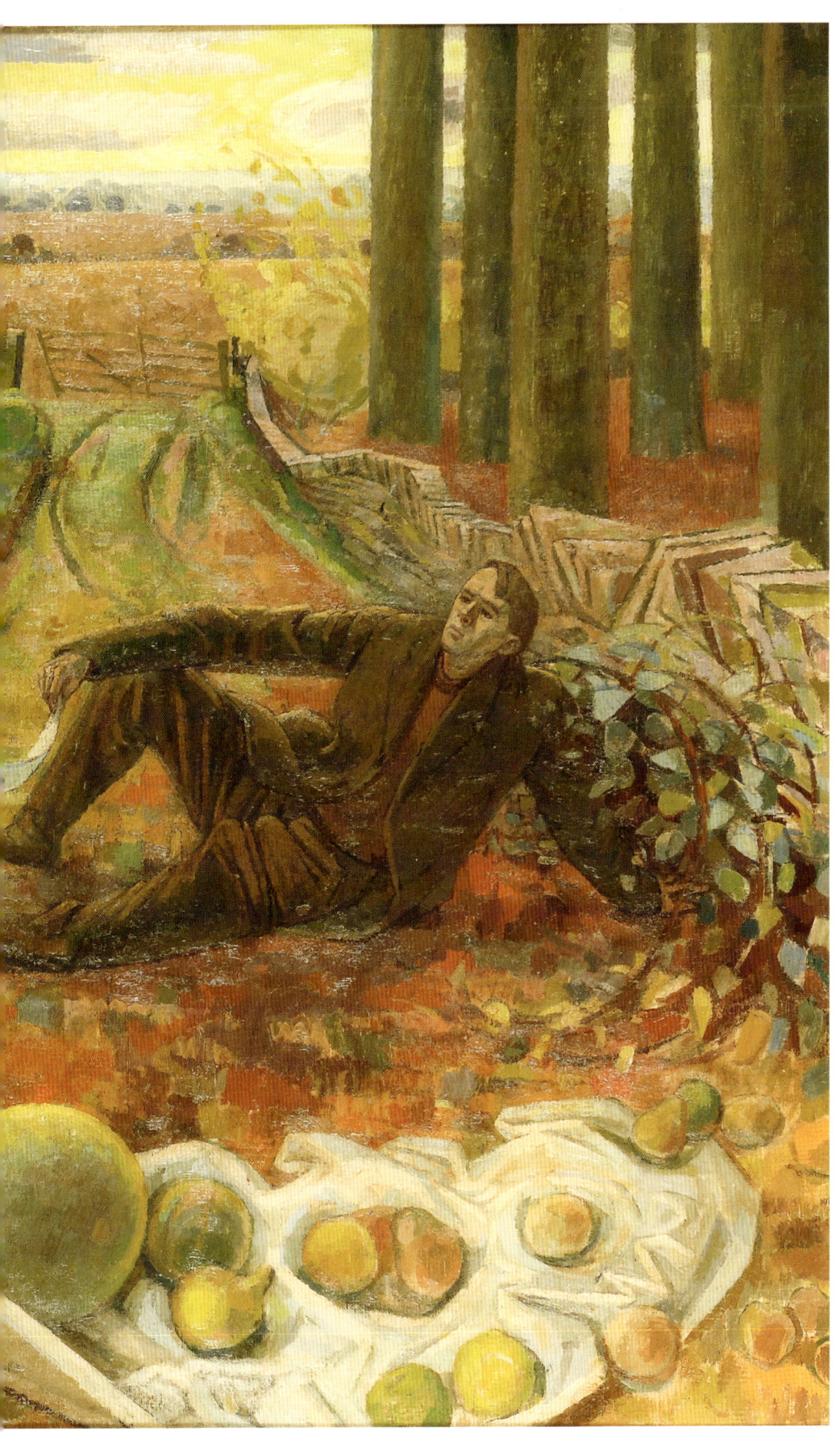

CAT 114
Autumn and the Poet, 1948-1960,
Signed, 'ED',
Oil on canvas,
35 ½ x 59 in. (90 x 150 cm)
Collection: Maidstone Museum and Bentlif Art Gallery

Autumn and the Poet, Dunbar's last allegorical painting, was begun in Oxfordshire in 1948/9 then laid aside for some years before completion in 1958-60. In the form of a traditional Annunciation, the fruit-laden but moribund figure of Autumn is urging the Poet (who closely resembles Roger Folley) to disseminate truths about the essential synergy between man and creation, without which mankind cannot survive.

Photograph: St Barbe Museum and Art Gallery, Lymington
© Christopher Campbell-Howes

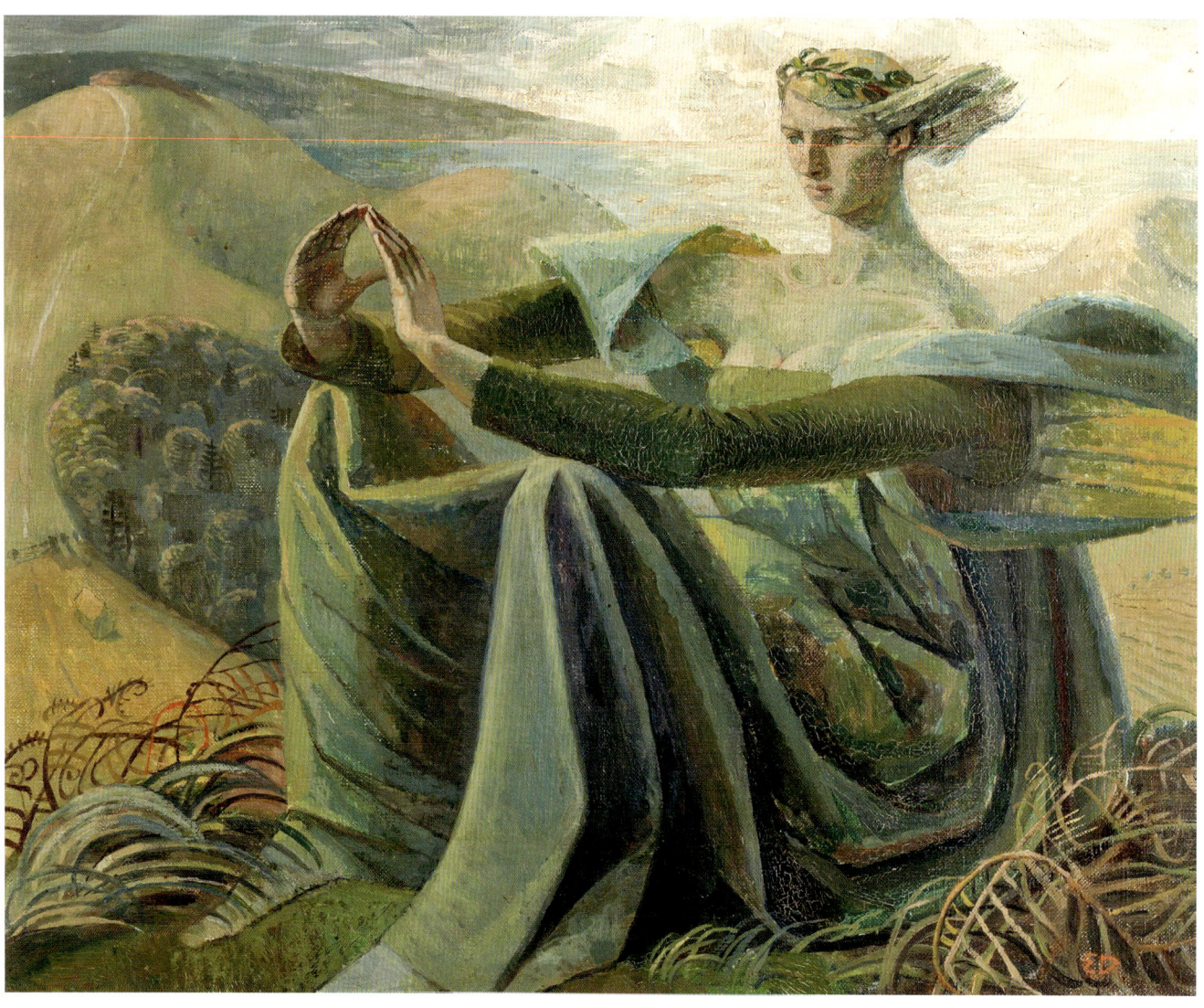

CAT 115 *Dorset*, 1947-8,
Oil on canvas, 19 x 23 in. (48 x 58 cm) Exhibited: Ruskin School, Oxford, 1950,
Private collection

Dunbar's experience of Dorset was largely vicarious, taken in though the novels of Thomas Hardy. In the first of her great post-war allegories she shows Anne Garland, the heroine of Hardy's *The Trumpet Major*, looking out to sea from a stylised representation of Portland Bill. Close reading of Hardy's novel reveals that what she is watching through her hands, at once prayerful and protective, is *HMS Victory*, outward bound for Trafalgar. But *Dorset* goes deeper than that, she is more than a woman yearning for her sailor lover: complementing the roles Dunbar assigned to so many women in her war painting, notably the principal figure in *A Land Girl and the Bail Bull* (FIG 19), she has made *Dorset*, one of the rare conventionally beautiful women in her work, also into a tutelary deity, a symbolic guardian of the English coast and the land within.

CAT 116 J*acob's Dream*, 1960, signed 'ED',
Oil on canvas, 20 x 12 in. (50.8 x 30.5 cm)
Private collection courtesy England & Co Gallery, London

Dunbar's last painting, on her easel when she died. The image is taken from *Genesis*, chapter 28, in which Jacob, asleep on the ground, dreams of a ladder to heaven, with angels ascending and descending. The 'angels' represent one of Dunbar's very few forays into the abstract. The background landscape is identifiable as the countryside near Wye, Kent, and where she finished this painting a few days before she died in May 1960. Some see in this painting a meditation on her own end.

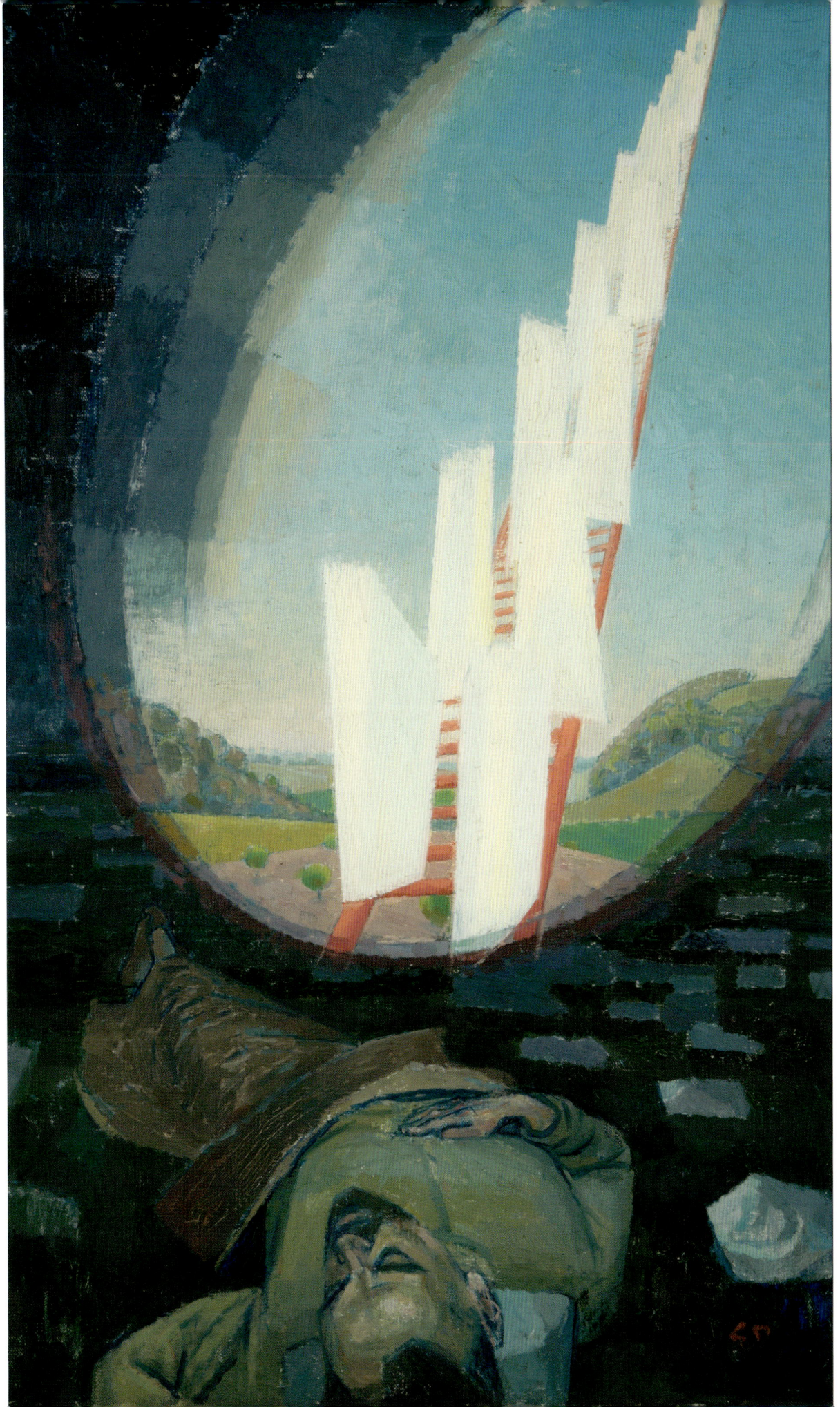

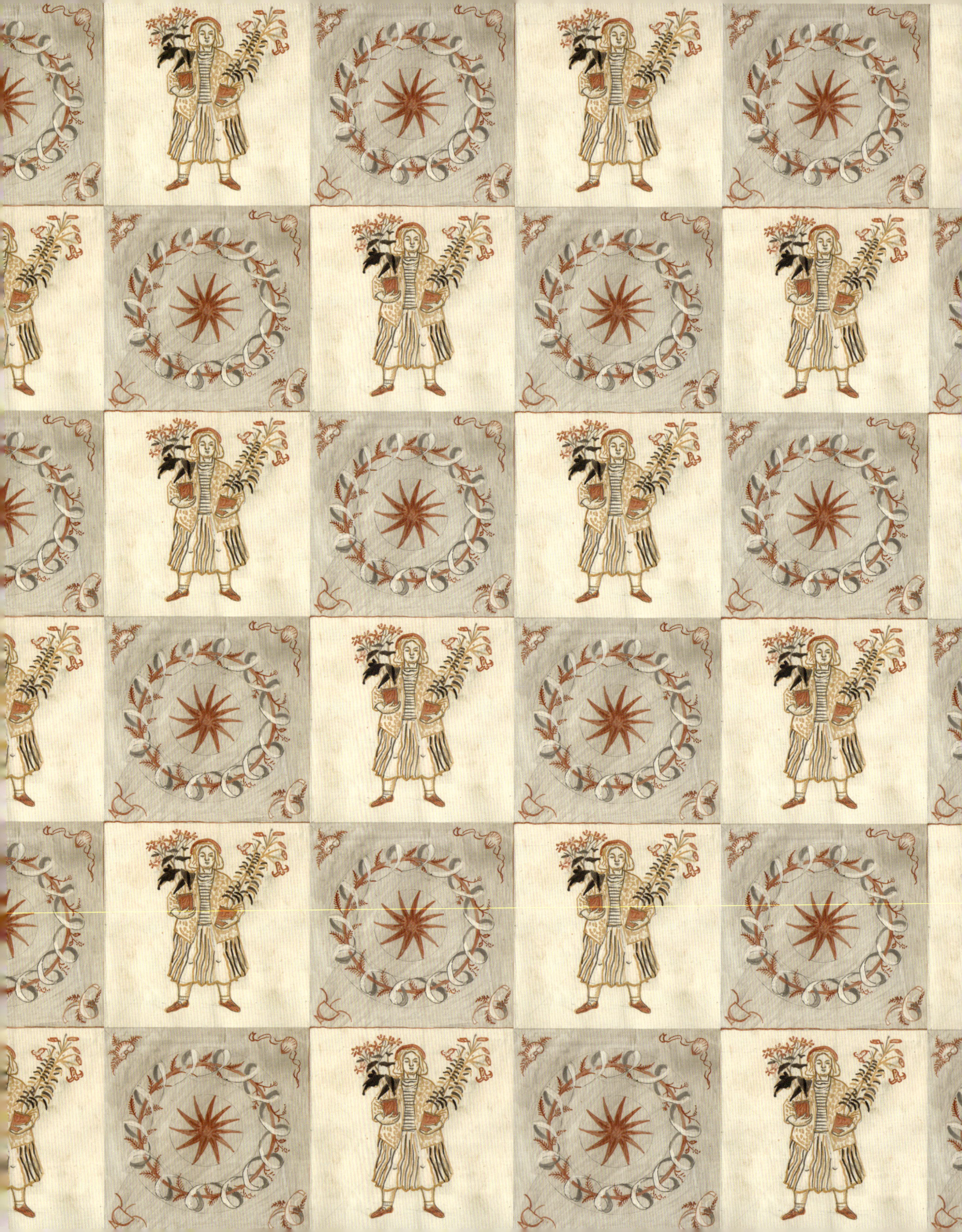

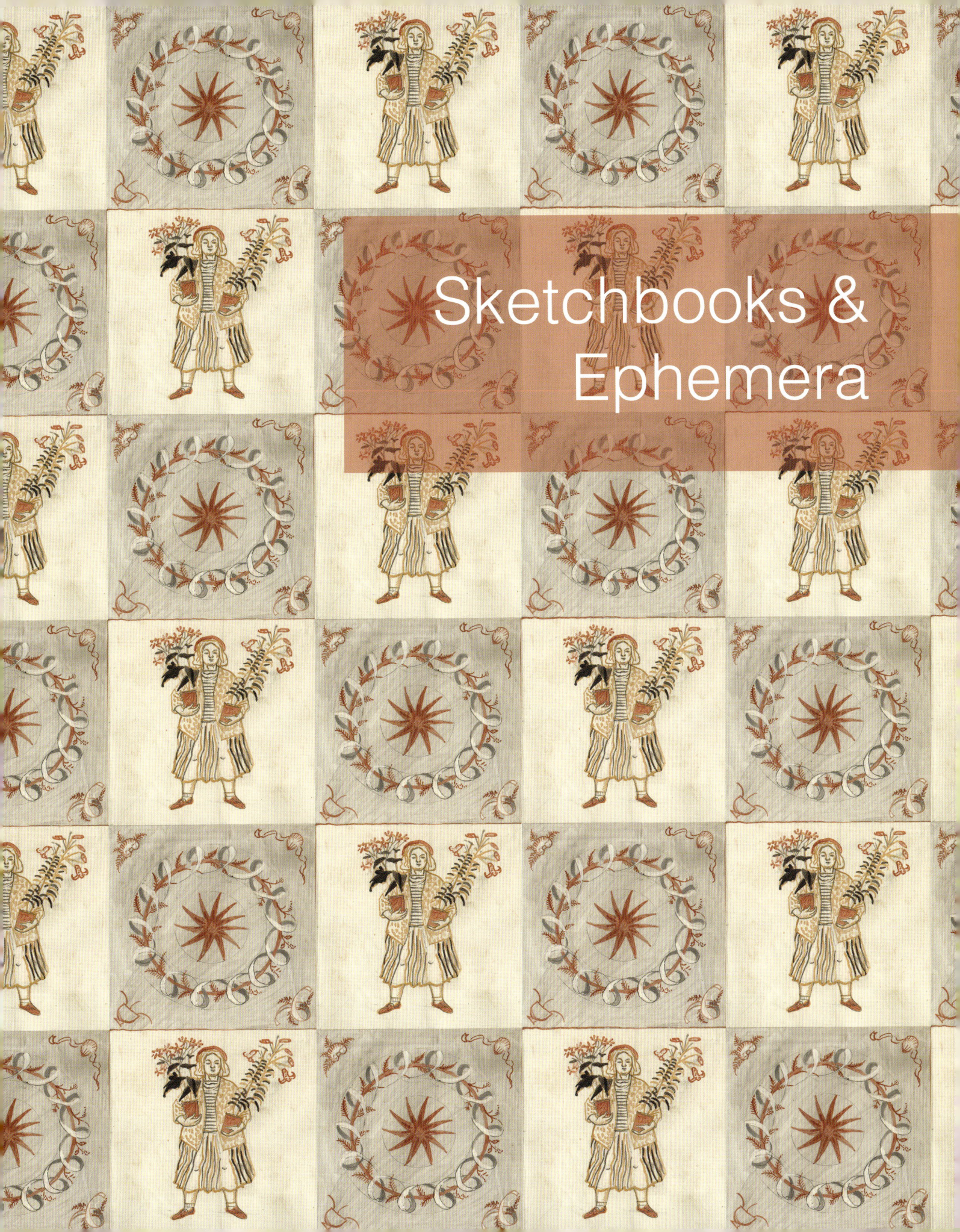

Sketchbooks & Ephemera

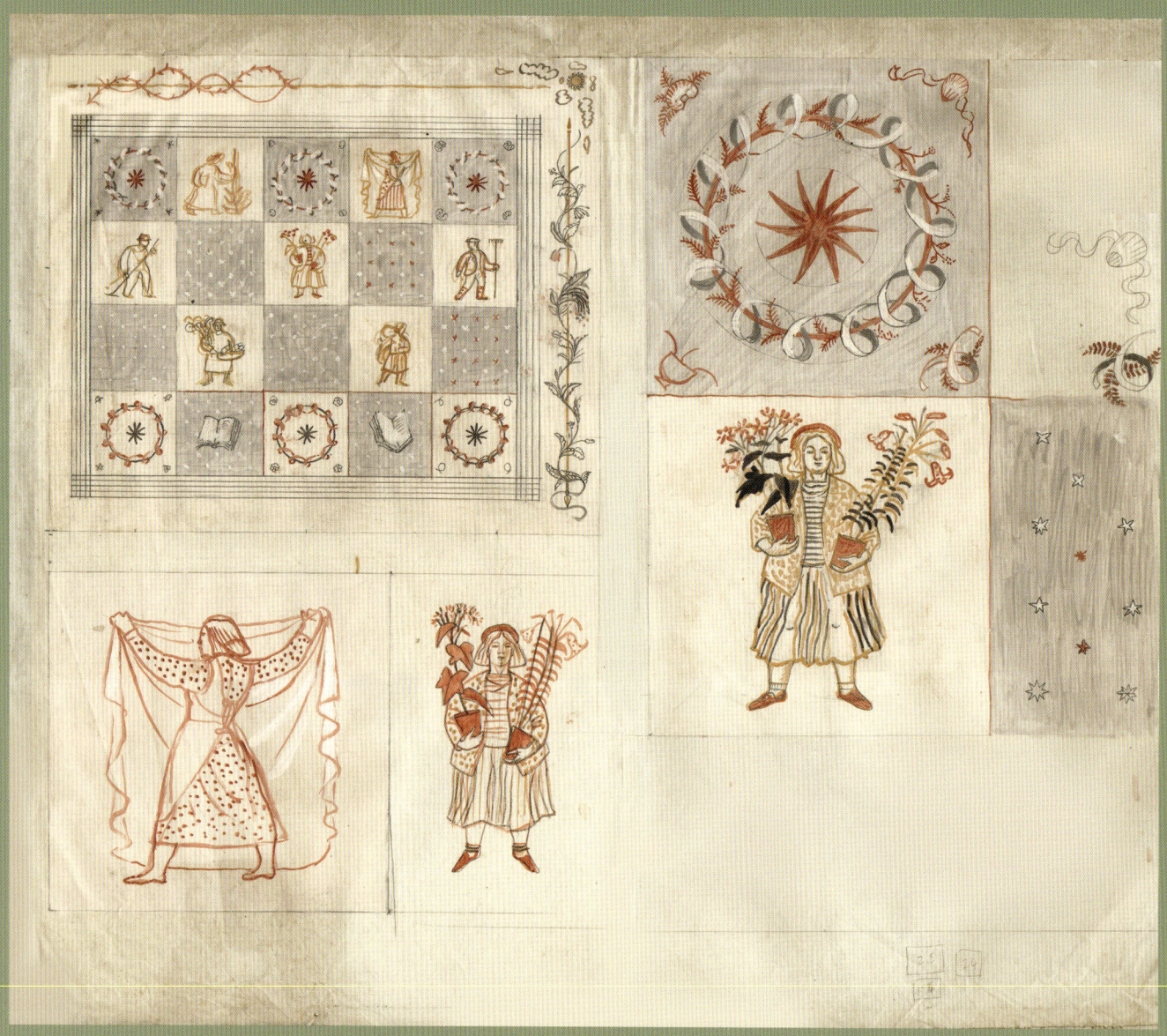

CAT 117 [HMO 689] Studies for designs for an embroidered quilt, 1935-36,
Pencil and watercolour on paper, 24 ½ x 29 ¾ in. (62.5 x 75.7 cm)

The quilt in question was to be made by Dunbar and Charles Mahoney as a gift for Mahoney's mother Bessie.

Sketchbooks & Ephemera

When Evelyn Dunbar enrolled at the Royal College of Art in 1929 it was a toss-up as to whether she would apply for the Design School or the Painting School and although Painting won she maintained a strong interest in design and included many designer-draughtsmen among her friends, particularly Edward Bawden and Barnett Freedman. Like them she enjoyed free-hand pattern-making and filled many sketchbooks with pictorial jottings of people, places and incidents which could be worked up later when required into vignettes to decorate such publications as *The Scots Week-End* (page 170) and *Gardeners' Choice* (pages 82-95). Equally, they could be incorporated into subject paintings like *The Days of the Week*, or used in any one of her other decorative projects. Whether working in sketchbooks or on loose scraps of paper she was happy drawing in line either with pen or pencil, or with clean strokes of a well-charged brush, using the latter particularly to create decorative patterns often reminiscent of Vanessa Bell's designs for Hogarth Press bookjackets for her sister's – Virginia Woolf's – novels. Through Mahoney and other Royal College contacts she would also have been familiar with the work of the Curwen Press, particularly the pattern papers inspired by the recently deceased Claud Lovat Fraser and produced by Paul Nash, Edward Bawden, Enid Marx and others.

In her early days she had a natural playfulness which is reflected in her illustrated letters to Jane Carrington and Edward Bawden; those to Charles Mahoney – who she addressed variously as 'Dear Chas', 'Dear Matey Cock' or 'My dear old potting shed' – stand out particularly. By the late 1930s this natural gaiety and *joie de vivre* gave way to a less light-hearted mood as the disparity between her Christian Science upbringing and Mahoney's atheistic socialism increasingly drove a wedge between them. Apart from the rift with Mahoney this mood of greater seriousness chimed with that of the country as a whole as the clouds of impending war grew ever darker. Her Shell poster designs (CAT 82-84) probably date from this time and it is probable that Barnett Freedman encouraged her to produce some possible ideas as, in the late 1930s, he was commissioned by his friend Jack Beddington, who ran the Shell publicity department, to create 'puzzle' advertisements for use in various technical journals. Dunbar may have thought that with their simple kitchen imagery of shelling peas combined with semi-humourous captions – 'I Shell', 'Thou Shellest' – they might appeal to various ladies' journals. (see Ruth Artmonsky, *Jack Beddington, The Footnote Man*, London, 2006, p.54)

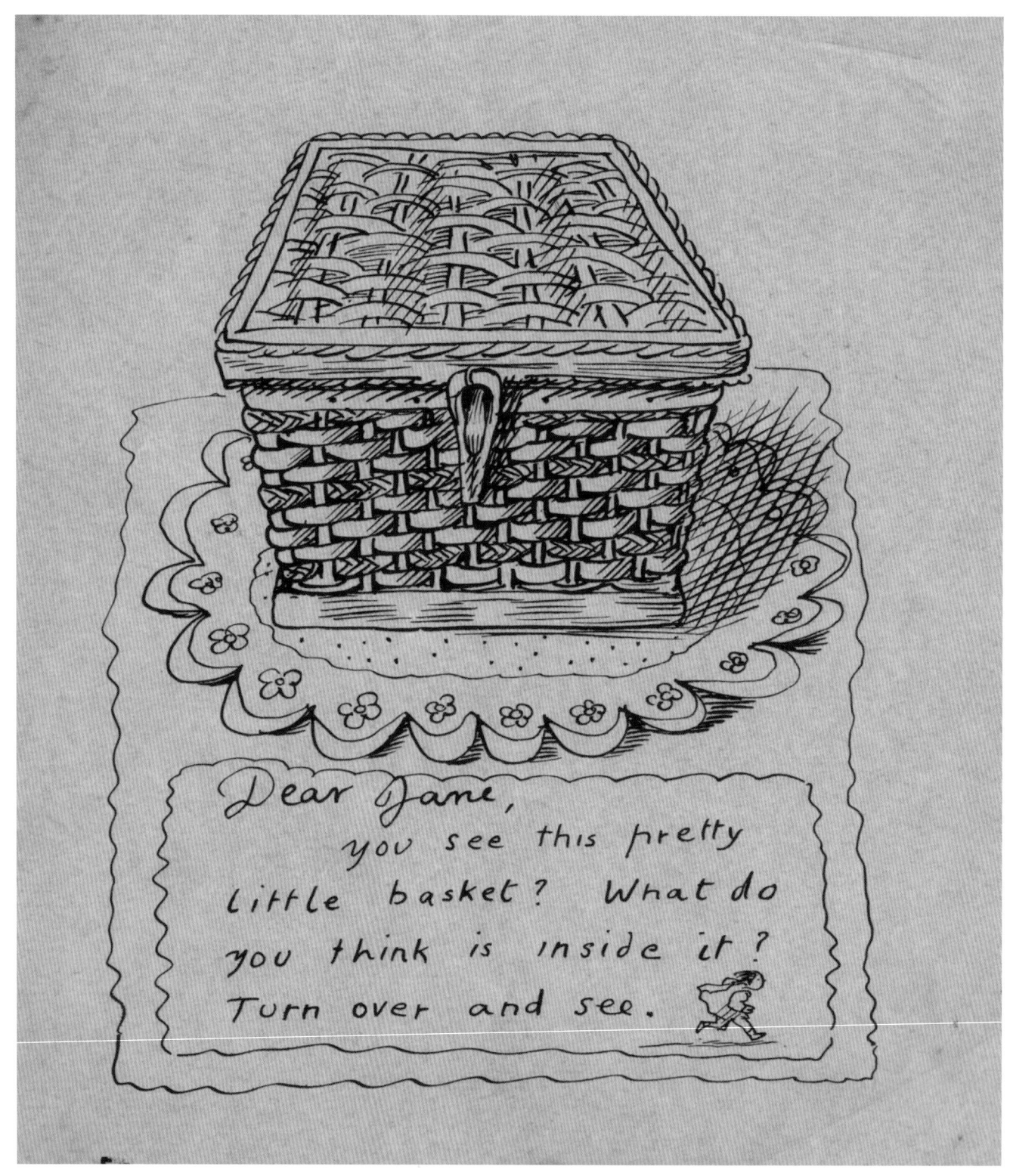

CAT 118 [HMO 688] First page of a letter to Jane Carrington, c.1936,
Pen & ink on paper, 10 x 8 in. (25.5 x 20.4 cm)

Jane Carrington was the daughter of Dunbar's Hampstead friends Noël and Catherine Carrington. Dunbar wrote several such letters to Jane, then a six-year-old in hospital with polio. Usually these letters were prettily water-coloured. Why this uncoloured example was never sent is not known.

It is not surprising that they were not developed further, but they were the precursors to Dunbar's *Mother Hubbard* (CAT 81) commissioned by ICI, and used for publication in a variety of different publications in much the same manner as Beddington's 'puzzle' advertisements.

Scrapbooks and artists' Christmas cards were a particular feature of the interwar period and beyond. Edward Bawden's and Eric Ravilious's scrapbooks in the collection of the Fry Gallery, Saffron Walden, contain many examples of cards from John Piper, Graham Sutherland, Geoffrey Rhoades and other artist friends, including Dunbar and Mahoney. After her marriage to Roger Folley Evelyn continued to produce her annual card usually accompanied by some verse by her husband: that for Christmas 1947 – one of the bleakest of postwar winters – depicts a particularly jolly figure of Pomona, the Roman goddess of fruit trees, gardens and orchards (FIG 23), reminding us once again of Evelyn's delight in animating the spirits of the months and seasons, virtues and ancient gods. Christian Science could not erase these pagan deities from her pantheon.

P.S.

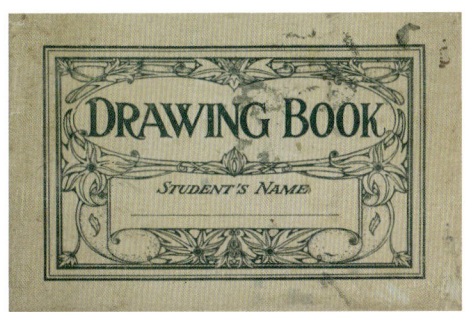

CAT 119

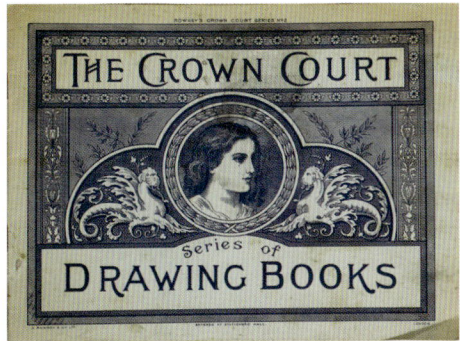

CAT 120

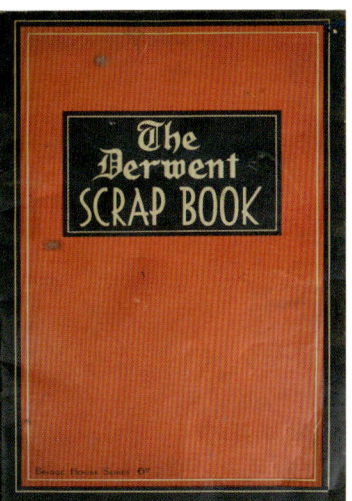

CAT 121

CAT 122

Four of Evelyn Dunbar's sketchbooks

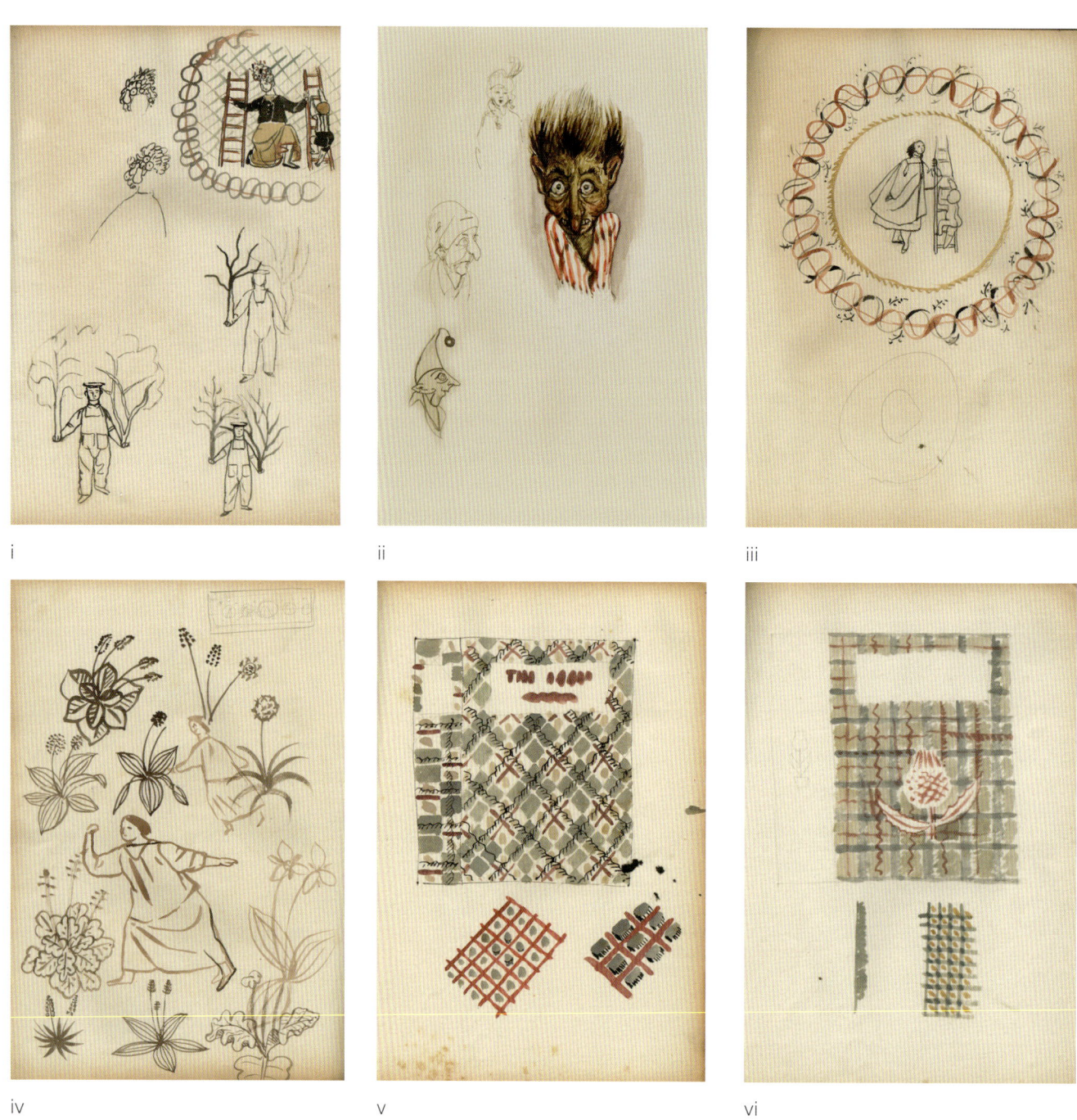

i-vii: Pages from Evelyn Dunbar's sketchbooks (see CAT 121 and CAT 122)

In general Dunbar preferred loose cartridge paper for her sketch work, but occasionally she resorted to cheap sketch books if ever she had a single idea to work out in many examples. One such dates from 1935, when Dunbar was working out tartan-based designs for the cover of *The Scots Week-End and Caledonian Vade Mecum for Host, Guest and Wayfarer*, a miscellany which she illustrated with line drawings.

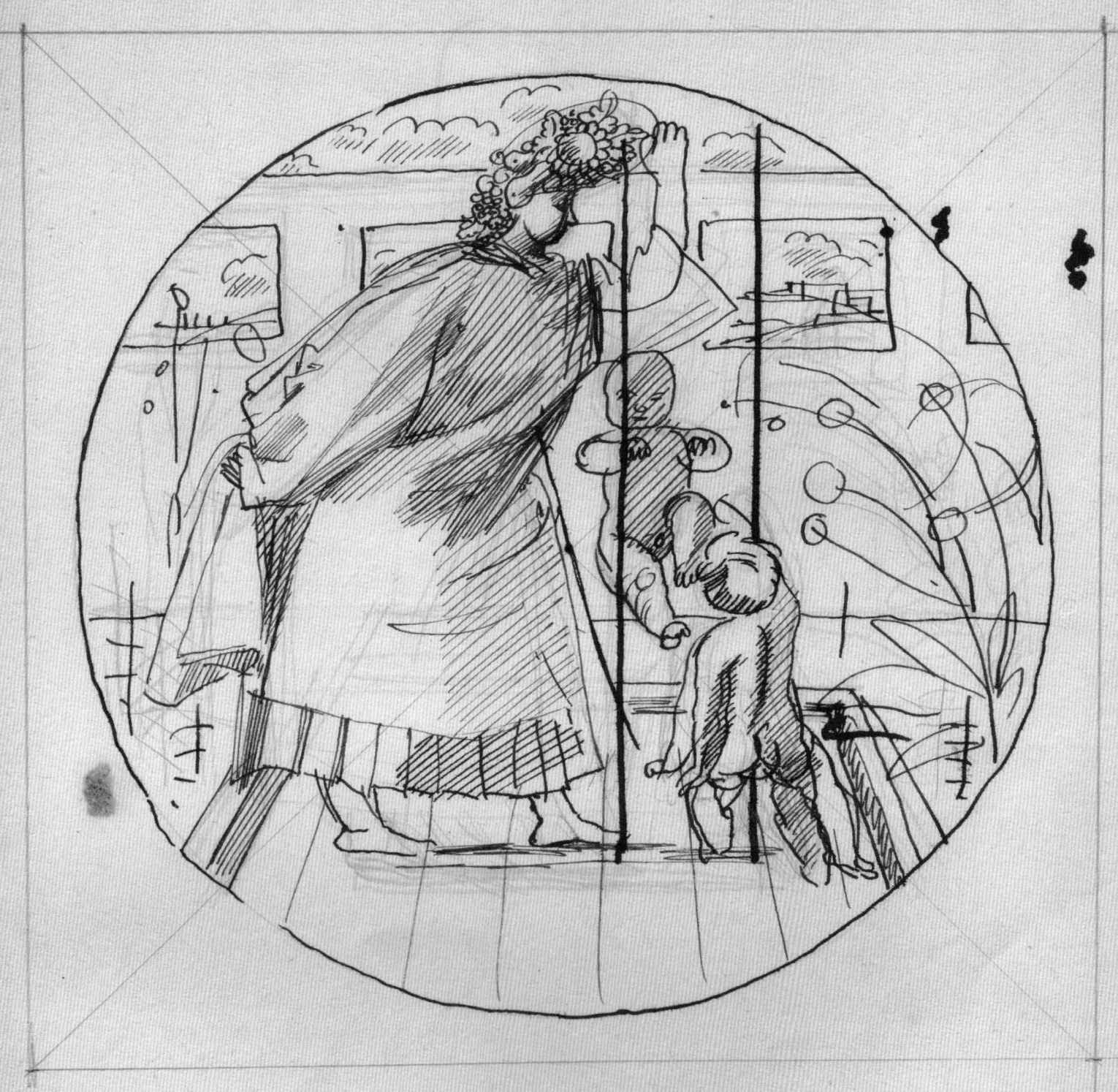

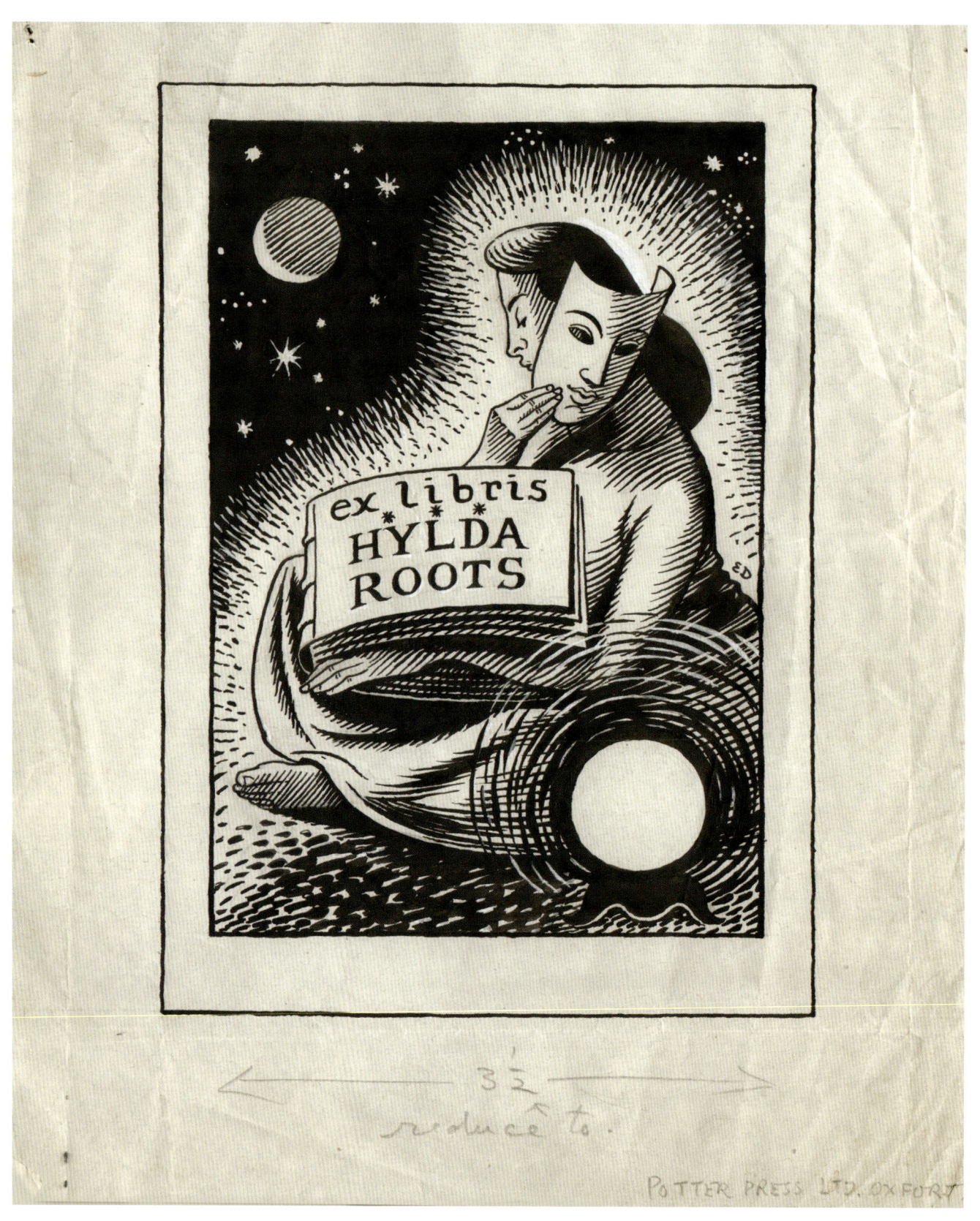

CAT 123 [HMO 337] Ex Libris Hylda Roots – Design for an Ex Libris commission,
Inscribed recto with instructions to printer (Potter Press, Oxford), c.1948,
Pencil, pen & ink and white gouache on paper, 8 x 9 ¾ in. (20.3 x 25 cm)

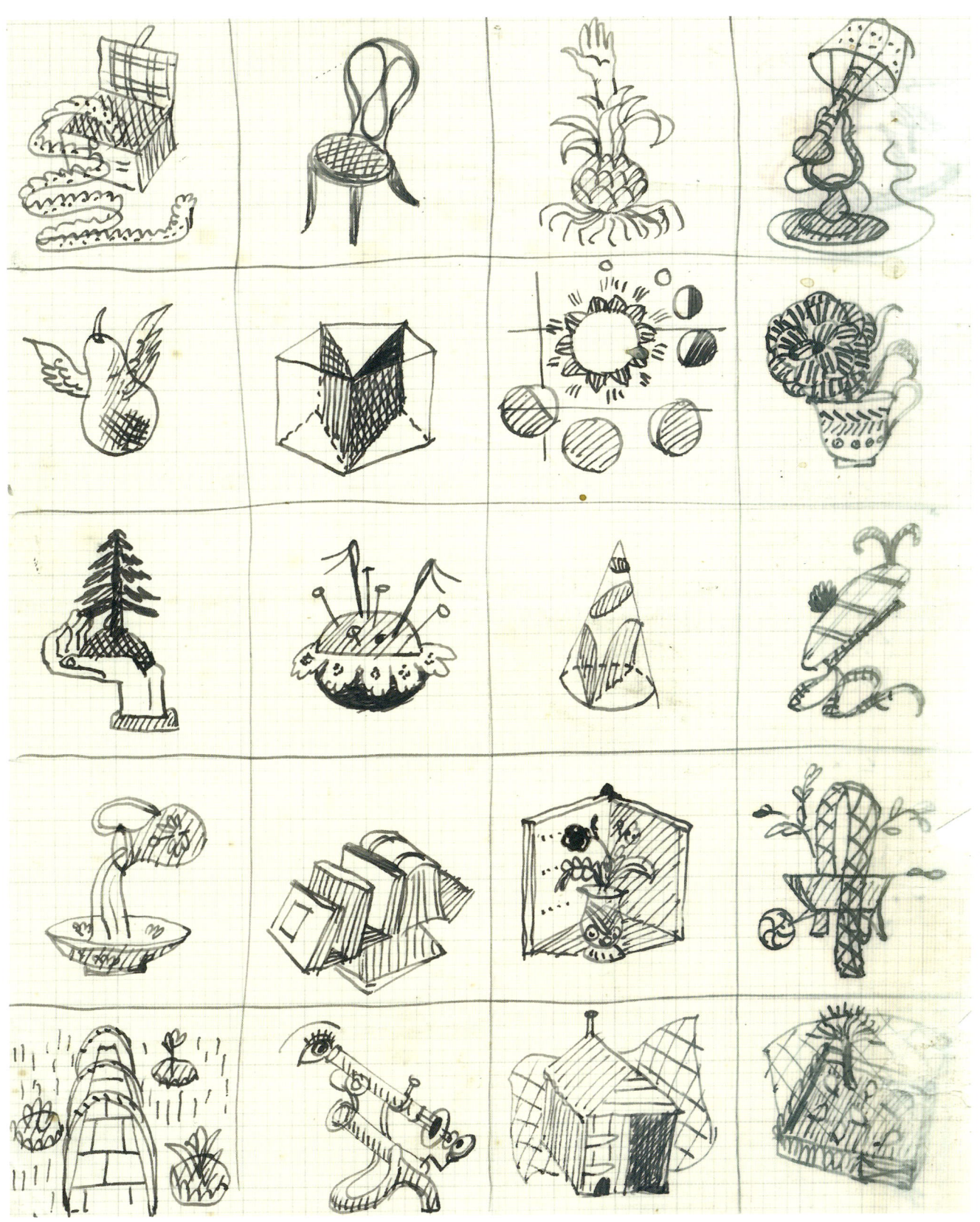

CAT 124 A set of 20 vignettes, purpose unknown, several of which can be associated with decorative projects Dunbar was involved with in the mid-1930s, ink on paper, 12 x 8 ¼ in. (30.5 x 21 cm)
Provenance: Charles Mahoney

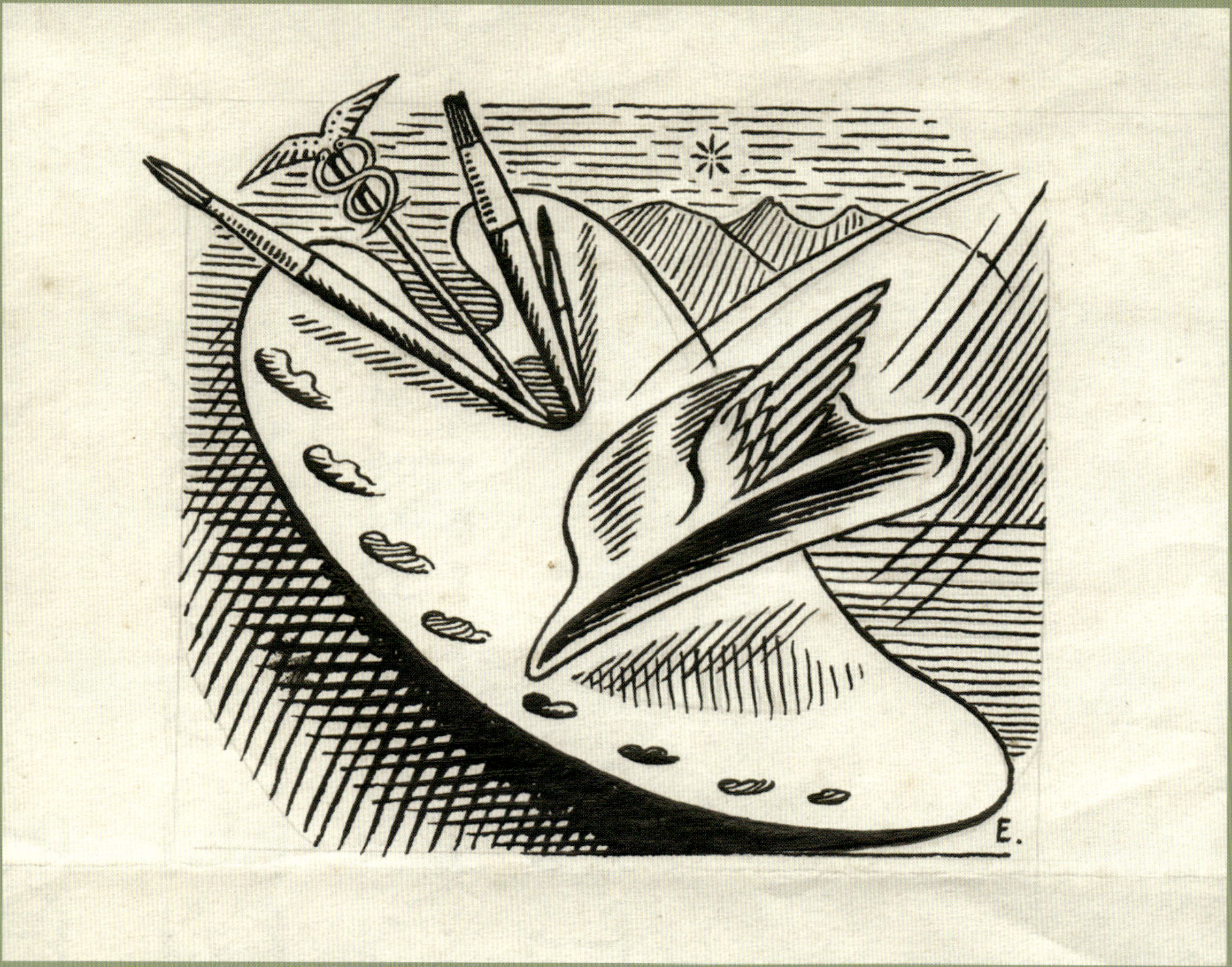

CAT 125 [HMO 340]
Study for a Christmas card design, 1942,
Pencil and pen & ink on paper,
8 x 10 in. (20.3 x 25.4 cm)

This is the first Christmas card sent jointly after the artist's marriage to Roger Folley in 1942. Dunbar wrote of it: 'Our first Christmas card. At that time Roger was in the R.A.F. and Evelyn an official war artist, so the symbolism is obvious. The distant peaks, one imagines, are meant to suggest the brief "leave" periods in the Lakes or Yorkshire fells.'

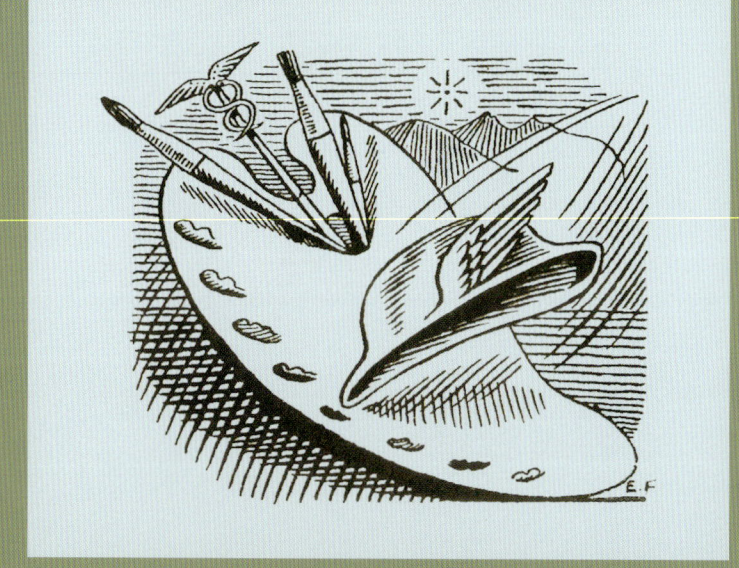

FIG 22 Printed version of the card.
Private collection.

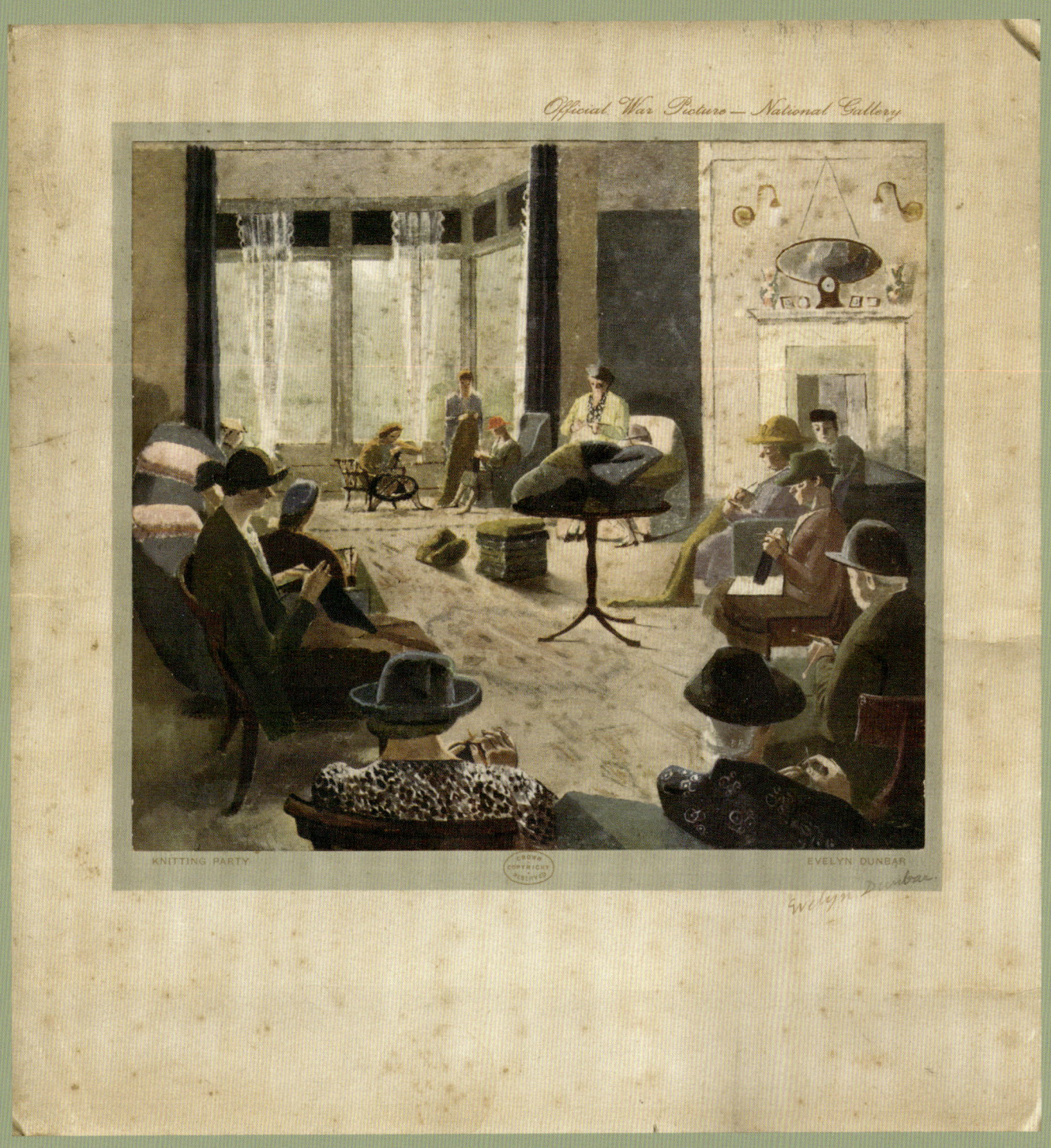

CAT 126 [HMO 81]
Greeting card, with space for a small calendar, c.1943,
Printed on corrugated cardboard, 12 x 11 in. (30.5 x 28 cm)

One of a series of Official War Paintings reproduced by the National Gallery. Dunbar's *A Knitting Party* ,1940, is featured, with about 16 women (among them Florence Dunbar, the artist's mother, surreptitiously looking at her watch in the window) from the WVS knitting balaclavas, socks, etc. for the troops. (See FIG 7, page 29)

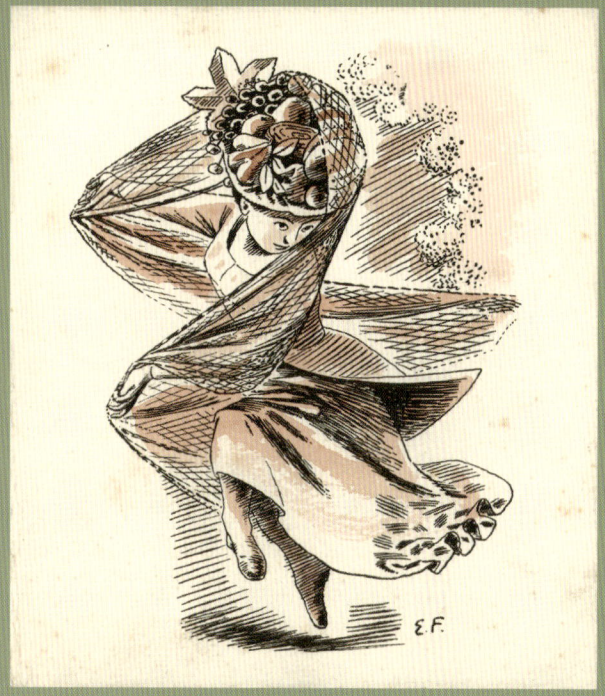

FIG 23 [HMO 77] Printed Christmas card, signed 'E.F.' in the plate, 1946-47, 7 x 5 ¾ in. (17.3 x 14.7 cm) with text by her husband Roger Folley. 'Pomona', shown dancing with a fruit-laden hat typical of Dunbar in certain modes, was a minor Roman goddess of fruits and produce, and clearly a major personage in Dunbar's pantheon.

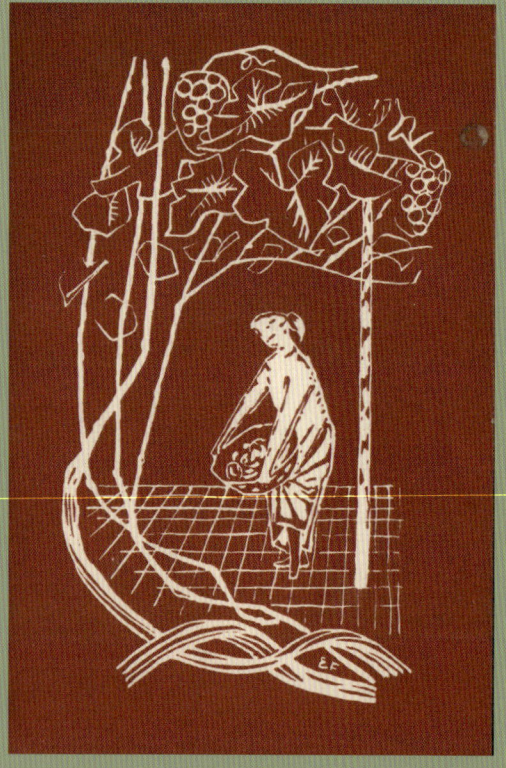

FIG 24 [HMO 76] Printed Christmas card, 1951, 6½ x 4¼ in. (16.9 x 10.6 cm) with text by her husband Roger Folley. 'Sous les vignes' refers to the vines in the conservatory at The Elms, the house near Ashford, Kent, in which they lived 1950-57.

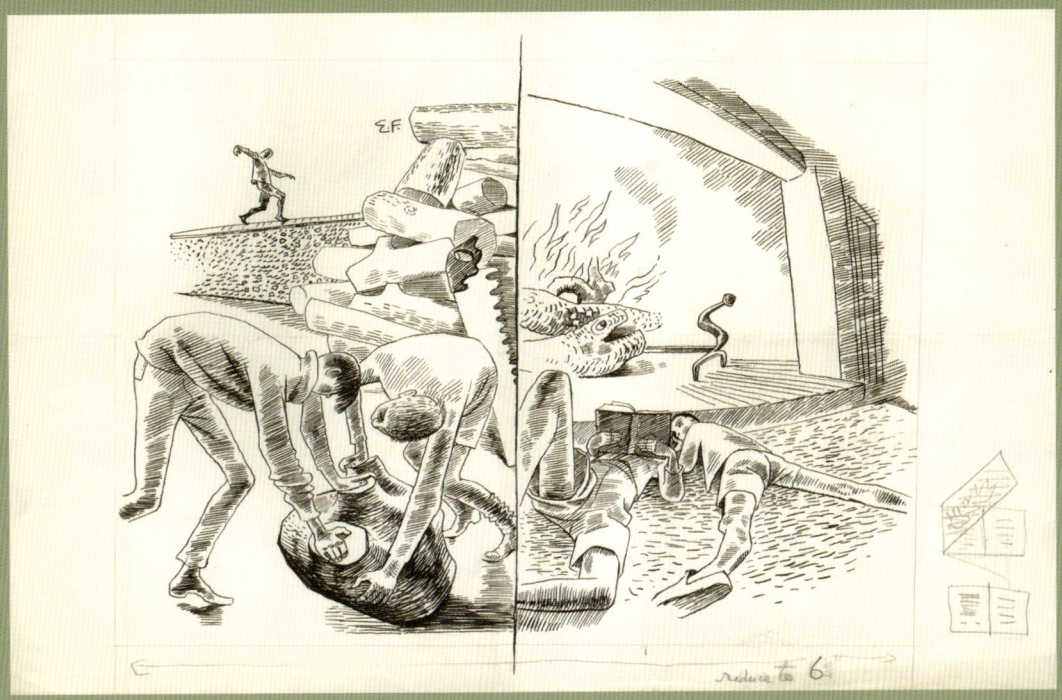

CAT 127 [HMO 60] Study 1 for a Christmas card design for 1959,
Pencil and pen & ink on paper 15 x 22 in. (38 x 56 cm), inscribed with printer's instructions

The subjects are her nephew Richard Campbell-Howes, then 11, and two boys whom Dunbar sometimes hosted from a nearby children's home.

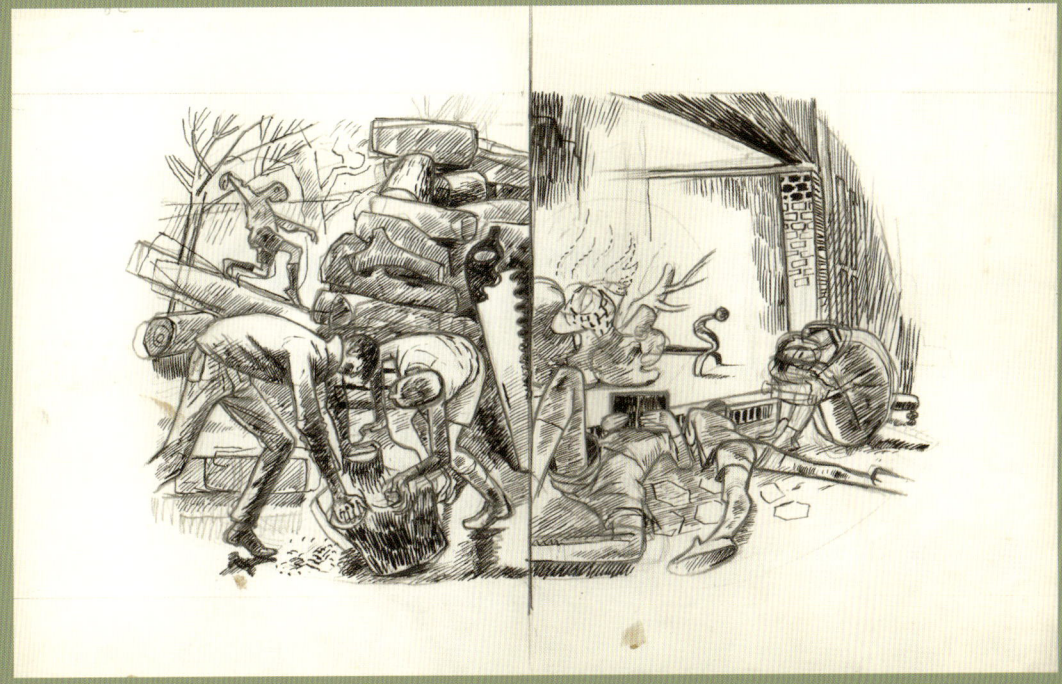

CAT 128 [HMO 62] Study 2 for for a Christmas card design for 1959,
Pencil and pen & ink on paper 15 x 22 in. (38 x 56 cm)

The subjects are as before, but with the third boy in front of the log fire at Staple Farm, near Wye, Kent, the last house Dunbar lived in.

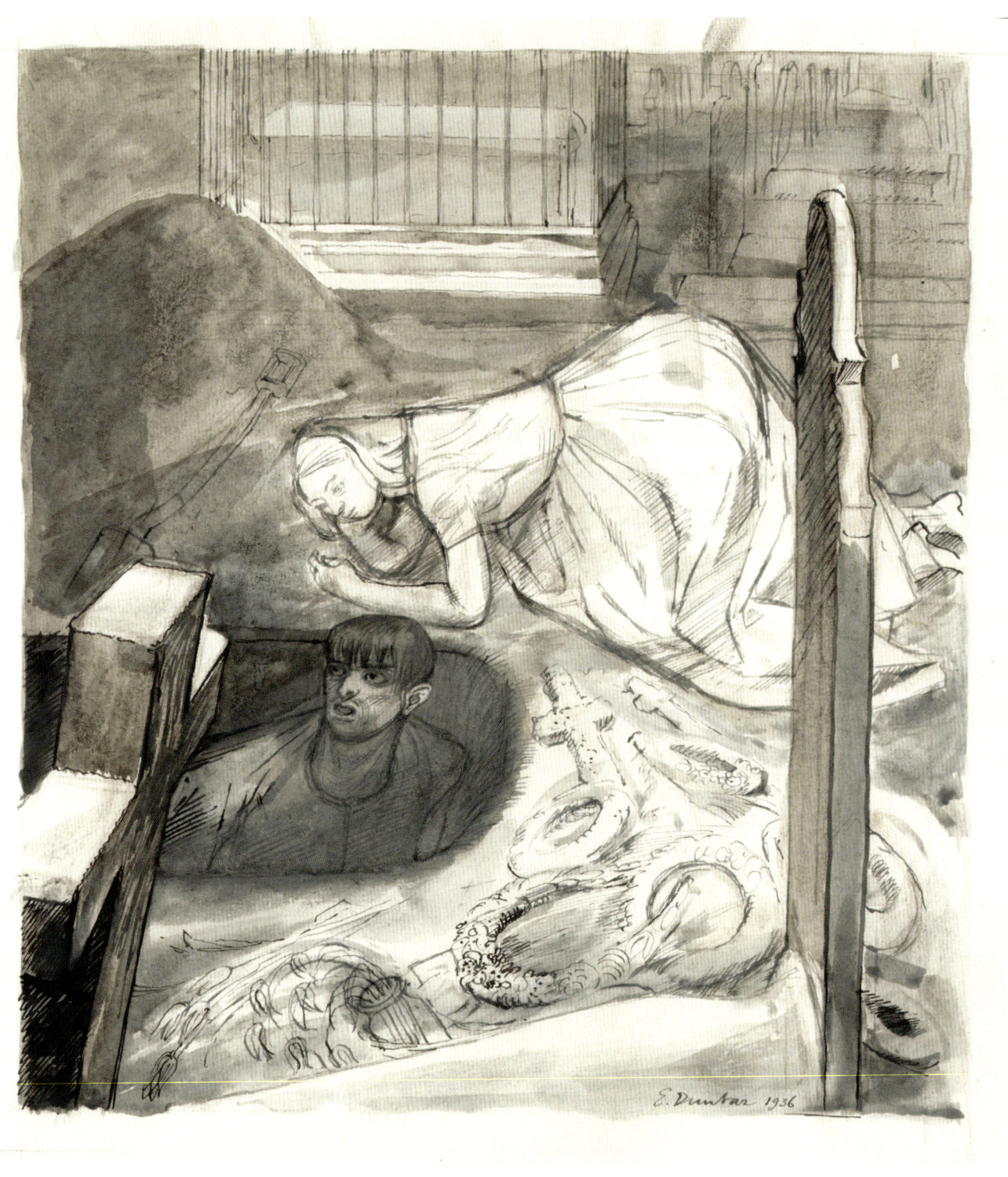

CAT 129 [HMO 510] Study for an illustration for Emily Brontë's *Wuthering Heights*, a commission from the magazine *Signature*, signed and dated 'E. Dunbar 1936',
Pencil, pen & ink and wash on paper 22 ½ x 15 ¼ in. (57.5 x 38.5 cm)

Dunbar's only known adult foray into the Gothic. In 1936 three prominent younger artists, among them Dunbar and Graham Sutherland, were asked by the magazine *Signature* to submit illustrations of an episode in *Wuthering Heights*, to be judged by Kenneth (later Sir, later still Lord) Clark. Dunbar included images from the graveyard of a local Strood church. Clark was unimpressed, feeling that Dunbar's drawing did not sufficiently enhance the text.

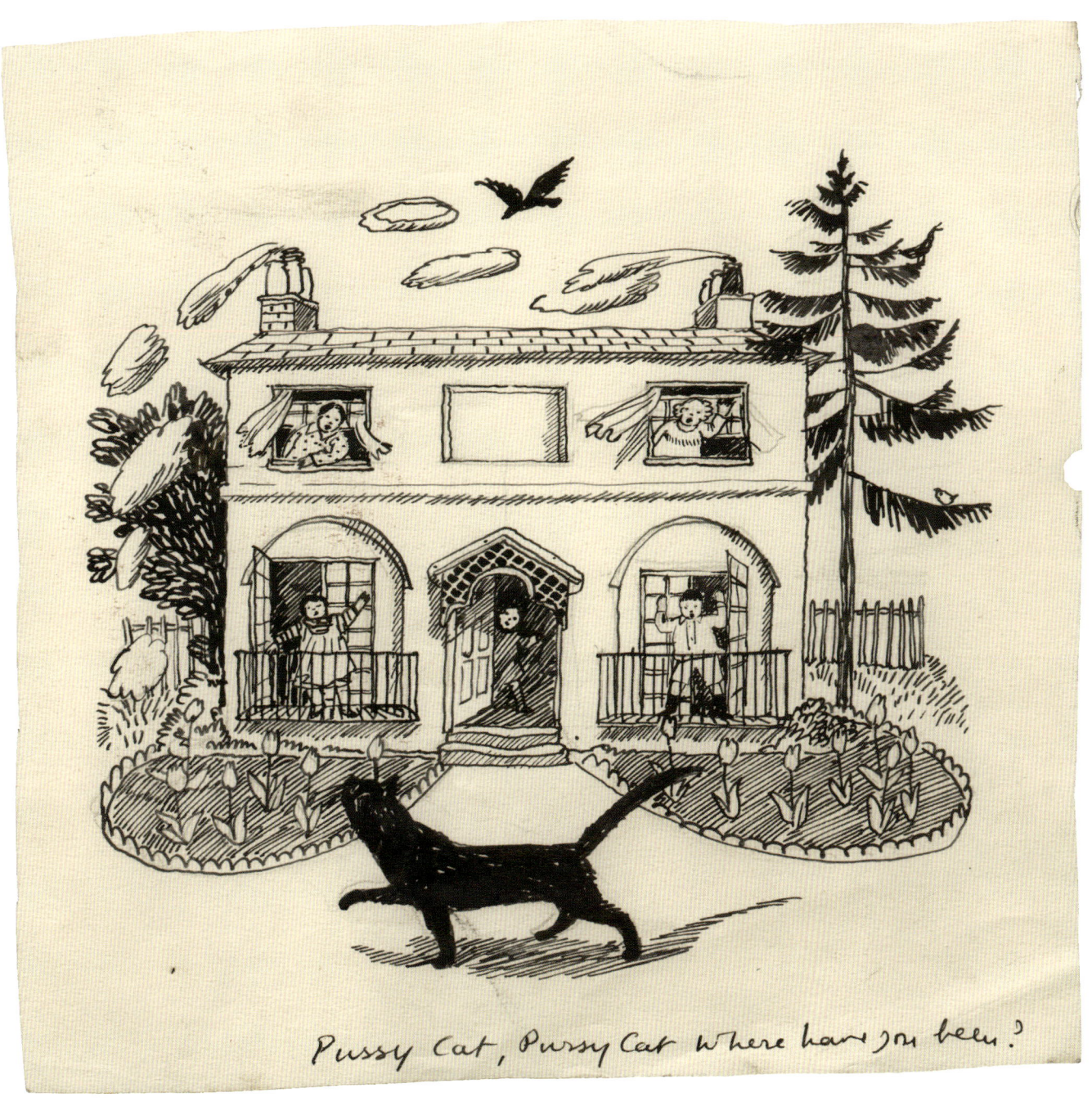

CAT 130 [HMO 333] *Pussy Cat, Pussy Cat, Where Have You Been*, no date, Pencil and pen & ink on paper, approx. 8 x 8 in. (approx. 20 x 20 cm)

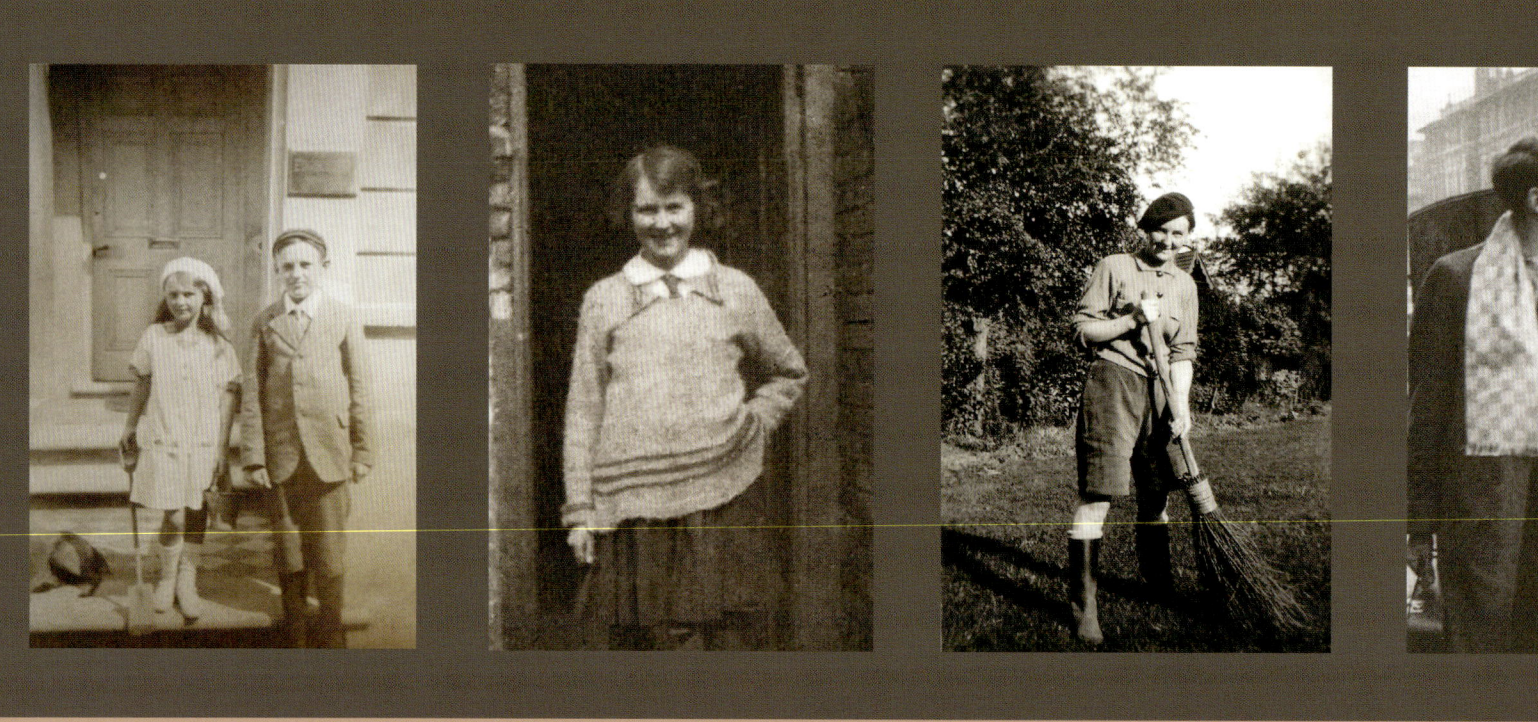

Evelyn Dunbar (1906-1960)
A Chronology

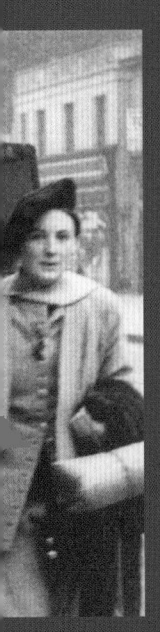
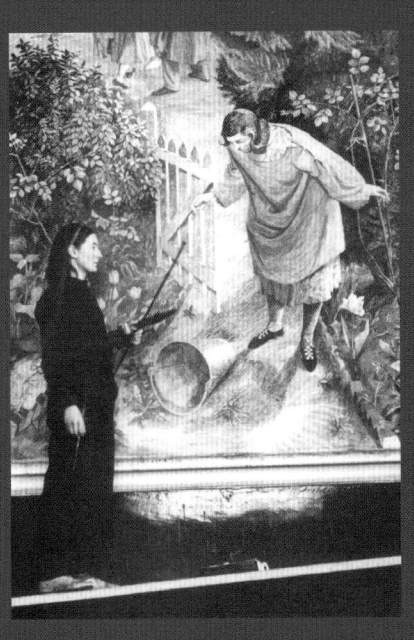
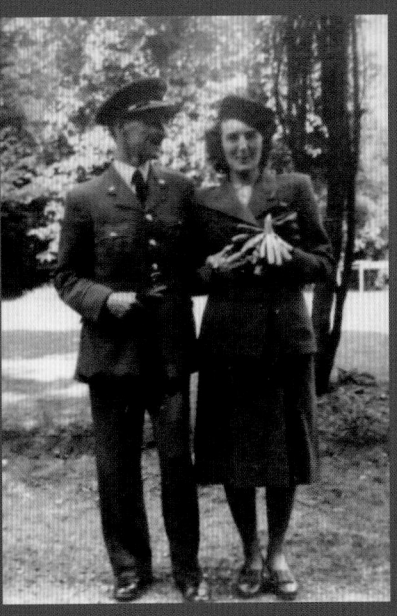
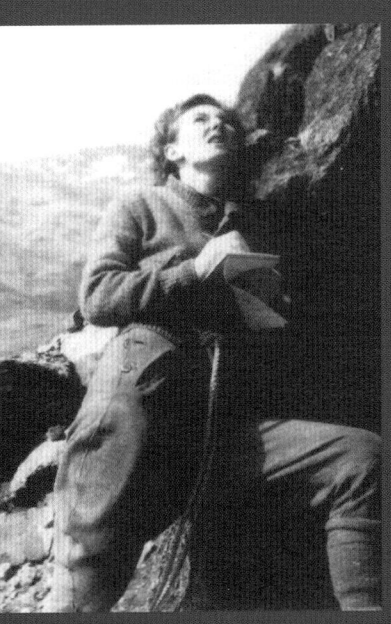

1895 — William Dunbar, originally from crofting stock in Cromdale, Morayshire, later draper and bespoke tailor from Reading, marries Florence Murgatroyd, daughter of a Bradford woolmaster. Their first four children are Ronald, Jessie, Marjorie and Alec.

1905 — The fifth Dunbar child, a girl, dies in infancy. In her distress Florence Dunbar turns to Christian Science, following the example of her sister Clara, and determines to bring up her children as Christian Scientists.

1906 — Evelyn Mary Dunbar is born on December 18th.

1908 — William Dunbar sells his Reading business and buys another in Kent. The Dunbars move to Snodland, a village between Maidstone and Rochester.

1913 — To run William Dunbar's expanding business more effectively, the family moves to 244 High Street, Rochester.

1914 — Encouraged by Florence Dunbar, herself an amateur artist, Evelyn begins to submit entries to Royal Drawing Society competitions.

1918 — Evelyn wins a Kent County Scholarship to Rochester Grammar School for Girls. She and Florence continue membership of West Kent Art Society, run by George Ward, also principal teacher of art at Evelyn's school.

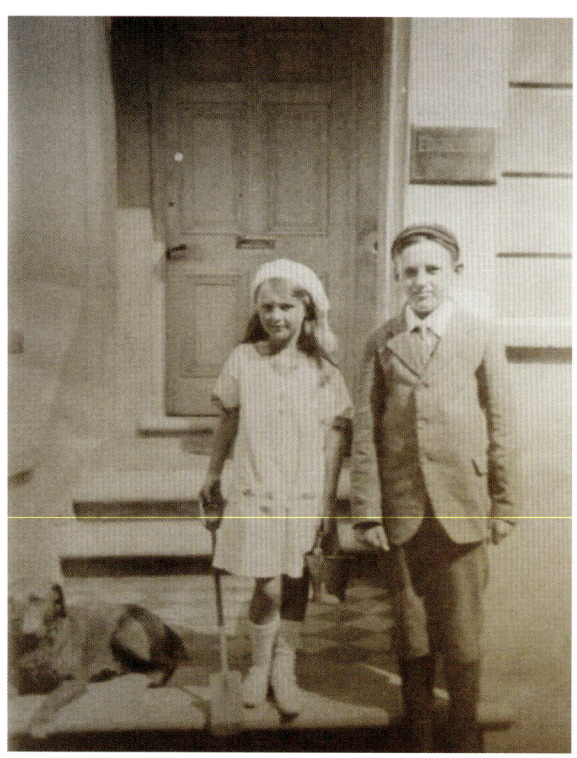

FIG 25 Evelyn, aged 7, with brother Alec, Felbridge (dog, left) and bucket and spade, on holiday in Folkestone as World War 1 broke out in August 1914. (Dunbar family archive.)

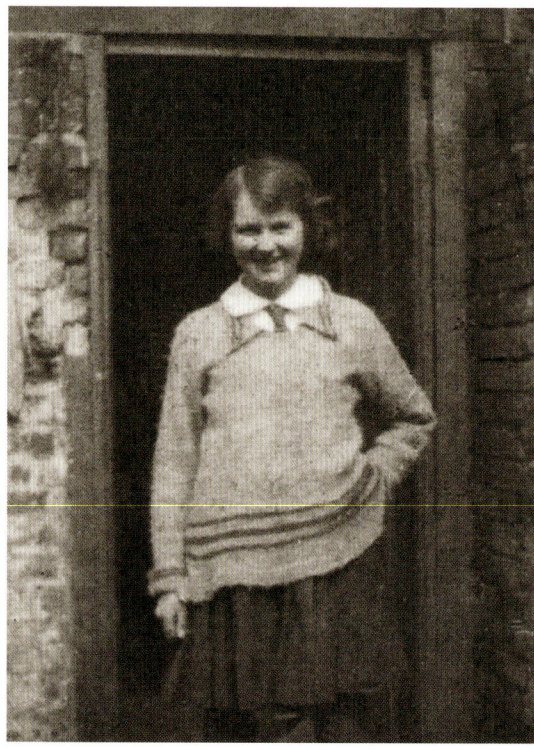

FIG 26 Evelyn aged about 10. Photograph by kind permission of Elizabeth Bulkeley.

1920	Florence's sister Clara, who also paints, and her wealthy husband Stead Cowling move from Yorkshire to Steellands, an estate in Ticehurst, East Sussex.
1923	Evelyn matriculates (i.e. qualifies for university entry) with passes in English, maths, history, botany and German, with special mention for oral German. Encouraged by George Ward, she wins certificates for excellence in competitions organised by the National Society of Art Masters.
1924	William Dunbar buys The Cedars, a 17-room late Victorian house with a large garden in Strood, that part of Rochester west of the river Medway. The tower room is converted into a studio for Evelyn and Florence.
1925	Evelyn leaves school and spends a year at home writing and illustrating children's books
1926-28	Evelyn has difficulty finding an art college that suits her. She enrols for but does not complete courses at Rochester School of Art, Royal Drawing Society and Chelsea College of Art and Design.
1928	Travelling via Holland, Evelyn spends some time in Germany, possibly visiting a male pen-friend, leading to a disastrous romantic entanglement. She subsequently drops everything German from her cultural baggage.

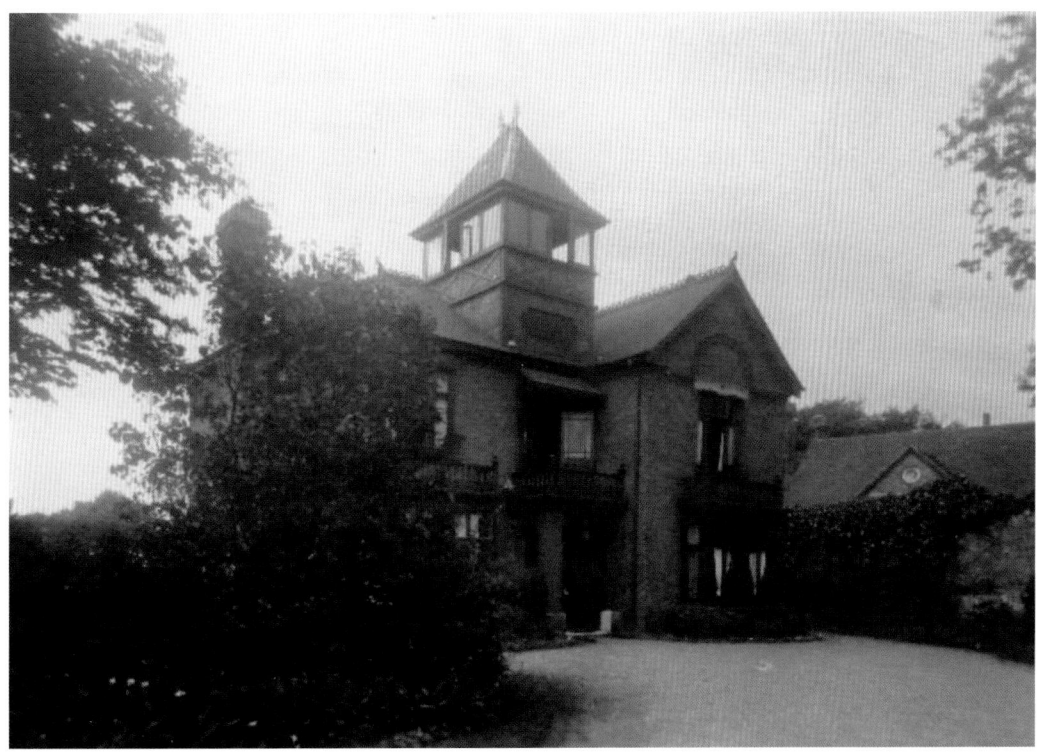

FIG 27 The Cedars, the Dunbar family home in Strood, Rochester, 1924-1946. (Dunbar family archive)

1929 Evelyn wins an exhibition to the Royal College of Art, where the Principal is Sir William Rothenstein. Her chief first-year tutor is Allan Gwynne-Jones, with whose mother she lodges in Hampstead for a while. She also lodges with Noel and Catherine Carrington, a literary couple on the edge of the now dwindling Bloomsbury group.

1931 Evelyn wins the Augustus Spencer prize.

1932 William Dunbar dies aged 70. Evelyn graduates as ARCA, but decides to stay on for a fourth year at the Royal College of Art, partly subsidised by her uncle Stead Cowling, to study mural painting under Cyril (usually known as Charles) Mahoney.

1933-36 On leaving the Royal College of Art Evelyn volunteers to take part in a mural decoration scheme at Brockley County School for Boys, Lewisham, later to become a unit of Prendergast-Hilly Fields School. The project, led by Mahoney, is unpaid. Working closely together at Brockley, Evelyn and Mahoney three years her senior fall in love. They discover a mutual love of plants and gardening, reinforced by artist colleagues and friends such as Edward Bawden, whom they visit regularly at Great Bardfield.

1934 Stead Cowling dies. For a time his widow Clara subsidises Evelyn, enabling her to rent a Hampstead studio from Noël Carrington. She shares this studio with Mahoney, who lives in it for occasional periods.

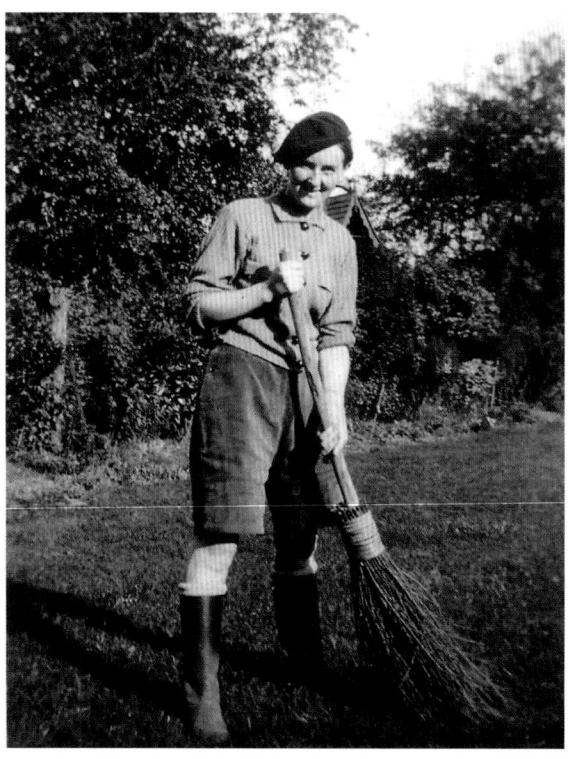

FIG 28 Evelyn in an unidentified garden, c.1933-36. At this time she and Mahoney were known jocularly as Adam and Eve because of their devotion to gardening. (Photograph by kind permission of Elizabeth Bulkeley.)

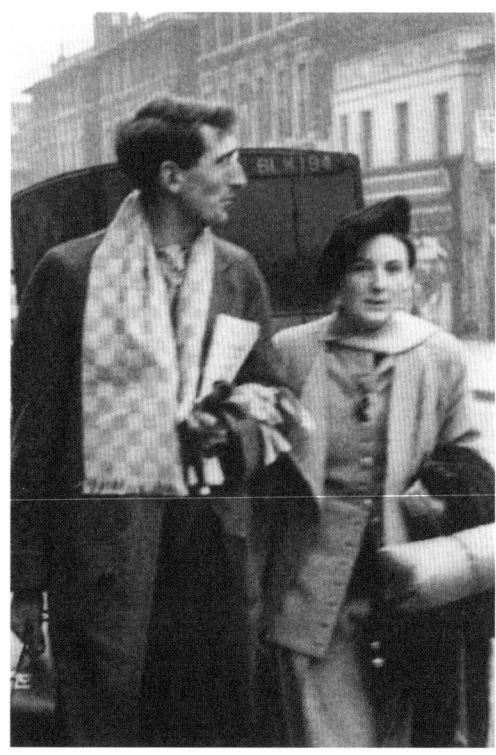

FIG 29 Evelyn and Charles Mahoney in London, 1936.
(Photograph by kind permission of Elizabeth Bulkeley.)

1935   Evelyn is commissioned, probably via Noel Carrington, to provide pen-and-ink vignettes for a dip-into miscellany called *The Scots Week-End and Caledonian Vade Mecum for Host, Guest and Wayfarer*.

1936   The Brockley Murals are inaugurated by Oliver Stanley, then Minister of Education. Evelyn is commissioned by the publishers Routledge to write and illustrate Gardeners' Choice. She invites Mahoney to share the project with her. He does so, but the relationship is beginning to come apart, not least because of the gulf between Evelyn's Christian Science and Mahoney's left-wing and atheist persuasion. Evelyn gives up her Hampstead studio.

1937   *Gardeners' Choice* appears. On behalf of the magazine *Country Life*, Noel Carrington commissions Evelyn to produce its *Gardener's Diary 1938*. A rich outpouring of plant and gardening images, allegorical and didactic, follows.

1938-40   The lowest period in Evelyn's career, although she paints continually. She lives at The Cedars, increasingly in professional isolation and at some distance from her shopkeeper siblings. She opens The Blue Gallery, a commercial art gallery above her sisters' The Fancy Shop, but it does not prosper. She is working behind the counter when on her 33rd birthday Sir William Rothenstein suggests she should apply for appointment as an Official War Artist.

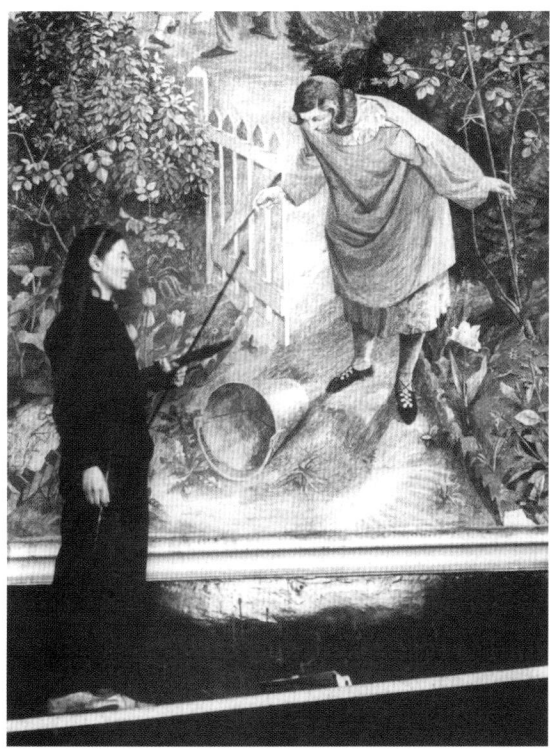

FIG 30 Evelyn with her Brockley mural panel *The Country Girl and the Pail of Milk*, 1936. Press photograph, staged for the inauguration.

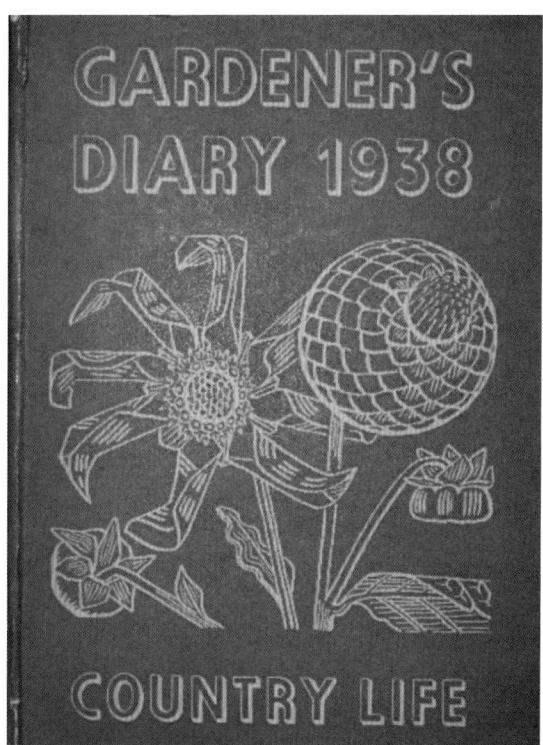

FIG 31 Cover of *Gardener's Diary 1938*.

1940-42 Evelyn is appointed Official War Artist, with a remit to paint women's war activities on the home front. She becomes particularly associated with the Women's Land Army. At Sparsholt Farm Institute, Winchester, she meets Roger Folley, an agricultural economist then serving in the RAF. They marry in 1942. Her remit is extended to include nursing subjects.

1943-45 Evelyn becomes the only female war artist to be salaried on a rolling periodic contract basis. She contrives to follow her husband's RAF movements with postings to Monmouthshire, the Scottish Borders, Gloucestershire and finally home to Kent. In 1944 Florence Dunbar dies. Subsequently The Cedars is sold.

1945-47 Following Roger Folley's demobilisation, he and Evelyn set up their first married home in Long Compton, Warwickshire, next door to his sister, Joan Duckworth. They move to Enstone, nearer Oxford, on Roger Folley's appointment to the University Agricultural Research Institute. In 1946 Clara Cowling dies, leaving Evelyn a substantial sum.

1947-50 Evelyn finds Oxford congenial. She takes up part-time teaching posts, including a Visitorship at the Ruskin. An outpouring of major allegorical and other paintings follows in possibly the most productive period of her life.

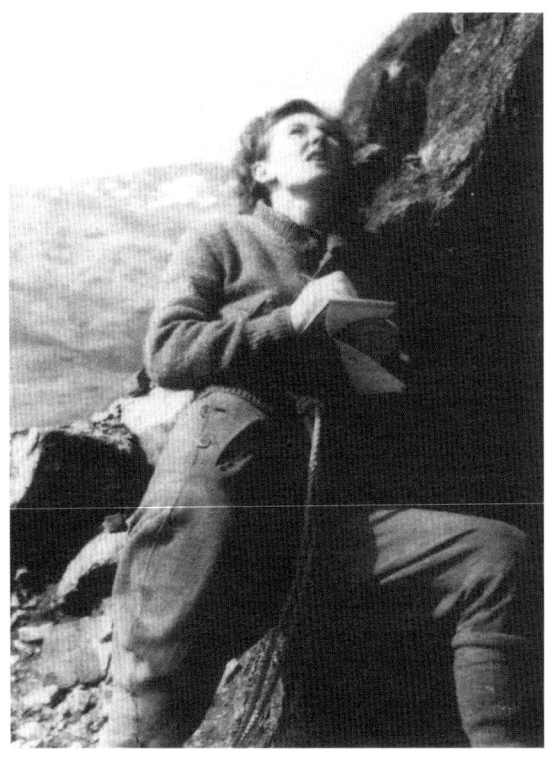

FIG 32 Evelyn sketching in the Lake District. Private collection

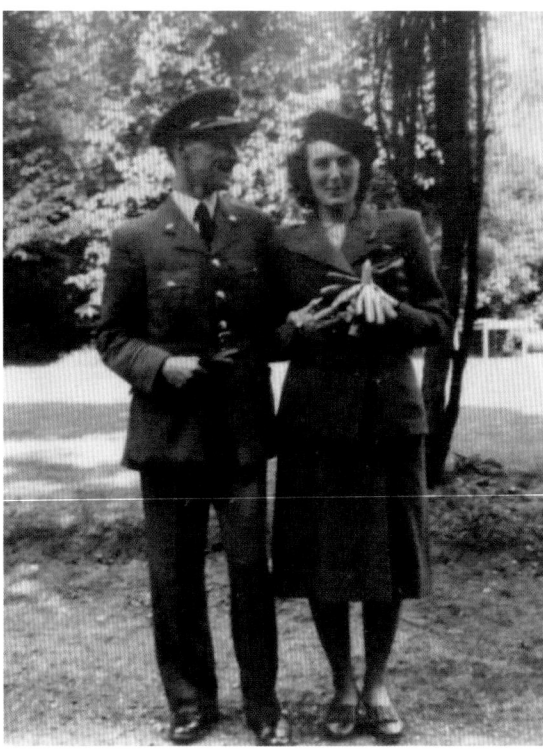

FIG 33 August 17th 1942: Roger and Evelyn Folley, newly married, in the garden at The Cedars. (Dunbar family archive)

1950-57   Roger Folley is appointed to the Agricultural Economics Department of Wye College, Kent. He and Evelyn leave Enstone and Oxford to live near Wye. Evelyn bolsters her Christian Science convictions with the discovery of a group of like-minded friends in Ashford, Kent. A hiatus in Evelyn's output is followed by a concentration on landscape and portraits. She gives many of her canvases away. She holds a small solo exhibition at Wye College in 1953.

1957   Evelyn is unable to complete a mural commission at Bletchley Park Teacher Training College, submitting two modest library panels instead. She and Roger Folley move house again, firstly into the village of Wye and finally to Staple Farm, a farmhouse up on the North Downs.

1958-60   For the first time ever she complains to Roger Folley of feeling unwell. She takes up work again on the large allegory *Autumn and the Poet*, set aside since leaving Enstone, and completes it. On May 12th 1960, while out collecting pea-sticks with her husband, she suddenly collapses and dies. Coronary atheroma is given as the cause of death. She is cremated a few days later. 'Unto the perfect day' is inscribed in the Book of Remembrance.

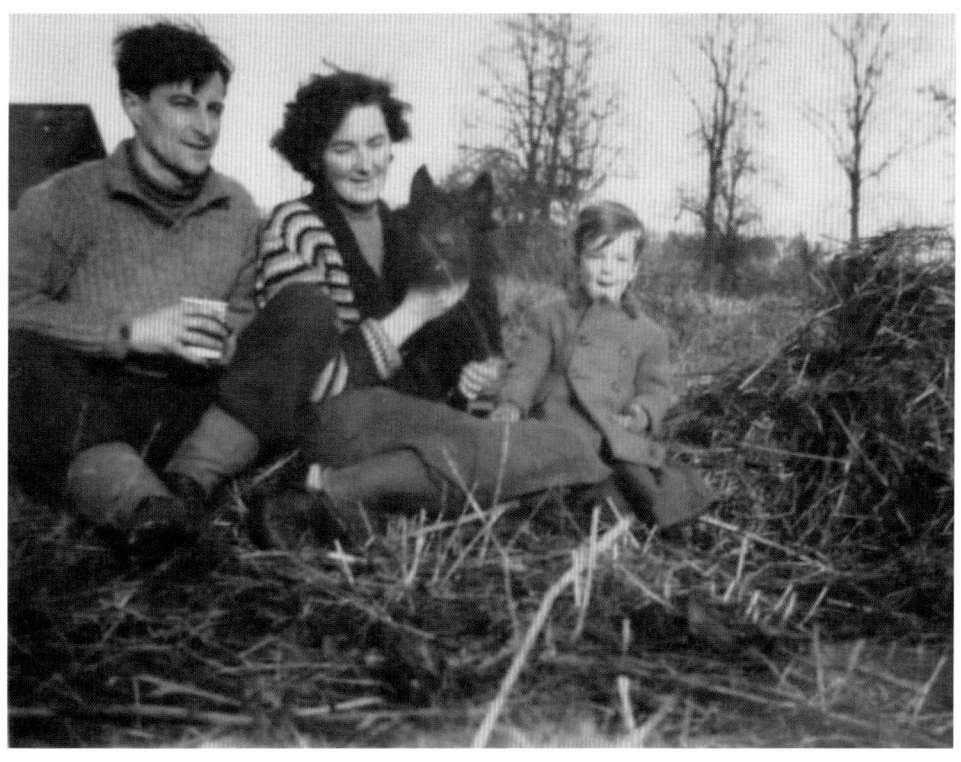

FIG 34 Roger and Evelyn Folley and dog ('Zim') with their nephew Christopher Campbell-Howes, aged 4, in the early spring of 1946. (Dunbar family archive.)

CONTRIBUTORS

Christopher Campbell-Howes
Christopher Campbell-Howes retired early from running schools in Scotland and settled in the south of France to devote himself to writing and musical composition. Evelyn Dunbar, a major influence in his youth, was his aunt. His newly completed biography of her owes much to recent discoveries of her work.

Gill Clarke
Gill Clarke is Visiting Professor at the University of Chichester and Guest Curator at the University's Otter Gallery and St Barbe Museum & Art Gallery, Lymington. Her books include *Randolph Schwabe: A Life in Art* (2012), *The Women's Land Army: A Portrait* (2008) and *Evelyn Dunbar: War and Country* (2006).

Andrew Lambirth
Andrew Lambirth is a writer, critic and curator. He was art critic of *The Spectator* 2002-2014 and his reviews have been collected in a paperback entitled *A is a Critic*. He has written books on many Modern British artists: his most recent is on the landscape painter David Tress.

Paul Liss
Fine art dealer and exhibition organiser, Paul Liss co-founded Liss Llewellyn Fine Art in 1991. He has curated numerous monographic exhibitions in collaboration with museums and cultural institutions in the UK and abroad.

Sacha Llewellyn
Art historian and exhibition organiser, Sacha Llewellyn co-founded Liss Llewellyn Fine Art in 1991. She is currently writing a monograph on Winifred Knights which will be published by Lund Humphries in 2016 to coincide with the exhibition she is guest curating at The Dulwich Picture Gallery. Other future projects include *Art of the Second World War*, *Portrait of an Artist* and *Sir Thomas Monnington P.R. A.*

Simon Martin
Simon Martin is Artistic Director of Pallant House Gallery in Chichester, and a Trustee of the Charleston Trust and HOUSE. He is author of numerous books on Modern British art, including books on *Edward Burra, Eduardo Paolozzi, Colin Self, John Tunnard, Leon Underwood* and *Conscience and Conflict: British artists and the Spanish Civil War*.

Alan Powers
Alan Powers studies mid-20th century Britain across the spectrum of art, design and architecture, with a particular interest in their intersections, such as mural painting and book illustration. His books include *Britain (Modern Architectures in History)*, 2007, and *Eric Ravilious*, 2013. He is currently researching a book on Edward Ardizzone.

Peyton Skipwith
Peyton Skipwith is a fine art consultant and writer. He worked at The Fine Art Society for forty-four years, retiring in 2005. Through exhibitions, books and reviews he has played a significant role in the revival of interest in the work of artists and designers of the interwar years, especially Edward Bawden.

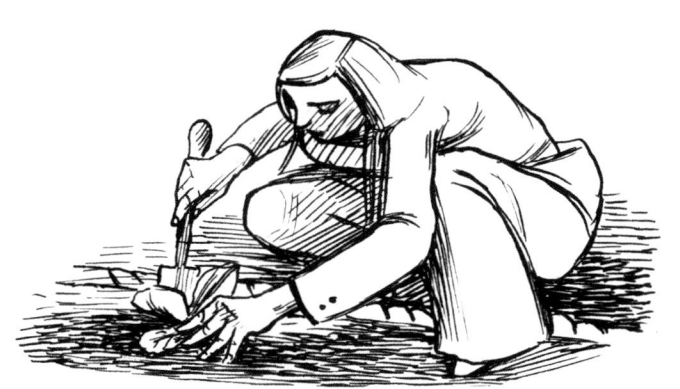

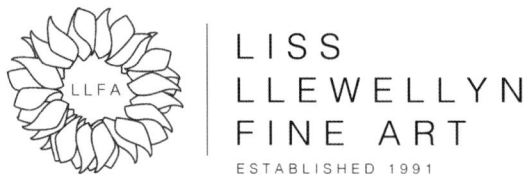

LISS LLEWELLYN FINE ART
ESTABLISHED 1991

paul@llfa.gallery   sacha@llfa.gallery

Founded in 1991 by Paul Liss and Sacha Llewellyn, Liss Llewellyn Fine Art specialises in the unsung heroes and heroines of British art from 1880 to 1980. For over 20 years Liss Llewellyn Fine Art has worked in association with museums to develop a series of in-depth exhibitions to encourage the reappraisal of some of the lesser known figures of 20th century British Art.

www.llfa.gallery

Design and Typesetting by David Maes

Text © Christopher Campbell-Howes, Gill Clarke, Andrew Lambirth, Paul Liss, Sacha Llewellyn, Simon Martin, Alan Powers, Peyton Skipwith

Photography:
Glynn Clarkson, Nigel Green, Petra Hogervorst, Richard Valencia

Printed by Zenith Media, 2015

ISBN: 978-1-869827-93-9